Patterns
of the Life-World

Northwestern University
STUDIES IN *Phenomenology &*
Existential Philosophy

Edited by

Patterns
of the Life-World

Essays
in Honor of John Wild

JAMES M. EDIE
FRANCIS H. PARKER
CALVIN O. SCHRAG

NORTHWESTERN UNIVERSITY PRESS

EVANSTON   1970

Contents

[vii]

viii / *Contents*

PART IV SUBJECTIVITY AND OBJECTIVITY

Preface

JOHN WILD is one of America's most distinguished philosophers. The contributors to this volume have sought to honor him, each in his own way. Among the contributors there are former students, former colleagues, and friends. The editors have chosen the title, *Patterns of the Life-World,* because it succeeds in expressing John Wild's philosophical interests succinctly and in a way that covers his work from the beginning of his career to the present. Some of the contributors do not share Professor Wild's current interests, and in some cases there are marked differences of opinion and point of view between a particular author and the man honored by his essay. The editors do not consider the clearly discernible philosophical differences among the various contributors to be at all unfortunate. Quite the contrary; they consider these differences to be illustrative of the practice of philosophy as a project of dialogue and dialectics. This is philosophy as Professor Wild himself practices it, both in his teaching and in his writing. The editors are of the mind that the most appropriate way in which to honor this eminent philosopher is not by simply rehearsing his manifold accomplishments but by honoring that spirit of philosophy which he himself so well emulates.

John Daniel Wild was born on April 10, 1902, in Chicago, Illinois. He received his college education at the University of Chicago, where he was awarded the Bachelor of Philosophy degree in 1923. In 1925 he earned the Master of Arts degree from Harvard University. He then returned to the University of Chicago for doctoral study and won his Doctor of Philosophy degree in 1926. He taught at the University of Michigan from 1926 to 1927. In 1927 he was appointed to the philosophy faculty at Harvard University and taught there as Professor of Philosophy until 1961. In 1961 he went to Northwestern University as Chairman of the Department of Philosophy, and, in 1963, moved to Yale University. He has served both as vice-president (1950–51) and as president (1960–61) of the American Philosophical Association. In 1953–54 he was president of the Metaphysical Society of America. He founded the Society for Realistic Philosophy and served as president from 1947 to 1950. He has been a member of the editorial board, since 1947, of *Philosophy and Phenomenological Research,* and, since 1951, of *Philosophy East and West.* While at Northwestern, he served as chairman of the original committee that established the Society for Phenomenology and Existential Philosophy in 1962, and, in the same year, he helped launch the Northwestern University Studies in Phenomenology and Existential Philosophy of which he is the General Editor. Twice he has been the recipient of a Guggenheim Fellowship, in 1930–31 to work at the University of Freiburg in Germany, and again in 1957–58, during which time he traveled extensively and lectured at various universities in Germany and France. He has held visiting professorships at the University of Chicago, the University of Hawaii, and the University of Washington. He gave the Mahlon Powell lectures at Indiana University in 1953.

One of the things about John Wild which impresses both critics and friends is the breadth of his interests. He is at home with most of the great minds of the past; he has contributed important works on Plato and Aristotle, on the Medievals, on Berkeley and Spinoza, on the existentialists and phenomenologists, and, most recently, on William James. It is a mark both of his peculiar philosophical temper and of his attitude toward life that when one thinks of comparisons with other historical philosophers, the names that come most readily to mind are those of Socrates and William James. For him philosophy has never been a "game," but always a matter of the most serious commitment. To it he has brought not only his intellect but his personality, and his ability to project his personal enthusiasm into what would otherwise remain the dry bones of argument is legendary to all those who have been associated with him either as students or as colleagues. Wild is a seminal and adventurous thinker, always restless, always ready to change, always impelled to take new and critical views of his own work and the works of his colleagues. To his students his genuine enthusiasm for philosophy was contagious; advance to eminence and age has made him not less but more radical and adventuresome in his ideas, because, in the manner of Socrates, he understands philosophy as a way of living as well as a way of thinking.

It is to the man John Wild, and to the cause of philosophy in which his whole life has been absorbed, that this volume is dedicated. It is hoped that the essays which follow will stimulate their readers to reflect upon and explore some of the questions which have been of primal concern not only to Professor Wild but to all the great minds in the history of philosophy whose thought his own work has helped to preserve and elucidate.

The editors wish to thank all those whose contributions have made this volume possible, and also those who expressed a desire to contribute to the volume but were unable to do so because of age and infirmity. We also wish to thank the staff of the Northwestern University Press, whose editorial help and suggestions have greatly enhanced this volume.

THE EDITORS

PART I
THE RELEVANCE
OF THE TRADITION

1 / Insight

Francis H. Parker

> All men by nature desire to know. An indication of this is the delight we take in our senses; for even apart from their usefulness they are loved for themselves; and above all others the sense of sight. For not only with a view to action, but even when we are not going to do anything, we prefer seeing . . . to everything else.
>
> Aristotle, *Metaphysics*

SOCRATES' INSIGHTS were rich, manifold, and variegated, and he therefore influenced his disciples in a variety of ways. John Wild is a twentieth-century Socrates, and the variety of his influence is reflected, although certainly not fully, in this book in his honor. Other essays in this volume express many other aspects of his influence; mine can express only his influence upon me, and all too little of that. That influence, distilled by twenty years of reflection, is epitomized in the single value of *insight*. To the theory of insight which he has taught and to the living insight which he has embodied—to his words and to his deeds, to the *logos* and to the *ergon*—this essay is devoted. What is the meaning of insight? What is its role in human life? What objections may be leveled against a theory of insight? And what is the value of insight? These are the questions which I now want to discuss.

[3]

II

JUST AS "being is said in many senses," as Aristotle rightly declared, we should expect that insight into being would, correspondingly, be said in many senses. And so it is. We speak of having insight into a chemical reaction, into the proper way to build a bridge, into the solution of a mathematical problem, into another person's joy or sorrow, and into the rightness or wrongness of an action—to cite only a few examples. All these manifold uses of the word "insight" have something in common, however—at least we certainly do not believe that we are equivocating when we use the same word in these and other very different situations. But just what is it that they all have in common? What is the essential nature of insight?

The essential nature of insight as I see it—or at least the meaning of the word which I wish herein to stress—may be brought out by means of a brief review of the way in which Aristotle intended and used the concept. For Aristotle, insight is one of the virtues or excellences, specifically one of the theoretical, intellectual virtues. By "virtue" (*aretē*) Aristotle meant, most generally, an acquired, ingrained disposition or habit or second nature (*hexis*) which causes one to act in such a way as to actualize one's basic potentialities or first nature. Since human nature or potentiality is most fundamentally both cognitive and conative, the most fundamental division of virtue is into the intellectual and the moral, into habits of actualizing one's cognitive nature and habits of actualizing one's conative or active nature. Since knowing may be engaged in either for its own sake or for the sake of the use to which the knowledge can be put, intellectual virtue is, accordingly, divided into the contemplative or theoretical, on the one hand, and the calculative or practical, on the other. Theoretical, intellectual virtue, the acquired, ingrained disposition to act in such a way as to know reality as it is in itself and for its own sake, involves, furthermore, two essential components and their relational totality. It involves, in the first place, the ability to demonstrate true propositions from relevant evidence, either deductive or inductive in character. This component of theoretical, intellectual virtue Aristotle called scientific knowledge (*epistēmē*). In the second place, however, such demonstration of true propositions from relevant evidence presupposes an intellectual grasp of the evidence itself, be it deductive or inductive. The habit of being able to grasp the evidence on which scientific knowledge is founded is a second, distinct component of theoretical, intellectual virtue; and it is this component that Aristotle called insight or intellectual intuition (*nous*). The union of insight or intellectual intuition with demonstration or scientific knowledge is, according to Aristotle, wisdom (*sophia*), the supreme theoretical, intellectual virtue.

Since, as we have just seen, the evidence upon which demonstration or scientific knowledge is based is of two kinds, deductive and inductive, insight or the habit [1] of being able to grasp such evidence is correspondingly of two kinds, according to Aristotle. The inductive evidence upon which scientific knowledge rests consists of particular sensory occurrences—pointer readings, color patches, etc.—and insight into them consists of intellectually seeing their nature and significance. This is one kind of insight. The deductive evidence upon which scientific knowledge rests consists of general propositions and, insofar as these are themselves deduced from higher premises, of universal and necessary first principles, and insight into them consists of intellectually apprehending their meaning and truth. This is the other kind of insight. In Aristotle's words, "Insight is concerned with the ultimates in both directions; for both the first terms and the last are objects of insight and not of demonstration." [2]

Thus scientific knowledge is based upon an insight into or an intuitive awareness of the concrete, particular items and situations we experience, on the one hand, and upon an insight into or an intuitive awareness of the most fundamental, universal principles of things, on the other. In other words, knowledge involves insight as well as demonstration; and knowledge also involves universals as well as particulars. Hence knowledge involves two kinds of insight: insight into universals and insight into particulars. But both kinds of insight are quite distinct from mediate, inferential apprehension (*dianoia, epistēmē*), for they are both immediate and intuitive. In sum, we have here two types of insight: (1) intuition of the most fundamental, univer-

---

1. Insight is a habit or disposition, not merely an activity, because we would refer to someone as an insightful person even if he were asleep.
2. *Nic. Eth.* (W. D. Ross translation, slightly modified) 6. 1143a35–b1.

sal principles of being and knowing (for example, the principle of noncontradiction); and (2) intuition of the concrete, particular individual or situation—of this particular situation here and now.

It might at first seem that one of these two types of intuition or insight is purely intellectual—insight into universal principles —and that the other type of intuition or insight is purely sensory —insight into concrete particulars. While I do not myself find Aristotle quite clear on this point, it is apparent to me that this dichotomy cannot be sustained. Insight into concrete particulars, into inductive evidence, cannot, on Aristotelian or any grounds, be purely an act of sensation, because the proper objects of acts of sensation are always the concrete particulars as such, as unique and unrepeatable, whereas insight is into the natures, essences, or meanings of these concrete particulars, which natures, essences, or meanings must be universal and repeatable in order that they may serve as inductive evidence for scientific knowledge. If this is not so—if it is not the universal nature or essence or meaning but only the unique, unrepeatable particular which composes the inductive evidence—then we are saddled with the insoluble problem of "the inductive leap" from particulars to universals, from the past to the future, which leads to the impossibility of scientific knowledge. It is clear then that the particular must contain the universal, and that insight into the particular must be insight into the universal nature or meaning of that particular. Such insight is itself, in its own proper being, an act of intellect rather than of sensation, though that act of intellect is and must be intimately fused with an act of sensation.

Correspondingly, insight into the abstract, universal principles of being—into the deductive evidence for scientific knowledge—cannot be merely an intellectual act all by itself, because the proper objects of intellectual acts are always the abstract universals as such, as general and repeatable, whereas insight is into the meanings and principles of real beings themselves, and real beings themselves are always, according to the evidence of Aristotle and of our common sense, concrete and individual. If this is not so—if it is not the meanings and principles of individual things but only abstract essences and principles in themselves which compose our scientific knowledge and the deductive evidence upon which it is based—then we have the dualism of extreme, "Platonic" realism, a mysterious and unbridgeable chasm between a World of Forms and a World of Particulars where our scientific knowledge cannot be *of* the concrete world of nature. It is clear then, again, that the universal must be in the particular and that insight into the universal must be insight into the universal nature or meaning of that particular. Such insight is, once more, in its own proper being, an act of intellect rather than an act of sensation (insight is, in Aristotle's language, *nous* rather than *aisthēsis*); but this intellectual act is and must be intimately joined with an act of sensation, and its proper object must be intimately in the object of sensation.

Thus both types of insight are intellectual grasps of the universal in the sensed particular, and they are therefore not so much two different kinds of insight as two different areas of occurrence of one and the same kind of insight. Insight is concerned with the ultimates in both directions. Inductively evidential insight makes explicit, direct reference to sensed particulars: "This, this, and this are particular instances of water boiling at 100 degrees centigrade," for example. Deductively evidential insight makes only implicit and indirect reference to sensed particulars: "Being (which is ultimately concrete and individual) cannot be other than it is," for example. But both occurrences of insight are intellectual apprehensions of universals in sensed particulars. It is this intimate fusion of two distinct acts and objects—an intellectual grasp of universals and a sensory grasp of particulars—which is, as we shall see in Section III, the very essence of insight.

Whereas insight into universal principles and insight into the natures of particulars are, therefore, basically and essentially the same, I wish to concentrate primarily, though not exclusively, upon insight into universal principles. My reason for this is that intuition of fundamental, universal principles is more essential and more peculiar to philosophical knowledge in contrast to other kinds of knowledge than is intuition of the natures of concrete particulars. Insight into particulars is necessarily essential to every type of knowledge which is empirical, for our primary experiences are of particulars (though, as we have seen, these particulars contain universals). But most types of knowledge other than philosophy take their universal principles or premises from types of knowledge other than themselves, or else postulate their principles without insight into their truth, whereas it seems to be the concern of philosophical knowledge to establish the truth or falsity of these first principles. Because of this fact, recent attacks on the idea that philosophy is a kind of *knowledge,* a *distinctive* kind of knowledge, have as their essence and focal point (as we shall see in Section III) an attack on insight of this first kind, on intuition into the first principles of things. Let us then examine the nature and role of insight as intuition of fundamental, universal principles.

III

THE GUIDING PRECEPT for understanding the nature and role of insight as intuition of first principles is the one which is so fundamental to and so revealing of the Aristotelian approach to human knowledge and reality: "What is first in the order of being and truth is last in the order of human knowing, and what is first in the order of human knowing is last in the order of being and truth." Aristotle asserted:

> The natural path of investigation starts from what is more readily knowable and more evident *to us* although intrinsically more obscure, and proceeds toward what is more *self*-evident and intrinsically more intelligible; for it is one thing to be knowable to us and quite another to be intelligible objectively.[3]

Now, "The intrinsically most knowable things," Aristotle said elsewhere, "are the primary causes—its being through these that other things, namely the subsumed particulars, are known, and not *vice versa.*"[4] In another place he made the same point somewhat more fully:

> We cannot know the truth of anything without also knowing its explanation. And just as a thing possesses a quality in a higher degree than other things when it is able to infect those other things with that quality (e.g. fire is the hottest of all things because it is the cause of heat in everything else), so in the same way that is the most true which is the explanation of other truths. Consequently the ultimate principles of the permanent aspects of

3. *Phys.* (Wheelright translation) 1. 184a17–21.
4. *Meta.* (Wheelright translation, slightly modified) 1. 982b2–4.

things must necessarily be true in the fullest sense; for such principles are not merely sometimes true, nor is there any ulterior explanation of their being, but on the contrary *they* are the explanation of other things. And so, as each thing stands in respect of being, it stands likewise in respect of truth.[5]

Last in the order of achievement but first in the order of being and truth—such is insight as here discussed, and such is the motto for climbing the ladder of truth up to insight and into the first principles from which all other truths hang. The meaning of this "last but yet first" is nowhere, perhaps, as vividly portrayed as in the upward and downward ways depicted in the famous allegory of the cave in Plato's *Republic*.[6] We human beings begin our lives as prisoners in the dark and shadowy cave of sense experience where our awareness is restricted to the "blooming, buzzing confusion" of the shadows on the wall and the reverberating echoes. In this imprisoned state what is most knowable to us is the darkness, not the light; and our "knowledge" is no more than a seeming, an imaging (*eikasia*). From this condition some of us are forced to freedom, perhaps by a Socrates, some great teacher, and made to turn our eyes away from darkness and toward the light of a fire whose brightness, cast on moving puppets, is the source of the shadows first most knowable to us. At first we are blinded by the firelight and wish only to return to the familiar darkness. Gradually, however, our eyes accommodate to the light and then, in a flash, the truth reveals itself to us. We had thought that the shadows were real and the light unreal; now we see that the shadows are only copies of illuminated realities. Having gained this insight (which turns out to be only a relative one) and having adjusted ourselves to it, we are once more forced away from the familiar, from what is most knowable to us, to climb on upward through the dark and rugged tunnel leading to the mouth of the cave. Coming out of the cave upon the surface of the earth we are once more blinded by the light and wish only to return to our earlier familiar life of relative darkness, but again our eyes gradually accommodate to the light. First we become able to make out the night sky and the heavenly bodies, then daytime shadows and reflections, then the

5. *Ibid.*, 2. 993b24–31.
6. The following account owes much to John Wild's *Plato's Theory of Man* (Cambridge, Mass.: Harvard University Press, 1948), Chap. 5.

various beings on the surface of the earth—trees, animals, people. Finally, we find that we can turn our gaze, though never for long, upon the sun itself, that ultimate source of all the light and life we see about us on earth and even, indirectly, of the things we once dreamed of in the cave. After having finally achieved this highest of all insights and wishing to remain in its light, we are obligated to return to the cave in order to understand and explain its shadowy interior in the light of the sun we have seen outside, and also in order to share our insight with those still imprisoned and to serve as guides for their journeys out of the darkness of the cave into the light of the sun.

The meaning of this allegory of the cave is given by Plato, just before depicting the cave itself, in his analogy of a divided line. A vertical line is divided into two unequal parts, and then each of these parts is in turn divided into two unequal parts according to the same ratio as the first division. The bottom portion of the line, corresponding to the seeing of the shadows and the hearing of the echoes in the cave, represents sensory experience of the superficial aspects of physical things (*eikasia*). The next higher part of the line, corresponding to the seeing of the puppets in front of the fire, represents empirical generalization, true belief (*pistis*) about physical things. The next higher, and third, portion of the line, corresponding to the perception of the shadows and reflections on the surface of the earth outside the cave, represents deductive science, the discursive reasoning (*dianoia*) or demonstration of lower truths from higher and ultimately the highest truths; this Plato identified with mathematics, but we today would identify it with all deductively formulated sciences. And the fourth and highest portion of the line, corresponding to the apprehension of the living beings outside the cave and preeminently of the sun, represents insight or intellectual intuition (*noēsis*) into the ultimate truths, the first principles of all things. The vision of the sun at the very top of the line which for Plato was the vision of "The Good"—that supreme Reality which is both the source of all existence and truth and yet beyond all (finite) existence and truth—is essentially religious insight into which intellectual insight imperceptibly merges. This ultimate Reality, "The Good," is so intense that no human being can gaze upon it for long, and so transcendent that no human being can ever express it properly or adequately in terms of human thought. Yet its immediate offspring, the living beings outside the cave, are accurately formulable by human thought; and they stand as true tokens of the transcendent Truth. The mounting up from deductive science to insight into first principles and the returning to the demonstration of the propositions of deductive science from these first principles Plato called "dialectic" (which should not at all be confused with what Hegel and Marx called "dialectic"), and it is this which for Plato is the heart and core of philosophy. After one has climbed out of the cave, up the divided line, to an insight into the first principles of all things, one is thereby enabled and also obligated, both intellectually and socially, to reenter the cave, to climb back down the line, in order to demonstrate and understand all lesser truths and experiences in terms of that insight and in order to guide others to that same insight and understanding.

What are these ultimate truths, the first principles of all things, which are the objects of insight in the sense now being discussed? Since it is not the specific content or detailed objects of insight but rather insight as such which is the present topic, I shall not attempt a proper answer to this question. Several examples of such first principles may, however, be given as illustrations: the principles of noncontradiction, of sufficient reason, of excluded middle, of goodness as actuality, and of the identification of things in cognition. But if it should be the case that one or more of these examples is not in fact truly a first principle, this does not matter for my present purposes. That there are first principles into which insight can be had is one thing; just exactly what these principles are is quite another. "In other words, the assertion of a necessity, the assertion that something has to be a certain way . . . can perfectly well be false," as Henry Veatch has said,[7] because the necessary and universal truth into which insight may be had is a property of the *objects* of the insight, not of the insight itself. Though I may be mistaken in any particular insight into any particular first principle, it is at any rate true that human knowledge requires insight into first principles. But this point must now be argued, especially in view of the serious and important modern objections to this thesis.

7. "Matrix, Matter, and Method in Metaphysics," *Review of Metaphysics*, XIV, No. 4 (June, 1961), 597. See esp. pp. 597–600 of this article for an elaboration and defense of this distinction.

IV

THIS THEORY of the dimension of insight that is an intellectual intuition into universal and necessary truths which are the foundations of all knowledge, a theory first clearly developed by Plato and Aristotle and continued and extended throughout medieval philosophy, involves important difficulties which cannot be adequately considered here. But it should at least be pointed out that this theory of insight has been rejected by the dominant movements characteristic of contemporary philosophy. What these modern movements object to in this theory is its thesis that there are some propositions (like the principle of noncontradiction) which are universally and necessarily true and yet at the same time are about the real world.[8] This objection has taken two main forms.

One form stems from Kant. Kant agrees that there are propositions which are both universally, necessarily true and also informative about reality, but he maintains that the reality about which they are informative is not *reality*, not things as they are in themselves, but only *appearance*, only things as they appear to the human mind. And things as they appear to the human mind cannot be identified with things as they really are in themselves, according to Kant, because the impact on the human mind by real things in themselves must be modified, altered, and reconstructed into phenomenal counterparts made knowable by and to the human mind. Kant's reasons for this position are well known to all those who have undergone the discipline of the *Critique of Pure Reason;* they cannot be reconsidered here except to suggest that the most fundamental reason is Kant's unexamined belief, inherited from both the rationalists and the empiricists, that experience is identical with sense-experience and that sense-experience is unintelligible in itself. "The sum of the matter is this [Kant wrote]: the business of the senses is to intuit, that of the understanding is to think." [9] "The understand-

8. This aspect of the present topic I have treated in a different but related way in my essay, "Traditional Reason and Modern Reason," in *Faith and Philosophy,* ed. Alvin Plantinga (Grand Rapids, Mich.: William B. Eerdmans, 1964), Chap. 2.

9. *Prolegomena to Any Future Metaphysics,* trans. Lewis White Beck (New York: Liberal Arts Press, 1950), p. 52.

ing intuits nothing but only reflects." [10] The intellect, that is, has no proper object or subject matter of its own; it supplies the mind no information; it only arranges the information supplied by the senses. The theory of insight presented here maintains, on the contrary, that it is the business of the understanding or intellect to intuit its own proper object, to supply its own unique information, the universal and necessary, in and through sense-experience. We have also seen, furthermore, that there is not and cannot be any such thing as a purely sensory intuition, for the senses alone present only the unique, unrepeatable aspects of things which explain nothing, not even themselves. It is clear from this, indeed, that the Kantian "intuition" has an entirely different meaning from the Aristotelian intuition. Kant's *Anschauung* is pure *Schau*, pure show, of the particular and contingent, whereas Aristotle's *nous* is insight into the universal and necessary.

The only difference which needs to be noted at the moment, however, between this Kantian view and the theory of insight presented here is the Kantian denial of the claim made by the theory of insight that real things in themselves are knowable. Various external and internal criticisms of this Kantian agnosticism might be made, but I shall content myself here with only one, an internal criticism. This criticism is that Kant contradicts himself, for he says, on the one hand, both that there do exist real things in themselves and that a certain few of their properties are known, and yet he also says, on the other hand, that these things in themselves are unknowable; and this I take to be a contradiction. While it might be argued that Kant escapes self-contradiction by maintaining merely that we don't know *anything at all* about things as they are independently of our cognition of them, he clearly seems to go further than this by assigning at least some known properties to these supposed unknowables. He claims, for example, that

> things as objects of our senses existing outside us are given, but we know nothing of what they may be in themselves, knowing only their appearances, that is, the representations which they cause [sic] in us by affecting our senses. Consequently I grant by all means that there are bodies without us, that is, things which, though quite unknown to us as to what they are in themselves, we

10. *Ibid.*, p. 36.

yet know by the representations which their influence [sic] on our sensibility procures us.[11]

To say that something is completely and in principle unknowable and yet at the same time to say something about its specific properties, for example that it possesses a causal influence on us, seems to me to be a flat contradiction. For real things in themselves to be completely and in principle unknowable would be for no one to be aware of or to express that fact. Hume knew this, and to him we must now turn.

The other form of the objection to the central thesis of insight as intellectual intuition—the thesis that there are propositions which are both universally, necessarily true and yet also about real existence—stems from Hume, and it is this objection which is today the more influential one. Hume and his followers agree that there are propositions which are universally and necessarily true ("relations of ideas"), but they insist that they are not true of any reality at all, not even of the human mind or of things as they appear to the human mind. On the contrary, such universal, necessary propositions are merely verbal or ideational tautologies. They are true only because of the way we happen to use words and become mentally acclimated, because of our linguistic mental customs; and our linguistic mental customs are not necessarily in tune with reality. Thus while there are, on this view, propositions which are universal and necessary, logically certain, they are entirely arbitrary or conventional since they arise only from linguistic and psychological conventions and not from the necessities of existence. They are postulates laid down arbitrarily on the basis of customary definitions or usages. From these postulates are derived by a process of logical deduction lesser propositions (theorems) which are verified or falsified by their correlation or lack of correlation with sensory data. And through this sensory verification or falsification of the theorems, the postulates are indirectly verified or falsified. Thus there is, as with Kant, no such thing as insight, as intellectual intuition; all "intuition" is of the unique and unrepeatable; the intellect can only postulate, not intuit.

The issues involved in this Humean objection to intellectual insight, an objection which is today so widespread among professional philosophers, are many and complicated, so it is not

11. *Ibid.*

possible to do justice to them here. But I would like to suggest two internal criticisms of the Humean view. The first criticism is that the Humean view concedes at least one case of insight into universal principles of being (one of Aristotle's two kinds of insight), and the second criticism is that the Humean view requires insight into the natures of sensed particulars (the other of Aristotle's two kinds of insight). At least the second of these two criticisms, and perhaps also the first, could also be made against the Kantian view just considered.

In the first place, the deduction of the theorems from the postulates, which is involved in making the postulates true of experienced reality rather than merely of words or ideas, clearly seems to require the assumption of the principle of noncontradiction as inescapably true, and thus the assumption of at least one proposition which is really and necessarily true, at least for reality as we humans must think it if not for reality itself, rather than being just arbitrarily or customarily postulated. This is so because deduction entails the principle of noncontradiction—a deductive conclusion *means* a proposition whose denial taken with the affirmation of its premises would involve a contradiction—and because such deduction is, according to this Humean view, necessarily involved in the verification of all propositions universally, in whatever language they might be expressed. And if one proposition, the principle of noncontradiction, can be universally and necessarily true of thought about reality, the door is open for insight into other such propositions also.

In the second place, the correlation between concepts and the propositions they form, on the one hand, and sensory data, on the other—which correlation is necessary, on this Humean view, to the factual or empirical verification of otherwise merely linguistic tautologies—requires that the universal forms signified by the concepts be *in* the sensory data as the foundations justifying the correlations. Two things which are correlated— the concept and the sense datum—must have something in common; that which is in the correlated concept must also be in the correlated sensory datum. But this means that universals can be intuited in sensory data, and this is insight working in its capacity as the supplier of inductive evidence. Furthermore, if universal *meanings* can be intuited in sensed particulars, the door is open as well for the intuition of universal *principles* in and from sensed particulars, which universal, necessary propositions are therefore true of empirical facts. The Humean conception of logical deduction and conceptual-empirical correlation therefore requires insight in both its roles: insight into universal, necessary propositions and insight into the natures or meanings of sensed particulars.

This brings us to the heart of the issue between the affirmers and the deniers of insight or intellectual intuition. The heart of the issue is this: Does sense experience contain intelligible, repeatable structures, or does it not? The answer dominant in modern philosophy is that it does not. As Kant said, "The understanding intuits nothing but only reflects." The answer dominant in classical philosophy is that it does. As Gilson has said, the senses bear a message which is meaningful to reason, though not meaningful to the senses themselves.[12] The basic issue concerning the possibility of intellectual insight is whether reason, as well as sense, is intuitive and possesses its own proper object, the universal and necessary forms of objective realities. And the thesis that there is intellectual insight, that reason is intuitive of the universal and necessary structures of independent realities, is conceded, I have suggested, by its opponents—by the Kantian knowing of properties of things in themselves and by the Humean presupposition of the inescapable truth of the principle of noncontradiction and of the universal structures in sensory facts correlating them with intellectual concepts. Thus there is such a thing as insight or intellectual intuition, and the denials of this thesis have only reaffirmed it.

V

WHAT IS THE VALUE OF INSIGHT as here interpreted, especially as intuition of the first principles of being? I want at least to raise this large question in my conclusion, though I shall do little more than touch upon its answer.

First of all, what is value or goodness in general? I suggest, without defense, that Aristotle was right in his statement, at the beginning of his *Nicomachean Ethics*, that "the good has rightly been declared to be that at which all things aim," where the aim

12. *Réalisme Thomiste et critique de la connaissance* (Paris: J. Vrin, 1947), p. 218.

is not an assumed aim of consciousness merely, since consciousness may be mistaken, but rather the existential aim of the very being of the thing in question. But what is it that all things aim at existentially? Their full, mature, developed being, the actualization of their specific potentialities, the realization of themselves. From this it follows that the human good is the fullest possible actuality of human potentialities: generically, those potentialities which humans share with other beings (their physicality, vitality, and animality); specifically, those potentialities which are distinctively human (rationality and all the other distinctively human characteristics which follow from it); and individually, those potentialities which are unique (those aims projected freely and uniquely by individual persons).

From this general background the specific value or goodness of insight necessarily follows. Insight is the most fundamental aspect of the existential actuality of human intelligence or reason, giving rise to knowledge and thus to that total actuality of human reason which is wisdom. Indeed, this conclusion was, of course, adumbrated in the approach taken to discover the meaning of insight, for that approach began by noting that insight is, according to Aristotle, a virtue. The value or goodness of insight as intellectual intuition of first principles is, therefore, the actuality of the specifically human potentiality or tendency to know the basic, determining principles of all things, which knowledge is the foundation of all science and wisdom.

Thus the achievement of insight is the fundamental project, the basic telic determinant or goal-cause, of *homo theoreticus*, of man as knower. And since specifically human action presupposes theoretical knowledge, insight is also the fundamental instrumental cause of all specifically human action. Men may have beliefs without insight, and men may act without insight; but men cannot know and they cannot act humanly, humanely, without insight. Hence insight has always been and will always continue to be vital to humans throughout history, since man cannot escape his drive to know and since the lack of specifically human action, of action based upon insight, always tends toward the destruction of man. Insight is thus a prerequisite of moral, social, political, economic, and all other human values. Insight is the peculiarly human good, the good which is intimately connected with and distinctively pertains to man as man. Something at least analogous to social, political, and economic goods characterizes other forms of natural life; and religious goods pertain to man not so much in that he is man as in that he is a creature of God and in relation to God. But the good of and for man just insofar as he is man, as a being between God and nature, of man insofar as his awareness is neither merely sensory nor divine but rational, is the good of insight. Insight, then, man's distinctive grasp of the principles and particulars which are the ultimate justifications of knowledge and action, of *logos* and *ergon,* is the good belonging peculiarly to that in-betweenness which is man.

2 / Why Be Uncritical
about the Life-World?

Henry B. Veatch

ONE MIGHT ASK, "How can one be uncritical about the
Lebenswelt?" Must not a concern with the *Lebenswelt*, in the
very nature of the case, be critical, and even Critical in a not
improperly Kantian sense? Thus when Husserl in the *Krisis*
called for an *epochē* with respect to the sciences and urged that
the *Lebenswelt* be made the theme of careful phenomenological
investigation, he was not urging any return to the natural attitude. On the contrary, the world of the natural attitude had long
since been bracketed, so that Husserl's own somewhat belated
interest in the life-world was quite consciously and explicitly an
interest directed toward phenomena, as over against things-in-
themselves, toward that which is wholly "immanent," as over
against the "transcendent." [1] In short, for Husserl the program
which he projected for a phenomenological investigation of the
Lebenswelt was a program set in what was admittedly a transcendental framework, and in what therefore could in an extended, though not improper, sense be called a Kantian framework.[2] And what could be more Critical than this?

1. These terms we are exploiting in the sense in which they are used
in Husserl's somewhat early work, *The Idea of Phenomenology*, trans.
William P. Alston and George Nakhnikian (The Hague: Martinus Nijhoff,
1964).
2. This is not to say, of course, that there are not radical differences
between Husserl and Kant. On the other hand, that Husserl took what
might be called "the transcendental turn" in philosophy and was thus a
transcendental philosopher in this basically Kantian sense, surely no one
would deny.

Nor is it any less the case with Merleau-Ponty that, in seeking "to return to things themselves," "to return to that world which precedes knowledge, of which knowledge always *speaks*, and in relation to which every scientific schematization is an abstract and derivative sign-language, as is geography in relation to the country-side in which we have learnt beforehand what a forest, a prairie or a river is," [3] he is indeed not projecting a return to ordinary common-sense objects, to forests, prairies, rivers, etc., taken as existing in themselves and as they are just in the natural attitude and before any and all operations of bracketing of whatever sort. Such a return to things themselves is a return not to things in themselves but rather to things as they are for us, as they present themselves to us, as they are perceived by us; it is not a return to ordinary common-sense objects existing independently of us and in themselves, but rather a return to things in a phenomenal field where they present themselves, as one likes to say, prepredicatively and preobjectively.[4]

And so it would seem that it could be affirmed with respect to Merleau-Ponty, no less than with respect to Husserl, that in each of their respective cases their urging of a return to the life-world must be understood not realistically but transcendentally. What philosophic reflection, as they understand it, is to concern itself with is not the everyday world considered as an external world in itself, but rather with how such a world, or for that matter any world, comes to be for us, or is constituted by us. As Merleau-Ponty remarks, "Normal functioning [in the case of the senses and sensation] must be understood as a process of integration in which the text of the external world is not so much copied, as

3. *Phenomenology of Perception,* trans. Colin Smith (New York: Humanities Press, 1962), p. ix.
4. It should perhaps be readily admitted that this represents a very cursory interpretation of Merleau-Ponty, and many will doubtless object that, so far from subscribing to any transcendental idealism of the type of either Kant or Husserl, it is in this very respect that Merleau-Ponty would wish to distance himself from these particular predecessors, to whom otherwise he would acknowledge himself to be much indebted. Suffice it to say that here there is neither time nor occasion to justify our admittedly superficial interpretation of Merleau-Ponty. Instead, we would simply urge that however successful Merleau-Ponty may have been in overcoming "the subject-object dichotomy," and in avoiding transcendental idealisms of the usual variety, there is surely no denying that he is no classical realist and that he quite decisively makes "the transcendental turn" in philosophy such as we are here characterizing it.

composed." [5] Or, more generally, phenomenology is said to be precisely "a study of the *advent* of being into consciousness." [6] For like any and every philosophy which has taken "the transcendental turn," as it is sometimes called, phenomenology directs its attention not to the way things are in themselves, but rather to how things come to be for us or for consciousness. The operative question thus becomes: what are the conditions for things' coming to be known by us? Or, to think of it in an even more rudimentary way, what are the conditions and circumstances of things' being for us, of their being presented to consciousness, and so coming to be things for consciousness or objects of consciousness? [7]

Now it is precisely some such question as this, we would suggest, that is *the* philosophic question for any philosophy that might be said to be a transcendental philosophy. In contrast, in the case of a more realistic, or, if you will, a more un-Critical, type of philosophy the fundamental question is simply: What is the nature of things? Or: What does it take for things simply to be? What are the "causes" of things and of their being? Accordingly, the issue which we should like to raise in this paper—and more particularly the issue which we should like to raise specifically with respect to John Wild's own version of transcendental philosophy—is why this transcendental type of question in philosophy should take precedence over the realistic question.

THE PROBLEM OF THE TRANSCENDENTAL TURN: ITS FURTHER SPECIFICATION

LET US, THOUGH, TRY TO GET CLEAR at the outset just what sort of an issue this is. For surely what we have called the

5. *Phenomenology of Perception*, p. 9.
6. *Ibid.*, p. 61.
7. See Kant's own characterization of transcendental knowledge: "And here I make a remark which the reader must bear well in mind, as it extends its influence over all that follows. Not every kind of knowledge a *priori* should be called transcendental, but that only by which we know that—and how—certain representations (intuitions or concepts) can be employed or are possibly purely a *priori*. The term 'transcendental,' that is to say, signifies such knowledge as concerns the a *priori* possibility of knowledge, or its a *priori* employment" (*Critique of Pure Reason*, trans. Norman Kemp Smith [London: Macmillan, 1929], A56; B80).

transcendental type of question in philosophy would appear, in one sense at least, to be no less proper in a realistic philosophy than it is in a transcendental one. Indeed, in any realism the question is not only proper, but even ineluctable, as to just what the conditions and factors are of our coming to know things in themselves and as they are in themselves.[8] It is a question, in other words, as to the principles and causes of our knowledge of things, as contrasted with the question as to the principles and causes of the being of things.

Nevertheless, it would seem that this question as to the conditions of things' coming to be known by us, or, better, the conditions of their coming to be objects for us, or, in a still more rudimentary way, the conditions of their even appearing to us in any way at all, surely takes on an entirely different cast when raised in a realistic context than in the context of a transcendental philosophy. In the former, the explanation of things' appearing to us in the way they do and of their coming to be known for what they are must ultimately be in terms of what they are and the way they are in themselves. For instance, my understanding of something as being an accident of a substance—e.g., my understanding of a certain height as being the height of a particular tree—must ultimately be based on the fact that the tree actually is of that height in itself and in the real world. In contrast, in the context of a transcendental philosophy, a tree's appearing to be of a certain height, or, more generally, a thing's appearing under certain attributes and as having certain characteristics, is not anything that must be explained in terms of an appeal to the way things are in themselves; instead, the explanation is, as it were, for the most part self-contained within the process of coming to know, within the process of appearing. In Husserl's earlier terminology the explanation must be within the domain of the immanent and without reference to the transcendent; as he expressly comments, it must not be thought that "things . . . exist in themselves and 'send their representatives into consciousness.' . . . Instead, the things are and are given in appearance and *in virtue of the appearance itself.*" [9]

---

8. For this reason, a realist, no less than a phenomenologist, may interest himself in questions, say, as to the means and manner of perception—e.g., of figure-ground, of perceptual *Gestalten,* of the relevance to perceptual knowledge of *Abschattungen,* etc.

9. *The Idea of Phenomenology,* p. 10 (italics added).

The Problem of the Transcendental Turn as It Pertains to John Wild

WE COME, THEN, directly to John Wild and to the way in which this issue impinges directly upon the sort of thing he has been saying in his recent writing.[10] It is true that, so far as I know, Wild nowhere expressly faces up to the issue of why there should be a transcendental philosophy as over against a realistic one. Instead, he seems preoccupied almost exclusively and, one is tempted to say, rather uncritically with his unceasing campaign for the *Lebenswelt* and against the scientific world. It is a "war of the worlds," as he calls it, and it is his constant concern to alert people to the seriousness of this war, and to what the dire consequences will be both for human society and for human beings as individuals if the war is won by the partisans of a scientific world-view. Our human freedom will be lost, the arts and the humanities will wither away, and our very lives as men will be reduced to a rigorous regimen of computerized behavior patterns. Certainly, in all of this John Wild is right and is to be commended for the vigor and earnestness with which he proclaims this message. Still, conceding both the rightness and the righteousness of his cause, insofar as it involves this kind of stirring defense of the life-world as over against the scientific universe, just why does he suppose that his defense of the lived world should have required him to take the transcendental turn? Why must he hold the *Lebenswelt* to be no more than a mere phenomenal world? Why could it not be the real world itself, in the sense of the world of things as they are in themselves, as over against the scientific universe—which might then be regarded as the world of things only as they appear to us, or of things merely as they are seen (in a not improperly Wittgensteinian sense of "seeing as") through the medium of prefabricated hypotheses, elaborate intellectual constructions, and countless other devices of a priorism in both science and philosophy?

Very well, then, just what would John Wild say to questions such as these, which surely must be adjudged critical, even if

10. That is, in his writing since about 1957.

somewhat un-Critical? How would he respond to them? Or, inasmuch as these questions are of a kind that he seems never to have occupied himself with directly, might it be possible for others to determine, from within the context of his present philosophical loyalties, just what sort of defense he might give of his having taken this sharply transcendental turn in philosophy, and how successful this presumed line of defense might be?

WILD'S INDIFFERENCE TO THE MORE USUAL ARGUMENTS IN JUSTIFICATION OF THE TRANSCENDENTAL TURN

ACCORDINGLY, in addressing ourselves to just this task of trying to assess the degree to which John Wild may be ad-judged to have been either critical or uncritical in having taken the transcendental turn in philosophy, it should be possible at the very outset to rule out any number of the more or less standard considerations which, in the history of modern West-ern thought, have led other thinkers to take this same transcen-dental turn. For instance, in Kant's case the decisive considera-tion was surely that of how synthetic judgments a priori are possible. But this question would hardly seem to be one that has occupied John Wild's attention at all, or at least not to any significant degree. Similarly, if one turns to Husserl, it would seem that the overriding consideration that led him to take the step of his celebrated *epoché*, and so to embark upon a course of transcendental phenomenological reduction, was none other than his concern for apodictic certainty in philosophy and for the turning of philosophy into a *strenge Wissenschaft*. But just about the last thing that would concern John Wild would be how to make philosophy a strict science, or how to achieve anything like apodictic certainty in philosophy.

Moreover, if we turn to the example of a distinguished contemporary figure in American philosophy, Wilfrid Sellars, who, at least on many interpretations of his work, has indeed taken the transcendental turn in philosophy, it quickly appears that Sellar's reasons for having taken this turn are surely not Wild's reasons. Sellars has apparently been strongly influenced by Popper's repudiation of induction as a proper method, be it either in science or in philosophy. Not only that, but Sellars has also decisively put behind him any appeal to anything like infallible sensory givens as providing ultimate atoms out of which all human knowledge must be built up and constructed. Instead, his view would appear to be that intelligibility is entirely a function of any one of the various possible conceptual systems which we human beings may choose to bring to bear upon experience and which, so far from having been in any way derived from experience, are at least in principle put together in terms of purely syntactically determined formation rules and transformation rules in complete independence of semantic considerations of any kind. It is then and only then, and in virtue of a transcendental type of argument, that such conceptual systems may in turn be brought to bear upon experience. That is to say, the reason a given conceptual system is adopted is not because things themselves "send their representatives into consciousness," thus insuring that the very structures of things in themselves are represented in the structures of the relevant conceptual system; rather, the relevant conceptual system is adopted on no other grounds than that it so orders and structures our experience as to render it intelligible, and it does so without the slightest regard to the question of whether things really are so ordered and structured in themselves.

Once more, though, what could be further from John Wild's mind when he makes his transcendental turn than all these various Sellarsian considerations, having to do with Popper's strictures on induction, with the current fashionable repudiation of sense data, with modern logical techniques for the construction of purely syntactical systems, and so on? But if John Wild has not been prompted to make his transcendental turn on the basis of such standard and traditional considerations, what sorts of considerations have prompted him to take this step? Our original question still presses for an answer.

TRANSCENDENTAL CONSIDERATIONS IN LIEU OF
ACTUAL TRANSCENDENTAL ARGUMENTS

IN ATTEMPTING to put forward an answer which we think John Wild might perhaps give to such a question, though he nowhere to our knowledge actually does give it, we would suggest that there are two basic lines of consideration which have led him either consciously or unconsciously, and critically or uncritically, to treat of the *Lebenswelt* as if it were set in a thoroughly transcendental framework. For one thing, there is a constantly recurring theme which runs throughout *Existence and the World of Freedom,* which might be paraphrased in some such way as this: Any and every attempt on the part of realistic philosophers to view things objectively and simply as they are in themselves can only lead sooner or later to a recognition of the modern scientific universe as being the only world there is. Sometimes this theme seems to be treated as if it were a historical thesis concerning the development of Western philosophy— as if the sort of philosophical realism associated with the name of Aristotle had as a matter of historical fact gradually developed and evolved into the modern scientific world-view.[11] At other times, this theme seems to be put forward not as a device for understanding the development of Western philosophy but as a direct interpretation of philosophical realism itself, as if any realism of the classical Western type (e.g., Aristotle's) were a philosophy which does not so much develop into, but actually itself is, a philosophy that views the world in terms of fixed unchanging relationships, that allows no proper place for human freedom, that either denies the existence of values altogether or else tries to paste them artificially onto a universe in which they have no real place, that treats of the human subject as if it were just one more object among other objects, and so on.

Whatever form this theme takes, however, be it that of a historical thesis or a direct critique of realism, it is a theme which seems to serve John Wild as a sort of inverted or *ersatz* transcendental argument. It is as if Wild were saying: Unless the *Lebenswelt* be susceptible of a transcendental justification, then there is no way that it can maintain itself as a genuine life-world; for, treated realistically, the *Lebenswelt* loses its character as a life-world altogether and becomes reduced to the stark, meaningless, lifeless universe of modern science.

Now let us look briefly at the second of those broad, general considerations which we are suggesting have been of decisive

---

11. In this paper we shall forego any attempt to assess this historical thesis. Suffice it to say that it is a thesis often associated with the name of Heidegger, and, so far as we have been able to judge, it is as a distinctively Heideggerian thesis that John Wild adopts it and makes it his own.

influence in leading John Wild to take the transcendental turn in philosophy. This second consideration arises directly out of one of Wild's most fundamental convictions regarding the freedom of the human subject or person. For he feels that man is free, not merely in the traditional sense of having free choice or a free will, but rather in the newer sense [12] of being no less than a freedom to determine the very way things appear to him to be, the way he takes them to be, the sense which he makes of them. In other words, the world, so far from being what it is in itself and independently of our human modes of apprehending it, is instead, and in a quite precise technical sense, a purely phenomenal world; not only that, but it is a phenomenal world with respect to which we human beings have had no little freedom in determining just how it will appear to us and what sort of structure and character it will have insofar as it presents itself to us. Thus, in Wild's expressive phrase, our human freedom is no less than a "freedom of world constitution" (pp. 77, 121).[13]

Given this basic conviction as to human freedom, it is little wonder that one of the operative considerations that must determine John Wild's entire philosophical outlook is that the real world, or the world in which we human beings find ourselves, the *Lebenswelt*, in short, can only be understood in a transcendental context, not in a realistic one. Indeed, to do otherwise would be to seriously compromise that "freedom of world constitution" which John Wild considers to be at the very foundation of his entire present personal and philosophic outlook. Accordingly, what we have here is not really a transcendental argument, or at least not a transcendental argument of the accustomed sort. For so far as I have been able to discover, Wild nowhere argues, in the manner of Kant, that without such things as the a priori forms of intuition and the pure concepts of the understanding there just would be no world of objects or world of experience of any kind. Instead, the argument that seems to be implicit in Wild—though once more it would not appear to be an argument that Wild spells out in so many words —is to the effect that unless our human world or worlds are regarded as being structured according to various a priori forms

12. That is, in the sense of so much contemporary phenomenology and existentialism.

13. All page references given in the text will be to Wild's *Existence and the World of Freedom* (Englewood Cliffs, N.J.: Prentice-Hall, 1963).

and patterns supplied by the human subject, then there could not possibly be that freedom of world constitution which in Wild's eyes is no less than the essentially human, and without which all that is of value and significance in human life would be lost.

A Suggested Rebuttal
of the First Consideration

HAVING THUS PRESENTED what would appear to us to be two of the more decisive considerations, which, while they could hardly be said to have provided John Wild with anything like a transcendental argument, would nonetheless seem to have given him the needed push for taking the transcendental turn in philosophy, let us now try to assess their legitimacy and defensibility. In regard to the first consideration, I must confess straight out that it strikes me as not really able to bear a very close scrutiny. What Wild would appear to be maintaining in this connection is that both as a matter of history and as a matter of logic any sort of thoroughgoing realism in philosophy is bound sooner or later to lead to a repudiation of the *Lebenswelt* and to an eventual installation of the modern scientific universe as the only reality; hence it is as if he were arguing that the only way to save the *Lebenswelt* were to renounce realism and embrace some form of transcendentalism in its stead.

Surely, though, these particular alarms and excursions on behalf of the *Lebenswelt* would seem to be largely misplaced. Suppose, just for the purposes of illustration, that one were to understand the so-called life-world more or less in Aristotelian terms. After all, the suggestion is not so farfetched, it being something of a commonplace in philosophy to use Aristotle as an example of a thinker who took the everyday world, or the common-sense world, or the world just as we human beings experience it in our daily lives, as being the real world. For that matter, no less orthodox a phenomenologist than Aron Gurwitsch has remarked that the *Lebenswelt* as understood by Husserl—i.e., "the world in the sense of the life-world common to the whole human race and invariant with respect to the conceptions that change from one cultural-historical group to another"—"would be a possible starting point for a new interpretation of Aristotelian science." [14]

Furthermore, we all know that in the context of Aristotelian philosophy things are regarded pretty much the way they are in what Husserl was wont to call the natural attitude—that is, realistically. Accordingly, in this kind of a realistic setting human beings find themselves in a world of real things or substances—trees and plants, men and animals, earth and sky and waters, sun and moon and stars. Also, these same things and substances are constantly undergoing changes of various kinds, of generation and corruption, of increase and decrease, of motion from place to place, of first having this feature or characteristic and then that. Moreover, these changes come about as a result of the exercise of real causes, one substance actually acting upon and changing another in certain determinate ways, and that other in turn suffering or undergoing such changes in accordance with its potentiality or capacity for being affected in this or that determinate way rather than some other. Indeed, because of the manifold capacities of things to act and to be acted upon in all sorts of different ways, one could almost apply to Aristotelian substances—although, to be sure, hardly in the same sense!—Sartre's famous characterization of men as not being what they are and being what they are not.

For similar reasons, this real world of changing substances with their manifold powers and capacities is a world shot through with chance and indeterminacy. To use the stock example, while the man was injured because he was struck on the head by a falling tile when he was on his way to the market place, and while the tile was dislodged from the roof because of the wind, it was nevertheless simply by accident that the tile happened to fall at the very moment the man was passing beneath the building en route to the market. And just as chance and indeterminacy are pervasive features of this Aristotelian natural world, so in a somewhat different way are ends, purposes, final causes, and values. In fact, for Aristotle "the good simply is that at which all things aim," which, being interpreted in more technical language, means that value is nothing other than actuality as over against the potentiality that is ordered to it. In other words, in the life-world of Aristotelian philosophy

14. *Studies in Phenomenology and Psychology* (Evanston, Ill.: Northwestern University Press, 1966), p. 120.

values are as pervasive and as inescapable as are actuality and potentiality.

However, it is scarcely possible or appropriate in a paper such as this to try to present a brief for Aristotelian realism, much less to make out an entire case for it. Nevertheless, it would seem that one could very properly invoke the example of an Aristotle simply for the purpose of showing how a philosophy, while scrupulously respecting most, if not all, of the salient features of what has now fashionably come to be called the *Lebenswelt,* may nonetheless remain a thoroughgoing realism. Accordingly, it would seem that the first of the two considerations, which as we have suggested must have led John Wild to take the transcendental turn in philosophy, itself turns out to be largely gratuitous: a realism in philosophy by no means condemns one to an acceptance of the modern scientific world-view; nor is it at all necessary, in order to save the *Lebenswelt,* to shift it from a realistic to a transcendental setting.

A DIAGNOSIS OF WILD'S PARTIALITY FOR THE FIRST CONSIDERATION

NEVERTHELESS, before we leave this topic, it might be well if we were to look a bit more closely to see if it might be possible to determine just why John Wild should have been so confident and so sure of himself in his equation of realism in philosophy with an acceptance of the modern scientific universe. For it is no less perplexing than it is surprising the way in which he repeatedly berates both what he calls the rationalistic and realistic tradition of Western thought and what he terms the purely objectivist approach of modern science. The result has been that the world has come to be conceived purely objectively and in such a way that everything is, as it were, fixated in its own static, unchanging essence, that all occurrences and happenings are rigorously determined in accordance with necessary laws, that the human subject is completely extruded from such a world of mere objects, that the only way a subject can be got into this objective scientific universe is by turning him into an object and so depriving him of any and every vestige of freedom, that values are rendered meaningless and as having no place in such a deterministic, objective universe, and so on.[15] Yet is it not patent to almost anyone that while for a philosopher such as Aristotle, no less than for the modern scientist, the natural world may indeed be regarded both objectively and realistically, it is scarcely the same universe or the same nature that the two are considering? Even the word "nature" or *physis* is scarcely univocal for Aristotle and for the modern scientist; and all of the key terms and notions have radically different senses in the two systems. Thus Aristotelian substances are hardly the same as "substances" in the modern scientific sense. Matter, as Aristotle conceived it, and potentiality certainly play no role at all in modern physics. Chance is construed in an altogether different way; and it would seem that the contemporary scientist construes causation simply in terms of causal laws, with the result that not even efficient causes in the Aristotelian sense are recognized any longer; and formal, final, and material causes have so completely disappeared from the modern scientific scene that not even the words have left so much as a trace behind.

To make Wild's understanding of the implications of realism in philosophy, and particularly of the traditional Aristotelian realism of Western philosophy, still more suspect, one has only to consider that, so far from its being possible to equate such a realistic outlook with the outlook of the modern scientist, it seems rather that in the eyes of a number of contemporary philosophers of science, modern science is to be understood as not being a realism at all. On the contrary, with the discrediting of induction and the glorification of the hypothetico-deductive method, both of which have become such marked features of recent discussions of the logic and philosophy of science, it tends to be more and more the fashion not to regard science as viewing nature objectively; rather, as Popper has remarked, quoting from Kant: modern scientists have "learnt that our reason can understand only *what it creates according to its own design: that we must compel Nature to answer our questions,* rather than cling

15. Of course, it is possible not only to question whether an Aristotelian realism in philosophy necessarily commits one to the modern scientific universe, but also to question whether the universe of modern science does indeed involve all of those features and consequences which Wild ascribes to it and which would appear to be so inimical to the life-world. This last question, however, is not one that we shall concern ourselves with in this paper.

to Nature's apron strings and allow her to guide us." [16] Clearly, though, when the activity of scientists is construed in this way, then it is the scientist who must be thought of as having taken the transcendental turn,[17] leaving it perhaps only to Aristotelian philosophers of the life-world to indulge in the realism of the natural attitude. Thus, so far from being able to condemn the traditional philosophical realism of Aristotle on the ground that it reduces to no more than the objectivist realism of modern science, it would rather seem that John Wild might well have acknowledged such a philosophical realism as being precisely distinguishable from modern science on the ground that while the former is indeed a realism the latter tends increasingly toward being no less than a transcendentalism.

What, though, could have led Wild to this seemingly rather mistaken account of traditional Aristotelian realism, denying that it has any feeling at all for the life-world and equating it simply with what he has taken to be the realism of modern science? To answer this question, I believe that one needs to single out a type of assertion which Wild frequently makes and which seems to function as little less than a fundamental philosophical principle with him. Perhaps we might best bring out the character and import of this principle by piecing together several sentences drawn from his very significant chapter on "Philosophy and Freedom." "In the central tradition of Western thought," Wild avers, "philosophy has usually been regarded as a purely theoretical or scientific discipline whose function is to understand the basic structure of the objective universe as it is in itself, apart from human desire and prejudice" (p. 120). "The objective perspective is outwardly directed toward external things and structures. . . . It aims at formulating propositions which will agree with the objective facts as they already are and have been determined to be. In this sense it is externally determined and passive" (p. 125). "In the rationalistic tradition of Western thought . . . reason has been conceived along objectivist lines, as externally determined by its formal object rather than spontaneous and independent, as passive and assimilative

16. This is Popper's own translation of the relevant passage from Kant and appears in *Conjectures and Refutations* (New York and London: Basic Books, 1962), p. 189.

17. It should be remarked perhaps that Popper himself does not take this turn, though with what philosophical consistency he is able to refrain from doing so is another question.

rather than active, and finally as receptive of what is already determined rather than as open to the ambiguous and indeterminate" (p. 126). "Traditional rationalism, still alive in the common sense of our time, has not only maintained that understanding is nonspontaneous and divorced from action; it has also held that our human awareness is directed toward an objective universe that is already fixed in its essential structure" (p. 129).

Now the principle which we would suggest is implicit in these passages is really twofold: reason or understanding is held to be essentially receptive and passive with respect to the character and structures of the objects which it comes to know; and, for their part, the objects that thus come to be known are already determined and are, as it were, ensconced in "an objective universe that is already fixed in its essential structure." Given such a twofold principle—which in fact serves Wild as a principle of interpretation when it comes to Aristotelian realism —it then becomes understandable why John Wild should have seemed to fly in the face of the facts and to have interpreted the supposedly lived world of Aristotelian realism as being in fact not a lived world at all but a rigidly determined and structured universe, from which all change, all indeterminacy, all freedom, and all value have been excluded. The reason is that on his principle of interpretation not only must a realistic type of knowledge be determined simply by its object, but that object in turn must itself be rigidly fixed and determined.

But why this last? Granted that in any genuine realism knowledge must indeed be determined by its object, why must this mean that any such object of knowledge must itself be fixed, determinate, and determined? Quite the contrary; suppose that the object which one was seeking to know and to understand were itself more or less indeterminate, being incomplete, in process of change, and open to various alternative lines of development. Would not one's knowledge of that object as it is in itself have to reflect these very indeterminacies and ambiguities? Indeed, the very requirement of utter passivity in knowledge with which Wild so repeatedly reproaches the realists,[18] so far

18. Granted that in any genuine realism knowledge must be in large measure determined by its object, I do not think, as Wild seems to think, that it necessarily follows from this that such knowledge must involve a complete passivity on the part of the knower, as if the knower could in no wise be the agent of his own knowledge. However, this criticism is one that hardly needs to be pressed in the argument of this paper.

from entailing any fixity or rigidity or determinateness or even necessity in the object of knowledge, might well entail just the opposite, depending upon the particular kind of object that one had to do with.

With this, however, it would seem that the very principle which John Wild appeals to in his assessment of traditional realism turns out to be not so much a principle as a decidedly unwarranted assumption. Moreover, once this assumption has been exposed, there would then seem to be no reason why our knowledge of the very world we live in, with all of its indeterminacies and ambiguities and uncertainties, should not be a straightforward, realistic knowledge of the real world as it is in itself. In other words, the first consideration which we have suggested might have been operative in influencing Wild to take the transcendental turn with respect to the *Lebenswelt* turns out to be a consideration that is not merely inadequate to this purpose, but perhaps even inaccurate.

A Suggested Rebuttal
of the Second Consideration

What, though, of the second consideration? Might this perhaps prove to be a more fruitful source for a properly transcendental argument in justification of Wild's quite patent transcendental turn? Already we have conceded, in the passing notice which we gave of this second consideration, that if in fact human beings do have a "freedom of world constitution," as Wild calls it, then the worlds that get constituted in this way must be understood transcendentally rather than realistically. That is to say, a philosopher cannot avoid taking the transcendental turn, as soon as world constitution in this sense becomes the order of the day. But then have we not got the very sort of transcendental justification that John Wild needs in order to support his general mode and manner of conceiving and treating of the life-world?

Clearly, though, before this particular line of transcendental justification can be made really telling, one must first ask just what the basis is for Wild's fundamental premise and point of departure in this connection. What he begins with is the conviction that human beings are free beings just in the sense that they have a freedom of world constitution; and, given the soundness of this conviction, then indeed Wild would appear to have a means of justifying the transcendental turn which he takes with reference to the *Lebenswelt*.

But what sort of evidence does he have for this freedom of human beings in this particular sense? He cannot legitimately say that his evidence lies simply in his experience of human beings in the lived world of everyday experience, for the lived world is a constituted world; and if the evidence for human freedom amounts to no more than the way men appear to us in the lived world—i.e., the way we take them to be, the sense that we make of human life and of our human existence—then this will not do. For the sort of freedom that provides the basis for Wild's argument is something that has to be presupposed by, and actually makes possible, any and all appearances of things in the lived world, as well as our taking them to be the way we do, and our giving them the sense and meaning that we do. Hence if such freedom is a presupposition of our making sense of things in our world, it cannot be a product of the sense that we make of human beings and their existence.

Put in more technical language, what this challenge amounts to is this: the kind of evidence which John Wild needs to support his thesis of human freedom cannot be an empirical evidence based on his experience of men in the *Lebenswelt*. Nor for the same reason can his thesis even be treated as an explanatory hypothesis that may be verified or falsified by the experience which we have of men in the lived world. The only sort of evidence that could properly count here would be transcendental evidence. And does Wild ever provide evidence of this sort?

Now it is true that in any number of passages in his work Wild inveighs eloquently against any mere relativism of human world constitutions. "Thus it is easy for us, in our everyday reflections," he remarks, "to confuse our life-world and its contingent accidents with *the* life-world" (p. 137). And he promptly charges Heidegger with having done just this; and not only Heidegger, but the medieval philosophers, Hegel, and even the present-day existentialists in their support of "their versions of radical humanism" (p. 137). Indeed, the list of offenders in this regard seems to include nearly everyone except Socrates, Kant, and, of course, John Wild himself. However, what Wild is really upbraiding the philosophers for, and in fact all of us, is that we are forever guilty of a "failure to distinguish between *the* world and versions of the world" (p. 168).

Could it be, then, that when one does draw this distinction, and does penetrate beyond mere versions of the world to *the* world, one will there discover that in the world men really and truly are nothing but resources of freedom, and of a freedom of world constitution no less? Unhappily, it is difficult to answer this question, because Wild studiously refrains from trying to give any very detailed account of what *the* world is like. In fact, at times he even seems to suggest that there is no such thing, the expression "*the* world" amounting to no more than a kind of formula for always going beyond any given version of the world, and yet without there ever being any final or ultimate or absolute world which might properly be called *the* world (see p. 134). At other times, though, Wild explicitly denies that his philosophy is one of mere "radical transcendence," as he calls it (p. 138). Indeed, on the very same page he proclaims that

> the time has now come to say emphatically that the noetic freedom of which I have been speaking does not mean irresponsible choice, or believing anything we please, irrespective of the evidence. At each of the levels to which we have referred, there is evidence against which our chosen interpretations must be checked. The life-world is not a chaos of arbitrary constructions.[19] It is marked by lasting structures of existence, like lived time and space, feeling, language, death, and worldliness itself, which condition and limit our choices (p. 138; see also p. 75).

True, in this list of the nonrelative and lasting structures of existence which are to be found in *the* world, the specific item of

19. One wonders if it may not be an analogous difficulty that Wild finds himself confronted with when he comes to ethics and the question of whether there is any basis for ethical norms and standards. Such standards can hardly be derived from the world, since they would then be no better than projections of our own in our activity of world constitution. But what, then, can be the source of our moral norms and standards, unless perhaps Wild were to set up a real world in opposition to the mere worlds we constitute, and were to trace our standards back to the former as contrasted with the latter? Note, though, that Wild struggles manfully, even if in our judgment unsuccessfully, with this ethical issue. See his essay, "Authentic Existence: A New Approach to 'Value Theory,'" in *An Invitation to Phenomenology*, ed. James Edie (Chicago: Quadrangle Books, 1965), pp. 59–77. See also Chap. 9 of *Existence and the World of Freedom*, entitled "Authentic Existence and Value."

man's freedom in the sense we are here considering is not included. Yet for purposes of argument let us suppose that it should really have been put there; it surely is there by implication, and, to paraphrase Wild's own words, it would seem that the evidence for such a human freedom is indeed an "evidence against which our chosen interpretations must be checked," and that the fact of such freedom is an undeniable feature of the life-world rather than any mere "arbitrary construction."

So be it. But then if such is the evidence for man's freedom, it turns out to be not a transcendental evidence after all. Instead, it is as if Wild, in toying with the idea that the life-world might be *the* world, had inadvertently converted them both into nothing less than the real world, and not merely the real world as it is for us and considered in a transcendental context, but rather the real world as it is in itself. But with this, Wild would have completely betrayed his own program of a transcendental philosophy and would have tumbled back into something like a most un-Critical realism. And that for John Wild would be not so much a regression as perhaps even an atavism, considering his own past intellectual history.

The more one reflects upon the second consideration, which at first glance seemed to offer the means for justifying John Wild's having taken the transcendental turn in philosophy, the more the internal dialectic generated by that same consideration exposes it as little more than a snare and a delusion. If the fact of man's freedom is what justifies man's transcendental constitution of his own life-world, then what is the evidence that such a human freedom is indeed a fact? It can hardly be made evident through our experience with human beings in the life-world, since such a freedom is presupposed if there is to be any experience of any kind in the life-world at all. On the other hand, if such a freedom is something which we recognize as pertaining to men simply as they are in themselves and not merely as we take them to be, then so far from one's evidence being a transcendental evidence, one has forsaken transcendental philosophy altogether and returned once more to realism. *Facilis descensus Averno!*

So it is then that our somewhat paradoxical earlier question turns out to be a really pressing one for John Wild, for does he not need to be far more critical in his seemingly rather uncritical Critical approach to the *Lebenswelt*? It is true that taking the transcendental turn in philosophy has become, nowadays, not merely *à la mode*, but almost *de rigueur*, and not merely among those influenced by phenomenology, but among the ordinary language philosophers as well. Yet for some strange reason this turn seems often to be made cryptically or in secret, or perhaps naively and without the thinkers involved really knowing what they are doing. Thus Norman Malcolm in a celebrated essay [20] some years ago sought to transpose or transform G. E. Moore's defense of common-sense realism into a defense of ordinary language. And yet the question seems not to have been faced at all as to whether one could legitimately assign such a privileged position to these ordinary uses and locutions, short of turning them into a kind of transcendental logic. True enough, Stanley Cavell has said in so many words that the necessity which we feel attaches to our ordinary linguistic uses is due to the fact that these latter are "instances (not of Formal, but) of Transcendental Logic." [21] He even goes so far as to set alongside the passage which we earlier quoted from Kant regarding knowledge of a transcendental sort, the following gnomic utterance of Wittgenstein: "Our investigation . . . is directed not towards phenomena, but, as one might say, towards the 'possibilities' of phenomena [§90]." [22] Yet however much Cavell seems here inclined to take Wittgenstein as a sort of gloss upon Kant, or perhaps Kant upon Wittgenstein, Cavell does not bother to amplify or explain, much less to justify, his notion of the transcendental turn as being the one and only primrose way to contemporary philosophy. Nor do Strawson and Sellars and others like them seem to be any less unsatisfactory and evasive on the score of their crypto-transcendentalism.

Accordingly, when one presses John Wild with the need not to let his transcendental arguments walk in darkness, but to bring them out into the light, the issue is not one of the lived-world as over against the scientific world, or of ordinary language as over against a presumed ideal language. Many a classical realist would be the first to grant either Wild or the ordinary

20. "Moore on Ordinary Language," in *Ordinary Language*, ed. V. C. Chappell (Englewood Cliffs, N.J.: Prentice-Hall, 1964), pp. 5–23.

21. See Cavell's essay, "Must We Mean What We Say?" *ibid.*, p. 86.

22. This is quoted in "The Availability of Wittgenstein's Later Philosophy," in *Wittgenstein: The Philosophical Investigations*, ed. George Pitcher (Garden City, N.Y.: Doubleday, 1966), p. 176.

language philosophers these points. The issue is rather one as to why the life-world, in order to be saved and defended, must be understood in some sort of transcendental context or setting. It is with respect to this issue that it would seem one can no longer afford to be uncritical.

3 / Homage to Saint Anselm

Robert Jordan

MOST DISCUSSIONS of arguments for the existence of God have a quality of unreality about them. Perhaps one reason for this is that the arguments continue to be advanced and refuted in spite of widespread agreement that the whole enterprise is misconceived. It has even become fashionable for theologians to dismiss the exercise as misguided from the start and to suggest, in certain moods, that there is something faintly ridiculous in the notion that finite and sinful man could actually demonstrate that the ground of his being is really there after all. But books and articles continue to appear and we can confidently expect to be told repeatedly and regularly what is *really* wrong with the ontological argument, not to mention other less suspect demonstrations. Philosophers seem unable to let go of the problem of God's existence even in the face of what appears to be solid evidence that they never should have picked it up in the first place. All of this seems the more remarkable when one notices that most of the participants in the debate apparently agree that the problem of God's existence is a purely theoretical or possibly a purely logical matter.

Occasionally, however, a different approach has been acknowledged, although rarely if ever adopted. Canon Van Steenberghen makes the following remark about the conclusion which his own argument leads to, namely, that the order of finite beings requires the affirmation of an infinite being:

This discovery would be exciting for a man who would actually live it, who would see directly into all its moral and religious implications.[1]

Indeed, as he goes on to say, such a discovery, when all of its implications had been worked out, might transform one's entire life and one's whole understanding of the world. Or consider the conclusion of Norman Malcolm's much discussed defense of the ontological argument of *Proslogion* III, a kind of concluding unscientific postscript to what has gone before. Malcolm says:

> But even if one allows that Anselm's phrase may be free of contradiction, one wants to know how it can have any *meaning* for anyone. Why is it that human beings have even *formed* the concept of an infinite being, a being a greater than which cannot be conceived? This is a legitimate and important question. I am sure there cannot be a deep understanding of that concept without an understanding of the phenomena of human life that give rise to it. . . . If one had the acuteness and depth to perceive these connections one could grasp the *sense* of the concept. When we encounter this concept as a problem in philosophy, we do not consider the human phenomena that lie behind it. It is not surprising that many philosophers believe that the idea of a necessary being is an arbitrary and absurd construction.[2]

If there ever was a philosopher who really *lived* an argument, a philosopher for whom the synthesis of philosophy and theology as the quest for wisdom was a "form of life," it was Saint Anselm. He was not alone in this because it is characteristic of the Augustinian family generally. But there is hardly a better example of the Augustinian conception of the relation of faith and reason than the two meditations called *Monologion* and *Proslogion*. I shall assume that these two works are intimately related, and that in a certain kind of way, which I shall try to indicate later, the second depends upon the first. Other people have taken this position and I am aware of the hazard in doing so. Some writers have maintained that the ontological argument presupposes the arguments of the *Monologion*, but Arthur

1. F. Van Steenberghen, *Ontology* (New York: Joseph F. Wagner, 1952), p. 141.
2. In *The Ontological Argument*, ed. Alvin Plantinga (Garden City, N.Y.: Doubleday, 1965), pp. 157–59.

McGill points out that Anselm says quite clearly in the preface to the *Proslogion* that he set out to find a completely autonomous argument which would require for its proof "nothing else but itself alone." [3] This should be decisive, I think, if one is thinking of structures of reasoning alone or of logical problems to be solved. Anselm was a formidable logician and skillful linguistic analyst, but it seems to me that one cannot say that the *Proslogion* is simply the solution to a logical problem. That would be false to its character of spiritual meditation. At any rate, I want to suggest that Anselm is not merely solving a logical problem or puzzle but rather completing a vision, a metaphysical or ontological vision. The vision is an intellectual "seeing," of course, but I can think of no more appropriate term for it. In fact, Anselm uses "vision" in this sense, or at least in a way very similar to it, as I shall indicate later. In any case, I am talking mainly about a habit of mind or mode of thought rather than a precisely defined method or a particular argument.

This mode of thought appears first in Plato's theory of participation and remains a constant in every variety of Platonism. It is everywhere in Augustine's writings and, indeed, it seems to be the natural mode of thinking for all the members of the Platonic-Augustinian family, from Augustine himself to St. Bonaventura. It is a mode of thought which represents one long line of meditation on and speculation about the analogy of being, the analogous modalities of being, even when the writers in question have no express doctrine of analogy.[4] Here it is essential to remember that the motto of the Augustinian family is "faith seeking understanding," and not only to remember it but to give it the central place it deserves. Why the central place? Because it must continually be kept in mind that for philosophers in this

3. *The Many-faced Argument*, ed. John C. Hick and Arthur C. McGill (New York: Macmillan, 1967), pp. 105–6.

4. I refrain from saying that the line is finally completed by Aquinas in his discussion of the analogy of names and of analogical predication. What Aquinas means by analogy is, at the moment, open to dispute. See Ralph M. McInerny, *The Logic of Analogy* (The Hague: Martinus Nijhoff, 1961), esp. pp. 33, 47, 166–69. McInerny argues that the analogy of names is a logical question, not a metaphysical one, that the analogy of being is simply the analogy of "being" (p. 167). Whether this is sound Thomism I must leave to others to decide. But I am convinced that it is not Anselm. It is surely true that the logical and real orders should not be confused. It is also surely true that they should not be divorced. See Battista Mondin, S.X., *The Principle of Analogy in Protestant and Catholic Theology* (The Hague: Martinus Nijhoff, 1963), esp. Chaps. 3 and 4.

tradition faith and reason do not come apart, that logical speculation, no matter how sophisticated, is never divorced from experience, which is to say that it is never separated, though it is
distinguished, from its ontological ground.[5] Although I can't
bring myself to accept his general assessment of the ontological
argument, R. W. Southern does recognize the importance of the
experiential element in the formulation of the argument. With
reference to Anselm's argument he says:

> If God exists, there must be a level of *experience* at which it is
> impossible to think of God as not existing. But at what level can
> this impossibility be made to appear? Must the demonstration
> await the experience of the Beatific Vision? Or can it, at the very
> opposite extreme, be made out at the level of linguistic-logical
> analysis? [6]

My contention is that the impossibility appears at neither extreme. Obviously, it does not await the beatific vision, nor does it
depend upon faith. Is it made clear at the level of linguistic-logi-
cal analysis? No, because such analysis only produces the means
by which an ontological insight is *expressed*. This is a thoroughly rational but not merely logical matter.[7] I shall now try to
support this contention.

I suppose that it is taken for granted by commentators on
Anselm's argument that there must be some crucial point where
the trouble starts, and that if we could only identify it precisely
we could then eliminate it and resolve the issue once and for all.
Perhaps it is because there has been no general agreement about
this precise point that no argument has resisted final refutation
as successfully as Anselm's. I have my own notion about the
crucial point in the argument and it is this: the trouble starts at
the very beginning of *Proslogion* II, with the phrase "something
than which nothing greater can be thought." I think that most
discussions of the argument pass too quickly beyond the phrase
itself to a consideration of the logic or the grammar of the
subsequent argument. The question which should be asked first

5. This is borne out by Anselm's discussion of truth in the *de Veritate*.
See *Truth, Freedom, and Evil: Three Philosophical Dialogues*, ed. Jasper
Hopkins and Herbert Richardson (New York: Harper & Row, 1967).

6. R. W. Southern, *Saint Anselm and His Biographer* (Cambridge: At
the University Press, 1963), p. 65 (italics added).

7. On this question, see D. P. Henry, *The Logic of Saint Anselm*
(Oxford: Clarendon Press, 1967), pp. 148–49.

is: Does the phrase "that than which nothing greater can be thought" have any positive content or meaning? What is it that is the object of this thought, and can one actually ever attain this notion?

In Descartes's version of the argument in the Fifth Meditation one is invited to ask a question about the content of the idea immediately and for two reasons. Descartes says:

> But now, if just because I can draw the idea of something from my thought, it follows that all which I know clearly and distinctly as pertaining to this object does really belong to it, may I not derive from this an argument demonstrating the existence of God? It is certain that I no less find the idea of God, that is to say, the idea of a supremely perfect Being, in me, than that of any figure or number, whatever it is.[8]

In the first place, even if it is understood that for Descartes an innate idea is not one which is always present in the mind but rather one that the mind can summon up, one is compelled to ask what the positive content of the idea of God is and to question, at least, whether this idea could be in *any* sense innate. Secondly, not only does Descartes have the idea, but it is both clear and distinct. This is a claim so bold that, while it seems absurd to tell a man that he does not have an idea which he confidently says that he has, we are bound to wonder whether Descartes is deceiving himself in some way. In what he goes on to say in Meditation V and in his replies to his critics we are given an answer. The term "God" stands for a supremely perfect Being whose existence cannot be separated from His essence. But we are inclined to raise the same question about these terms. What is the actual content or actual reference of these conceptions? We may write or say the words "Supreme Being," "existence of God," and "essence of God," but unless they stand for something actual they cannot be genuine conceptions. Hence we are further inclined to state the argument as a hypothetical one, which must always remain hypothetical because the terms can never really be filled in.[9]

8. *The Philosophical Works of Descartes*, trans. E. S. Haldane and G. R. Ross (New York: Dover Publications, 1955), I, 180.
9. On this point see Charles Hartshorne's essay in Plantinga, *The Ontological Argument*, esp. p. 135, where he gives as the form of the hypothetical, "If 'God' stands for something conceivable, it stands for something actual." The same problem is encountered in arguments em-

This Cartesian digression may appear to have little or nothing to do with Anselm and, generally speaking, I think it is only misleading to compare Anselm and Descartes. There is nothing in Anselm which is remotely like an innate idea and there are other obvious differences between the two philosophers, both epistemological and metaphysical. But on the particular point in question a comparison is legitimate and relevant. *Proslogion* IV, following the demonstration that God not only exists but cannot be thought not to exist, explains why, in that case, the Fool can say in his heart, "There is no God." The explanation is that "to think" can mean two different things:

> For in one sense a thing is thought when the word signifying it is thought; in another sense when the very object which the thing is is understood. In the first sense, then, God can be thought not to exist, but not at all in the second sense. . . . Whoever really understands (bene intelligit) this understands clearly that this same being so exists that not even in thought can it not exist. Thus whoever understands that God exists in such a way cannot think of Him as not existing.[10]

Plainly, only the person who understands *well*, who *really* understands what is meant by "God," will see the force of the preceding argument. Anyone who does not *really* understand and yet denies that God exists simply does not know what he is talking about.[11] He has the word "God" in his mind but he does not have the conception of God *in intellectu*. Here I follow Charlesworth and McGill in interpreting the phrase *in intellectu* not as meaning "mental" or "in the mind" but rather "intelligible," "conceivable," or "standing in relation to the understanding." [12] I take it

---

ploying the analogy of proper proportionality. Thus we might say that God is to His being as the creature is to its being, as a way of asserting that essence and existence are identical in God, but not in creatures. The objection would be that both the essence and the existence of God are unknown terms. Whether there is an adequate answer to this objection is another question altogether and a large one. But, clearly, the problem is common to all arguments for the existence of God. It simply makes its appearance more quickly in the ontological argument.

10. *Proslogion* IV, pp. 119–21. All quotations from the *Proslogion* are from the translation of M. J. Charlesworth, *St. Anselm's Proslogion* (Oxford: Clarendon Press, 1965), hereafter cited as Charlesworth.

11. On this point and on the significance of the prayer which closes *Proslogion* IV, see D. P. Henry, *The Logic of Saint Anselm*, pp. 149–50.

12. Charlesworth, p. 63; Hick and McGill, *The Many-faced Argument*, pp. 4–5, 82.

that what this comes to is that to *really* understand the word "God" is to engage in an act of thinking which has an intentionality pointing outside of itself.

The same distinction seems to be made in Section III of Anselm's reply to Gaunilo:

> In short, if anyone says that he thinks that this being [that-than-which-a-greater-cannot-be-thought] does not exist, I reply that, when he thinks of this, either he thinks of something than which a greater cannot be thought, or he does not think of it. If he does not think of it, then he does not think that what he does not think of does not exist.[13]

The only reasonable way to interpret this is to say that the word "God" can be thought of in conjunction with the words "does not exist," but this does not mean that, in Anselm's terms, the word "God" has been understood. One might hold in mind the words "that-than-which-a-greater-cannot-be-thought" together with the words "does not exist," but the words are not *in intellectu* in the sense required by Anselm for real understanding. However, while this reading of Anselm removes some difficulties by clarifying his intention, it leaves others untouched. It answers the Fool, but it does not meet the objections of those who speak on the Fool's behalf. If we are to be concerned with no more than the contrast between thinking a notion verbally and really understanding it, then either we understand it or we don't understand it, either we see it or we don't see it. And we are left, apparently, with only one conclusion, that the existence of "that-than-which-a-greater-cannot-be-thought" is a self-evident truth and therefore needs no argument. But it is obvious from *Proslogion* II that Anselm thinks he is proposing a genuine argument. Indeed, *Proslogion* II and III are unintelligible on any other assumption, something which is clearly reflected in the literature about the ontological argument.

Perhaps Anselm is not quite consistent in his conception of who the Fool is. In *Proslogion* II it is the Fool who says in his heart that there is no God, and who raises the question about whether it is possible that what Anselm believes is false. But the Fool here is not one who entertains in his mind merely verbal connections between words. For Anselm says:

13. Charlesworth, pp. 176–77.

But surely, when this same Fool hears what I am speaking about, namely, "something-than-which-nothing-greater-can-be-thought," he understands what he hears, and what he understands is in his mind, even if he does not understand that it actually exists.[14]

Almost immediately, in *Proslogion* IV, the distinction between thinking words and understanding "the very object which the thing is" is introduced. There are three states of mind, then, which we are to reflect upon. Something can be "in thought" in the sense that the word signifying it is in thought, and in this sense God could be thought not to exist. Something can be in thought in the sense that the person thinking it possesses a meaningful concept, not just a word. But according to *Proslogion* II such a person "understands what he hears, and what he understands is in his mind, even if he does not understand that it actually exists." This must mean that such a person could think the notion of "something-than-which-nothing-greater-can-be-thought" while withholding assent to its existence. What he thinks has meaning for him, but, although he understands it, he does not understand it *well*. His understanding is incomplete. It is completed by the last part of *Proslogion* II and by *Proslogion* III.

It might be objected that these two chapters present quite different arguments. Norman Malcolm has argued persuasively that this is indeed true and that the ontological argument can be understood only by distinguishing carefully between the reasoning in *Proslogion* II and the very different argument of *Proslogion* III. In terms of the logic of these two passages I think that Malcolm's recommendations can hardly be resisted. But in terms of the ontological vision which, as I have suggested, is being completed in Anselm's argument, it is more helpful, I think, to regard *Proslogion* II and III as continuous although they represent different moments in the movement of the mind which Anselm is describing. Malcolm's distinction is important for his interpretation of Anselm, because he wishes to defend the argument of *Proslogion* III but to reject the argument of *Proslogion* II, on the ground that in II Anselm argues that existence is a perfection but that in III he argues that necessary existence is a perfection, which is not the same thing at all. Therefore, it is of

14. *Ibid.*, p. 117.

the greatest importance not to confuse the two kinds of reasoning.

"The doctrine that existence is a perfection," Malcolm says, "is remarkably queer." [15] I am not persuaded that it is as queer as he makes it out to be. He believes that his objection to it amounts to a repetition of Kant's well-known contention that existence or being is not a real predicate. The point is important for what I shall say later, and I want to consider it briefly. Malcolm uses several illustrations to support his position, including the following:

> A king might desire that his next chancellor should have knowledge, wit, and resolution; but it is ludicrous to add that the king's desire is to have a chancellor who exists. Suppose that two royal councilors, A and B, were asked to draw up separately descriptions of the most perfect chancellor they could conceive, and that the descriptions they produced were identical except that A included existence in his list of attributes of a perfect chancellor and B did not. (I do not mean that B put nonexistence in his list.) One and the same person could satisfy both descriptions.[16]

Well, one and the same *real* person could satisfy both descriptions. It seems ludicrous to add existence to the other attributes for the simple reason that nobody would desire a nonexistent chancellor. Existence is taken for granted. But there is a more important reason for the oddness of the language here. Existence is not the same kind of attribute as those that make up the description of the most perfect chancellor. The attributes of the description will all be powers, capacities, or other characteristics which a person might have and would then actualize or act upon, provided that there actually was such a person. One cannot add existence to the list as though it were a property or quality, like skin color or the ability to dissimulate. The properties described all belong to the essence of the ideal chancellor. But this does not mean that existence may be disregarded. Ontologically speaking, it is not ludicrous to "add" existence; it is in fact necessary to do so, although it might be wise to use less odd-sounding language in doing it. Indeed, existence *is* added in the description of the most perfect chancellor just because it is taken for granted. There may be good reasons for taking it for granted, but that this is being done should be acknowledged. Suppose that a person possessing the qualifications of the ideal chancellor is, in fact, discovered. Such a person will *actually* possess the attributes of the description. Now, existence is not something actualized along with the other attributes. It is the act of existing which supports all of the attributes collectively and in the most fundamental way possible. And this is the reason why existence cannot be "added," except by using language which produces such a bizarre effect that the crucial *importance* of existence is actually obscured. That is to say, the capacity to be at all is more fundamental than the capacity to act in various ways, once the thing in question, whatever it may be, exists.

Malcolm quotes with approval Gassendi's objection to Descartes:

> Existence is a perfection neither in God nor in anything else; it is rather that in the absence of which there is no perfection. . . . Hence neither is existence held to exist in a thing in the way perfections do, nor if the thing lacks existence is it said to be imperfect (or deprived of a perfection), so much as to be nothing.[17]

If an example of remarkably queer language is wanted, I submit that this specimen will do nicely. Its apparent sense disguises its real non-sense. But to go along with this particular language-game, let us say that we should not include existence in the description of the most perfect chancellor. Whether this has force against Descartes I leave aside. Perhaps it does, since Descartes speaks explicitly of existence as a perfection. But in a kind of backhanded way, the quotation makes the point that I tried to make. A little further on in the same letter Gassendi chides Descartes for comparing existence with a property.[18] The reason is, of course, that by doing so we are inevitably led to include existence in the description of the ideal chancellor. Now, Gassendi's antecedent metaphysical commitments may prevent him from understanding perfections in any way other than as properties, as this term is commonly understood. But this cuts no ice against Anselm, who has quite different metaphysical commitments. I am not persuaded that it even counts against Descartes. In his reply to Gassendi, Descartes says that he finds

17. *Ibid.*, pp. 140–41.
18. Haldane and Ross, *Philosophical Works of Descartes*, II, 185.

no incongruity in the notion that existence is a property of God, "because it belongs to Him and forms part of His essence alone." With things other than God this is not true, of course, but Descartes adds the following interesting comment.

> I do not, nevertheless, deny that existence is a possible perfection in the idea of a triangle, as it is a necessary one in the idea of God; for this fact makes the idea of the triangle one of higher rank than the ideas of those chimerical things whose existence can never be supposed.[19]

Perhaps more to the point is the statement which opens this passage of Descartes's letter: "Here I do not see to what class of reality you wish to assign existence." And here Descartes is squarely on target. In other words, if I may put it in my own way, if existence adds nothing to the description of the most perfect chancellor, it does something else which one would suppose is at least worth noticing, although nobody seems interested enough to notice it—it adds *the chancellor*.

To return to the *Proslogion,* the question which should be asked before one scrutinizes the logic of the argument is an ontological question. What kind of thinking, what kind of metaphysical vision, informs Anselm's mind and provides the background for *Proslogion* II and III? My contention is that the ontological argument itself is the expression of a long process of ontological meditation, that the argument is the completion in words of a movement of the mind which is prior to the statement of the argument and without which the argument is purely formal. I think, further, that the argument cannot be understood without taking into account what I would call the metaphysical or ontological reach of Anselm's speculation. I suppose that what I am saying here is that the ontological argument has exactly the right name. It remains an ontological argument, regardless of the logical machinery which can be brought to bear upon its interpretation.

In other words, I am taking up Malcolm's suggestion, which, at the close of his paper, he makes in the following way:

> At a deeper level, I suspect that the argument can be thoroughly understood only by one who has a view of that human "form of life" that gives rise to the idea of an infinitely great being, who

19. *Ibid.,* p. 228.

views it from *inside* not just from the outside and who has, therefore, at least some inclination to partake in that religious form of life. . . . This inclination can hardly be an *effect* of Anselm's argument, but is rather presupposed in the fullest understanding of it.[20]

I also hope that, at the same time, I am addressing myself to the kind of existential concern which John Wild has discussed in his recent books and, in particular, in his essay, "An Existential Argument for Transcendence." [21] I don't mean that what I shall say supplements Wild's position or that it is directly supported by it. But I think that on the whole it is compatible with that position. My reason for thinking so is my conviction that what precedes Anselm's argument is, allowing for the obvious differences between the forms of thought of his time and our own, a phenomenology of being. In summing up his own argument concerning the passage from the limited and finite to the transcendent, Wild says:

> This existential argument is based on motions rather than notions. One must live through this passage to really understand the argument, which simply brings out the sense and clarifies the original lived experience.[22]

I would not say that this is all that Anselm is doing, but it is a part of what he is doing, and an important part, perhaps the most important part. It is also what Augustinians insist upon wherever one finds them. The inseparability of thinking from living, willing, and loving is one of the marks of the Augustinian family.

I said earlier that one might be baffled by Anselm's argument even before attempting a logical analysis of it simply because of the pivotal phrase, "that-than-which-nothing-greater-can-be-thought." If this is more than verbal trickery or self-deception, what could the phrase refer to? How is it possible to relate the expression to its content? What would it mean to form this conception? What am I thinking of when I think this notion? [23]

20. Plantinga, *The Ontological Argument*, p. 159.
21. *The Journal of Bible and Religion*, XXX (October, 1962), 269–77. At the end of his argument Wild points out that it has affinities with the arguments of Anselm and Bonaventura.
22. *Ibid.*, p. 273.
23. The question is raised by Gaunilo in his reply, § 4 (Charlesworth, p. 161).

In the first place we know from *Monologion* I that Anselm was not only a follower of Augustine but that his intention was to remain loyal to Augustine on all substantive issues. But this does not mean that Anselm appealed to Augustine as an authority; nor does it mean that he was only concerned to repeat Augustinian doctrines, although, as Gilson observes, many of those teachings find their clearest expression in Anselm, including the family motto, faith seeking understanding. It does mean that Anselm shared the Augustinian mode of thought or habit of mind, which is not difficult to recognize and identify because it includes, as functional moments in the quest for wisdom (to borrow Albert Balz's phrase), faith and reason, the experiential and even existential, and the conceptual. What characterizes this mode of thought is a continual preoccupation with the metaphysical contrast between the temporal and the eternal, the mutable and the immutable, the limited and the unlimited, a sustained meditation on the modalities of being.

Regardless of the importance of logic in Anselm's time, and granting that Anselm was a redoubtable logician, one must wonder whether Gilson is correct in his judgment that the ontological argument is a purely logical demonstration.[24] Such a position ignores the experiential nature of the quest for wisdom which is a constant in the tradition with which Anselm identifies himself. To think in terms of the modalities of being is not to pose purely conceptual problems. It is to *participate*, at the same time, in the contingency which this speculation brings to light. It is very easy to lose sight of this fact, or to ignore it altogether. For example, Régis Jolivet offers the stock criticism of Anselm, that the argument deals only with ideas and that there is, accordingly, no guarantee that there is anything real, corresponding to the idea, outside the mind. Recent discussions of Anselm have shown, convincingly, that this kind of criticism misses Anselm's point entirely. There is another way of missing it which is even more serious. Jolivet concludes his short critique with the following statement:

> This idea only acquires validity and consistency if it is truly formed by the mind as a consequence of the demands of real being and is grasped through experience.[25]

24. *Reason and Revelation in the Middle Ages* (New York: Scribner, 1938), pp. 23–26.
25. *The God of Reason* (London: Burns and Oates, 1958), p. 46.

The imagination boggles at a comment like this because this is precisely what Anselm does and it is only by recognizing that he does it that the ontological argument makes any sense at all. There must be some reason why the ontological argument can be decisively refuted several times a year and still retain its fascination. Apparently, its spell is so great that the demand for new refutations far exceeds the supply. Part of the answer must be that Anselm had an unusually complex mind, capable of holding in balance a theology of grace and a philosophy which did complete justice to the life of reason.[26] It may be difficult for the contemporary mind to appreciate such a delicate balance, but to recognize in Anselm only a resolute logician is to overlook the vision which informed the expression of his thought.

It is for this reason, I think, that the *Monologion* and *Proslogion* can be interpreted as significantly related. I have said that, in my judgment, Anselm was completing an intellectual vision in the *Proslogion*. The vision begins to take shape in the *Monologion*. Beginning with the notion of degrees of goodness, Anselm moves to degrees of existence, presenting a causal argument to the effect that limited beings must exist through something which

> does not exist through any efficient agent and does not derive existence from any matter, and was not aided in being brought into existence by any external causes.[27]

Such a being exists through itself, and the contrast is between the being that exists through itself and the beings that exist through something other than themselves.

> But whatever exists through another is less than that, through which all things are, and which alone exists through itself. Therefore, that which exists through itself exists in the greatest degree of all things.[28]

Anselm goes on to argue for an unlimited ground of the limited perfections which we see everywhere around us, contrasting

26. A very sensitive discussion of this aspect of Anselm's thought can be found in Maurice Nedoncelle, *Is There a Christian Philosophy?* (London: Burns and Oates, 1960), Chap. 3.

27. *Monologion* VI, p. 48. All references to the *Monologion* are to the Sidney Norton Deane translation (Chicago: Open Court, 1939), hereafter cited as Deane.

28. Deane, III, 48.

always what is changing, temporal, and conditioned with what is the necessary termination of our meditation on mutability—that which is changeless, immutable, and unconditioned. All of this is not a mere piece of ratiocination but a philosophical meditation on the substance of faith.[29] The fact that Anselm broke new ground in composing these works by refraining from any appeal to Scripture does not make either of his meditations a work of pure reason. They are, indeed, perfect illustrations of the *enactment* of the Augustinian ideal of wisdom, that life of the spirit in which faith and reason are distinguished, but a life in which, as Albert Balz put it so well, "reason and faith are dynamically coimplicative." [30]

I want, now, to propose a question and to try to suggest an answer. However, the question is very difficult to frame because what I am asking about is the nature of a spiritual life in which nonconceptual thought is as important as conceptual thought, and where reason, imagination, emotion, and love are functioning together as elements of a total experience. But I think we must ask what is happening in this kind of thinking. What is the character of the experience which Anselm then expresses in the words of his meditations? I suggest that it is the experience of the analogical structure of being, a partly nonconceptual intuition of the modalities of existence. Of course, when it gets expressed, it will be conceptual, unless it takes the form of poetry, prayer, or perhaps soliloquy.

That analogy has some role in Anselm's thinking is, obviously, not a new discovery of mine, and a reader of the two meditations could scarcely miss the clues. The question is: What are we to make of them? Charlesworth says, in his commentary, that "Anselm is feeling his way tentatively towards the theory of analogy that plays a central role in Aquinas's theology," and again, with reference to *Proslogion* V, "Anselm is here hinting at the theory of analogy which Aquinas was later to develop more

29. R. W. Southern, *Saint Anselm and His Biographer*, pp. 52–55, has some helpful comments on the phrases *Fides quaerens intellectum*, the original title of the *Proslogion*, and *de ratione fidei*, which was originally part of the title of the *Monologion*. He suggests that the best translation of the latter phrase would be "a meditation on the rationale of the faith." Cf. the Preface to the *Proslogion*.

30. In *Descartes and the Modern Mind* (Hamden, Conn.: Shoe String Press, 1952), p. 28.

fully." [31] I suppose that in a way this is the natural conclusion to draw, but in this negative form it obscures something which is very important in Anselm. Besides, a *theory* of analogy would be, presumably, a theory of analogical predication or of analogical *terms*. But I don't see that such a theory would have done Anselm any good, especially if the theory of analogy is a logical matter rather than an ontological one. Such a theory would not give *content* to the analogates, particularly the primary analogate in the statement of a metaphysical analogy. The only thing that would give content to the terms would be the experience of being as analogous.

I suggest, then, that it is just this experience which Anselm is reflecting upon in his two meditations. The meditations are not about "Being" but about Being, over its entire range—the multidimensional structure of existence. And he is not so much anticipating Aquinas as he is remembering Augustine. [32]

Admittedly, this is an interpretation, but I think that it is the only interpretation that makes any sense. [33] It is supported by the general movement of thought in both meditations as it bears upon the degrees of being. There are so many passages of this kind that it would take too much space to cite any substantial number of them. The subject of all of them is the act of existence, proportioned to the possible, of which William Lynch has written so discerningly that I shall allow some words of his to serve as commentary:

> As existence descends in the initial creative act and in all its later dynamic processes of becoming through space and time, it is articulated, jointed, membered, shaped according to all the forms of all the things that can be, of all the possibles. . . . The act of existence descends analogously, *ana-logon*, "according to a proportion." The degree of existence is always measured by the degree of

31. Charlesworth, pp. 39, 78.
32. Anyone who believes that Augustinians think in terms of essence without ever reaching existence should consult the excellent monograph by James F. Anderson, *St. Augustine and Being* (The Hague: Martinus Nijhoff, 1965), esp. Chaps. 8 and 9.
33. I don't mean that everything Anselm says is automatically justifiable by an appeal to the experience of being as I have described it. I am concerned only with the passages that are directly relevant to the ontological argument.

possibility, by the degree of fullness of being any possibility may receive.[34]

Fullness of being in the Augustinian sense of so-much-being-and-no-more, this being but no further being, limited being, contingent being, conditioned being in which, in a relative sense, there is non-being as well, a mixture of being and non-being and therefore being that cannot account for itself—this is the object of Anselm's meditation in the *Monologion*.

There are some passages which further support my interpretation, especially the suggestion made earlier that vision is the appropriate word to use in this connection. In *Monologion* LXIV Anselm says:

> It seems to me that the mystery of so sublime a subject transcends all the vision of the human intellect [*transcendere omnem intellectus aciem humani*]. And for that reason I think it best to refrain from the attempt to explain how this thing is. For it is my opinion that one who is investigating an incomprehensible object ought to be satisfied if his reasoning shall have brought him far enough to recognize that this object most certainly exists.[35]

Again, in *Monologion* LXV, Anselm puzzles over the paradox that the object he is seeking is and remains ineffable because our familiar words are alien to it and cannot strictly be predicated of it:

> And often we see a thing, not precisely as it is in itself, but through a likeness or image, as when we look upon a face in a mirror. And in this way, we often express and yet do not express, see and yet do not see, one and the same object; we do not express it and do not see it by virtue of its own proper nature.[36]

The only way I can see of resolving the paradox is to regard the attributions which Anselm discusses in so many other passages as derived from faith, and that he is not yet prepared to focus on the one similarity which might be adequately expressed—ontological similarity. He is getting close to it when he says that "the

---

34. *Christ and Apollo* (New York: New American Library, 1960), p. 150.

35. Deane, pp. 127–28. I have consulted the Latin of Dom F. S. Schmitt, *S. Anselmi: Opera Omnia*, 6 vols. (Edinburgh: Nelson and Sons, 1946–61), Vol. I.

36. Deane, pp. 129–30.

more earnestly the rational mind devotes itself to learning its own nature, the more effectively does it rise to the knowledge of that Being." [37] I take this statement to mean that the reason is alone ordered to being as to its proper object. Faith is what tells reason where to look, and even continually supports the quest, but the completion of the ontological vision is the work of reason alone, not forgetting, all the same, that rational insight is only a functional moment in the life of the spirit moving toward the goal of wisdom.

I have said that the vision is completed in the argument of *Proslogion* II and III. By this time Anselm has found a way to express it in purely ontological terms, "that-than-which-nothing-greater-can-be-thought." [38] I have indicated earlier in what sense existence could be regarded as a perfection. All of the relative perfections which Anselm discusses can be reduced to, in the sense that they are dependent upon, relative perfections of being —that is, so-much-being-but-no-more. I want to cite in this connection a passage in Charlesworth's commentary:

> The validity of the *Proslogion* proof depends, then, upon the possibility of comparing things as "greater" or "better" in an *absolute sense*. But, as we have seen, outside the context of causal dependency it is difficult to see exactly how such absolute comparisons can be made. Within our experience we can only make comparisons *in particular respects*, and it would have to be *proved* or demonstrated in some way that it is possible and licit to make absolute comparisons. [39]

With all respect to a writer whose book I have found enormously helpful, I think that this is to put the whole problem backwards. Causal dependency, which here means dependency in being, can make sense only if it is possible to compare relative degrees of perfection in an absolute sense, not the other way round. The reason is that the notion of cause, that is, transcendent cause, can have no content, so far as the idea of the causal agent is

37. *Ibid.*, pp. 131–32.
38. On the background of this expression, see D. P. Henry, *The Logic of Saint Anselm,* Chap. 5, "The Modal Complex," esp. pp. 134–50.
39. Charlesworth, pp. 60–61, 77. Charlesworth says quite rightly that if he is correct in his judgment about the necessity for appealing to causality, Anselm's argument is unnecessary. But he also acknowledges the fact that Anselm does not himself appeal to causality in the *Proslogion*.

concerned, if the notion of complete perfection of being cannot, antecedently, have content. It seems to me that a first cause is a term which is really without meaning until the notion of unlimited being can be said to have meaning. I shall return to this point later.

Suppose that we now ask whether the notion of *limited* being is intelligible. If "unlimited being" is not intelligible, what would it mean to talk about "limited being"? One answer might be that a thing is limited in the sense that it contains less being than something else which is greater. For example, a human being might be said to be greater in being than a stone, and in relation to man, a stone, or any sentient but nonrational being, is limited being. But these are comparisons in relative terms. Some things are greater than others in particular respects, but, the answer might continue, why insist that relative perfections must be related to some absolute perfection? All we need is something greater *in some way*. To use the word "lesser" meaningfully we need only something greater, and, similarly, to speak of "greater" meaningfully we need only to be able to point to something less than what we are calling greater, leaving it open whether there might be something greater than anything we know and which might even be the greatest.[40]

But this will not do. Anselm is talking about perfection of *being*, about existence as a perfection, and this is quite different from the comparisons I have just been talking about. The issue here is confined to the relation of possibility, the capacity to be or exist, and existence. That relation applies to any limited being whatever. It applies as much to a man as to a sea urchin or a diamond. The formula, so-much-being-but-no-more, refers in this context primarily to essence, but whether this essence is to *be*, to *exist*, must be understood in an absolute sense. Either it is or it isn't, but antecedently, on the basis of essence alone, we cannot say that it must be or that it cannot be.

I turn now to Chapter VIII of Anselm's reply to Gaunilo, which contains, it seems to me, the clearest statement of the possibility, and, indeed, the necessity, of comparisons in the

---

40. It is sometimes argued that "that than which a greater cannot be thought" might be simply what there is, the totality of things, the universe, Nature. But, in Anselm's terms, that would merely be the greatest, relatively speaking. It contains nothing but limited beings and, therefore, we can think of something greater in an absolute sense.

absolute sense. Furthermore, it raises explicitly what I have called the crucial question, namely, how "that-than-which-noth-ing-greater-can-be-thought" can be meaningful. Unfortunately, he combines the only claim he needs to make with another claim which, if I understand him at all, he has no right to make:

> For since everything that is less good is similar in so far as it is good to that which is more good, it is evident to any rational mind that, mounting from the less good to the more good we can from those things than which something greater can be thought conjec-ture a great deal about that-than-which-a-greater-cannot-be-thought.[41]

It is difficult to see what the "great deal" (*multum*) could be. Even if "good" is understood as a transcendental term, goodness follows being, it does not precede it. Besides, only a few lines later, in Chapter IX, he comes close to, without actually repeat-ing, his admission, in *Monologion* LXIV and in *Proslogion* XIV–XVII, that what we are seeking is ineffable, in the sense that its nature cannot be fully comprehended. Leaving this aside, Chapter VIII argues for a minimum meaning for "that-than-which-a-greater-cannot-be-thought," but this is all he needs. The other illustrations in the chapter bear strictly upon limita-tion of existence—temporality and changeableness. With re-spect to these limitations, he says:

> Again, whether something of this kind actually exists or not, that which does not lack anything at all, nor is forced to change or move, is very much better still. Cannot this be thought? Or can we think of something greater than this? Or is this not precisely to form an idea of that-than-which-a-greater-cannot-be-thought from those things than which a greater can be thought? There is, then, a way by which one can form an idea of "that-than-which-a-greater-cannot-be-thought." [42]

If one is willing to acknowledge the analogical nature of being or existence, I do not see how it is possible to resist Anselm's conclusion. The claim he is making, philosophically speaking, can be understood as a minimum though sufficient claim that the conception of being without limit is a meaningful conception, that "that than which nothing greater can be

41. Charlesworth, p. 187.
42. *Ibid.*

thought" can be *in intellectu* in the sense required by Anselm's argument. This does not mean that the argument moves from concept to existence. For we cannot form this conception except by participating in the structure of existence within which our struggle with our own limitations takes place. The vision cannot be completed without the enactment in our own lives of the creative possibilities which point beyond themselves. Anselm found his freedom in obedience to the demands of a religious life which was perfectly supplemented by his philosophical meditations. Perhaps it is impossible to understand his concept of a perfect being in precisely the way he himself understood it. But he describes a movement of life and thought which is never wholly absent from reflection on the human condition at any time, the attempt to discover a sense-making instrument which will support our conviction that limited being is not incompatible with fullness of being, although the latter may require something which we cannot summon up within ourselves. As Josef Pieper says somewhere, we become philosophers in order that we may hope.

As a postscript, I would suggest that the ontological argument, as Anselm understood it, is fundamental to all other proofs or arguments for the existence of God and is presupposed by them.[43] I cannot discuss this in detail at this stage of the essay but, briefly, my contention is that the movement of the mind which Anselm exhibits is best described as analogical thought determined by the analogous nature of what it thinks about. The analogy of being, not to mention the analogy of "being," does not in itself prove the existence of God; it only shows you how you could *have* a proof or argument once you have got it. Any kind of argument of the sort described as *a posteriori,* whether based on causality (either efficient or exemplary), motion, contingency, or purpose, moves from the existence of something finite to the necessity of something infinite. But it seems to me that this movement presupposes that the conception of "that-than-which-nothing-greater-can-be-thought" is meaningful, and that Anselm's subsequent argument, that this being exists so truly that it cannot even be thought not to exist, has force. If this is not so,

43. I am not, of course, agreeing with Kant any more than Kant was really disagreeing with Anselm. As far as I can see, Kant's criticisms could have no force against Anselm because they are employing, if I may bring myself up to date by using the phrase, quite different "language-games."

then any causal argument will argue to something that is without meaningful content. The conclusions may be in the mind verbally, but they are not *in intellectu* in Anselm's sense. Truly, in that event, one would not know what one was talking about and the only reasonable position left open would be agnosticism. This is a very large question, but I think it is such an important one that it should be discussed outside the familiar context of Kant's critique, which simply suppresses the important questions.

It has not really been my purpose in this essay to come down on either side of the dispute about the validity of the ontological argument. I have, rather, tried to do something which, I think, is a necessary preliminary. That task is nicely stated by Charlesworth. In discussing Anselm's view of existence as a perfection, he says:

> One cannot be completely confident in rejecting it. But we may at least say that the comparison between real and conceptual existence is such a different kind of comparison from those we ordinarily make that we may reasonably place the onus on Anselm to show what sense can be given to it.[44]

I hope that I have succeeded in lifting that burden, if only a little. But, as Augustine would express it, I say this without prejudice to any other equal or better understanding.

44. Charlesworth, p. 69.

4 / Art and Philosophy

John M. Anderson

WHATEVER ELSE PHILOSOPHY MAY BE, it is also a language, and it is fruitful to consider its nature and function in these terms. Here such a consideration is developed indirectly, that is, not through the use of the language of philosophy, but by reference to examples and illustrations of its use. This indirect approach permits sketching the nature of the language of philosophy in the perspective of different cultures and epochs, and comparing it with other, nonphilosophical languages. But the analytical language of such an indirect consideration must also serve to suggest what it cannot say; it must itself comprise a *reductio ad absurdum* of its own use as the language of philosophy. To make this *reductio* more evident the language of philosophy is sketched here as a language based upon, but transcending and epitomizing, the language of art. Thus we begin with a consideration of an example of philosophical language which is based upon and yet epitomizes art—the Platonic dialogue. These dialogues are at once dramas and transcend dramas, that is, they are based upon the drama in order to attain a mode of expression which is not only impossible in a language without this basis, but is impossible in the drama as such.

Greek culture was characterized by an appeal to tradition and to ultimate origins as the basis for understanding the events and circumstances of human life and society. In the course of Greek history such an appeal was made in a variety of ways and so resulted in divergent interpretations and accounts of these events and circumstances. In part, Greek philosophy comprises

responses to this resultant relativism and confusion, and develops, before Plato, along three lines. First, there are those Greek
thinkers who seek to replace the appeal to traditions and origins
by hypotheses about the nature of the cosmos. Their assumption
is that a clear and definite account of the events and circumstances of human life and society may be given in such terms.
Second, there are the Sophists who accept the relativity to man
of any interpretations and accounts, but who claim that the
confusion of this relativity can be avoided by explicit reference
of all interpretation to the standard of man's nature. Third, there
is the Socrates who appears in Plato's dialogue and responds to
the diversity and multiplicity of human beliefs, behavior, and
expression by incorporating them in the developing matrix of
discussion. There, Socrates claims, confusion is avoided by the
interrelation of the variety of interpretation and belief in such a
way as to refer to the Whole within which these are parts.

These pre-Platonic responses of Greek philosophers to the
confusions and relativisms attendant upon an appeal to traditions and origins as the basis for understanding human life and
society have a common characteristic. They claim to free an
understanding of human nature from any reference to traditions
and origins; that is, they assume that human life and society
may be understood independently of such a reference, solely in
the terms of the cosmos itself, or of man's nature, or of the
Whole which incorporates man and his expressions as its parts.
Yet this common characteristic of these early Greek responses is
hardly consistent with a second characteristic which they also
exhibit. Each of these responses is formulated in the terms of a
language which claims to have the broadest appeal to men—to
be, that is, both intelligible and convincing to all. Thus the
philosophers of the cosmos express their esoteric insights concerning its nature in a language with a clear empirical reference,
so that these insights will be apparent. The Sophists' language
justifies their peculiar claim that human nature is the measure
of things by means of the art of persuasion, which as a craft
appeals to all. And Socrates, whose insight concerning the
Whole is the most strange, is always willing to begin a discussion with anyone's beliefs and opinions, to talk with anyone.

Each of these modes of expression claims to provide a
breadth of appeal which makes the esoteric claims expressed
evident to all. Yet the claim to universal appeal in these lan-

guages is based, not on a reference to traditions and origins, but on a reference to beginnings in another sense. Thus experience, the craft of persuasion, and anyone's beliefs and opinions constitute beginnings. Yet in each of these three cases, although the reference to beginnings carries an evident and broad appeal, it is formulated as an *ad hoc* reference to just those beginnings which are required to support the esoteric insights expressed in each philosophy. Thus these ways of escaping from the confusion and relativism of an appeal to traditions and origins seem to be based upon the appeal to an arbitrarily limited beginning.

Plato makes use of art as a constitutive element in philosophical language to avoid the paradox of making an appeal for universal acceptance which is based upon a reference to arbitrarily limited beginnings. The reference to beginnings through art is not the same as a reference to traditions and origins; yet as measured by the breadth of its support of communication and its persuasiveness, art is not arbitrary in its reference to beginnings —it speaks to all. Its mode of expression blends experience, the craft of persuasion, and the beliefs of individuals in such a way as to avoid a reference to arbitrarily restricted beginnings. Moreover, as Plato shows, the art of the drama can be developed into dialogue, where ultimate things can be expressed. In Plato's view the language of philosophy combines a reference to beginnings made through art and a reference to completion made through the epitomization of art in dialogue. Thus the language of philosophy can speak to all without an arbitrary restriction of reference to beginnings, and it can express ultimate things without esotericism.

II

THE HOPE FOR A LANGUAGE which avoids ambiguities and confusions and attains the expression of the truth is perennial. In modern times the threat to the realization of such a hope has often been seen in the possibility of slipping back from the language of science into the ambiguities and polyvalence of meanings found in common usage; or into the figurative and symbolic usages characteristic of custom and social behavior, for example, in the language of law or politics or religion. The dissolution of this threat has been found in the pursuit and attainment of clear and definite meanings of words and the precision of an exact syntax. The achievement of such definite meanings and exact syntax seems a special characteristic of modern times, when ideal languages have been constructed to comprise an intelligible realm which truly represents what is.

In modern times one such formulation of intelligible realms has been in the terms of axioms and a deductive apparatus for developing their consequences. Axiom systems seem to provide a language for interpreting experience, that is, for attaining a clear and objective account, a view, of things; they seem to constitute a model of reality.

Yet there are different ways of constructing axiom systems, so that their variety provides a variety of views of things, and their axioms—and even their deductive apparatus—appear as hypothetical. Impressed by the definiteness and precision of the language of axiom systems, some modern men have sought the resolution of this peculiar ambiguity by explicitly relating any axiom system and its function as a model of reality to man's interests and needs, to human nature. In this relation the hypothetical character of an axiom system does not introduce ambiguity and confusion; the significance of the hypothesis is interpreted and fixed by its reference to human nature. This modern effort to resolve the ambiguity of axiom systems evidently has an analogue in the view of language held by the Greek Sophists.

There is a second modern effort to resolve the ambiguity implicit in the hypothetical views afforded by axiom systems which is characteristically Socratic in tone. Thus the alternative views afforded by different axiom systems are often interpreted as parts of a more inclusive system into which they can be incorporated. This fixes their hypothetical character, since it is understood as a consequence of partiality and has its significance in reference to a whole. It is the reference to a whole which serves as the standard for the resolution of the ambiguity attendant upon the hypothetical formulation which marks the construction of such an ideal language as an axiom system.

These two interpretations of the hypothetical character of such a language do reflect insights characteristic of Sophist and Socratic thought, yet there is a fundamental difference between Greek and modern thought. The view of nature offered by the Greek cosmologists, the Sophists' reference of any expression of views to human nature, and the Socratic reference to the Whole in order to interrelate what would otherwise be a congeries of human beliefs and views are interpretative modes for resolving the threat of ambiguity and confusion implicit in the pervasive Greek reference to traditions and origins. In the context of modern culture, however, apparently similar interpretations of language are offered, not as resolutions of problems arising from traditional and customary usages of language but as resolutions of problems arising in the usages of a precise and definite language, as exemplified in axiom systems. The fundamental problem implicit in the modern use of language is the variety and hypothetical character of the views generated by its very precision, clarity, and definiteness. Modern man has almost forgotten the historical source of his explicit quest for precision and definiteness in language in his concern over the problems arising as a consequence of the success of his quest. Yet any understanding of the ultimate problems resulting from the search for and the use of a precise and definite language must take into account the need for such an ideal language, which has its source in a reference to traditions and origins.

The impact of science on modern culture, its pervasive influence within all aspects of human life and society, is attributable to the breadth of its appeal to mankind as much as to the power of its precise and definite language. The protean character of science—its emergence in engineering, in industry, in social and economic planning, its place in medicine—testifies to the capacity of the scientific enterprise to speak to broad classes of men. If science is considered as a language, this pervasive influence in culture must be understood as a function of its power to communicate to, to appeal to, and so to involve many people. Yet the power to communicate in this almost universal way is not simply a function of the clarity and precision of the language of science; indeed, it constitutes a regression from the development of science as a language possessing ideal precision and definiteness. The broad appeal of science is a consequence not so much of its attainment of clarity in its theoretical structures as of its incorporation of those human orientations toward traditions and origins whose attendant confusions give rise to the effort to achieve precision and definiteness. No doubt the achievement of ideal languages defines modernity. In consequence, a central problem of modern culture is to relate clear and precise expression, once achieved, back to the context to which it is an interpretative response, the context of traditions and origins which involves the very confusions this response seeks to correct.

The modern conception of science as a creative enterprise reflects a partial awareness of this central problem. Understood as a creative enterprise which determines (or manifests) progress, science both contributes the clarity of theoretical formulation and relates to the context of traditions and origins in which all men are involved. Understood as creative, science becomes a mode of history, and it is history which modern man understands as developing beginnings to their ends, as completing and so clarifying beginnings. History provides the concept for the modern interpretation of social change, so that, for example, science is understood as aiming at the development of social forms, just because these are to be understood as a part of historical evolution.

The modern conception of history reflects the characteristic emphasis of modern man on precision and definiteness in the expression of his views and the understanding of his place. History is conceived as a movement in which man participates by commitment to completion, and so by identification with a movement forward. For example, modern man understands himself to be committed to progress, and so to be involved in a movement in which his commitment is expressed as a drive toward mastery and control. Hegel's view of history as dialectic illustrates this commitment and expression, for man's commitment to each moment in the Hegelian dialectic is an identification without recourse, necessitated by the need to carry the movement of the dialectic forward. Other modern views carry this same suggestion of a history comprised of stages of progress in which each stage occupies a necessary and definite, if transient, place. Thus, the development of a people and a locale is seen to culminate in a nation, and the extension of applied science to all aspects of human life is held to be an essential step in the evolution of human culture.

Modern man's historical sense of his participation in the coursing of events is intended to and does refer to traditions and customs as well as to completions; but his sense of the connection of these beginnings and completions is carried by his involvement in events as this is expressed precisely and definitely in the moments of history. Thus modern man often comes to identify himself with the coursing of events, to see himself written large there; and his sense of involvement comes to be defined in purely human terms, or at least in the terms of a movement springing *ex nihilo* from inscrutable beginnings and moving toward that ideal Whole in which all confusion is resolved.

III

GREEK CULTURE was characterized to some extent by that human drive for mastery and control which is so dominant in modern times. Indeed, Thucydides' criticism of the political thrust of Athens in the Peloponnesian War is directed against just this trait. As a historian Thucydides is concerned to show that political development need not and should not be a movement of imperialistic expansion. Similarly, as a philosopher Plato criticizes just such expansion in the *Republic*. There he uses the language of dialogue to formulate a conception of political development in terms suggesting a quite different understanding of its end than mastery. Plato uses the language of dialogue to refer to the development of political order without expressing man's involvement in it as a drive toward mastery and control; this is possible for in dialogue reference to beginnings develops in terms of their positive character as this emerges in the artistic context of the drama. It is the dramatic basis of dialogue which ensures that beginnings can be incorporated as positive elements in development and so qualify the mode of man's commitment to political ends—and to other ends as well.

Plato uses a dialogue to present protagonists whose specific natures and temperaments are initially suggested and then emerge and develop more clearly in the course of their discussions. Certainly in the course of these discussions the explicit views of the protagonists come to a clearer formulation and are interrelated and contrasted to reveal their partiality and lacks. But in the course of the dialogue the temperaments, attitudes, and beliefs of the protagonists also emerge and serve to guide its development. Thus in the course of the *Republic* Glaucon is disclosed as a rash man and Thrasymachus as a violent one; and this emergence of rashness and violence in the movement of the drama modifies the formulation of the nature and significance of political order as this develops in the dialogue. Such emergent events in a dialogue are attributable to its dramatic basis and also guide its course toward the formulation of its theme, its completion. Whoever and whatever appears in a dialogue risks transmutation in its course. Even readers find themselves picked up by the flow of the drama, involved in it and modified by it as a consequence of their contributions to its development.

Art alone does not fully achieve the development and completion of what begins in the context it provides. Even very good art, such as that of Aristophanes—which is Plato's example in the *Symposium*—seeks to develop and complete the positive elements which emerge in the context it provides by the use of novel forms. Thus it is Aristophanes' "originality" which explicitly presents and develops the beginnings evoked through his art. Such "originality," however, is so close to beginnings that the structure it affords dissolves back into their movement, failing to do more than suggest the possibility of completing what art has begun. In epitomizing art, however, dialogue both accepts what begins in the context afforded by the art of drama and handles the very difficult task of developing and completing these beginnings.

The completion of beginnings in the context of the dramatic basis of dialogue requires the transmutation of them in such a way as to maintain and develop, to complete, them. As more than art, dialogue must accomplish just this task. It must constitute a connection of the reference to beginnings, and the reference to a whole. But in order to express this connection the language of dialogue modifies the conception of the standard implicit in a reference to a whole so fundamentally as to reformulate this standard quite radically. Thus the language of dialogue cannot be said to refer to the Whole, but rather to the Good, that is, to perfection. The language of dialogue carries in its reference to the standard of perfection a reference both to positive beginnings and to a whole. Thus a dialogue expresses a transient manifestation of the Whole and a perpetually recurrent manifestation of beginnings. In Plato's terms a dialogue is daimonic.

The daimonism of a dialogue carries a continuation and development of beginnings as well as a recurrent exemplification of the Whole. But this daimonism is not to be found, Plato tells us, in the direct reference of dialogue to perfection. It is to be found in the orientation implicit in the concrete unity comprised of the balanced elements of the human soul. It is the balance of the elements of the human soul of its author, its protagonists, and its readers which is daimonic, and the achievement of which grounds the reference of the dialogue to perfection. A dialogue expresses this reference through the orientation implicit in the balance of each and every participant in it.

Art has a very broad appeal to men, for art appeals to actual individuals in the terms of their transient natures by reflecting them in artistry—in novel forms, topical approaches, and new media. Art appeals to all men because each man recognizes through it the signifiance of his own beginnings. The language of dialogue also has a very broad appeal to men, for its basis in the art of the drama serves to provide the context for the emergence of the elements of the human soul. But dialogue appeals to men through the emergence of the elements of their souls only as these are recognized as approaching balance. This grounding of dialogue in the balance of the elements of the soul enables it to transcend art. The language of dialogue appeals to every man, as does art, yet it epitomizes art.

If the language of dialogue escapes the criticisms Plato directs against Aristophanes and the best art, does it escape those he directs against Socrates and the best theoretical philosophy? Plato's criticism of this philosophy focuses on Socrates' peculiar intellectualism. It is the purity—perhaps the pride—of Socrates' intellectual orientation which makes it impossible for him to participate in any eros except the love of the Whole. Thus Socrates himself cannot participate in the eros peculiar to art. His soul *is* oriented toward the Whole and he has no need for that awareness of initial balance for which only the evocation of man's beginnings through art can prepare the way. Socrates really is possessed of no Platonic daimon. He can be brought to speak of his daimon only in the context of a Platonic dialogue. It is the dramatic basis of dialogue which enables *Plato* to present Socratic eros as daimonic, as involving the elements of the soul which suggest balance, and so as oriented not toward the Whole but toward perfection.

The difficulty in Socrates' philosophy is his failure to take account of the beginnings which lie behind the conflict and contradictions of precise and definite expressions, theoretical views. Plato's own use of art in dialogue to disclose beginnings is a fundamental step toward correcting Socrates' philosophy and redefining the ultimate standard of language as the standard of perfection. The potential balance of the emergent elements of the soul in the author, the reader, or the protagonists of a dialogue implies an orientation toward perfection. That is, a dialogue is grounded not in the potential balance of the elements of the soul, but in the orientation of the soul toward perfection. For Plato this balance is potentially an orientation toward perfection; and so the task of redefining the ultimate standard of language is a task of overcoming a lack of balance. When this lack of balance is overcome, the whole soul is wheeled around and oriented toward perfection. Thus the reference to the ultimate standard of language is not carried by dialogue, but by the activity of the soul in achieving its ultimate orientation: the reference of dialogue to perfection is not carried by dialogue, but in the souls of those who participate in dialogue.

Plato does not fully escape his own criticism of Socrates' intellectualism. But it is only Plato's reference to a ground extrinsic to language, the balance of the elements of the soul, which prevents his redefining the ultimate standard of language, the standard of perfection, adequately. The best theoretical philosophy, that is, Socratic discussion, does not constitute a universal language; its appeal is restricted just because it fails to take into account the elements of man's soul, man's beginnings. Yet a dialogue is also restricted in its appeal just because it is grounded in the special unity of these elements of the soul which constitute a balance. This unity, the quasi-substantive daimon of the human soul, can orient the soul toward perfection only by overcoming its lack of balance, by incorporating its elements. For this reason, dialogue can appeal only to those souls who are prepared for this reorientation; its speaks only to these few.

IV

No DOUBT Plato's sense of the apparent breadth of appeal of dialogue was reinforced by the fact that the drama constituted an especially appropriate mode of expression in later Greek culture. His use of the drama as the basis of dialogue must have seemed to him to be supported by the wide and diverse audience which found the theater significant and attractive. Neither to him nor to this audience would his conception of dialogue have appeared as anything more than a claim to state the essence of drama by an extension of its language to philosophy.

Yet Plato need not have based philosophy upon the drama. He might have looked to the Homeric epic or to poetry. If he had returned to the epic, his sense of the central place in art of the protagonists, and so of the author and reader, would have been much less. And his extension of the drama to philosophical dialogue, as well as his grounding of dialogue in the unity of the elements of the souls of its protagonists, its author, and its readers, would have seemed less natural. If he had returned to the epic, the extension of the drama to dialogue would have seemed less a development of the place of art in philosophy than a possibility peculiar to the drama itself; and so Plato's conception of philosophy might have been less dependent upon that balance of the elements of the soul which is so specifically the harmony suggested by the drama.

Certainly in modern culture the appeal of art to a wide and diverse audience is not a special trait of the drama. The patterns of modern society do not reinforce the sense of the central place of the individual which the drama carries. The appeal of the drama to a modern audience has been weakened by changes in society. The sense of individualism supported by modern society is that of a more or less anonymous participant in broad social movements and historical developments, and modes of art which reflect this have a wider appeal to a modern audience. Modern society thus provides support for the appeal of such an art form as the novel and affords the opportunity for a radical restatement of the way in which philosophy epitomizes art. Today when philosophy is understood as based upon art it is most natural to see it as an extension of the novel; but then the language of philosophy need not involve an *extrinsic* reference to perfection via the unity of the soul.

If it is to Montaigne rather than Descartes that one must look for the enrichment of the skeptical method through a basis in art, it is in Hegel's early work that art and philosophy appear together most significantly in an odd but peculiarly modern vein. Something of the significance and importance, as well as the curious reluctance, of modern thinkers who interpret philosophy on the basis of an art form supported by the modern social context is to be found in *The Phenomenology of Mind*.[1] Indeed, in one sense this work is an emphatically modern formulation of the language of dialogue. In another sense, however, it anticipates a much more radically modern conception of philosophy as an extension of art.

Certainly *The Phenomenology of Mind*, with its puns, its exaggerated examples, its contrasts and conflicts of views, its comic relief, and its suggestive richness of historical example and parody, makes use of artistic devices and techniques in as evident a way as does a Platonic dialogue. The series of typical views offered there may be taken as a comedy of errors, and, as such, a version of Plato's use of the drama as the basis for philosophy. But where Plato appeals to the classical drama, with its emphasis upon the central place of individuals as protagonists, Hegel, with a deep sense of the modern temper, appeals to a drama in which typical persuasions and cultural epochs are protagonists. Philosophy epitomizes this comedy of typical human errors to reveal the course of events as the sweep of progress which harmonizes these elements of the Absolute. The basis of philosophy in art evokes the dramatic moments of history; but philosophy develops these emergent elements to reveal the very harmony of the Absolute itself. Hegel's reinterpretation of the nature of drama as a comedy of typical persuasions and cultural patterns makes it much more relevant to modern man's deep sense of his anonymous and functional participation in the sweep of events. And it enables Hegel to present this participation with modern emphasis, as involvement in a romantic history which expresses the dynamic harmony of elements that is both the beginning and the Whole of the Absolute.

An explicit task of *The Phenomenology of Mind* is to reintroduce that reference to beginnings which is often forgotten as a consequence of the dominant intellectualism of modern thought, and to formulate the essential reconsideration of the significance and meaning of beginnings for modern life. Thus Hegel penetrates to the significance of beginnings in the terms of the moments of a dramatic history which develop to their completion, as philosophy shows, in the dynamic structure of the

1. G. W. Hegel, *The Phenomenology of Mind*, trans. J. B. Baillie (New York: Humanities Press, 1964).

Absolute itself. His completion of the emergent elements in art through philosophy reflects the intellectualism as well as the sense of anonymity of the modern age. For Hegel, philosophy is Absolute Knowledge. The language of philosophy is not grounded in the balance of the elements of the human soul which, in turn, reflects the harmony of Being; it penetrates directly through the diverse structure of romantic history to the unity which reveals this history as the representation by the Absolute to itself of its beginnings, that is, the completion of these beginnings.

Those beginnings which are the moments of a dramatic history are also, for Hegel, the parts of the Whole. They occur in history in such a way as to reveal their nature as parts, that is, they occur as typical and as conflicting or contradictory. Hegel's interpretation of the nature of drama as romantic history makes of drama just that sweep of typical moments which can be represented within the unity of the Absolute—and therefore makes of drama just that mode of language which grounds the abstraction of theoretical philosophy and loses any reference to the concrete beginnings evoked in art. One essential of the language of philosophy is its reference to beginnings; and these beginnings are carried by its basis in art. Yet if the drama is reinterpreted so that these beginnings occur as representations by the Absolute to itself, they can be no more than typical and contradictory moments entailing the Whole of which they are parts; they cannot be those positive beginnings which the language of philosophy must take into account.

Perhaps Plato might have appealed to some art other than the drama, and to one less readily brought to abstract philosophical focus through the conception of the balance of the elements of the human soul. Hegel certainly should have appealed to some art other than the drama, for as a modern philosopher his appeal to art must carry both the modern sense of man's anonymous and functional participation in the course of events and the possibility of a philosophical epitomization of art. Yet his abstraction from individual protagonists in his interpretation of the drama, which defines a romantic history that carries both a sense of anonymous and functional participation and philosophical structure, achieves this only at the price of losing contact with its basis in art. In consequence of this loss of contact, Hegel attributes to modern man's anonymous participation in the course of events a quality which it rarely has when seen from the perspective of the individual; he identifies this anonymity with that total submergence of the individual in history which defines mass culture and the totalitarian significance of the masses. Yet *The Phenomenology of Mind*—complex book that it is—also formulates a method which imposes no such necessity for submergence of the individual in history and entails no such conception of the overwhelming movement of a romantic history. The method of phenomenology which Hegel develops in this book might well have been used to relate more generally to art rather than specifically to the drama, and to provide access to a philosophical epitomization of art without abstraction.

As Hegel develops the method of phenomenology, it is peculiarly well adapted to reflect the anonymous and functional participation of man in the sweep of events which is so characteristic of modern times, for it can disclose what appears in those broad social movements and historical moments which set the pattern and tone of modern culture. As Hegel uses this method in his early work it provides a very free and broad access to circumstances, so that it evokes things themselves as continually slipping beyond the focus of human perspective and as of more than merely human relevance; indeed, Hegel's phenomenological disclosure of epochal changes places human participants in the stream of history. The breadth of the dynamic panorama which Hegel's phenomenology evokes is too great to be attained by the use of the artistic context of the drama, even when this is strained to constitute a dramatic history. Nor does Hegel's phenomenological method support the extension of a dramatic history to reflect the explicit structure of the dynamic unity of the Absolute. Hegel's method requires a different basis in art and a different epitomization of art in philosophy than the drama on the one hand, and Absolute Idealism on the other, afford.

If Hegel intended to make the method of phenomenology a technique of the language of modern philosophy, as his early work suggests he might have done, then his first step should have been the selection of an art form as the basis for philosophical development which, like phenomenology, could reflect the panorama and diffuseness of modern culture. He might well have selected the novel, for the novel develops the participation of individuals in the color and tone of social contexts and change, in the trend of political and social revolution, and as highlighted against the slower movement of the seasons and the appearances of nature. An appeal to the novel might have provided the key to a more general artistic basis for phenomenological insight into the broad patterns of human participation in events and also permitted the epitomization of art to give full philosophical significance.

Although Hegel did connect art and philosophy in his epitomization of the drama as romantic history, he did not use the phenomenological method as the support for such a connection. Apparently he did not see the possibility of appealing to an art form such as the novel and then developing, in the terms of a phenomenological appeal, a philosophical epitomization of art.

V

THE LANGUAGE OF THE DRAMA suggests that the beginnings emergent in the context it provides develop toward completion through the resolution of conflicts of attitudes, beliefs, and views in the balance achieved in the persons of its protagonists. The development of a drama turns upon the pivots of its protagonists, and so is readily, almost inescapably, understood as taking place in the terms of their characters through the formulation and resolution of the conflicts they express and encounter. Such a development tacitly attributes a unifying function to the persons in the drama which serves to extend the significance of emergent beginnings beyond their occurrence in this context. Such an attribution supports the philosophical extension of art through the transcendence of the person in conflict and oppositions between persons in the achievement of individual and collective balance. In a novel, by contrast, conflicting attitudes, beliefs, and views, and so the place of the protagonists, can hardly emerge so centrally as to make them the pivots of its development; the place of the protagonists in a novel is more passive, more that of participants in a movement to which they contribute but which they do not resolve. The participative contributions of the protagonists in a novel afford little support for its philosophical extension through their achievement of balance and so of their service as the pivots of transcendence.

All art carries human return to and acceptance of beginnings, but in the novel such acceptance develops from a return to beginnings in the movement adumbrating their immanent completion in the panorama and sweep of events of which life is an aspect. This *participative* contribution by its protagonists to the development of a novel reflects modern man's sense of his anonymous and functional place in his world. It suggests that the mode in which beginnings are brought to immanent completion in the novel affords a more fundamental insight into the significance of the basis of philosophy in art and a radical suggestion concerning the way in which philosophy epitomizes art. If this insight is sound and this suggestion correct, the task of modern philosophy is to show how the context evoking beginnings which a novel affords may be extended to a grasp of the world as a context in which beginnings also develop toward completion. The key to the fulfillment of this task is the special nature of the participative contribution of the author and reader of the novel which constitutes the basis for its development and for this philosophical extension of it.

The language of a novel is free in principle from the requirements of descriptive representation and commitment to abstract intellectual structure. Thus the novel carries its own beginnings in the sounds, rhythms, images, and structures of its medium. This reference of the novel to its own beginnings is an essential reflexive reference; that is, these beginnings of the novel in the terms of its medium emerge not merely as appearance, but constitute what appears. Such reflexive reference is found, too, in the initiatory events, the climactic events, and the occurrence and influence of characters in the novel. These beginnings not only appear, but also constitute what appears. Thus the world of the novel is a development from moments in which what appears and its appearance are merged in a beginning which serves as a standard guiding this development.

The novel affords a context for the emergence of positive beginnings, which, in turn, guide its development. Within the novel the artist formulates this sense of a standard by introducing explicit artistic techniques, forms, and media, as well as human emotions, ideas, and personal and cultural involvement. These creative contributions to art are intended to open the artist and reader to beginnings, and so ensure participation in them; but they are also intended to contrast the artist and reader with beginnings. The tension between the artist or reader and the beginnings emergent in the context of a novel is carried by the creative introduction of artistry and human meanings as, relative to the limited participation in beginnings attained, these express both an incompleteness of the creative human contributions and the incompleteness of beginnings. It is the demand for the resolution of this tension which establishes beginnings as standards and limns the sense in which they should be completed.

Yet the formulation of this standard of development in the terms of the artistry and human meanings contributed to the novel is weak. If the tension produced by these creative introductions carries a suggestion of the development of beginnings and thus of the possibilities of completing them, it also suggests that this completion apparently might be attained by the resolution of the tension through an identification of the artist or reader with beginnings as such. Certainly the creative contributions which introduce artistry and human meanings into the novel require a modification of the persons of the artist and the reader which reflects their transmutation into participants in the movement of beginnings. But such a transmutation, if understood as identification, dissipates the tension which creative contributions formulate and dissolves the requirement that beginnings should be developed; it fails to provide the matrix for the possibilities of their completion. The artist often seeks to avoid this loss of tension through an identifying transmutation by the use of novelty of form, medium, and technique; that is, he claims for artistic novelty the formulation of an irreducible tension between the creative contributions of man and the beginnings emergent in the context of the novel. The artist's creative powers thus introduce and claim to maintain this tension. Yet the tension between man's creative contributions and beginnings as formulated by artistic novelty is too easily dissolved into the exercise of human creative power to support the claim that such devices enable the novel to provide the context for the completion of beginnings.

The fact that the artist can formulate and the reader can grasp the matrix of possibility for the completion of beginnings in the novel depends upon the implicit opposition there, as in any art, between the medium and the creative human contributions introduced into it. The medium of the novel is stubbornly

resistive to human demands on it. It obtrudes as a *given* independent of man's creative contributions. The artist who appeals
to the medium of the novel can express through his response to
it an irreducible tension between human creative contributions
and elements in art which are alien to man. This emphasis upon
the medium and its use provides the matrix in which beginnings
may be developed toward completion. The appeal to and use of
the medium, as a given to some extent independent of human
creative contributions, make of the artist's creative contributions
to beginnings a much more precarious and uncontrollable transmutation of his nature than the exercise of his creative powers
suggests. Such use of the medium of the novel prevents both the
artist's and the reader's identification with beginnings in art and
their total mastery of them by the use of novelty; it characterizes
human involvement in art as participative contribution.

In the novel, this tension between the medium and creative
contributions can more easily be understood than in the drama,
as allowing indifferent as well as threatening circumstances,
images, and events to take a positive place in its context. In
consequence, such alien elements can be used more readily in
the context of the novel to make explicit the tension between
beginnings and human contributions, through the negative responses of the author and the reader, without interpreting this
tension as a strong contradiction. These elements thus come to
be understood by the artist and the reader as demanding that
transmutation of their natures which supports nonhuman contributions to the novel. The formulation of the contrast between
the medium and man's creative contributions to art projects a
matrix of possibility in which beginnings emerge in a movement
connecting and connected by dual contributors. The transmutation of man required by the participation of alien elements in
the novel, and the transmutation of these elements in turn required by man's participation defines a context which is open
to the emergence of beginnings and provides the matrix in which
this emergence can be supported and enriched through that
dual transmutation which enhances participative contribution.
This contrast of human and alien elements in art, together with
their initial, limited participation in beginnings, comprises a
projection of a realm of possibility which is continuously rede-
termined as the movement completing beginnings, as the matrix
of the movement enriching them.

The task of philosophy is to constitute a language whose reflexive reference carries this sense of the enrichment of beginnings and so refers to perfection. One essential part of this task is to introduce the reference to beginnings which is so often ignored or poorly handled by modern thinkers. This reference requires a basis for the language of philosophy in art, for there beginnings occur as positive and immanent. The language of art can be used to carry a reference to the movement toward the completion of beginnings without identifying the artist and the reader with them, or attributing creation of them to the artist or the reader. But at best, the language of art formulates this movement toward completion as recurrent development. What art, even at its best, does not quite do is to carry the nature of this movement as guided both by a reference to beginnings and to completion. The language of philosophy, which as having a basis in art carries a reference to immanent beginnings, must also, as the epitomization of art, formulate a reference to the completion of these beginnings in such a way as to return repeatedly to them and to suggest the possibility of carrying through alternative lines of their development. This language must formulate that tension which enables it to carry the matrix for the alternative possibilities of completing beginnings in the special sense which permits the determination and modification of this movement in its course.

If the formulation of this tension in the language of art as a tension between creative contributions of the artist or the reader and the medium in its broadest sense cannot carry the matrix of alternative developments of beginnings, this is only because here this tension can be expressed no more explicitly than the contrast between the creative contributions to art and the restricted medium of an art. The epitomization of art by philosophy thus must strengthen the statement of this tension as a means of carrying the matrix in which beginnings may move to completion. But in strengthening the expression of this tension care must be taken to avoid the error of Socratic discussion and, even, the dialogue—the error suggested by, although not inevitable in, the use of the drama as the artistic basis of philosophy. This error epitomizes the tension between the artist or reader and the medium of the drama (its language, scene, and protagonists) as a conflict of elements of personality, beliefs, and views, to be resolved through the attainment of unity in the persons of the artist and reader. This is an error because in extending the language of art to philosophy it shifts this tension from language to a locus in the persons of the creative users of language. As a consequence, it strips language of its fundamental power, the power it has of constituting the context in which its creative users are participants in what is alien to them.

The use of the novel as the artistic basis of philosophy suggests that this error may be avoided. Here the tension between the artist or reader and the medium of the novel (its language, circumstances, and opaque movements) can be epitomized as holding between man and what is alien to him. This extension of the language of art to philosophy leaves this tension as an aspect of language, as a development within the context of language. As a consequence, it reinforces the power of language to constitute the context in which its creative users are open to and so participate in what is alien to them, and who are, in fact, participative contributors to the context of language. Such a development of tension formulates the matrix in which the movements completing immanent beginnings as the embodiments of the contributions of man and what is alien to him can occur; and it formulates this matrix as the realm of the possibility of alternative completions reflecting the unqualified potentialities which immanent beginnings introduce and which are supported by this dual contribution. It is this realm which must be carried by the language of philosophy. It is this reference to perfection which epitomizes art, which connects beginnings to completions.

A Platonic dialogue is very far from a drama, and the language of modern philosophy could not be a novel. Yet the epitomization of art is not a speech about the nature of language, simply because to speak about language is to sharpen to a contradiction that weaker contrast between medium and man which alone affords in language an openness to beginnings and permits the recurrent development which reflects their enrichment. The access art affords to beginnings supports philosophical speech: man knows too much to remain silent. But to use language as if it were independent of these beginnings is to claim the power to create them: man does not know enough to speak forever. The tormenting difficulty in philosophical speech is to say neither too much nor too little.

PART II
APPROACHES TO
THE LIFE-WORLD

5 / The Phenomenon of World

Robert R. Ehman

THERE IS no more decisive move in contemporary phenomenological thought than that from transcendental subjectivity to the world as the horizon of phenomenological investigation. While this move alters phenomenology, it does not turn it into something wholly other. The task of the phenomenologist remains the disclosure of the structures and meanings through which beings appear rather than simply the realistic explanation and fact-gathering of the natural sciences. However, in opposition to the Husserlian view, there is now an attention to the real independent beings that surround us and to the world ground against which we discover our own subjectivity. There is no longer a pure stream of consciousness essentially independent of the world and describable without reference to any larger reality. The radically new dimension in the recent phenomenological thought of Merleau-Ponty, Fink, Heidegger, and Dufrenne is the attempt to correct the idealist bias of the Husserlian approach without returning to the naive ontological realism of the tradition.[1] These thinkers do not reduce being to meaning; nor on the

1. The movement from transcendental subjectivity to world as the horizon of phenomenology is found not only in Merleau-Ponty and in Heidegger but also in E. Fink (*Sein, Wahrheit, Welt* [The Hague: Martinus Nijhoff, 1958], and *Spiel als Weltsymbol* [Stuttgart: Kohlhammer, 1960]); in M. Dufrenne ("L'*A priori* comme monde," *Annales de l'Université de Paris*, 1966, No. 1); and in Paul Ricoeur (*Freedom and Nature: The Voluntary and the Involuntary*, trans. Erazim V. Kohák [Evanston, Ill.: Northwestern University Press, 1966], esp. pp. 466–81). The move of Heidegger to world as the horizon for the understanding of Being is pointed up emphatically by W. Marx: "Es scheint uns, als sei es

[85]

other hand do they pass over meaning in favor of an exclusive concentration on being. They attempt to put them both in a dialectical interrelation in which each has an equal part in the constitution of a world in which we find our place. While there remains a tension between the idealist and realist poles, there is a genuine endeavor to transcend the old dilemmas between idealism and realism in which Husserl is still enmeshed. The endeavor to transcend these dilemmas focuses on the phenomenon of world: it is world that is to provide the perspective from which we can do equal justice to both poles without allowing either to suppress the other.

In an essay in honor of John Wild, it is appropriate to turn our attention to his role in this movement. There is no more powerful attempt to articulate the phenomenon of world and to interpret freedom and value, science and religion in terms of it than that found in his recent work. In this essay I shall examine Wild's interpretation of the world. In the first part of my discussion, I shall consider his approach to the world from the traditional realist and idealist conceptions of being; and in the second part of my discussion, I shall deal with his distinctions between the world and versions, the world and transcendence, and the life-world and the universe of science. I shall argue, in regard to the issue of the relation of the world to being in the traditional senses, that Wild succeeds in demonstrating a world horizon prior to and inclusive of independent beings with a place in addition for meanings without a real foundation in beings. I shall argue, with regard to the distinctions between the world and versions and the world and transcendence, that these are defensible in the light of the evidence to which Wild appeals in spite of some ambiguity in his treatment. Finally, raising the issue of the relation of the world to the universe of science, I shall attempt to further clarify Wild's interpretation of science, giving a larger place to the positive disclosive contribution of science. I shall argue that Wild succeeds in maintaining that the life-world is prior to and more inclusive than the universe of science even when we take science as revealing dimensions of

---

Heideggers Bestreben, Sein uberhaupt nur noch as Welt zu denken" (*Heidegger und die Tradition* [Stuttgart: Kohlhammer, 1961], p. 191). Wild's own phenomenology must be seen against the background of these contemporary continental developments.

beings that remain hidden at the level of prescientific experience.

II

IN HIS *Ideas I* Husserl moves from the naive, outward directed realism of the "natural attitude" to the phenomenological perspective by contrasting the one with the other. The phenomenological perspective reveals itself against the background of the natural standpoint. While from the point of view of the natural attitude consciousness is simply a psychic dimension of man as a part of nature, from the phenomenological point of view consciousness appears as the field of all that has being or meaning for us and constitutes being and meaning through its own synthetic activities. The transcendental status of consciousness is based on its function of constituting the natural world that appeared to include it, and transcendental reduction consists in winning the insight that consciousness is prior to and more inclusive than the natural and social worlds. For Husserl, the world is nothing else than the system of meanings and references that consciousness constitutes so far as it is able to attain wide-ranging unities of meaning. From the perspective of consciousness the world is contingent. The imaginative "nihilation" of the world reveals that consciousness could conceivably exist apart from a world, apart from a coherent field of meaning. Beings are unities of meaning.

For Wild, there is no transcendental reduction. However, in the same manner as Husserl, he moves from a nonphenomenological to a phenomenological perspective by contrasting the one with the other and revealing the one against the ground of the other. For Wild, the fundamental contrast to the phenomenological perspective is not the natural attitude but rather the traditional conceptions of being and the objective universe of science. The phenomenological "reduction" for Wild, therefore, consists not in a move to a stream of pure consciousness that might conceivably survive the nihilation of the world and which constitutes all beings as unities of meaning, but rather in a move to an ultimate horizon of being and meaning that might conceivably survive the nihilation of particular beings (BMW, 420).[2] The world for Wild is prior to and more inclusive than the beings within it in a manner analogous to that in which for Husserl transcendental consciousness is prior to and more inclusive than its objects. The background of our experience of any particular being for Husserl is, in the end, the past and future horizons of our conscious experience; for Wild the ultimate background is something beyond past and future experience and transcendent of its relation to our self.

In order to understand the manner in which Wild moves from the traditional concepts of being to the world, it is necessary to see how he interprets these and to indicate the sort of experience that on his view these traditional conceptions fail to cover. For the traditional realist, as Wild interprets him, being applies to things which exist in their own right, "absolutely independent of man and his human interpretations" (BMW, 421); for the traditional idealist, being applies to beings as they really are, "with their meaning fully revealed, free from any dilution or confusion with alien factors" (BMW, 422). However, as Wild himself goes on to point out, this manner of contrasting these positions is misleading on two counts. In the first place, and this is essential for Wild, the realist as well as the idealist assumes that beings are meaningful in themselves, that there is no real discrepancy or clash between meaning and being. Both traditional views assume that "being and meaning are originally identified" and that "there is no basic tension between them" (BMW, 424). The distinction between the two classical views is therefore not as fundamental as it might at first appear to be. Neither allows for the possibility of real absurdity nor has a place in a final account of the world for illusion and evil. The main distinction between the views, and this is the second point, is simply that while for the realist, mind is passive and "finds" meaningful beings, for the idealist, mind is active and constitutes beings through an unfolding and synthesis of meanings (BMW, 423).

The crucial experience to which Wild appeals against both of the traditional views is already apparent: it is the experience of

2. In this essay I shall abbreviate Wild's "Being, Meaning, and the World" (*Review of Metaphysics*, XVIII [March, 1965], 411–29) as BMW, and his *Existence and the World of Freedom* (Englewood Cliffs, N.J.: Prentice-Hall, 1963) as EWF.

a discrepancy, a clash, between meaning and being found both in the presence of illusions and "mere appearances" where our meanings stand over against real beings and in the presence of real beings of which we cannot make sense (BMW, 425). The traditional views, as Wild sees them, rule out the experience of sheer meaning without being and sheer being without meaning. "The two cannot clash and absurdity has to be interpreted as a mere absence of being or meaning" (BMW, 425). The appearance of illusion, error, absurdity, and brute beings is, on these classical views, nothing but a transitory phenomenon, a phase on the path toward a mode of understanding in which these will be corrected and canceled out. Being is meaningful and intelligible. In opposition to this, Wild interprets the very experience of absurdity as disclosing independent beings that might turn out to be unintelligible, "as the patient in the accident ward may turn out to be incurable" (BMW, 425). There might be no meaningful account possible of the beings that we encounter and the events that befall us. The only meaning that we might find is that of a meaningless clash with meaning. In this context one is tempted to think of senseless suffering, malice, failure, blindness, and accident.

For Wild, *being* denotes real things that are present regardless of the degree to which we succeed in fitting them into a coherent field of meaning. On the other hand, *meaning* denotes a field through which we disclose things in their bearing upon one another, as being something of a certain sort having a value and a place in a context (BMW, 425). The thrust of Wild's distinction between being and meaning might be seen by putting his view in contrast to Husserl's. For both, to apprehend something as something, to find its meaning, is to see it as referring beyond itself to something else, not simply to see it as an isolated unit. The table as a table belongs to a room of furniture and refers, together with the chairs and other furniture with which it is related, to the purpose of a person who puts it to use. To interpret a table as a table is to place it in a coherent world of instruments. For Husserl, the meaning tends to coincide with the being, and the real being becomes nothing more than the referent of a never completed synthesis of meanings vivifying a sensuous given. On the other side, for Wild, the real object is not simply constituted of a synthesis of meanings with a sensuous embodiment but might stare us in the face even in the absence of a harmonious synthesis. For this reason, the object cannot be "bracketed" in Husserl's sense, cannot be reduced to the product of the constituting activity of an ego. The real being of a table is not simply constituted of given sensuous material so synthesized in terms of meanings that it has a place in a world of furniture and of human purposes. While the being could not be revealed as a table apart from a field of meanings of this sort, it is conceivable that, out in a desert and with a form other than that of all other tables with which we are familiar, it would appear as absurd and unintelligible and we would be unable to find appropriate meanings for it or to give it a meaningful place in our world.

In opposition to Husserl, the real object, for Wild, is there prior to any synthesis of meanings, prior to our taking it as something and giving it a place in a meaningful context, even though it must be put into such a context in order to be revealed as what it is. For Husserl, the experience of absurdity and meaninglessness is an experience of the nihilation of the world and the non-being of the things that we seem to find around us. The lack of meaning is equivalent to a lack of being. For Wild, the beings remain even though we might make no sense of them, might not be able to sustain any of our interpretations of them. They are indeed precisely that with which our meanings would in this case clash. When one interpretation after another is canceled out, this only the more radically reveals the independence of the being. There is a distinction between a mere incoherence in meaning, as when a patient is unable to carry on a coherent dialogue and to think coherently, and a clash between meaning and being. The paranoiac patient might have a wholly coherent field of meanings. The problem is that it fails to fit the facts. For Husserl, the clash between meaning and being is reduced to a clash among meanings.

Finding the meaning of a being takes place for Wild against the background of an actual or possible discrepancy; and the failure to find meaning and the experience of discrepancy take place against the background of a minimal relation of being and meaning (BMW, 427, 425). The meaning that we find might in any case turn out to fall short of the being, or hide its real being rather than reveal it; and the very disclosure of a brute being, of something absurd, presupposes an attempt to find a meaning and some meaning with which it clashes. In the very experience of this distinction between being and meaning, we become aware of a field in which they are together. This is not a mere field of beings or of meanings, but a field that includes both in relation to one another. There is a world for Wild wherever there is a field of this sort; and a world consists precisely in meanings partially revealing beings and beings standing over against and in relation to meanings. The world is therefore the field of all disclosure. However, it is at the same time a field of illusion, error, and dream. The world is distinct from a mere sum of beings in including meanings through which these are revealed, related, and covered up; it is distinct from a mere system of meanings in including beings that might not coincide with our meanings and might not be meaningful at all. In contrast to being in the traditional senses, the world is a concrete whole that includes being that might not be meaningful, as well as meanings that might not disclose things as they really are. For a being to be in a world is for it to have some meaning, since even to be out of place and meaningless is itself a sort of meaning. However, there is no a priori identity of being and meaning.

There are two sides of this initial interpretation of world that must be put to the critical test. These are in the end simply the two sides of the distinction between meaning and being. The one is the supposed presence of beings independent of meanings; the other is the alleged presence of meanings without a real foundation, mere appearances without truth. In maintaining that there are absolutely independent beings, does not Wild violate the fundamental phenomenological demand that we remain within the limits of the evidence? The beings that we experience are never revealed apart from our meanings. On the other side, in maintaining that there are mere meanings without a real foundation, does not Wild fail to recognize the intentionality of meaning toward being, its openness to being? The beings that we experience seem to be nothing more than terms of a synthetic unity of meanings; in the measure that meaning collapses, the being itself seems to reduce to a mere dream or hallucination. On the other side, meanings are not final objects in their own right but media for the disclosure of beings. They fail to reveal beings only so far as they are not properly synthesized with one another. The supposed distinction between being and meaning appears to be nothing else than the distinction between the complete ideal synthesis of meaning at which we always aim and the partial synthesis that we actually attain. Being is itself a meaning: the full synthesis of meanings.

In regard to the first of these issues, there is no disputing that we disclose beings through our meanings. However, it does not in the least follow from this that they are disclosed as products of the synthesis of our experiences of them. The perception of a being as something is a finding of meaning in something that reveals itself as apart from our meaning. The being is not revealed to be simply as what we take it to be. The "as" is a partial disclosure of something given as already there, as something that might belie our interpretation and might resist it. The disclosure of the being beyond our interpretations is found in the sense of the limits of our perception of the thing, its unexplored horizons and unexhausted depths, as well as in the recognition that our interpretations might be false, that they are problematic. Husserl interprets the impossibility of a complete synthesis of the being, of a complete disclosure of it, as implying that the real being is the ideal referent of an infinite synthesis of meanings. However, on this interpretation, the thing itself in its real being would be problematic in precisely the measure that our interpretations of it are, and the failure to make sense of it would put its very existence into question.[3] But this does not conform to our experience. The real being is present and is not an absconding referent of a synthesis that we cannot complete; it is present even when all of our meanings are "disappointed." The naked brute being of the thing is in fact never more apparent than when we fail to make sense of it, when it clashes with our meanings. In the very experience of the failure of our meanings to reveal the thing as it is, we confront the independence of the thing: it is there as transcending our meanings.

When I meet a stranger I might find that I constantly misinterpret his words, gestures, and actions, and that at each stage the interpretations with which I replace my previous ones fail to make sense of his behavior as a meaningful pattern. I might be forced to recognize the possibility that, in the words of Husserl, "Every illusion [might] not as it were *de facto* proclaim a deeper truth, and every conflict in its proper place be precisely what is demanded by more widely connected systems for maintaining the harmony of the whole" (Ideas I, 137). The behavior of the

3. *Ideas*, trans. W. R. B. Gibson (New York: Collier, 1962), I, 137. Hereafter, references in the text to *Ideas* will refer to this translation.

person might not make sense, might be incoherent; on the other hand, I might simply fail to grasp its meaning. However, and this is the important point, my failure to make sense of his behavior not only does not lead me to doubt the existence of a real being there, but it does not even lead me to doubt the presence of a man. What it does put into question is the meaningfulness of his behavior and his existence. He might be so confused, so disintegrated, that his gestures are really absurd. The absurdity of his gestures only points up the more radically his *existence* as something independent of meaning, as something that might mean nothing.

However, it might appear that the existence of the person in this case is not put into question only because the perception of him as a person is meaningful and consistent with the larger context. The absurdity in this case falls within the horizon of a meaningful field. The very existence of the person might become problematic as soon as the larger context begins to become incoherent and not only the figure of the person himself but also the surroundings begin to resist our interpretations. The figure of the person needs only to become amorphous, the surroundings need only begin to change in unexpected and chaotic ways, we ourselves need only lose our bearings and forget where we are, and we will no longer be certain what it is that we perceive around us, we will begin to fear that we are dreaming or hallucinating, and we will begin to doubt that we ourselves are who we suppose ourselves to be.

While all this might be admitted, it does not put into question the distinction between meaning and being. In the measure that the beings resist our meanings, it becomes problematic what they are, but even in this chaos of terrifying absurdity it is still impossible to doubt that there is something there, that we ourselves exist. The naked existence of other things and of our own self is revealed in this case the more radically. While for a moment we might suppose that we are dreaming, we can at any time assure ourselves of the opposite by simply reflecting on the brute adumbrated presence of the beings around us, on their retreat from our meanings. When we are really dreaming, there are only images, no adumbrated real beings. The distinction between waking and dreaming is not simply a matter of coherence but of the presence of real beings. When we are asleep, we allow real beings to move to the fringe of our awareness; and when we dream, we fill up the space that we in this manner leave empty by images and projections that may have no real foundation and may reveal nothing about the real beings that surround us. However, even to speak of dreaming as distinct from waking experience, we need to appeal to the waking experience, for it is this that provides the standard for the distinction; and there would be no distinction unless at the horizon of the dream there were a real field of beings to which we could return and against the standard of which we could reveal the images of the dream for the fictions that they are. The experience of dreams or hallucinations does not put into question the presence of real beings apart from our meanings but reveals these real beings as their background. The distinction between meanings and beings is revealed every time we wake up from a dream and discover that we had been living among meanings that fail to conform to real beings.

While it is indeed the case that meanings intend real beings, it does not follow that there are any corresponding real beings, nor does it follow that the meanings have any role in revealing the real beings that there are. Meanings might hide reality as well as disclose it, as is the case with illusions, dreams, hallucinations, and idle chatter. The distinction between meaning and being implies the necessity of appealing beyond meanings to the actual presence of beings in order to evaluate the meanings. In the measure that phenomenology remains at the level of a bare hermeneutic of meanings, it will be unable to distinguish meanings that conceal from those that reveal the real nature of being. However, and this is the essential and novel point in Wild's view, the very presence of empty meanings reveals a world wider than real beings and real meanings. The empty meanings have their own irreducible significance and must be included in a final description of the world. They constitute a part of the versions of the world in which people actually exist. The paranoiac really lives in a world that is in part constituted by the illusory meanings that he gives to things, and he cannot be understood without reference to these meanings. In spite of the fact that they are without a real foundation and do not reveal things as they really are, they are in the world and must be given a place there. The world must be "broad enough to encompass 'subjective' as well as 'objective' factors in one single overarching frame" (BMW, 415).

When we reveal a meaning to be unreal, illusory, we do not for that reason remove it as a phase of our experience of the world. The meaning of an illusion, error, or hallucination as lived through is not the same as that of the same as corrected: to see a submerged stick as bent is an irreducibly different experience than to see it as merely *looking* bent, and the difference must be respected. In the traditional conceptions of being, there is in the end a place only for illusions and errors as corrected. There is no place for the error as actually experienced.

III

WHEN HE DISTINGUISHES the world from being in the traditional senses, Wild puts the emphasis on the separation of being and meaning. In opposition to the traditional conceptions of being, the world includes beings that might fail to conform to meanings and, in addition, meanings that fail to correspond to any real beings. There might appear to be such meanings allowed in the traditional views. These do not deny that we can refer to nonexistent entities. However, while it is possible on these views to imagine or dream of things that do not really exist, the basic elements of meanings, the "simple ideas," all refer to something real. The fictional referent is simply an arbitrary synthesis of meanings each of which has a real referent. There is no world of meanings that might have no reality corresponding to it at all, no ultimate independence of being and meaning. On Wild's view, the possibility of an ultimate failure of the two to coincide remains open.

However, the world does not on his view for this reason constitute a field in which there is a necessary final opposition between meaning and being. In all of Wild's writings on the topic, he distinguishes between the world and human versions of the world and tends to regard the world as a union of meaning and being, "the field of beings actually gathered together in such a way as to make sense" (BMW, 417). The discrepancy between meaning and being might apply only to the human versions of the world. While the world includes these versions, it is nevertheless distinct from them. In order to arrive at a more adequate understanding of Wild's view in this regard, it is necessary to enter more deeply into the distinction between versions and the world.

For Wild, "It is only through working out our different versions that we have any access to *the* world at all" (BMW, 416), and, as a consequence, it is necessary to approach the distinction between the world and versions from the perspective of the versions. The version of the world in which an individual or community exists is not simply the global meanings through which it interprets its total existence and place in the world, even though, to be sure, it embraces this. The version includes independent beings as well, so far as these are revealed and interpreted in terms of these meanings (*EWF,* 48). In the same sense as the world itself, a man's version is a field in which independent beings are gathered together with meanings that reveal them in their bearing on one another. The distinction between a version of the world and the world itself is revealed in the experienced limitation of the version. These are revealed in the first instance in the presence of beings that are independent of and inexhaustible in terms of our meanings, in the second instance by the encounter with other persons and cultures with different versions in which all beings appear to take on a different significance and value, and in the third instance by a sense of mystery that reveals the limits of all meaning and disclosure. The person who takes his own version of the world as the world fails to recognize the independence of the beings that surround him, fails to open himself and communicate with persons with versions other than his own, and is oblivious to the mystery of the world. He takes beings as nothing more than he reveals them to be. He is closed and fanatical.

Up to now, *the* world appears simply as the horizon, the limit, of our versions. In the measure that the world is revealed through the presence of independent beings, it appears to reduce to nothing more than the limit that they impose on our meanings and to consist in nothing more than their opaqueness and transcendence of our meanings. However, in the measure that the world is revealed through the presence of diverse versions, it appears to reduce to simply the wider human world that includes and yet surpasses our own individual or cultural worlds. On the other hand, so far as it is revealed in a "sense of mystery," the world appears to coincide with an absolute mysterious transcendence beyond beings and meanings. There is something strangely elusive about *the* world; and it might appear that there is here no unambiguous, univocal phenomenon. There is indeed an important ambiguity in Wild's interpretation of the world. There seem to be two diverse interpretations. On one, the world tends to coincide with the totality of our versions as opening up to independent beings. These beings retreat beyond our versions and meanings and find their root in a transcendent mystery. On this interpretation, the world is the field of meanings and independent beings as together *and as apart.* The world is a horizon in the sense of being the limit of our versions, of the disclosive range of our meanings. When interpreted in this manner, the world tends ultimately to be distinguished from a totality of our versions, from the human world, only in the measure that it is unintelligible, a limit of meaning. However, there is a second interpretation. On this, the world is the projected union of being and meaning, "the field of beings actually gathered together in such a way as to make sense and to appear as what they really are" (BMW, 417; cf. *EWF*, 82). On this interpretation, the place of a being in the world is its ultimate meaning and the world reconciles all opposition between being and meaning. When interpreted in this way, the world is distinguished from the totality of our versions in the measure that it gives a higher and more complete intelligibility. The world is a horizon in being a limit to our partial versions, but in its own right it is a horizon only in pointing beyond itself to a transcendent and mysterious origin of its own unity and meaningfulness. On the first interpretation, the world does not denote a final union of meaning and being and does not imply a final disclosure in which things may be revealed without distortion as what they really are; on the second interpretation, the world is precisely the idea of such a final union of meaning and being.

From the one point of view, the world is a concrete presence, the actual field of our struggle to reveal the meaning of beings; from the other point of view, the world is an ideal, something toward which we might strive but which might not really "be there." There is always the possibility that the experienced discrepancy between meaning and being might be ultimate; to hold that the union between these is necessary is to return to the traditional conception of being. The two views appear to imply a different attitude on the part of the philosophical inquirer. The first view allows for the possibility of an ultimate relativism with regard to global interpretations of being by opening up the possibility of an ultimate unreconcilable diversity of versions finding their limit in opaqueness. The second view, on the other side, prescribes that we strive for a final understanding that will reveal things as they are, for the world may very well be a final union of meaning and being, might contain no unintelligible beings or ultimate conflict of meanings.

In our ordinary understanding of "world," there is a counterpart to the ambiguity in Wild's interpretation. When we speak of being-in-the-world, we may mean to focus on the fact that we are not fully at home, are pilgrims, and cannot make final sense of our existence. In this sense, the world is a scene of struggle to find meaning in which we might fail to find it and are delivered over to a destiny that we cannot fully understand or master. On the other side, when we speak of being-in-the-world, we might mean to focus on the fact that we dwell in an ordered field of meaning through which we make sense of things and make ourselves at home among them. In this sense, the world is the successful outcome of the struggle to find meaning, a field where we reveal things as they really are.

There is ground for both interpretations in the fact that to some degree we both succeed and fail in our attempts to find meaning for our existence and for the beings that we encounter. The struggle to find meaning presupposes a belief in the possibility of finding it and is guided by the idea of the world as a final union of meaning and being. On the other side, the very need to struggle and the inevitable limits of our understanding put the belief in the possibility of a final meaning into question and open up the possibility that the world might not include a full union of meaning and being. However, in the end, there is no opposition between these points of view. The world is present as a problematic union of meaning and being; as a horizon of our present understanding, it opens up possibilities of further disclosure without assuring them. The world as an idea of a final union of meaning and being is only regulative; we cannot establish it as constitutive. However, it is necessary to guard against a nihilistic skepticism that gives up in the face of apparent absurdity and fails to search for meaning. The phenomenological evidence does not reach far enough to decide on the final meaningfulness of being. However, in resting with absurdity, we fail to pursue the meaning which might lie right beyond the present horizon of our understanding.

For Wild, the world opens to an absolute transcendence. There is consequently a need at this point to distinguish the world from transcendence and to consider the evidence for transcendence. In some cases Wild approaches transcendence by pointing to the restlessness with which we move beyond all of our versions, all of our meanings (*EWF*, 210). In other cases, he regards transcendence as the ultimate referent of the fundamental freedom by which we originate global interpretations and constitute our versions of the world. However, this does not suffice to distinguish the world from transcendence. The restlessness might be simply a struggle to achieve the union of meaning and being projected in the idea of the world as a full union of these factors; and the ultimate referent of our freedom of world interpretation might be the meaningful world whole. The sense of mystery rather than restlessness in fact discloses a transcendence beyond the limits of the world. In some passages Wild appeals to this sense of mystery to distinguish the world from versions (*EWF*, 215). These passages are misleading. In the measure that the world is a final union of meaning and being, it is not itself mysterious; indeed, it is the reverse. The mystery does not pertain to the place of things in the world—it is not an intramundane mystery; rather, it pertains to the origin of meaning and being—the mystery is transmundane. There might be no world, no meaningful being. The ultimate origin of being and meaning transcends both; it is a limit of meaning. While our meanings ultimately point toward an ultimate source beyond all beings and beyond the world, they cannot dispel the mystery of the source.

There might appear to be an opposition between the mystery of transcendence and the idea of the world as a full union of meaning and being. The sense of mystery is a sense of the limits of intelligibility. However, it does not have to do with the meaningfulness of beings but, as already pointed out, with the ground of the union of meaning and being. The union of meaning and being cannot have its source in either term since it is precisely the mysterious *relation* of the two terms that is at stake in this case. The mystery lies on a higher plane than that of particular beings. These might be intelligible and meaningful while at the same time the ground of their being and intelligibility remains hidden. Here we come to a limit of a phenomenological inquiry. The phenomenologist can seek for the meaning of beings. He can attempt to find the place of beings in a world whole. But he cannot move to the origin of the world. When he attempts this, he finds a mystery that puts a limit to his inquiry. The phenomenon of mystery might be regarded as a limiting, a horizonal, phenomenon.

There are two further fundamental concepts in Wild's interpretation of the world to which we must now turn—that of the life-world and that of the universe of science. These are dialectically interrelated in that for Wild the one is to be approached through the contrast with the other. The life-world is the counterpart of the universe of science. For Wild, the latter universe is not a final horizon; it is included in the life-world and science is an "abstract perspective on things in the *Lebenswelt*" (*EWF*, 94). The life-world is the broader and richer horizon. In order to assess this claim, it is first of all necessary to understand the meaning of life-world. The life-world seems to be distinguished from the world as in some respect narrower. For this reason it is puzzling that Wild interprets science from the perspective of the life-world rather than from that of *the* world. What is the relation between the world and the life-world, and why does Wild approach science from the perspective of the second rather than of the first?

While Wild fails to address himself to this question as directly as he might, there is no doubt that there is on his view a distinction between the life-world and the world when we take the world as the ideal union of meaning and being, the field of things revealed as they really are. The life-world is the field of our versions; it never attains a full union of meaning and being; and as a phenomenologist striving to reveal the final meaning of things, we must not restrict ourselves to an interpretation of the meaning of things for individuals or groups, or even to an interpretation of the meaning of things for human history, but we must inquire into their meaning in the world transcending the human world. For Wild, there are accordingly three phenomenological epochēs. The first opens us to the meaning of things for the person experiencing them; the second opens us to the meaning of things for human existence and human history; the third opens us to the meaning of things in a final world horizon (*EWF*, 36–37).

However, while the distinction between the life-world and the world in this sense is clear enough, the distinction between the life-world and the world as the totality of human versions opening to resistant independent beings and finding its ultimate horizon in an indeterminate transcendence is not at all clear. The life-world is open and ambiguous; it is "surrounded by mystery" (*EWF*, 91); it includes independent beings which we know that we do not know as well as beings that we partially reveal; it includes illusions, hallucinations, and other "subjective" factors as lived through; it is the field in which we struggle to find meaning, in which we develop global interpretations of being, and in which we restlessly put these interpretations to the critical test or fanatically close ourselves off from wider horizons; it is our field of care in which we exist, act, and face death. The life-world transcends any given version in including diverse versions that clash with our own and in opening to independent beings beyond any given version and to transcendence. The life-world appears to be precisely the term used by Wild to denote the world so far as it falls short of the ideal union of being and meaning, so far as it is an actual presence, so far as it appears in our actual existence.

From this point of view, we may attempt to understand why Wild approaches science from the perspective of the life-world rather than from that of the world itself. To approach the universe of science from the perspective of the world as a field of final meaning would be to evaluate it from the perspective of its ultimate or final meaning. While this is indeed the ultimate philosophical task, it requires as a first step the interpretation of the phenomenon in its meaning within the human world, from the human point of view. The interpretation that Wild provides of science must therefore be read as a preliminary, and not a final, interpretation. He does not attempt to give the final significance of science but merely to show its place in the human life-world and to put into question the attempts to reduce the life-world to the universe of science. In order to evaluate Wild's treatment of the scientific universe, it is therefore unnecessary to decide the issue as to the final meaningfulness of being and the ultimate validity of the idea of the world as a full union of meaning and being.

The main lines of Wild's interpretation of science and its relation to the life-world may be easily seen. The fundamental distinction between the two is that the one is an abstract perspective on the other. The universe of science is "derived" from the life-world "by abstraction" (*EWF,* 114). For Wild, the abstraction consists primarily in regarding concrete facts of our life-world from a detached point of view in which they are isolated from their wider context, from the meanings through which they are revealed, from the illusions and errors and other "subjective factors" which are corrected and eliminated in the scientific result (cf. *EWF,* 50–56). The natural scientist is concerned with facts only so far as he can subsume them under causal laws and in this manner explain and predict them (*EWF,* 69). He has no concern for the global meanings in which we attempt to interpret our total being-in-the-world and to evaluate our existence. He simply leaves these meanings out of account unless he takes them simply as objects of anthropological research. However, in this case, he distorts them since he puts them into the world frame of science and does not see the world as do those who live in the framework of these meanings. For these persons, the global meanings are not objects, not one possibility among many seen from a detached point of view, but the very manner in which they interpret the world. In its procedure of taking all beings and meanings as bare objects, science also abstracts from the freedom through which we originally project global meanings, from the sense of mystery and transcendence, and from the direct sense of our own existence as we live it.

The life-world for Wild is prior to the universe of science precisely in being the "primordial source" from which the universe of science is derived by abstraction. The life-world provides the original disclosures and evidences upon which the natural scientist depends, and it is the ultimate source of the meaning of the categories that he employs. For Wild, the scientist does not create altogether new categories. He simply uses the fundamental categories of our life-world—time, space, event, law—in a more abstract and formal manner than the ordinary person. The time and space of science are "derived" from the lived temporality and spatiality from which we gain our "original sense" of the meaning of time and space (*EWF,* 96). The causes of science that are expressed in abstract functional relationships are originally met with as active forces and powers pervaded with positive or negative value (*EWF,* 114). On the other side, the life-world is more inclusive than the universe of science in including the beings and events that the scientist abstractly interprets in terms of the "abstract essences or variables, laws, and theories" which constitute scientific meaning. There appears on Wild's view to be nothing more in the scientific universe than in the life-world.

Put in this form, it is not hard to object to Wild's view. There are two features of the scientific universe that put radically into question the claim that science does no more than abstract from the life-world. The first is that science attempts to complete and give a nonperspectival view of its object, to consider it as apart from the human meanings through which it is revealed, and indeed as apart from the human world altogether; the second is that in this attempt science moves beyond the perceived object to interpret it in terms of micro-theoretical particles that do not appear to have a place in the life-world at all. The first feature is dramatically apparent in the accounts that science gives of astronomical and geological events that are pre- or post-human; the second is dramatically evident in the accounts that science gives of the micro-structures of common-sense objects. While in these cases the data of the scientific account are certainly abstract aspects of objects as revealed in the life-world, the objects of the theories appear to fall outside of the life-world and to limit it. When he regards the objects of the scientific universe as abstractions from the life-world, Wild appears open to the criticism of failing to distinguish the data of science from its own proper objects. The observed fossils and genetic processes that serve as data for evolutionary theory are not the objects of that theory; the observed movements that serve as the data for theories of submicroscopic structures are not the objects of those theories.

There can be no question that Wild fails to do justice to the full cognitive contribution of science. He cannot maintain that science does nothing more than abstract. However, it does not follow that he cannot do justice to the constructive element in science and nevertheless maintain that the life-world is prior and more inclusive. He does not work this out, and he gives only fleeting suggestions. However, these may be developed, and in doing so we may move to a deeper understanding of Wild's view of the life-world. There are two factors about the life-world that open the possibility of its including even pre- and post-human events and beings and the submicroscopic particles that have no sensuous appearance and appear to have properties incompatible with those of the perceived objects that science interprets in terms of them. The first of these factors is the *openness* of the life-world; and it is to this that Wild himself explicitly appeals in his all too brief remarks with regard to pre-human and post-human time and history and with regard to submicroscopic particles (*EWF*, 95). "The *Lebenswelt* is not a fixed 'expanse.' It is a moving historical world that is open at either end. Science has extended these borders and given us information concerning its prehuman and posthuman history" (*EWF*, 95). In the same vein and with regard to submicroscopic extensions of the life-world:

> I do not see the whole of this yellow pencil, but only through partial, ambiguous perspectives. Each of these leaves the way open for an indefinite number of further aspects to be revealed by different points of view. The concrete object of direct perception is infinitely rich. There is no reason, therefore, why it should not have room for the submicroscopic perspectives of the physicist, and the further aspects revealed to him through his special techniques and instruments. In the open field of the *Lebenswelt,* there is room for all of these aspects and for many more as well (*EWF*, 95).

The discoveries of the scientist extend the life-world, reveal dimensions of it that remain otherwise unrevealed and on the horizon. The new horizons of science serve as a limit only to the prescientific life-world. The life-world for Wild is no longer the prescientific world that it was for Husserl and Merleau-Ponty; it is rather, as we have already seen, the whole world as centered in our own existence, as historical, as including beings that we are unable to reveal in their full and final meaning.

This leads directly to the second factor in the life-world that makes it possible to include science within it. This is the presence of independent beings. There are some passages in which Wild speaks of science as giving us a view of things as they are apart from us (*EWF*, 53); and it is indeed possible to interpret all of the diverse forms of abstraction found in science, as well as its constructive activity, as an attempt to reveal beings in their nonhuman meaning, as they are apart from us. There are indeed paradoxes with this interpretation when it comes to science of behavior, but in the measure that this remains a pure natural science it is open to the objection of putting man in an alien frame and treating him as nonhuman. If it is indeed the project of science to reveal things as they are apart from us, science becomes the project of interpreting and articulating the adumbrated depths of independent beings. When it "completes" its objects, "abstracts" them from human meanings and values, and interprets them in terms of invisible microparticles, it reveals a dimension of things hidden from perception and from our ordinary practical dealings with them. However, science does not for this reason transcend the life-world, since that life-world itself includes independent beings and all that we actually succeed in revealing about them. In emphasizing the abstractness of science and the priority of the life-world, Wild tends to give the impression that science makes no real advance, that it is merely negative, that it merely covers over. He ought to have balanced this emphasis with an equal emphasis on the positive role of science in penetrating the hidden depths of the beings that surround us.

The universe of science is therefore included in the life-world as its extension and completion in certain domains; and, in its application to technology, it gives us a certain power of control and prediction over independent beings and events within the life-world. But the universe of science falls short of the life-world, is more limited, in all of the meanings and aspects of being from which it abstracts. In the measure that it transcends the diversity of our global world interpretations and historical versions of the world, the universe of science might appear to have a higher status, to be nearer to the world as a union of being and meaning than the wider life-world in which it is included. However, the union of being and meaning achieved from the point of view of science is achieved only within a limited domain. There is no science of the world as such; science deals with particular beings or regions of being and not with the whole. The advance of science does not succeed in answering the basic questions of the meaning of the world and our existence as a whole, and it is unable to give direction in matters of ultimate value. There is no more dramatic illustration of this limitation of science than the fact that while persons in diverse cultures with diverse versions of the world share the same scientific universe, this does not in the least unite them in other matters.

The term "world" is fraught with ambiguity and is in some respects open and indeterminate. However, in spite of this, there is a hard core of meaning; and in regarding the world as the fundamental phenomenon, Wild overcomes three limitations of the traditional phenomenology. First, he overcomes the idealist limitation. While phenomenology on Wild's view remains concerned with the full range of meanings, it never attempts to reduce beings to meanings or to remain within the sphere of a pure hermeneutic of meaning or pure analysis of consciousness. Instead it puts meanings to the critical test of the real beings that constitute the world together with meanings. Second, Wild overcomes the threat of relativism and skepticism that emerges in the phenomenological accounts that remain wholly within the limits of the human world. The idea of the world prescribes a search for meanings that are not relative to particular cultures or versions but are valid for all. While Wild respects the diversity of versions, he is never content to rest with these as final. Third, Wild overcomes the tendency of the traditional phenomenology to treat science as a mere construction or a mere abstraction. There is an element of this disparagement of the disclosive role of science in Wild's own interpretation. However, in regarding the life-world as being open to the hidden depths of independent beings, he allows for a positive interpretation of science as revealing dimensions of beings hidden from the perspective of prescientific experience and as expanding the horizons of the life-world itself.

6 / The Life-World and Its Historical Horizon

Calvin O. Schrag

THE CONCEPT OF THE LIFE-WORLD has become increasingly common in the growing literature on phenomenology and existentialism. Indeed, some contemporary philosophers, such as John Wild, place the concept of the life-world at the center of their philosophical investigations. In many of these investigations and discussions, however, the relevance and the weight of the historical as it pertains to the life-world, if not neglected, is given only a kind of implicit acknowledgment. It is the purpose of this essay to render more explicit the relevance of the historical for a phenomenology of the life-world.[1]

History as a philosophical problem has been with us for some time now, and particularly since the time of Hegel. It may well be said that Hegel intensified and consolidated the historical consciousness. This intensification and consolidation of the sense of the historical by Hegel was not, as is sometimes believed, the result of a wholly abstract and somewhat fanciful project of pure thought. It received its impetus from an attentiveness to the French Revolution and an assessment of its ineluctable consequences. It was thus that the modern consciousness of the historical was born as a consciousness of crisis. During the unsettling developments of the French Revolution, suppressed freedom erupted in the guise of political liberty; the

1. An illuminating discussion of Husserl's understanding of the historical world and use of the historical sciences can be found in Robert Welch Jordan's article, "Husserl's Phenomenology as an 'Historical' Science," *Social Research,* Vol. XXXV, No. 2, 1968.

edifice of the traditional absolute state collapsed, and with it fell its metaphysical supports. With this came the disquieting awareness of the imminence of widespread social change and the openness of the historical future. The events of the times conspired to produce a deeply felt cultural anxiety. Reflection on the patterns and meaning of history was thus occasioned by a profound consciousness of crisis.

The consciousness of crisis continued to play a dominant role in the reflections on history and the sense of the historical by succeeding European thinkers. Indeed, one can trace the orchestration of this theme from Hegel's *Vorlesungen über die Philosophie der Geschichte* (1837) to Husserl's *Die Krisis der europäischen Wissenschaften und die transzendentale Philosophie* (1954). Yet various modulations and some instances of counterpoint are discernible in this orchestral development. A variety of attitudes and programs came to expression in the reflections of those thinkers who addressed themselves to the element of crisis in man's historical experience. Hegel came to a resolution of the problem fully equipped with an idealistic metaphysics in which the victory over the discontinuities occasioned by the eruption of crisis was assured by the rational movement of the Absolute Spirit. This metaphysics of history, as understood by Hegel, was at the same time a theodicy. Hegel made this explicit when he wrote: "Our mode of treating the subject is, in this aspect, a Theodicaea—a justification of the ways of God . . . so that the ill that is found in the World may be comprehended, and the thinking Spirit reconciled with the fact of the existence of evil." [2] The answer to the question of the meaning of historical experience, according to Hegel, is thus to be found within the framework of theo-metaphysical ruminations.

The legacy of Hegel's reflections on historical consciousness revolves around the conceptual maneuvers of two interrelated projects: (1) the drive to formulate a universal and unified philosophy of history; and (2) the search for a substrate of historical experience. The drive to formulate a system can be properly understood as the mainspring of Hegel's mature philosophy. Reality, according to Hegel, comes to its fulfillment as it is comprehended (*begriffen*) within a system of concepts. This thesis, applied to historical experience in the interests of con-

2. *The Philosophy of History*, trans. J. Sibree (New York: Dover Publications, 1956), p. 15.

structing a philosophy of history, makes possible the comprehension of the crisis situations in human life from the standpoint of rational unity. Coupled with this drive to formulate a rational and unified philosophy of history on the part of Hegel was a search for a stable substrate of historical experience. Hegel found this stable substrate in the Absolute Spirit, which enjoys its self-actualization as it moves from subjectivity and particularity to objectivity and universality. It is noteworthy that in his search for a substrate Hegel abandoned the Cartesianized cosmological category of substance as self-contained and static, resting in itself. Absolute Spirit is posited as a dynamic and restless subjectivity that yearns for a self-unification and self-objectification, whereby the crisis of its own development might be sublated. But in marking out the path of this dynamic struggle and securing the vantage point of an "end of history," from which the development of historical consciousness could be comprehended, Hegel ultimately had recourse to a nonhistorical concept of reason. Reason, as understood by Hegel, is in the final analysis nonhistorical; it is reason in the form of a "logic of science" which arrogates to itself universal, necessary, and objective knowledge. The immanent logos that structures the development of history is an abstract and objectifying reason, which requires that the historical process be completed as a condition for its being known. The owl of Minerva is not able to discern the sense of the historical as it occurs in the light of day. She must wait until dusk to comprehend the historical as *that which has transpired*. To understand history in terms of these criteria of rationality, Hegel was forced to place himself at the end of history. Thus the Hegelian resolution to the crisis-experience of historical consciousness remains a nonhistorical resolution.

After Hegel, a great deal of attention was given to history as a philosophical problem by a variety of thinkers who continued to define historical consciousness in terms of a consciousness of crisis, but who provided different diagnoses of the crisis and offered different cures. Karl Marx, one of the more celebrated spokesmen for the anti-Hegelian movement of the nineteenth century, diagnosed the cultural crisis of his times as the result of the conflict of economic classes. This diagnosis led to the elaboration of his economic interpretation of history. What interests us in the present context is not the doctrinal details of his economic theory, most of which have been discredited by subsequent theorists of economy, but rather the philosophical motivation which led Marx to ask the question about historical reality. It could be said that the moving force behind Marx's reflections was a desire to return to the concreteness of the historical as a counterthrust to Hegel's abstract theo-metaphysics of history. The crisis of consciousness, according to Marx, has its source in man's concrete socioeconomic existence, and it is within this existence that a solution is to be found. For all that Hegel had to say about the rational movement of the Absolute Spirit and the reconciliation of that which is estranged, the concrete facts of everyday life, says Marx, offer testimony that estrangement or alienation is still very much in force. The laborer as he is pitted against the depersonalizing system of capitalism remains alienated from the products of his labor, from those who use him as a source of labor, and ultimately from himself. Thus spoke the early Marx—the Marx of the *German Ideology* and the *Economic and Philosophic Manuscripts of 1844*. This was the *existential* Marx, whose attack on Hegel's philosophy of history contributed a formative influence in the development of the existentialist movement. Marx addressed Hegel with two searching questions: (1) Where is the reconciliation or synthesis of opposites that overcomes estrangement? (2) Where does Hegel himself stand when he issues his proclamation of synthesis? The answer to the first question, says Marx, can only be that the synthesis is in Hegel's head. It is a synthesis in abstract thought but not a synthesis in concrete reality. The continuing estrangement and depersonalization in our concrete socioeconomic existence attest to this. Marx's answer to the second question was that obviously Hegel himself stands within history when he asks the question about it, but the nature of Hegel's answer in which a final synthesis is proclaimed would require that he stand at the end of history and view it from above. Hegel's answer is thus at best irrelevant and at worst comic. His answer is not an answer to a *real* problem. It is not an answer to the alienation within man's concrete, social existence.

In our present project we are not interested in evaluating the force and cogency of Marx's attack on Hegel. Suffice it to say that it would seem to merit some attention. What needs to be pointed out, however, is that Marx himself did not remain true to his original insights. The irony of the intellectual odyssey of

Marx—and particularly of later Marxism—is that he and his followers began to fashion their own metaphysical heaven, in which the lion and the lamb were to feed together in the harmonious and undisturbed existence of a classless society. As a consequence, Hegel's "State," as a unified cultural consciousness, was simply replaced by the "Classless Society" as the end of history; economic forces were substituted for the Absolute Spirit as the substrate of history; and the meaning of history was alleged to be known by a "science" which, like that of Hegel, put claims on universality, objectivity, and necessity. According to the Marxist, the economic forces that propel history are discernible in all cultures; they can be objectively formulated so as to yield causal laws; and they conspire to produce an inevitable historical result.

The themes of historical consciousness and historical meaning came to the forefront of philosophical reflection in an unprecedented manner in the thought of Wilhelm Dilthey. Dilthey, whose thought was a formative influence in the rise and development of historicism (*Historizismus*), set himself the task of charting a human science (*Geisteswissenschaft*) which would provide an interpretive understanding of history as an expression of lived experience (*Erlebnis*). According to Dilthey, the basic fact of historical experience is the development of individual life-styles. The substrate of history is thus no longer the Absolute Spirit (Hegel), or economic forces (Marx), but the reality of individuated, lived experience. Philosophy of history finds its interpretive notions in the project and designs of a "philosophy of life" (*Lebensphilosophie*). This project, in turn, rather decisively modifies the complexion of philosophy of history as a special discipline. Indeed, it places into question the possibility of such a discipline under the categorial determinations of objectivity, universality, and necessity. Dilthey offers no unified view of history, replete with metaphysical explanations. Rather he presents an imaginative interpretation of various world-views arising out of particular life-styles. In short, a *historicist* approach replaces a metaphysical approach.

This historicist approach is accompanied by an expanded view of reason. The relationships of life, on which history rests, are not comprehended through the objectifying reason employed in the science of nature. The comprehension which yields a sense of the historical is a process of grasping a life-form within the concrete context in which the individual himself stands. Dilthey designated this process of comprehension through a consistent and technical use of "understanding" (*Verstehen*). By *Verstehen* Dilthey meant neither the knowledge borne by causal explanation nor the process of subsuming a particular under a universal or class concept. It is rather the imaginative interpretation, and hence a hermeneutic art, of the organization of an individual or communal life-style in terms of the purposes that it projects and the values that it realizes. Understanding, as the peculiar form of historical reason, does not prescind from value solicitations, as does scientific reason. The life under consideration is that which is organized by a self or a community of selves within the context of purposive activity and the self-evaluation of this activity, and it is from this point of view that it is to be understood. Understanding is geared to the reentry into, and imaginative reenactment of, a life-style that is extant or once flourished.

One is able to discern in Dilthey's philosophy a singular discontent with the objectivism and essentialism that characterized much of the thought of his time, and a gravitation toward a species of historicist subjectivity. This is discernible not only in his skepticism with regard to the use of objective reason in the project of historical understanding, but also in his location of the substrate of history more on the side of the subject than on the side of the object. There is indeed a thread of residual Kantianism that runs throughout the thought of Dilthey. He anticipated a "critique of historical reason" that would have the forms of historical understanding anchored in the *historical* subject, as Kant's *Critique* anchored the categories in the *transcendental* subject. Understanding would thus supply the forms of subjectivity of our present historical life by virtue of which the past could be imaginatively reenacted and comprehended. That this should raise rather poignantly the problem of relativism is perhaps inevitable, and we know that Dilthey wrestled with this problem throughout his lifetime. Whether his philosophy contained the resources for overcoming relativism is one of the proverbial moot questions.

Husserl's attack on historicism, and indirectly on Dilthey, in his essay on "Philosophy as a Rigorous Science," was sharp and forceful. Yet Husserl's rejection of Dilthey's historicism did not compel him to abandon his interest in the general theme of the historical. Indeed, he again addresses himself to this issue in a more thematic way in his lectures and essays later published under the title, *The Crisis of European Sciences and Transcendental Phenomenology*, which includes his rather remarkable essay, "The Question of the Origin of Geometry Considered as a Problem of Intentional History." [3] History becomes a philosophical issue for Husserl as he interrogates the crisis that has erupted in the development of the European sciences. Here Husserl would seem to follow the general pattern of modern historical thinking as it moves from the consciousness of crisis to reflections on history. The crisis within the European sciences is understood by Husserl as having its source in the failure of objective science to remain cognizant of its source. Reflection on our historical existence must, according to Husserl, take as its concrete point of departure the situational "breakdown" of our time (*"Zusammenbruchs"-Situation unserer Zeit*), which has been produced by the breakdown of science itself.[4] Contemporary science has everywhere lapsed into "objectivism," using for its model the objectivizing procedures of Galileo and Descartes. This lapse into objectivism, however, is not to be indicted because of the search for objective knowledge on the part of science. Objective knowledge *must* remain the ideal for all theoretico-scientific thought. Husserl does not for a moment question this ideal. What has occasioned the crisis is not the appeal to objectivity in the methodological designs of contemporary science, but rather the failure to recognize that the scientific-objective explanation of the world has its origin in a concrete life-world (*Lebenswelt*) of perceptual, social, and praxis-oriented experience. The application of the phenomenological reduction (which still remains in use in the later Husserl) requires that one suspend or put out of play the objective-scientific view of the world, without as such contesting it as a legitimate perspective, so as to move back to and become clear about the world as presented in our everyday, lived-through experience. Only when this is accomplished will the theoretico-scientific world be properly

3. *Die Krisis der europäischen Wissenschaften und die transzendentale Phänomenologie*, ed. Walter Biemel, *Husserliana* VI (The Hague: Martinus Nijhoff, 1954); the essay on the Origin of Geometry is published as Beilage III in this work. Translated as *The Crisis of European Sciences and Transcendental Phenomenology*, by David Carr (Evanston, Ill.: Northwestern University Press, 1970).
4. *Krisis*, p. 59.

understood as having its origin and foundation in the concrete life-world, and the tide of crisis within the European sciences will be successfully stemmed.

The return to the life-world, as projected by Husserl, brings with it the discovery of a historical horizon of interpersonal relations in which both actual and potential associations with others are experienced. This horizon, he continues, is open and endless (*offen endloser Horizont*), extending from a tradition which is already laden with sense and adumbrating a future which occasions the formation of new or original meaning.[5] The historical horizon displays an internal temporality, retentional and protentional, which occasions the sedimentation of sense in memory and the origination of sense in anticipation. Thus Husserl is able to define history in his essay on the origin of geometry as "from the beginning nothing more than the living movement of reciprocal involvement and interpenetration of original sense-formation and sense-sedimentation." [6] And it is at this point that we are able to see the paramount significance of the category of repetition (*Wiederholung*) in Husserl's explication of the sense of the historical. Repetition is the process of reclaiming the past in such a manner that its sedimented sense is made visible, or disclosed, through a projective sense-formation. Without repetition, recollected events would remain factually isolated and ultimately unintelligible.[7]

The phenomenological concept of horizon, as used by Husserl, would seem to have a peculiar applicability to the problem of historical meaning or sense. In Husserl's discussion of the "horizon-structure of experience" in *Erfahrung und Urteil,* he elaborates the thesis that all of our seeing, doing, and comprehending occur against a background of spatial and temporal intentionalities which mark out on a prepredicative level certain prereflective significations that undergird the formulation of predicative judgments. All experience and all judgment take place within this horizon-structure.[8] Now to speak of the historical as a

5. *Ibid.,* p. 167.
6. "Geschichte ist von vornherein nichts anderes als die lebendige Bewegung des Miteinander und Ineinander von ursprünglicher Sinnbildung und Sinnsedimentierung," *ibid.,* p. 380.
7. Jordan, "Husserl's Phenomenology," p. 252.
8. *Erfahrung und Urteil: Untersuchungen zur Genealogie der Logik,* ed. Ludwig Landgrebe (Hamburg: Claassen, 1964), see particularly pp. 26 ff.

horizon of the life-world has some noteworthy conceptual consequences. It is to reject any prejudgment of the historical as an
isolated element or separable feature of the life-world. The historical is not a quality adventitiously attached to a predefined,
naturalistically conceived, historically neutral life-world. The
historical enters into the very constitution of the life-world. It
determines the world as a historical field of intentionalities in
which facts, objects, and events are imbued with significations
that reveal the genealogy and teleology of human experience.
The historical horizon, quite clearly, is not a rigid boundary. It is
an expanding field of concerns from which and toward which
experience moves.

But, unfortunately, Husserl's reflections on the historical as
a horizon of the life-world, however suggestive, remain fragmentary, and the larger issue of the relation of his later reflections on
history to his earlier program of transcendental idealism remains unresolved. This becomes particularly evident when the
question as to the substrate or the bearer of the historical is
asked. In his essay on the origin of geometry Husserl proposes
that it is the individual person, who by virtue of his "internal
historicality" (*inneren Geschichtlichkeit*) is communalized with
other persons, that constitutes the proper subject of historical
consciousness.[9] But what remains unresolved at this juncture is
the discrepancy, real or apparent, between his claims in this
later essay and the egology of his transcendental idealism in
which the transcendental ego furnishes the ultimate source of
consciousness. In elaborating his phenomenology as a transcendental idealism in the *Cartesian Meditations*, Husserl appears to be anything but a historical thinker. In tracing the
intentional structure of consciousness back to its source in a
constituting transcendental ego, Husserl seems to be committed
to a pure nonhistorical subject which functions as an identity
pole in the presentative acts of consciousness. What manner of
connection, we ask, obtains between this pure, nonhistorical,
transcendental ego and the internal historicality of the communalized person? Are these separable perspectives? Do they comprise different levels of intentional analysis? Are they to be
explained in terms of different stages in Husserl's intellectual
development? Does the former in some manner find its genesis

9. *Krisis,* p. 381, n. 1.

in the latter? Husserl himself, unfortunately, provides us with little help in arriving at answers to these questions.

It is precisely at this point that Heidegger takes over the problem of the historical and makes an effort to rethink it from the standpoint of an *Existenz-ontologie*. In Heidegger's existentialist ontology the source of meaning resides not in a transcendental ego but in the *Existenz* of a historical *Dasein*. Heidegger abandons the idealism of Husserl's transcendental phenomenology and recharts the phenomenological program as a phenomenology of *Dasein*. This phenomenology of *Dasein*, particularly as it relates to the question of the historical, proceeds along the lines of a critical dialogue with Dilthey. Heidegger seeks to clarify what is at issue in speaking about the historical by moving out from an investigation of Dilthey's philosophy of life.[10] The basic flaw of Dilthey's analysis, according to Heidegger, is that it never penetrates to the *ontological* problem of life. Dilthey succeeds only in elucidating lived experience on the ontic level. As a result, life, which for Dilthey provided the source and substrate of history, remains an elusive and unfathomable succession of relativistic styles and orientations. Heidegger, in his phenomenology of *Dasein*, ontologizes the lived experience of which Dilthey speaks so as to make transparent its constitutive structures of finitude, temporality, and historicality. Historical consciousness thus no longer finds its genealogy of meaning in a relativistic life-style, and much less in an Absolute Spirit, or even a transcendental ego, but rather in the intrinsic historical existence of *Dasein*. The sense of the historical emerges from the ontological character of *Dasein* itself.

The crisis of consciousness, which in Hegel had already been correlated with the sense of history, is relocated by Heidegger within the existential structure of *Dasein*. The finite and historical temporality of *Dasein* provides the ontological source of crisis-consciousness. To be finite means to be subject to the threat of non-being, to the threat of a possible loss of historical time and historical space. *Dasein*, by virtue of its very constitution, is subject to the danger of being cut off from its historical past, separated from the meaningful content of its cultural heritage. Correspondingly, it is subject to the anxiety of the future, to the disquietude of disturbing possibilities that might become

10. See *Sein und Zeit*, 7th ed. (Tübingen: Max Niemeyer, 1953), pp. 372–404.

actual. The anxiety-ridden *Dasein* has nothing to remember and nothing for which to hope. It is estranged from its historical past and from its historical future. Its existential space falls under a similar threat. At every turn it is confronted with the threat of displacement. It can lose its finite space, both physical and social, as it can lose its finite time. Historical existence affords no ultimate security, for the forms of existential time and space which provide the ontological horizons for the "life" of history are indelibly finite and subject to dissolution. At the center of this anxiety of finitude is *Dasein's* most disquieting existential possibility—the possibility of death. As historically temporalized, *Dasein* exists between birth and death. Death belongs to the temporal projection of *Dasein* itself. Thus it is in man's being-unto-death that the crisis of historical existence reaches its apotheosis.

In the thought of Heidegger the interest in the historical is coextensive with the interest in human existence. This may, more generally, constitute the distinctive inquiry-standpoint of the so-called existentialist interpretation of history. Yet Heidegger, in distinction to some of the other existentialists, makes the problem of the historical an explicit theme for ontological analysis. The meaning of history is ontologically derived from the historical constitution of *Dasein*. This provides a new standpoint for dealing with the problem of historical relativism, a problem generated by the tradition of historicism but never successfully surmounted by any of its representatives. Heidegger is able to surmount the problem in a novel way, even though his own resolution may not be beyond the pale of criticism. If the possibility of the sense of history is ontologically grounded in the historicality of *Dasein,* then there is no historically neutral subject which *relates itself* to history in terms of relative claims and obligations. It is not that man *has* a history of varying contents, subject to the flux of coming to be and passing away; it is rather that man *is historical* by virtue of his being-in-the-world. Historicality is a structure of *Dasein's* finite and world-oriented existence. Such a being can no longer be relative to an external world-historical process. In the end the Heideggerian interpretation affords both a new understanding of man and a new approach to the meaning of history. History as an external succession of events is history only in a secondary sense (*sekundär geschichtlich*), and achieves significance or meaning only when it is viewed with respect to its ontological grounding in the primary historical (*primär Geschichtliche*), which is the historical *Dasein* itself.[11]

Has Heidegger's herculean effort to lay bare the ontological source of the meaning of history succeeded? Admittedly it is difficult to measure success or failure in matters such as these, but it would appear that a number of critical questions could be profitably posed. Some of these questions pertain specifically to the program of Heidegger, and others have to do with the wider tradition of modern historical thinking out of which Heidegger's own philosophy at least in part emerged. Given the unavoidable limitations of brevity which attach to our present project, these questions cannot be pursued in any depth or detail. We will need to be satisfied with adumbrations and tentative suggestions.

Although Heidegger may have succeeded in surmounting the historical relativism of historicism by tracing the origin of the sense of history back to a radically historicized *Dasein,* it would appear that the concrete historical participation of man in a community of persons is jeopardized as a result. Heidegger's ontology of *Existenz* surmounts historicism at the expense of losing the concrete-communal. As soon as history is grounded in the quasi-formal structure of the historicality of *Dasein,* the resonance of the concrete in the interpersonal life of man stands in danger of being neglected or obscured. In the last analysis Heidegger's ontology is geared toward a meta-historical standpoint which shuts itself off from history as it is lived.

An elucidation of the historical as a horizon of the life-world will need to remain more proximate to the experienced phenomena. This may require a shift from a phenomenology of *Dasein* to a more explicit phenomenology of world-experience. In such a phenomenology of experience, as it pertains to the historical, close attention will need to be given to the solicitation of meaning in man's concrete interpersonal existence. This will include specific investigations of speech and bodily comportment as these two interrelated phenomena provide access to the lived concreteness of the social world. An ontological analysis of the existential structure of historicity will remain philosophically anemic if it is not supported by concrete analyses and descriptions of the dialogical character of living speech and the disclo-

11. *Ibid.,* p. 381.

sure of the other through the motility of the lived body. Reflection on history as a source of meaning needs to be reinserted into the context of a concrete social life-world in which person-to-person encounters through speech and action conspire to produce a sense of the historical. The historical as a horizon of the life-world is a form of life concretized by the shared experiences of men speaking, acting, and working together to achieve communal goals. Historical consciousness comports a sense of the communal, however prereflective and inarticulate this sense of the communal may at first appear. The radically isolated *Dasein* of Heidegger's ontology, anxiously confronting its death within the structure of its historicality, does not allow for the sense of the communal in the concrete interpersonal life-world in which historical memories and anticipations are always already deployed.

A sense of the concrete-communal would thus appear to be an essential ingredient of historical world-experience. The historical as a horizon of the life-world encompasses the communal, and in such a way that it provides it with a past and a future and a sense of presence evaluated from the standpoint of past and future. In short, the sense of the concrete-communal in the life-world is determined by historical time. The historical life-world includes within itself not only a world of contemporaries but also a world of predecessors and a world of successors, and the sense of the historical finds its origin and development in an integration of these three temporalized world-regions. According to Heidegger (and also Husserl on this point), this integration is achieved through repetition. A sense of the historical is thus garnered through a repetition of the possible, and repetition is here understood as an explicit "handing-down" (*Überlieferung*), a going back into and a reclaiming of the possibilities of a *Dasein* that has already-been-there.[12] This reclaiming of the past as possibility secures the sense of the historical by combating its dissolution into a mere collection of isolated and objective facts. The sense of the historical is thus a continuing *achievement* rather than a given set of conditions. In his further elaboration of the notion of repetition Heidegger introduces the role of anticipation and the weight of the future. The authentic repetition of a possibility of *Dasein* that has been, says Heidegger, is existen-

12. *Ibid.*, p. 385.

tially grounded in anticipatory resoluteness.[13] The past is re-opened and reclaimed through anticipatory or projective thought and action. Historicality is thus structured by anticipation of the future as well as by retention and repetition of the past. This anticipation of the future confers upon the present an urgency and decisiveness. The present becomes the moment of historical decision, in which *Dasein* confronts the crisis of its finitude, courageously faces the future, and delivers the past as a repeatable possibility.

Heidegger's analysis of historical temporality is seminal and suggestive. However, as we discovered a problem in his derivation of historicality from the ontological constitution of a solitary *Dasein,* so we find a problem in his use of repetition as the integrating factor, and hence the source of meaning, for historical time. In granting to repetition a privileged status, he tends to restrict the future horizon of historical possibilities. We suggest that interpretive understanding within historical experience is as much occasioned by possibilities of a new and open future as by possibilities delivered from a repeatable past. We are not denying that past possibilities can be reclaimed in the present—so far Heidegger's analysis seems to be fundamentally sound—but what is at issue is the need for a more explicit recognition of the *openness* of history and the emergence of novelty. To emphasize the achievements of repetition in the posturing of historical meaning so radically as Heidegger does is to invite a species of historical fatalism, which would then require justification on other grounds. Admittedly, Heidegger allows for the accomplishments of the projective understanding and anticipatory resolution in the reclamation of the historical past, but in the end these appear to be servants employed for the purpose of discovering the repeatable possibilities in a world of *Dasein* that has been. Hence, it should come as no surprise to learn that Heidegger's "use" of the history of philosophy—and particularly the pre-Socratics—is determined by the project of reclaiming an originative understanding and articulation of the meaning of Being. We suggest an elucidation of the historical as a horizon of the life-world more cognizant of the possibilities of the future. History as it is lived is conditioned as much, if not more so, by a hope for that which has not yet happened as it is by a reclama-

13. *Ibid.*

tion of that which has already happened. The historical horizon opens up toward the new, the creative, and even the unimagined.

Our third critical point, although related to the above, extends beyond a critical assessment of Heidegger's approach to the historical. It pertains to a salient feature in the understanding of historical consciousness already found in the reflections of Hegel and in a variety of post-Hegelian thinkers. We have already shown, at least in a sketchy manner, how the modern European consciousness of history has been inextricably bound up with a consciousness of crisis. We now wish to contest the privilege that has been given to the phenomenon of crisis as the driving force in the development of historical consciousness. Does a description and interpretation of the historical life-world require that the experience of crisis be granted such a status of privilege? It is not at all clear that such must be the case. Without denying that the consciousness of crisis does at times occasion, and particularly intensify, concern about and reflection on the meaning of history, we wish to suggest that the genealogy of historical meaning has a more proliferative base. Historical consciousness can be occasioned by the experience of enjoyment as well as by the experience of crisis. Hope as well as anxiety can become a driving force in historical reflection. Love, as the cohesive factor in the development of a sense of community, plays as much of a role in the emergence of historical consciousness as does estrangement. Finitude has its positive as well as its negative expression.

One of the more disturbing tendencies in a strictly existentialist interpretation is that of viewing the negativity of estrangement as a necessary implication of finitude. Heidegger does not even make an effort to distinguish estrangement and finitude as distinct moments of historical consciousness. *Existenz* as determined by finitude is already determined by estrangement. *Dasein*'s being-in-the-world, by virtue of its ontological constitution, is "fallen" (*verfallen*) and subject to a structural guilt. Kierkegaard sought to maintain a real distinction between finitude and estrangement, mainly because of theological interests, but it is questionable whether he succeeded in doing so. This tendency to collapse the distinction between finitude as unified and finitude under the conditions of estrangement has some far-reaching consequences for an understanding of the historical. In such a scheme history is fated to become the domain of the "unhappy consciousness" and is subject to the curse of crisis. History becomes not only the cradle of transience but also the arena of conflict. Such a negative reading of the historical does not appear to be consonant with the wider range of life-styles that are possible. Enjoyment, hope, and love are as valid interpretive categories of the historical consciousness as crisis, anxiety, and estrangement. Time and space, as forms of finitude, are not fated to be factors of a discontinuous and fractionated existence. They also provide the conditions for the unification of experience. Admittedly, one can experience varied discontinuities within historical time and space. But an ascription of a status of privilege to these discontinuities in an ontology of estrangement is not warranted by the world facts of lived experience. Lived time and lived space can be deployed in a positive as well as a negative way. They occasion the appropriate places and the opportune times for the actualization of purposes and the approximation of value-bearing goals. The historical horizon of the life-world affords its unities as well as its discontinuities; it solicits hope as well as anxiety; it provides enjoyments as well as crises. A proper assessment of the historical will thus view it under the guise of ambiguity, and avoid on the one hand a utopian essentialism which views history as a heaven of self-realization, and on the other hand an unmitigated existentialism that views history as a hell of self-estrangement.

7 / The *Lebenswelt* as Ground and as *Leib* in Husserl: Somatology, Psychology, Sociology

Enzo Paci

HUSSERL'S CONCEPTION OF PHENOMENOLOGY as a grounding of the sciences is a familiar theme for readers of the *Krisis*. The ground is there shown as *Lebenswelt,* and it consists of a number of operations grouped by types. The various sciences are classified in terms of the types of operations that ground them. Phenomenology itself should be interpreted in terms of the particular type of operation that we could call "pragmatic"—that is, if the *epochē* is strictly presupposed.

As long as the *epochē* is maintained, there would be no harm in viewing phenomenology as a critical, non-naive pragmatism fully aware of its implications and of the importance of language as a ground. Such interpretation would be supported by certain aspects of the philosophy of Peirce, namely, those centered around phaneroscopy and phenomenology. From Peirce we could connect with James, Mead, and with certain themes of Dewey also present in Whitehead. Thus one could link Wild with Peirce through a winding and not quite continuous line.[1] This

Translated by Angel Medina.

1. For a fruitful discussion of the realistic-pragmatist-phenomenological point of view, see the following by John Wild: "Is There a World of Ordinary Language?" *Philosophical Review,* LXVII (October, 1958), 460–76; "Contemporary Phenomenology and the Problem of Existence," *Philosophy and Phenomenological Research,* XX (December, 1959), 166–80; *Existence and the World of Freedom* (Englewood Cliffs, N.J.: Prentice-Hall, 1963); "Husserl, Life-World and the Lived Body," in *Symposium Sobre la nocion Husserliana de la Lebenswelt, Proceedings of the XIII International Congress of Philosophy,* Universidad Nacional de Mexico, 1963, pp. 77–93.

line, however, loses much of its significance if the factual and methodological importance of the precategorial sphere and of the *Lebenswelt* is neglected.

It goes without saying that the *Lebenswelt* presupposes the return to a meaning of the *cogito* that is both concrete and transcendental. This meaning does not fit within a realism in the tradition of Perry, or of Plato and Aristotle. From this writer's point of view, one must acknowledge as valid only the first-person experience of a subject. It is only possible to come to intersubjectivity by starting from such experience. Furthermore, essences, ontological frameworks, and being must be considered as *non-realities*. Phenomenology can unfold only within the relational frameworks of time and truth. In this perspective, time modalities are based on the modal character of presence, and are experienced as forms of the temporal flux of the type: past-in-the-present, or future-in-the-present, or *otherness*-in-the-present (Plato would have said otherness-in-the-same). "Reality" is just one among several facets of the *cogito-presence*. On a different level, being could be seen, for example, as intention, direction, *telos*.

The *Lebenswelt* and its correlative science can be traced back to the *Logical Investigations* and, more clearly, to the period of 1906–7 when Husserl begins to talk consistently about the transcendental. The science of the *Lebenswelt* is a novel and incipient science, yet the forms of subjectivity and of history can again and again be transformed and actualized by it. Through the agency of this science we learn of a series of dialectical turns taken by humanity, turns which can be understood only by leaving behind the idols of truth and by looking upon mankind's illusions about the possession of its *telos* as a negative drift leading to fetishism, idolatry, and the petrification of values.

In one of my earlier works,[2] which represented a step in the resurgence of phenomenology in Italy, I elaborated, particularly in its conclusion (p. 253), on the substitution of "time and truth" for "time and being." My position there was, in part, autocritical with regard to the second and third parts of a previous work, *Principi di una Filosofia dell'essere*,[3] where the underlying intention of my discussions of forms and types of being

2. For further discussion see E. Paci, *Tempo e Verità nella fenomenologia di Husserl* (Bari: Laterza, 1961).
3. (Modena, 1939).

and/or ontologism was the study of possibly complementary angles in the phenomenologies of Husserl and Hegel.

It is possible to find in American pragmatism what Husserl would have termed an *a posteriori* longing for phenomenology. What is meant by this is that pragmatism, as operationalism, must sooner or later feel the need of a phenomenology radically concerned with the grounding of the sciences. Only a phenomenology can appropriately do this inasmuch as it conceives of the study of pragmatic operations as a study of constitution.

The problem-set that emerges from the above interpretation leads us to a consideration of phenomenology as a new type of encyclopedia of human operations, and consequently of the sciences. Husserl thought repeatedly about this prospect, which in his mind was tied to the understanding of phenomenology as first philosophy, and, later on in the *Krisis*, as *Lebenswelt*. Husserl's own efforts did not exhaust, but rather opened up, the possibilities of confronting new issues and antinomies deriving from logical and psychological analysis, where logic itself seemed unreconcilable with psychological approaches. Still, Husserl was able to find a new way for psychology conceived as phenomenological psychology. In the last analysis the *Lebenswelt* came to assume the grounding role, but not without absorbing some of the impact of negativity, for if it is true that in the *Lebenswelt* man acts in his full concreteness, this level can only be reached after an *epochē* that erases from the human condition neither error nor evil.

In this connection there appear, in the Italian interpretation of phenomenology, two themes that Husserl left undeveloped. I am thinking of the theme of *want,* a form of the *Lebenswelt* from which economics derives, and of the "holistic," encyclopedic character of the works of man. There can be a division of the sciences but never a corresponding division of man. Man is always an open field of interrelations in which economics and praxis, for instance, may be fused as a group of policy operations. The encyclopedia that we have in mind, however, is always *in fieri,* and if in it the *Lebenswelt* effects the interrelation of praxis and science, the policy operations will first of all take the form of political confrontation with whatever can conceal, stifle, or destroy constitutive subjectivity by making an object out of man.

Thus it can be said that Husserl opened the way for a

grounding of politics in which there is implicit the work of a dialectic whose phases always demand new and non-identical manifestations. The human *telos* is the content of truth toward which both politics and the encyclopedia tend, while seeing themselves in conflict with worldliness and fetishism in man. These remarks go beyond anything that Husserl ever said, but it seems to me that they can be developed in a direction that is not simply faithful to phenomenology but carries it to fruition, perfects it, and makes it relevant to present circumstances. If there is a crisis, we must acknowledge its encompassing presence today throughout the planet earth. Undoubtedly this crisis has something to do with the reductive character of scientific thought, of its uses in ways that ignore its genuine ground and goals. These uses are the true sources of the objectification and alienation of men and nations. Phenomenology thus takes a new meaning and becomes the firmest assertion of freedom ever achieved or undertaken by mankind. All of this is made more momentous by the fact that an alienated science loses its role as a science in conjunction with the other human operations and opens up the way to total war. The phenomenological encyclopedia acquires in this connection a new and more concretely constitutive role: as a totality of the sciences which, through the impact of scientific progress, negates war as a negation and transforms man in both his *Umwelt* and his intersubjectivity. Man must take cognizance of the process of grounding; he must experience the grounding of the scientific entity (*Ding*), of the lived body (*Leib*), of the mind (*Seele*), and of human historical society (*Geist*) always transcended in new goals. The entire planet as a civil society will in this way rediscover its own goals and meaning.

I do not believe that Husserl, were he alive, would oppose this interpretation, as he might have opposed Scheler's or Heidegger's doctrinal development of phenomenology. Husserl had a very clear notion of a phenomenology that would lay the groundwork for the sciences. He was aware that phenomenology, when conceived in this fashion, would have to meet squarely such issues as the problem of meaning and the problem of the *telos*. He therefore did not undertake the elucidation of questions such as "the meaning of Being" (*Sinn des Seins*) or the need for a *fundamental ontology* in a Heideggerian sense. Husserl's own problem is that of the import and actualization of truth, an actualization that can never be completed, just as the human *telos* can never be completed.

Man, however, finds in his positive kernel of subjectivity want, error, and evil. And in replacing, within the *Lebenswelt,* the role of "being" for that of intentionality, he emerges as struggle against negation, as work, as human creativity victorious over negation, through a total intersubjective reconstruction, an encyclopedia, and a planetary interrelationism. One must therefore avoid giving the term "ontology," as Husserl uses it, a realistic connotation. Ontology, for him, must be placed strictly in the context of intentionality. In conclusion, Husserl's attempts at laying the groundwork for the sciences open up new dimensions in his philosophy which demand a reexamination of it as a whole. In this dimension "being" cannot substitute itself for *epochē* and constitution.

We saw above that the thing and the body (*Leib*) must be constituted. As for mind, the entire fifth *Cartesian Meditation* is devoted to its constitution through empathic interaction (*Einfühlung*).[4] In these texts the relation between solipsistic constitution and intersubjective constitution begins to take a primary role. *Einfühlung* is not merely a reciprocal interaction among subjects. Subjects have their own body (*Leib*) and are, in their own way, things. In this particular area Husserl's thought is not always clear. To grasp it in its main features one must mark well the fact that every lived body (*Leib*) is for Husserl an orientation center (*Orientierungszentrum*). In peculiar ways this also applies to that physical body, owned by man and by humanity, which is the planet earth. Concerning this viewpoint, and because of the role of the *Lebenswelt* as origin, Husserl shows himself to be not a Copernican but a Ptolemaic. Our own body is a subjective object. Science must not reduce it to a lifeless, mechanical object without a history. All other objects are over against our body, which remains a subject among objects. In the presence and centrality of our body is rooted the localization of all our sensations, which are "ours" insofar as they are thus centered. Moreover, this centrality is relevant to all

4. The expression "empathic interaction" is needed here to render a shade of meaning in the concept of empathy (*einfühlung*) as understood by both Paci and Husserl. There is no empathy by mere imaginative understanding (*verstehen*). A transfer of roles in group activity dominated by an emerging common *telos* is necessary. This represents an important step beyond the psychologistic notion of *verstehen.*—Trans.

of our actions and behavior. In Husserl's formula the body is *Zentrum aller Handlung:* center of all acting.[5] It is also the organ of the will (*Willensorgan*). Since it is the locus of sensations and the center of animation, the body can interact with "other" bodies, and in thus overcoming the solipsistic self it establishes the sphere of culture—Hegel's Subjective, Objective, and Absolute Spirit are Husserl's lived-world as culture (*Lebenswelt-Geist*).

The fact that the body is mine and living allows me then to encounter the others and to understand the meaning of the sociability relation in general. Step by step the pattern of a genuine human nature takes shape, and we see the world of man growing within an inhabited and cultivated nature where centers, subjects, monads are apparent. Bodies are acting centers, but an acting center has meaning only if "nature and body, and the mind insofar as it is intertwined with the body, are all constituted together with each other, in mutual rapport."[6]

The grounding and the encyclopedia of the sciences are both theoretical synthesis and praxis. The regional ontologies of the sciences take their roots in constructive operations such as "positing a center," "volitive" pursuit of a meaning, and all the other experiences that we have called *Lebenswelt-Geist* within the interactive medium of a social community.

In the first chapter of *Ideen III* all of these factors are shown in relation to the ultimate source of legitimacy of knowing and acting, namely, experience. Experience precedes all thought, but most of all scientific and theoretical thought. Thought can have an orientation only if active, performative experience moves it. It is absolutely indispensable that thought keep its ties to the living, experiencing man. The typical varieties of experience are critical for the division of the sciences and their grounding in prescientific life. By 1912 Husserl had already begun to under-

5. This expression and the expression *Orientierungszentrum* can be found in a 1912 manuscript that contains many indications pertaining to the topics of *Ideen,* Vol. II, and which is now presented as Beilage I of *Ideen,* Vol. III. See Husserl, *Ideen zu einer reinen Phänomenologie und phänomenologischen Philosophie* (The Hague: Martinus Nijhoff, 1952), III, 124.

6. Husserl says textually that he can clearly see—and this clarity is an important by-product of phenomenological clarification (*Klärung*)—that "die Natur und der Leib, in ihrer Verflechtung mit diesem wieder de Seele, sich in Wechselbezogenheit aufeinander, in eins miteinander kostituiren" (*ibid.*).

stand the role of the *Lebenswelt* in the formation of regions and regional ontologies basic to the sciences.

It is well known that Husserl's themes are rich in motives that appear and reappear, as melodic lines in a symphony. Those who consider phenomenology as a philosophy of essences must never forget that "the original positing act is that of material perception" (*materielle Wahrnemung*), to which Husserl assimilates the perception of things and the perception of bodies (*Dingwahrenmung, Körperwahrnemung*). All perceptions, including "external" perceptions with their originating sensations, have their locus in the lived body (*Leib*).

What is interesting in Husserl's foundational work is that the resulting structure of the *Lebenswelt* shows in its features, and in the interrelations of these features, the precategorial bases of the sciences as they specifically present themselves. These bases are always intersubjective, and "objective nature" always appears in its grounding role as "a reciprocal understanding within a plurality of experiencing egos," rooted in lived bodies, all of them having to do with matter. The scientist is involved with nature both in body and in mind, and the objectivity of nature itself results from the "entire community of scientists." [7]

Here two divergent attitudes, and their corresponding expressions, may emerge. On the one hand the scientist has an overall grasp of the material sphere with its inherent components, including the somatic-psychic component; on the other hand he can focus on the lived body and on the psyche manifested in it, which will orient research in the direction of physiology and psychology. These attitudes (*Einstellungen*) are prefigured in ways of apprehending. In any case, the constitution of the various sciences and their subject matters must take place at the level of materiality as the initial step. The discernment of levels, degrees, and regions here gives rise to a descriptive clarification (*Aufklärung*) which is not the same as scientific explanation though it serves as its ground. This entire problem-set is the source of numerous phenomenological investigations [8] seeking to determine the relative position of regional ontologies, or ontological regions, and the subject matter pertaining to each science.

Reality for Husserl requires as a necessary condition explana-

7. *Ibid.*, p. 2.
8. *Ibid.*, p. 3.

tion in terms of causes, and anything in reality has identity only insofar as it is causally explained. Causality here is not a category but a mode of explanation, and is closer to the White-headian notion of "causal efficacy" than to the classical notion criticized by Hume. As with Whitehead, causality in Husserl has not an absolute sense but a relative one. What we encounter is always a field configurated in terms of concurrent causal laws. Even substantiality has a role among such laws configuring an environment. Substance in an absolute sense, as conceived by Descartes and Spinoza, is senseless.[9] Thus we learn that at the precategorial base of the sciences—Husserl is speaking in partic-ular about physiology and psychology—we do find a subjective process presenting some of the features of the causal relation, namely, connections, central organization, or polarity. The whole discourse about cause and substance becomes an analysis of the modes of the *Lebenswelt*. And with the new, noncategorial insights that the latter affords, the Humean critique of the for-mer concepts loses much of its strength even though some of its elements are incorporated here. Reality then has been defined as an experiential environment for the presentation of correlative causes configuring substances, and is adumbrated through spe-cific operational attitudes that will give way to the various sci-ences.

If we carefully follow Husserl's discourse it will become clear that grounding is possible for the scientist because he has first-person experience of reality, of its various modes of adumbra-tion as well as of the circumstances in which realities present themselves. Basic materiality is experienced insofar as the ap-prehending subject is material (as any other object in nature), besides being a lived body (*Leib*). The *Leib* assumes a central role within the precategorial design of the *Lebenswelt,* and this role is even more central as regards what we have called the phenomenological encyclopedia. It is not only that the body, even though an object, is and always remains a subject, but also that the animation of the lived body brings about a mingling of psychological experience with the experience of matter and of material bodies. On the one hand we now have matter in gen-eral, and on the other hand we have the lived body with its sensory fields (*Sinnesfelder*). What counts here is the disappear-

9. *Ibid.,* p. 4.

ance of the distinction between *res cogitans* and *res extensa*, between mind and body. Reality then is material not just in terms of extension, along quantitative lines, but also because the very bodies of men of science must enter into the picture. We can see here some intimations of Husserl's critique of Galileo for having neglected the lived body (*Leib*), and we cannot help but think of Heisenberg's principle.

It is to be noted that things both imply and respond to the sensory fields, and that the sensory fields themselves appear other than as organs or as kinds of matter. A material body is discovered by means of sensations localized in my sensory organs. I myself perceive my apprehension of material things and interpret it. Matter is not an *in-itself* but is discoverable and localized through the sensations of another portion of matter. This interrelation has the sense of an interperception. Matter at the basic level of experience is interacting matter. The fact that I have my own body makes me understand the sense in which nature is constituted by corporeality in general, and is, in various degrees, owned in terms of centrality by numerous interacting centers. I possess sense organs such as touch and sight—but nature is owned as a world by animated beings all of which have their sense organs. This factual datum cannot be neglected. Technology itself enters into the picture in this particular respect.

Every instrument is an enrichment of my owned body. Since instruments are extensions either of the sensing body, or of the acting body, or of the body as organ of will and *praxis*, they represent a fusion of the self and nature in the body. Technology therefore keeps enlarging the horizon of the owned body and of the living human being. However, this is the case only if we do not dissociate technology from the human subject, if we never forget his role concerning the grounding and the *telos*. The only other alternative would be the fall from subjectivity: interaction among subjects then becomes a mutually inflicted alienation.

Categorial sciences depend upon our ability to study our owned corporeality and psyche without turning them into objects. This is made possible by two precategorial sciences. By 1912 Husserl was aware—though he did not exploit his insights at that time—of the possibility of such sciences. One of them, somatology, would deal with the lived body (*Leib*), and the other, psychology, with the lived experience of the psyche. An important question would be that of the limits and common territory between the two.

Both of these sciences are "spheres of being"—but being is not here a category that would essentially determine an absolute reality. Somatology is possible insofar as there is perception and apprehension of the lived body. It sets a task for theoretical thought. It must not be considered as setting up a sphere of "separate realities," even though it moves at a level above pure and simple, passive and inert materiality, or what appears to us to be so. Yet since actual somatic experience introduces something "new"—emergent, in Whitehead's sense—in the sphere of materiality, a progressive analysis of the ways in which the lived body functions becomes necessary. This analysis will reveal the following levels: matter, the living owned body, the object in a field of objects, the for-itself, and "concrete subjectivity" or subjectivity as our own. Now if somatology is accepted, we will find not only the basis for physiology and psychology, two specific "scientific regions," but we will also be in possession of their concrete, precategorial outline. Since the lived body (*Leib*) is the zone of encounter between corporeality and the psyche, the aspects which appear in that zone "permeate all zoological sciences," for instance, human and animal physiology. Such sciences are "natural sciences" (naturalistic), but their foundation must be somatological, specifically with respect to the physiology of the sensory organs and of the nervous system. Here the result would be a grasp of localized sensation and a demonstration of relational patterns of influence among the various spheres of somatic activity, all of which is thematic for the phenomenologist.[10]

In the last analysis the basic data handled in these studies are always connected with direct somatic perception, which for each subject is exclusively his own. When modern science forgets this it becomes antihuman and has to face contradictions in spite of its most rigorous formalization. The deep antinomies of private experience cannot, however, be solved by eliminating subjectivity altogether.

Indeed, phenomenological themes, in a disguised manner, are active at the heart of neo-positivism. "Verification" itself represents a return to nonabstract experience, and consequently

10. *Ibid.*, p. 8.

to perception and to an awareness of the given in somatic presence (*Beweusstsein von leibhafter Selbstgegenwart*). Temporal presence and its modalities are very significant in these matters, and so is intersubjective constitution: the ways in which I see and am seen, my interpretation through visual perception of the modes of presentation of the other. Interpretations of this type are always in terms of somatological, spatial, and temporal patterns (modalities). There is no zoology if we do not "see" animals, or thus interpret the sight of them. Whatever we cannot see directly requires an interpretative activity focusing upon pictures or designs, or any other firsthand information. This makes it possible for us to discover at times, when we are confronted with live specimens, things that could not be seen upon inspection of pictures or designs. The great wealth of types of perception and sensation results in a precategorial "unification" of sensing, of the awareness of sensing, and of the feeling of sensing.

Somatic life is grasped by subjective processes in spite of the difficulties in the determination of the underlying experiences.[11] Husserl points in this respect to the affinities between plants and animals, and, had he known them, he might very well have accepted and elaborated Goethe's insights on the metamorphosis of animals and plants, as well as some related suggestions on mineralogy. Husserl, however, did not interpret the plant as a lived body. That would have meant, from his point of view, the possibility of interacting with the plant as with a psyche. However much one can make of the structure of interrelations at this level, it is not safe to interpret it in that sense. It is not possible, however, to exclude the idea of sensation with regard to plants; and, as a matter of principle, a methodological coordination of physiological botany and general biology is not impossible. While Husserl may be unaware of it, his efforts at this point reflect the remote, almost lost background of Goethe's harmonious and dramatic polymorphism. In any case, Husserl assigns here to phenomenology the responsibility for the transition from impressions, sensations, and perceptions to a whole new level of

11. I have translated, here and on p. 137, various Italian expressions used by the author to render the meaning of the German *Erlebnis* as "subjective process." For a justification of this usage, see the translation of Paul Ricoeur's *Husserl: An Analysis of His Phenomenology,* by Edward G. Ballard and Lester E. Embree (Evanston, Ill.: Northwestern University Press, 1967), p. 7, n. 3.—Trans.

interpretative experience, a task which should be entrusted to "ground-breaking phenomenological analyses." [12]

In somatology the perceiver apprehends his own body, but furthermore he perceives himself as a perceiver. He, the concrete *and* transcendental subject, perceives in space and in time. Thus somatology, insofar as it actualizes some modes of the *Lebenswelt,* presupposes both continuity and change between the "activity" and the "passivity" of the self. We now gain access to the dialectical dimension of the *Lebenswelt.* The self, or any group of selves, need protection from the danger that other things or men bring about. They must persuade or confront adverse positions. Instruments and rationalized use of instruments are a part of this struggle. [13]

We must now recapitulate our conclusions on somatology before making some further suggestions. Whatever is perceived is perceived by means of the lived body; zoology and physiology belong among the precategorial structures; even if we do not focus on it, we can have physiological experience by means of subjective process; [14] "pure consciousness" does not constitute a sphere apart from physiological, precategorial experience, but rather the former is constituted by the latter; sensations and their physiology are, according to Husserl, at the material root of "all fundamental types of noesis"—therefore if noesis is subjective and intends a noema, it is also physical, or, more precisely, physiological. Husserl reminds us that, as far back as the *Logical Investigations,* he had insisted that concreteness "essentially" implies sensations and consequently somatic presence. [15] Hence, somatology can easily become precategorial psychology or, as it

12. *Ideen,* III, 9–10. What is said here is in perfect accord with what we find in Husserl, *Zur Phänomenologie des inneren Zeitbewusstseins* (1893–1917) (The Hague: Martinus Nijhoff, 1966). Specifically, concerning the connection between time and perception, see Beilagen III and V as they refer to Husserl, *Analysen zur Passiven Synthesis* (The Hague: Martinus Nijhoff, 1966). This work begins with *Selbstgebung in der Wahrnemung:* passivity as life and duration pattern of a monad or center must be felt precategorially and thus it can be related to biological activity and passivity. We are dealing here with the relations between animals, plants, and minerals, as well as with the overlapping of somatology and psychology.

13. *Ideen,* III, 130.

14. See E. Paci, "Fenomenologia e fisiologia," *Aut, aut,* No. 81, 1964, *passim.*

15. *Ideen,* III, 11–12.

is called in the *Krisis,* transcendental psychological phenomenology.

These investigations, together with somatology, will be placed at the ground level of all sciences, and in particular of all the branches of psychology, from the most experimentally oriented to intersubjectively constituted branches of somatological, psychological, and even psychosomatic exploration. Somatic experience and psychic experience converge and diverge. Husserl observes that the "specialists" may reject these suggestions. In that case the specialists will ignore the operations that fulfill their self-understanding. This understanding is possible only after one grasps the essence and *telos* of the grounding operations. Otherwise, scientific research becomes dogmatic.[16]

If it is true that origin, presence, and evidence are in the lived world, it must also be kept in mind that it is the human subject that has the final capacity for clearing and unveiling, and for carrying out foundational work. If sensation is not an in-itself, but is localized in the body, it is therefore true that it belongs to the human subject, as does the matter of which it is made. For phenomenology, given any part of man, the whole follows. In the *Krisis,* we read that things are not abstractions but *plena.* Somatology and psychology lead to integral man, and to a society which does not impinge upon man's integrity.

The theme of the whole man contains, as well as establishes, three types of reality—lived materiality, perception insofar as it is aware of itself as well as of its contents, and lived body which gives way to the intersubjective realm of lived bodies and to society, science, culture, and reflection. In reflection we encounter the supreme egological consciousness that is capable of tracing its basic stages down to the passive apprehension of the somatic character of subjectivity, and to the very ambiance, to the world, implicated in the material basis of sensation. Given this grounding coimplication, we are never faced with an isolated self whose operations would be operations of pure consciousness (*Vorkommnisse eines reinen Bewusstseins*).[17] The fact of the matter is that man is neither pure self nor pure soma. Between these two extremes we interpose somatology and psychology and, above all, the encyclopedia of all the sciences.

16. *Ibid.,* pp. 13–14.
17. *Ibid.,* p. 15.

We must still distinguish between somatic and psychic sensations. The first are localized sensations which are identical with the behavior of the lived body. The second are psychological phenomena, and, at bottom, they reduce to feeling. Even though material sensations are at the basis of psychological sensations, and even though both are deeply entangled, it is possible to distinguish the one from the other. The "manifestations" of sensation are not the same at each level. These two levels may presuppose each other, or they may overlap. According to Husserl, they may necessitate or influence each other. They are never identical. Their causal actions differ too. Basic sensations are circumscribed by their material nature, which is the very model of psychological causality, i.e., psychological conditioning. This permits activity, spontaneity of movements, and kinesthesis. For Husserl the psyche is dynamism, never inertia, and that is why it is impossible for it ever to return to an identical material state. Husserl does not go any further. What he says is enough for us to reject psycho-physical parallelism.[18] He opens up the access to the psycho-somatic sphere where certain relations are traced from one to the other of these two levels. In any case he leaves us with the conviction that the import of physio-psychic research, as well as its limitations, has been made clear.[19]

What is less than clear in Husserl is the concrete determination of the limits and overlappings of the various precategorial sciences, and the extent to which the various levels of the *Lebenswelt* are autonomous or dependent. We are now back to the theme of interrelations and determinations of parts/wholes first confronted by the *Logical Investigations*. But by now we know that we have been helped in the elucidation of this theme by the understanding of the homogeneities and discontinuities typical of the *Lebenswelt*. We also know that the peculiarly distinctive fact in the precategorial grounding of the sciences is that the epistemic distinctions between the self and the body proper, the subject and the object, are absorbed by the identity of the transcendental ego with the concrete ego; in a classic formula, Fichte's transcendental ego *is* the man Fichte. On these bases a phenomenological encyclopedia becomes possible.

The encyclopedia is a whole whose parts manifest quite

18. *Ibid.*, p. 17.
19. *Ibid.*, p. 18.

diverse kinds of unity. The material world manifests itself multilaterally to the ego that lives in it with a living body, that sees itself in it as an object while continuing to be exploring subject.

Phenomenology must take responsibility for the clarification of implications and distinctions among all these sectors and levels. Phenomenological *Klärung* of the various modalities of subjective process and apprehension will show structured objects whose constitution can actually or possibly be effected through the mediation of the lived body that occupies the zones between materiality and selfness and constitutes, through its various attitudes, objects and types of objects, structures and areas of intentionality. All of these are ideal, unreal, if considered as thoughts, but very real when considered in their own experiential settings, in relation to their constitutive operations and to the causal and circumstantial influences active in each sphere. We have then many intentionally constitutive attitudes and, correspondingly, many kinds of cultural objects (objectivations) [20] which in fact "mingle" so well with each other that they can never be constitutively sorted out. The study of this constitutive "overlapping" gives us some grasp of the peculiar ways of "objectivism," insofar as we can return to multilateral grounding in the body proper (*Leib*). The various kinds of "objectivations" that we find in the sciences are grounded in "communities" of constitutive acts (Whitehead would have called them "communities of events").

All of these groupings that we find in the sciences lead us step by step to the society of subjects, the human community, with its ground in the *Geisteswissenschaften,* and ultimately in the *Lebenswelt-Geist.* Societies are not things, or, even less, abstract complexes. Without the reality of its centers, the subjects, societies become such abstractions. If we speak of a societal psyche we cannot forget that each self has its own psyche. Still it must be said that "collective personalities" have a ground in somatology and in the reality of precategorial conditioning, as well as in environmental interactions.

20. I use the word "objectivations" for "objects" in this context to dispel an ambiguity between its connotation as *recurrent abstract entities* (as in the expression "theories of objects") and its connotation as *culturally constituted meanings,* including all *institutions* (and in particular institutions involving the use of language). I am indebted to Professor José Ferrater-Mora for suggestions concerning the above distinction and terminology.—Trans.

We can assume that had Husserl proceeded along this road he would have thrown further light, beyond somatology and psychology, upon the precategorial attitudes basic to sociology. A sociology thus connected with the *Lebenswelt* would have mediated between naturalistic—not founded—sociologies and the subjective and intersubjective attitudes of human beings.

8 / Life-World and Structures

C. A. van Peursen

Recent Developments

Two significant developments can be remarked in the philosophy of the last fifty years. One is related to the notion of structure, the other to the notion of the life-world.

Philosophical, as well as scientific, research has always been the investigation of structures. It is by a process of structuring that chaos becomes cosmos, that human behavior is guided by reason, that human society can be organized according to the rules of justice—these were the themes of Greek philosophy, stimulating the rise of natural and social sciences. These structures were often indicated, in Greek and later philosophy, by terms like "articulations" (*eidē*), "schemes," and "laws." They had primarily an ontological status; the logical relationship expressed in these structures was rooted in a metaphysical or a physical reality. In the Middle Ages and the Renaissance this status was disputed by nominalism and empiricism, but neither current of thought succeeded in defining the proper status of structures and laws, having separated them from their ontological basis. Kant's epistemology provided a solution to this problem, but only by basing the structures on unchangeable laws of thought; renouncing a metaphysical foundation of the laws of nature and of ethics, he offered a new type of metaphysics—a "metaphysics of reason."

The new turn in philosophical reflection on structures came

when they were no longer investigated within an ontological or even an antiontological framework (like the more skeptical solution of nominalists and empiricists), but within the framework of logical meaning. This approach had been anticipated by many earlier thinkers. Kant himself analyzed analytic and synthetic propositions. A more ontological philosopher like Leibniz has been of special importance, because he promoted the investigation of a *mathesis universalis* and a "pure grammar." It was not, however, until the beginning of the twentieth century that a widespread philosophical discussion on the status of the "meaning" of a sentence or proposition came to the fore. Frege, Meinong, Husserl, Russell, and Moore developed their conceptions —often by the exchange of letters or in response to publications —about the realm of meanings as a field of logically describable rules that are not only separate (nonempirical) but also different (nonontological) from the laws of physics, psychology, or social science. Other thinkers, such as Wittgenstein, Schlick, and Carnap, have contributed to this discussion since about 1920, and many contemporary philosophical debates, marked by the influences of the aforementioned divergent philosophers, are concerned with the same theme.

What is striking in the contemporary discussion is that the investigation of structures, which are not at all identical with empirical data (ontological, physical, psychological, etc.), is no longer confined to philosophy or logic. Many trends in various scientific disciplines are toward the study of pure structures that have a logical status and that control empirical phenomena but are not dependent on them. A few examples may be mentioned. Mathematics, which around 1920–30 was often considered to be a branch of logic, appears not to be reducible to logic but to have a status of its own; this does not mean at all that it is an empirical science—on the contrary, it is a "science of structures" (Bourbaki). The concept of "structure" has become particularly dominant in the field of linguistics, where the idea of a "universal grammar," in many respects already anticipated by the structuralistic approach of de Saussure, can be found, for instance, in the work of Chomsky. The empirical manifestations of a language are controlled by general and formal rules that are not dependent upon them. Those rules constitute the "deep structure," whereas the empirical-physical aspect of a language, the "surface structure," has to be derived from the deep structure by transformational rules. In the field of psychology and logic, the work of Piaget and his collaborators must be mentioned. Piaget also speaks of structures that are constituted as it were through the empirical medium of psychic development, gaining nevertheless a pure logical, nonempirical status. Modern social science, particularly cultural anthropology, has incorporated the term "structure" in its vocabulary. Lévi-Strauss in particular has evolved a structuralism by which rules of kinship and so on are formulated and even formalized, making them subject to mathematical operations.

All these trends are well known and have been mentioned only in passing, to illustrate the closer relationship between the empirical and the structural that is coming to the fore in contemporary development. What kind of evolution in thought will take place when the meaning of a statement, and the logical rules governing it, which have been liberated from empirical and ontological discussions during the first decades of this century, will have to be correlated anew with the field of empirical reality? Old and new questions are converging here: How can syntactical and statistical study of language, deep and surface structures, mathematical structures and patterns of social behavior, logical and psychological rules, *quaestio iuris* and *quaestio facti,* be interrelated?

This focuses attention on a second theme in contemporary thinking: the life-world. Here the logical trend goes in the opposite direction: logical structures are not being disentangled from empirical phenomena; rather, empirical reality is, in a way, absorbing logical structures. No long survey of the history of modern philosophy is necessary; one illustration may be sufficient. Kant made a very fruitful and important distinction between empirical and mere structural questions, between the *quaestio facti* and the *quaestio iuris.* This has led various neo-Kantian schools of philosophy, and in their wake many of their opponents (such as the realists), to make a sharp contrast between the "naive experience," which does not yield any reliable information about the structure of knowledge, and the critical epistemological analysis of experience, which does. Much of the old Greek discrimination between *doxa* and *epistēmē* can be found again here.

A new turn in philosophical reflection occurred when this naive experience came to be considered as a source of important epistemological information about the structure of knowledge, and, in later development, even of human action. Husserl used the term *Lebenswelt* or *Lebensumwelt*. The life-world is the field of implicit knowledge that constitutes in many ways the horizon, the framework, for the more restricted fields of scientific knowledge. Husserl was influenced on this point by the work of Lévy-Bruhl, who had studied primitive mind and primitive experience; thus a more empirical impact on Husserl's philosophy became visible. Husserl evolved the idea of the life-world in the last period of his philosophy (around 1930). However, this later period does not contradict the much earlier phase of his thinking, around 1900, when he denied any deduction of the logical rules governing the structures of thought from empirical data, for instance, from laws of psychology. Although new tendencies in Husserl's thought became visible, he never forsook the hope of analyzing the life-world as a field of logically describable, although implicitly given, structures constituted by a nonempirical (transcendental) ego.

Husserl's idea of the life-world has been elaborated by many other phenomenologists, mostly in ways that are in closer contact with the empirical status of the phenomena. Merleau-Ponty, rejecting idealistic tendencies in Husserl's phenomenology, places the lived experience (*expérience vécue*) at the source of all scientific thinking. John Wild has also elaborated the idea of the life-world in a very interesting way. There is a kind of "war of the worlds" going on: the opposed claims of the life-world (characterized by the self-conscious activity of man, the global meaning related to values, and the perspective of transcendence) on the one hand, and the restricted, inclusive, and coherent world of scientific objectivity on the other hand. Wild sees in this confrontation a basic philosophic issue of our time.[1] For Wild the conflict is not between empirical sciences, with their methods of objectivation, and the life-world, as is the case in Merleau-Ponty's works. The restricted world of scientific objectivity only comes into conflict with the life-world when the latter is no longer considered as the wider, encompassing horizon of scientific as well as of practical and social human activities. The conflict arises when the world of science is proclaimed the only valuable world. And at that very moment scientific thinking

1. *Human Freedom and Social Order: An Essay in Christian Philosophy* (Durham, N.C.: Duke University Press, 1959).

itself becomes a type of rather dogmatic philosophy, as is the case in more narrow-minded branches of positivism and empiricism.

Wild's opinion has been underlined by new developments in logical positivism and analytic philosophy. Here also the idea of the life-world has made a breakthrough. The logical analysis of language started with too narrow an approach for the investigation of meaning. Daily language, at the beginning as much neglected a field for valuable information as daily experience in neo-Kantianism, has become the center of philosophical analysis in the work of the later Wittgenstein, of Moore, of Austin, and of Ryle. At the same time, thinkers more interested in logical and formal structures of language have become profoundly critical of oversimplified separations between the empirical and the logical. Quine's influential critique of the dichotomy of analytic and synthetic propositions places logical investigation within the wider horizon of the empirical uses of language. From the point of view of terminology Wittgenstein comes closest to the idea of the life-world, for he uses the notion of "forms of life" as the broadest frame of reference for the analysis of ordinary language. Other thinkers, relating the logical structures of language to daily actions, such as Stuart Hampshire in *Thought and Action*,[2] give an even more elaborate analysis of the life-world. In this way we arrive at the same point of necessary convergence as in the first theme of the structures: the interrelationship between *quaestio facti* and *quaestio iuris,* between the life-world and its patterns or structures.

LIFE-WORLD AND EMPIRICAL REALITY

THE WORK OF HUSSERL, especially, has clarified the position of a notion like life-world within the wide range of philosophical reflection. The life-world is not simply identical with empirical reality, but is reality within the horizon of human interpretation and experience; it is not a thing, not a static reality, but a process, the process of disclosure that takes place in human life, including man's scientific reflection, his artistic activities, his prescientific awareness.

2. (New York: Viking, 1960).

This means that the life-world as it is used in Husserl's phenomenology brings closer to each other the two focuses of empirical data (*quaestio facti*) and logically analyzable structures (*quaestio iuris*). The life-world is on the one hand the directly experienced world before man starts any scientific objectivation, even before man pronounces any structuralizing statement (Husserl also calls the life-world the sphere of the "prepredicative," that is, the prepropositional awareness). The life-world is on the other hand a field of activity: even simple things such as a cube are not given as such but are constituted in a process of concentrated awareness ("apperception"); the perceiving subject has to synthesize the various perspectives (*Abschattungen*) from which the cube is apprehended into one and the same cube, and to interpret, not explicitly but in a prepropositional way, the perceived side of the cube as the front of the cube, thus anticipating the back side, as yet unseen. Such processes demonstrate certain rules or structures that cannot be changed—the back side, for example, cannot be round—and these logical rules of anticipation manifest the activity of the subject. This subject is not the changeable human psyche but the logical function already at work in the prepropositional field of daily experience and perception.

Recent studies on the work of Husserl have developed in detail these aspects of his concept of the life-world. Many of them have pointed to the tension between the transcendental or logical aspect and the empirical one, as is being done in this essay. There is, of course, a clear shift in Husserl's thought toward daily and empirical reality. In some texts Husserl goes so far as to state that transcendental phenomenology, described somewhere as the science of all possible worlds, has the task of clarifying this empirically given world. It is as if, for example, on some pages of Husserl's *Erste Philosophie*[3] the wide range of phenomenological structures, with their all-embracing lines of logical rules, are converging toward empirical, contingent (nonlogical) reality. Even the terminology turns in that direction. In his *Logische Untersuchungen*, Husserl qualifies the logical structures or entities such as the intuited "redness" of an object or the meaning of the proposition of Pythagoras, as "eternal," "atemporal." Husserl in his later work localizes these structures within

3. (1923–24), *Husserliana* VII, VIII (The Hague: Martinus Nijhoff, 1956, 1959).

the process of constitution by the transcendental ego (the logical subject-function), and this process operates in the field of the life-world. Therefore, the logical structures come into closer contact with the process of history, and Husserl reformulates the qualification "eternal" as "all-temporal" (*Allzeitlichkeit*).

More instances of this tendency to move toward concrete empirical reality could be given. Only two of them, which are important for the trend of this discussion, need to be mentioned. General propositions of science, even mathematical truths, find their origin in the activity of the transcendental ego and its rationally regulated process: reason in history (*Vernunft in der Geschichte*). What are called "laws of nature" and even "facts" and "objects" are the result of such processes where the act of objectivation is at work. This is of special importance to the analysis of the objects. Our world is not the sum of objects, as is often stated; under the influence of the operations of natural science we are inclined to consider everything that surrounds us as mere objects. The things of our life-world are, however, valued; they represent a certain value as they are given—as houses, statues, utensils, etc. The "objects" are derived from things invested with value.

A second theme in Husserl's later philosophy is closely related to the previous one. All things and events have a certain time-structure. This structure is quite different for objects such as rocks, clouds, tones, mathematical propositions. All those structures are centered in the "now," that is, at the point where such an object is actually present to the subject. This "now" is not a mere moment, nor is it describable through the categories of scientific operations (time-measuring by clocks, by light signals, etc.). The "now" has a certain extension that cannot be defined merely theoretically; it is constituted, in the field of the life-world, by praxis, the awareness and apperception of the subject in its practical attitude.

These themes, where structural and empirical analyses converge, are of great importance, as we shall see below, for the contemporary philosophical discussion. We have already indicated how the correlation between structures and life-world, between logical and empirical analysis, presents a central issue for the modern philosophy of the various scientific disciplines. Husserl's phenomenology has undoubtedly failed insofar as it could not provide a sufficient basis for the methodology of the sciences. Even in the social and human sciences Husserl's fruit-ful notion of the life-world has had almost no direct influence on contemporary methodological discussions.

The reason for this is not difficult to discover. Husserl never bridged the gulf between the transcendental and the empirical aspects of the life-world. The transcendental ego, origin of all processes of constitution, remains, as he often formulated it, an anonymous ego. It has to acquire names, Husserl repeatedly acknowledges, and he frequently hints at the names of concrete, historical men as those where the operations of the anonymous ego become apparent within a contingent, empirical world. This tension in Husserl's work has often been called the tension between idealism and realism. The many discussions about whether Husserl's phenomenology is realistic or idealistic have not been very conclusive, nor have the efforts to reformulate his philosophy in more realistic terms. It is clear that for Husserl himself this tension was mainly between *quaestio iuris* and *quaestio facti*, between logically reducible rules and irreducible empirical contingency. His idealism was a transcendental ideal-ism, that is, the continuing effort to safeguard the status of the meaning of acts (for example, of the perception of redness, the understanding of a mathematical proposition) from their reduc-tion to empirical data (for example, of the laws of thought to psychological processes). The rules structuring empirical pheno-mena cannot be derived from those phenomena: this is the core of his transcendental phenomenology.

This issue is a common one for quite divergent schools of philosophers, as has already been remarked. It remained a cen-tral tendency of the whole development of Husserl's philosophy. At the beginning Husserl set the status of meaning apart in a third realm, in addition to the two empirical realms of physical and psychic reality. The main difference in logical positivism, which also made a sharp distinction between the logical (*quaes-tio iuris*) and the empirical (*quaestio facti*), has been formu-lated by Ryle: It is not at all necessary to claim a third realm of reality in order to safeguard the meanings, for these are the rules, as in a game of chess, not reducible to the empirical material (for example, of the chess set, of factual thought proc-esses); meanings are not logical entities, as Frege and Husserl assumed, but are a style of operation.

When Husserl develops the idea of the life-world he comes

closer to Ryle's philosophical analysis. The status of the meanings is not to be found in a timeless realm but in the operations of the logical subject. Nevertheless, there is still a difference between Husserl's phenomenology and analytic philosophy. The transcendental ego constitutes a source of meaning quite separate from empirical reality, whereas analytic philosophy reduces the subject (words like "I," "now") to objective human behavior or to given language-games. The result is that Husserl's phenomenology shows a tension between the transcendental ego and the given empirical reality, whereas analytic philosophy has great difficulties in relating the formal structures of scientific language to the self-commitment expressed in ordinary language, that is, to the empirical and historical subject. It is also from this point of view that the interrelationship between the life-world and the logically analyzable structures appears to be of crucial importance for philosophy as well as for a methodology.

STRUCTURING THE HUMAN WORLD

JOHN WILD belongs to a varied group of philosophers who stress the subject as agent and who derive the theoretical activities of man from his practical attitude. Wild does this in many of his works, and he relates this idea to that of the life-world: this is not mainly a pretheoretical sphere, but must be defined in a positive way as a practical and personal way of being. "To express this lived awareness is the task of what is now called phenomenology," Wild states. Other thinkers influenced by phenomenology as well as by existential philosophy, such as Levinas and Thévenaz, give priority to the ethical dimension of the human attitude over the theoretical and ontological human acts. Outside the school of phenomenologists many thinkers stress in similar ways the importance of human acts. Polanyi evolves a philosophy of science where the act of commitment is at the source of the more methodologically restricted acts of observation, verification, deduction, and so on. Also, in analytic philosophy illustrations of this priority of "the self as agent," formulated by John MacMurray,[4] can be found in the titles, and more so in the contents, of works like J. L. Austin's *How to Do*

4. *The Self as Agent* (New York: Humanities Press, 1957).

Things with Words,[5] and Stuart Hampshire's *Thought and Action.*

The contrast between naive experience (*doxa*) and theoretical reflection (*epistēmē*) in Greek philosophy has already been mentioned. It was perhaps the outcome of a society dominated by a leisure class, where the unsophisticated opinions of the working class were not positively valued. Much later, Descartes writes in his Sixth Meditation that the knowledge deriving from the unity of soul and body has only a relative value. Man experiences feelings of pleasure and pain, and he apprehends the world through the organs of sense. But all this cannot serve as theoretical truth; it is only useful for the preservation of life, since man can in that way shun what is harmful and pursue what is apt to promote well-being. The senses serve practical purposes, but only the mind, which is detached from practical activity, can discover the truth.

It is clear that as soon as priority is given to man as agent the roles are reserved. Theoretical truth is of importance, but in no case does it present the origin of truth as such. The practical attitude of man, "shunning what is harmful and pursuing what is apt to promote well-being," is of more importance. Husserl brought philosophy an important step forward by his concept of the life-world, which implies, as he stated, that *doxa* is more important than *epistēmē*. His phenomenological analysis remained, however, too much within the boundaries of a pure transcendental, that is, theoretical, deduction instead of broadening the horizon of transcendental analysis into that of praxis.

In what way can an analysis of man as agent clarify the interrelationship between the concrete, not phenomenologically reduced, life-world and the logical status of the structures? It is necessary, in order to arrive at this point of convergence, to consider the rules, patterns, structures, and laws neither as entities nor as description or pure rules of operations. They have, primarily, not a theoretical or logical-operational character, but a practical one. The structures are themselves the sedimentation of the process by which man tries to structure his surrounding world. Man is a living organism gifted with a sharply discriminating function, eliminating what is harmful and promoting well-being. This function, a feature of all living

5. (Cambridge, Mass.: Harvard University Press, 1962).

organisms, has become particularly specialized in man—physiologically by the development of his central nervous system and psychologically by his learning capacity. Man is a responding being that evolves various strategies of a practical character in order to cope with the challenges and the possibilities of the surrounding world. Rules of logic, laws of nature, the identity of objects, and so many other structures can be considered as the sedimentation of lines of approach taken by man in the history of his existence. One has to place historical man anew within the field of his personal and social action in order to discover the structures, the *quaestio iuris*, as a human way of shaping the contingent, often resistant, world (the *quaestio facti*).

The connection between philosophy, methodology, and daily praxis is stressed in this way. But an objection might be raised here: does not this approach reduce the *quaestio iuris* to the *quaestio facti*, logical structures to mere empirical data, philosophy to physiology and behavioral science? It is clear that in the contemporary development of, for example, brain research, a close relationship has become manifest between neurophysiological circuits and our laws of logic; elementary logical operation, for instance, such as conjunction, disjunction, and negation, correspond to neurophysiological switching operations such as, respectively, summation, facilitation, and inhibition. But such an empirical basis can never guarantee the validity of logical structures, as Husserl repeatedly argued. Husserl, therefore, set his logical-phenomenological analysis quite apart from any empirical investigation. This separation could also be found, at the beginning of this century, in the work of thinkers like Frege and Russell. It comes to the fore in logical positivism in the form of a strict separation between analytic and synthetic propositions.

Such a separation appeared to be impossible. Husserl's project of a pure grammar (*reine Grammatik*) was already mixed up with more elements derived from empirical language than he was conscious of, as Bar-Hillel pointed out in a study on this theme in Husserl's phenomenology.[6] The later development of the notion of the life-world made it still more convincing that empirical-historical, even anthropological, aspects cannot be eliminated from phenomenological research. Husserl's analyses

6. "Husserl's Conception of a Purely Logical Grammar," *Philosophy and Phenomenological Research*, XVII (1957), 362–69.

remained, however, within the boundaries of a pure transcendental-idealistic investigation. There was no answer to the question how it is possible for empirical patterns, like those of neurophysiological development, to correspond to logical rules. The same difficulty was presented in a different perspective when logical positivism discovered the impossibility of a strict separation between mere linguistic conventions (analytic propositions) and empirical fact-finding (synthetic propositions): In what way are the rules of various language-games related to empirical forms of life?

The answer to this central problem, as it is given mainly by modern biology, is rather simple. The evolution of man is characterized by a continuous and dynamic effort to gain control over his surrounding world; he organizes his behavior along lines of optimal approach; rules of logic and categories of scientific thinking are patterns of organization controlling human behavior. This answer needs, however, a philosophical interpretation, even a more interdisciplinary investigation. The danger of reducing logical rules to empirical facts has already been mentioned. Structures cannot be the outcome of a mere haphazard development; mere biological and subjective forms of adaptation cannot result in logically valid laws—unless, of course, random events fit into the chain of challenges constituted by the surrounding world. Empirical facts as such never have any power of organization unless they form a response, a timely answer, to the stimuli of the environment. A multidisciplinary investigation is necessary in order to understand under which circumstances and along what lines a response is adequate, timely, gaining control over the environment. Biology, physiology, neurology, psychology, cultural anthropology—a whole range of natural, behavioral, and social sciences is involved here. Philosophically, all this means that rules cannot be explained by mere subjective behavior; behavior must be adequate, and this demand submits empirically analyzable behavior to the norm of a given objective situation.

It was stressed earlier that man is primarily a practical subject. The stimuli he receives from the outside world are not simply bearers of empirical information, as empiricism thought; the things and the regularities he discovers in the surrounding reality are not simply theoretical objects, as rationalism thought. What is immediately given are not the pure logical laws of idealism, nor the mere facts of positivism. The objectivity of the world is a practical one: stimuli are clues for action; the identity and regularity of processes and things are possibilities for organizing behavior; laws are persuasive hints for future action; facts are the results of responding to values. The correspondence between empirical behavior and logical rules can only be clarified when, on the one hand, the empirical information is recognized to be more than pure data: the content of perception is the already selected starting point for well-directed action. It has to be recognized, on the other hand, that such action is not purely subjectivistic or random but that it is a response referring to evaluation and interpretation of situations.

The nonempirical, logical aspect of human action is rooted in this reference which implies the transcending of purely empirical data. This transcendence is a dynamic activity, not a theoretical or merely ontological concept; it is the act of disclosing the meaning that sense stimuli have for total human life. Such a disclosure is not primarily a theoretical or philosophical one. The whole pattern of human behavior already manifests such an interpretation and evaluation. Such practical evaluation, including daily activities as well as logical and scientific systems, pertains to the whole range of human social, cultural, and ethical activities. Facts are, in this perspective, reduced values, that is, empirical or theoretical restrictions of a more practical objectivity, visible only through acts of evaluation. This implies, lastly, that the correlation between the empirical and the logical aspect of human action is given only by transcending any empirically delimited field, including those of the empirical sciences. The fight of Husserl and others against psychologism, biologism, sociologism, and so on, remains of acute importance, especially when the interrelationship between *quaestio iuris* and *quaestio facti* is recognized.

It would be a mistake to think of phenomenology as being a special scientific method by which to investigate the life-world. Some authors consider phenomenology along this line as an intuitive method to be used, for example, in psychology or in social science. The contemporary developments in the methodology of behavioral and social sciences make it clear that in these fields no special intuition is needed, but only more refined logical networks that can do justice to the more intricate character of these phenomena. Modern structuralism, especially, mentioned at the beginning of this paper, shows how sharply discriminating and consistent methods can be evolved in order to discover the patterns and structures of the human life-world.

The importance of phenomenology for the scientific investigation of the life-world, therefore, has to be found in another direction. It is precisely the perspective of transcendence within the empirical data that is of extreme importance. This becomes clear, in the first place, when one is reminded of the phenomenological theme of subjectivity. Structures and logical rules can never be investigated without taking into consideration the activity of the subject. This subject must not be detached, as we saw, from the empirical (biological, cultural) subject; a phenomenological investigation must join the reflection and research of the empirical sciences. It is only in this case that structures can be described as sedimentation of the organizing power of a historical, human subject. This means a refutation of objectivism and reductionism: the structures are never given as such or prefabricated as physical, biological, social structures; they are part of a process of structuring reality by man. This also means a refutation of the dichotomy between the logical and the empirical, between analytic and synthetic propositions. Analytic propositions are, at a specific time, the most adequate expression of invariant and consistent statements; they are a historical recommendation for the organization of data—but they have to be renewed, again and again, by synthetic experience. Knowledge is not logically fixed, but logical fixations are steppingstones in a continuous process of restructuring experience and the life-world.

All this implies, in the second place, that the various scientific disciplines, those of nature as well as those of man, come about only by strict methods and logically regulated networks. But these methods are always ways of selecting and restricting the phenomena. They do not present photographs or objective panoramas of reality but only methodologically restricted models. They do not stand for reality but are approaches to reality, brought about by practical organizing human action. It is for this reason that the strict and exact sciences need a wider horizon. The phenomenological disclosure of the life-world enables such an integration of scientific networks within a wider awareness that can stimulate the always needed restructuring of scientific methods. The life-world constitutes the wider realm, where the transcendence of the necessary methodological restrictions becomes visible and where the horizon of evaluation can stimulate the further extension of scientific networks with their logical rules and their verifications. The integration of scientific reflection and research within social action and ethical responsibility will have to be the outcome of any phenomenological investigation where the life-world and the structures of scientific knowledge converge.

PART III
THE INDIVIDUAL
AND SOCIETY

9 / The Miser

Erwin W. Straus

SOME TIME AGO newspapers reported with sensational headlines the death of a man whose life had never aroused any public interest. Since he lived among people, but not with them, his death remained unnoticed for two weeks. Yet the posthumous recognition was not altogether undeserved, for the police unearthed more than one hundred and fifty thousand dollars in cash and securities in the quarters of the dead man, who had led a pauper's life.

Heralded by two headlines—AMID TRASH AND TOKENS and ECCENTRIC'S APARTMENT YIELDS $150,000 IN CASH AND SECURITIES—the following story appeared in the *Louisville Courier* on August 16, 1961:

More than $150,000 in cash and securities was unearthed Tuesday in the Yorkville district apartment of an eccentric, who piled about him the accumulated trash and tokens of year upon year of solitude. Amid the debris were faded reminders of life in New York half a century ago.

George Aichele, 73, was found dead Monday of natural causes. It took police all night to ferret out and count $47,000 in cash in the five-room flat, including $500 and $1,000 bills casually tucked amid rubbish.

More than 80 bank books also were turned up, noting deposits of more than $112,000. Some of the deposits, of only $10, were made, a friend said, because Aichele coveted the minor gifts with which banks encourage new depositors.

Aichele was an incredible hoarder. He even wrapped a single

penny and tucked it away with a notation he had found it outside his 86th Street apartment building.

"In the living room the junk was piled 5 feet high," said Patrolman James Pyne, first to enter the apartment after Aichele's lawyer missed the old bachelor for many days. There were radios, including new ones still in their cartons. There were razors and blades, newspapers and magazines dated at the turn of the century, unopened cases of liquor, phonograph records, thousands of packs of safety matches, dozens of wedding bands and diamond rings, a carton of more than 100 harmonicas, a birdcage. There was even a zither.

Aichele was a recluse as far as his home was concerned. No one but himself was known to have set foot inside it since a brother with whom he lived died 13 years ago. This brother, John, presumably took part in the hoarding, since much of the trash antedated his death in 1947. Another brother, Henry, a bank executive, died in 1956, also amid rubbish accumulated in his home. It took six months to clear it out. The brothers inherited money from their father, Charles, who made a fortune in Manhattan real estate. He died in 1932; the mother, Julia, in 1940.

Dickerson, Aichele's lawyer, reported that he had never been allowed into the apartment, although he had been Aichele's attorney for a quarter of a century. During all those years, Dickerson said, Aichele wore the same outfit, a brown sports jacket, brown trousers, old-fashioned high shoes, and a battered gray hat.

Similar stories appear with some regularity. The space allotted to them by the newspapers usually varies in accordance with the amount of money found. A dozen lines were deemed adequate to report the discovery of $18,000 in the home of two dead brothers in Mt. Vernon, Ohio:

A cleanup crew found $18,085 in cash hidden in old buckets, tobacco cans, and glass jars in a shed owned by two bachelor brothers who died last year. The money, eight $50 bills and the remainder in $5, $10 and $20 bills, was stuffed in ancient, dirt-covered hiding places in an old shed.

Yet the rule establishing a reasonable relation between the number of lines printed and the amount of money found is not always strictly observed. In a short column, a New Orleans paper reported on August 4, 1960, that the respectable amount of

$350,000 had been given to the National Institute of Health. The donor, in this case, was an 82-year-old Spanish-American War veteran named Shepard, who had identified himself in his will as a "Sergeant in Company G of the Missouri Infantry in the War with Spain." He designated that the funds left to the Public Health Service be used "for research wholly in cure and prevention of chronic spastic constipation." Actually, the National Institute never received the bequest, since Shepard's will was successfully contested, on a formal legal basis, by a nephew.

Shepard had spent the last decades of his life in a sort of voluntary confinement, making his home in a truly modest hotel where he occupied a room rented for $1 a day. He gained scanty support through a pension, paid by the Veterans Administration, and successfully reclaimed after his death when it became known that Shepard, besides having other assets, had left untouched a dividend account of more than $60,000 in one of the well-known brokerage houses. Shepard's nephew and heir first learned, it seems, about his rich uncle's life and death when he was requested to attend Shepard's burial in the National Cemetery of Iowa, an honor demanded in Shepard's last will. We were not able to find out when and how Shepard happened to meet Fortuna; neither do we know whether the "Sergeant in Company G" ever came into close contact with the enemy. Yet there can be little doubt that in the four score years of his secluded life the months of military service represented the one memorable event.

The newspaper reports—fragmentary as they are—leave unanswered many of the questions a psychiatrist would like to raise. Only under unusual circumstances may we have an opportunity to study a miser during his lifetime. Even if he should regard his behavior as morbid and should consider the possibility of medical help leading to a drastic change in his situation, he would be the last one to spend money on psychotherapy. Yet there is a kind of compensation for the inadequacy of the reports: the newspapers, wherever published, tell practically the same story, varying only in minor details. Through the available fragments of information we recognize a striking uniformity of conduct. As a rule, the miser remains a bachelor, but he may live in the company of another sibling. Such brotherhoods keep any visitor from their home. The possessions defended by the misers usually are inherited, not acquired. In the early years of their lives, as long as parental, especially maternal, protection lasts they may remain inconspicuous. They do not show any marked deficiency of intelligence. It is after the death of the mother that the drama begins. Single—or in a kind of *folie à deux*—the miser clings to his inherited wealth. He seldom entrusts his money to banks or invests it in securities. Instead, his treasures are hidden somewhere in his lodgings, a place into which no one is admitted. The entrance is frequently blocked by more or less elaborate barricades, and the window shutters are closed so that all direct contact with the outside surroundings is suspended. Inside is a chaos of refuse—never discarded—and of some new things—never used—where the miser resides, "a king of rags and patches." The actual economic and social conditions matter little in this development. Obviously, the personality is the decisive factor in the miser's career.[1]

According to Freud, orderliness, parsimoniousness, and obstinacy are the three characteristic traits "which are almost always found together." Freud concluded "from the analysis of persons possessing them that these characteristics proceed from the dissipation of their anal eroticism and its employment in other ways." [2]

"It appears, then, that when in the course of development the

---

1. Even before this paper went to the printer the Associated Press reported from Hollywood, Florida, in December, 1968, under the headline, FRAIL LADY WAS WORTH A MILLION, a case which resembles that of Aichele in many respects, down to the wrapped penny: "The frail, grayhaired widow in the flannel nightgown was just another unattended death. Then police found her secret fortune. 'I've never counted so much money before in my life—and I never will again,' Detective James Hampton said Sunday. A maid peeked through a window of the unpretentious home Saturday and saw the lifeless body of Mary MacMahon on the bed. She called police. Patrolman Tom McGuire and Sgt. Fulton answered the summons. They discovered stacks of stocks and cash in cardboard boxes on the floor, on shelves, everywhere. Green cord bound the money in bundles. The bills ranged from ones to hundreds and totalled $242,283.87. A neighbor said, . . . 'Nobody knew her very well. She played her radio loud and kept to herself. Lots of times she didn't want the neighborhood children to bother her.' The detective said, 'The funny thing about this thing is that she had a safe inside the house, a very good safe cemented into the floor. All she had in the safe was approximately $150 worth of pennies.' Rather than put the money in the safe, 'she put it in purses and boxes,' he said. 'We counted a little over 9,000 single bills that were in the house. One of the boxes contained approximately $165,000 in bills.' One of the pennies found in the home was carefully wrapped in paper and bore the notation: 'Found while shopping on Van Buren Street.'"

2. Sigmund Freud, *New Introductory Lectures on Psychoanalysis* (New York: W. W. Norton, 1933), p. 140.

individual comes to feel disfavor for his own feces and excrements, his instinctual interests arising from inner sources pass over to objects which can be given away as gifts. And rightly so, for feces were the first gift that an infant could make, and he parted with them out of love for the person who looked after him. . . . Subsequently, the old interest in feces turned into an appreciation of gold and money." [3]

Yet orderliness certainly was not an outstanding trait in the case of the Aicheles, nor of any of the other misers whose curriculum vitae has become familiar to me, for instance that of the Collyer brothers:

On Tuesday, April 8, 1947, the New York World Telegram carried two front page obituaries.[4] On the lower left-hand portion of the page was the story of the death of Henry Ford. . . . The center of the front page was taken up by a large square shot of what might appear to the uninformed eye as an incredibly cluttered up still life: dozens of old cartons, bits of furniture, etc., etc. . . . The news of Ford's death had been eclipsed by a full length, four-inch headline that read COLLYER FOUND DEAD IN OWN BOOBY TRAP. The story of the Collyer brothers, hermits who died in an old Fifth Avenue house, . . . had reduced Henry Ford's news appeal to the "also ran."

The Collyer case began when the butcher from whom Langley Collyer used to receive handouts of food became suspicious after Langley had not appeared in his shop for three weeks. The police were informed and began to search at the Collyer home. When they opened the front door of the old mansion they found an incredible blockage composed of thousands of boxes, pieces of furniture, junk, cans, waste of every sort imaginable—the fantastic accumulation of two brothers who secluded themselves from the outside world behind this barricade erected of debris. The only entrance space through this mountain of cardboard and broken glass was a two-foot tunnel through which a slender adult body might crawl. . . . The tunnel, as it turned out, was constructed ingeniously through a vast net of booby traps which would catch any intruder who might attempt to enter the Collyer house. . . . The three-story house contained an estimated 350 tons of variously assorted heaps of furniture, clothing, books, instruments, mechanisms, and masses of pure rubbish: rags, newspapers, bot-

3. *Ibid.*, p. 138.
4. Maurice Natanson, "The Rock Cried Out," *Prairie Schooner*, Vol. XXIV, No. 1 (Spring, 1950), reprinted with the permission of the author.

tles, dirt, wood, dust, and cartons filled with human excrement.[5] There were 14 pianos and an almost complete Model T. Ford, a buggy, thousands of books, two doll carriages, and two sections of a dead tree, each section about 10 inches in diameter and 7 foot long, etc., etc. The stacks of boxes, cans and furniture reached from floor to ceiling, and through this tower of filth and dust the wreckers made their way to the body of Homer Collyer, the older of the brothers, who was finally found on the second floor of the home in a tiny clearing amidst the wreckage. The search for Langley went on for the next two weeks. At the end of that time his body was found only a few feet away from that of his brother; the explanation was that one of the booby traps had come down on Langley as he was crawling through the second floor tunnel to reach his brother. Homer had been a blind paralytic whom Langley had bathed and fed in this bottled-up mansion for years. The booby trap had collapsed on Langley, just as he was in reach of Homer. . . .

The Collyers are an old American family. They came to this country on the Speedwell, shortly after the voyage of the Mayflower. The family flourished in the last half of the 19th century and the early years of the 1900s. . . . The father of the brothers was a distinguished and wealthy New York City gynecologist. . . . Both brothers held degrees from Columbia University.

It was about 1910 that the brothers broke all their social ties. They lived alone with their mother, for in later years Dr. Collyer separated from his wife and resided in another part of the city. The mother died in 1929. Since that time the brothers had been utterly isolated. Neither of the two brothers married. Although several bank accounts available to the brothers had been drawn upon, the account of the mother was never touched after she died. No attempt was made to consolidate her account with the others. . . . At night, Langley would leave the house to fill a pail with water at a nearby restaurant or in a park in the summer, and he would visit his grocer for some food which was freely given to him.

Most probably the patients seen by Freud and Abraham [6] were but duodecimo editions of the true miser. Since the patients reported for treatment to the doctors' offices, neither Freud nor Abraham had an opportunity to get a firsthand impression of

5. Since the brothers had not paid their utility bills for years, they had been cut off from the supply of water and light.—E.W.S.

6. Karl Abraham, one of the early psychoanalytic writers, contributed many studies to the problem of the anal character. See his *Selected Papers* (London: Hogarth Press, 1927).

their homes. It is only through police action, following the lonely deaths of misers, that we learn something about their squalid homes.

In the *New Introductory Lectures,* Freud confirmed and elaborated his ideas about the development of the "anal character," first mentioned twenty-five years before in a footnote to *Three Contributions to the Theory of Sex,*[7] where he had defined an erotogenic zone as "a portion of skin or mucous membrane in which stimuli produce a feeling of pleasure of definite quality." The sexual aim was formulated "by stating that the main object is to substitute for the projected feeling of sensitiveness in the erotogenic zone that outer stimulus which removes the feeling of sensitiveness by evoking the feeling of gratification." Freud added: "The action is puzzling only to some extent as one stimulus seems to want another applied to the same place for its own abrogation." However, Freud finally overcame such scruples. The concept of reaction-formation helped him to save the hypothesis. Indeed, whoever holds these three cards—fixation, sublimation, reaction-formation—cannot lose the game. His position resembles that of the gambler who set the rule: Heads I win; tails you lose.

Immunized against critical attack, the theorem of character formation endured the passage of time unchanged. It comes without surprise, therefore, that we should read in a handbook of psychiatry published half a century after Freud's initial observation: "Persons whose instinctual life is anally oriented show certain character traits which are partly reactions against and partly sublimations of anal-erotic activities; specifically orderliness, frugality, and obstinacy are clear indicators of the anal orientation."[8]

"Orderliness,' Michaels adds, "is an elaboration of the obedience to the environmental demands to be clean. Obstinacy, on the other hand, represents the rebellion against these environmental demands. . . . Frugality represents a continuation of anal retention. It can be motivated either by a fear of losing or by erogeneous pleasure."

7. In *The Basic Writings of Sigmund Freud,* trans. A. A. Brill (New York: Modern Library, 1938).
8. Joseph J. Michaels, "Character Structures and Character Disorders," in *American Handbook of Psychiatry,* ed. Silvano Arieti (New York: Basic Books, 1959), I, 360.

The term "frugality" refers to a simple type of life: cautious, humble, prudent, restrained in spending money—literally, content with the fruits of the season. A miser, to be sure, will not be listed as a contributor to the Community Fund; thereby he finds himself in the company of many others who have never realized that it is "more blessed to give than to receive." Not to give to others, although willing to spend money for one's own pleasure, is an attitude far removed from that of not using a penny for one's own outfit, like Aichele who for 25 years wore the same suit, hat, and shoes. The paradoxical habit of starving in the midst of plenty, Michaels explains, results from "the training for cleanliness in infancy when a child must forego an instinctual pleasure in deference to the demands of society." This Declaration of Dependence has been repeated so often that the many sons and daughters of the founding father ignored the statistical facts [9] and forgot to consider the peculiarities of the local apparatus involved in that ominous procedure.

Actually, before mothers ever started to act as representatives of society, Nature had already played tricks of her own, placing sphincters, i.e., striped muscles under voluntary control, at the exit of bladder and rectum. This local device, however, was not yet fully connected with the wire system of the mental apparatus at the time the baby was born—prematurely, in any case, according to zoologist Adolph Portmann.[10] Therefore control was not possible, and a sacrifice of instinctual pleasure couldn't be made until the neural connections began to function, which happens approximately at the time a child is able to stand, and—what is not unimportant in this context—to sit down; for the act of voiding is a rather complicated performance, not accomplished simply through relaxation of the sphincter alone. What is required is coordination of the diaphragm (contracting) with the sphincter (relaxing) and, in addition, sympathetic cooperation of the peristaltic apparatus, which is not under control of the Ego. Obviously, in the process of toilet training, parents

9. Compared with the untold millions, nay, billions, of human beings who since Olim's days cooperated with the demands of society, the number of certified misers is surprisingly small.

10. Portmann, zoologist at the University of Basel, emphasized that human children, in contrast to animals, are prematurely born, e.g., a young horse a few hours after birth stands on his own feet, while a human baby needs almost a year.

help their children to develop natural capacities. Also, Michaels concedes that in yielding "to the demands of society" a child acquires an active mastery of his instinctual drives. One might as well argue that society, with its requirement of prolonging retention, must have intensified the instinctual pleasure of voiding—an instinctual pleasure that, by the way, persists from childhood into old age, in spite of the vicissitudes encountered by the infantile instincts.

While psychoanalysis revolutionized psychology and psychiatry, and while Freud gave a radically new answer to the Delphic exhortation, *Know Thyself*, he never freed himself from the fetters of reductionism. In his contempt for consciousness "as a sense organ for the reception for psychic qualities," [11] he never acknowledged the problem as such; instead, like the majority of physiologists and psychologists, he identified stimuli with objects and confounded objects with stimuli. [12] Yet the stimulation of an erotogenic zone, or of any other receptor, does not transform the physical agent into an object. Manufacturers and retailers, spendthrifts and misers—all deal with goods and money, not with stimuli. Nobody can trade his itch, sell his toothache, or bequeath his appetite to someone else. Pleasure and pain cannot be transferred like merchandise from one person to another.

In order to equate feces with gold and money, Freud had to: (a) substitute a pleasure gained in retaining for the initial pleasure of voiding—exactly contrary to the doctrine of the pleasure principle; (b) replace, then, the pleasure of retaining through the interest in the matter retained; and (c) substitute objects (not stimuli) for the inner sources. Finally, he had to invent the fable that "feces were the first gift that an infant could make, parting with them out of love for the person who looked after him." In this statement the word "parting" obviously was used in a double sense: (a) as producing the excrement; and (b) as giving the product away afterwards. Certainly, young children may be proud of their excretory accomplishments, and they may perform better in the presence of a friendly adult. However, while a child may like to play with his brother's toys, while he

11. *The Interpretation of Dreams*, in *Basic Writings*, Bk. II, Chap. 7, § F.

12. See my general criticism in "Norm and Pathology of I-World Relations," *Diseases of the Nervous System*, Monograph Supplement, Vol. XXII, No. 4 (April, 1961).

may ask for a lollipop when his sister gets one, he neither wants to possess his brother's excrement nor to offer his own as a present. If Freud's account were correct, an infant would be terribly disappointed when his "precious gift" was immediately flushed down the drain by the loved person. Since this tragedy of offering and rejection is repeated day after day, Michaels may well consider adding cynicism to the triad of the anal character.

Obviously, the pleasure in making a present, for instance of transferring a valuable object—whatever it may be—from my possession to yours, is radically different from that feeling produced in "a portion of skin or mucous membrane by some sort of stimuli." It is hard to see how the latter could be transformed and survive in any tergiversation.

In Ovid's *Metamorphoses* miraculous transformations are enacted by the gods. In Freud's metamorphoses supernatural powers do not interfere. When a scientist of Freud's rank posits a relation between the vicissitudes of toilet training and a prevailing interest in possession and money in later years, one would expect that he would explore—at least cursorily—the structure and function of money, with its service indispensable in commercial transactions all over the world. Unfortunately, the genetic regressive method keeps his attention fixed on the early stages, factual or fictitious.

In his standard text *The Psychoanalytical Theory of Neuroses* Fenichel tried to fill the gap. Moving in a zigzag of contradictions, he ended with an identification of possession with incorporation. On the last angle before reaching the summit, Fenichel, speaking *loco infantis,* declared: "Everything that is pleasurable I should like to put in my mouth and swallow; everything that is painful I should like to spit out." Yet things, for instance a whip, a knife, a hot iron, are not painful by themselves. What is painful is being beaten, being cut, being burned! In such an impact I feel my body hurt. While I wish to get rid of my pain, I should not try to get relief by spitting out the bloody scars. There can be no doubt that young children manifest a strong tendency to put things in their mouths; since, however, this reflex act is performed without any discrimination, the results are often far from being pleasant. Fortunately, the grasp-and-snout reflexes disappear without any sacrifice of instinctual pleasure to the demands of society.

Unimpressed by facts, Fenichel used the formula "Everything pleasurable I would like to put into my mouth" as an upbeat for the final chord: "But there are pleasurable things that cannot be taken into the mouth. Those things are, sooner or later, called 'mine' and that means: I should like to take them into my mouth but I cannot do so; I declare them as symbolically-put-into-my-mouth." Fascinated by the goal to be reached, Fenichel forgot the starting point; he forgot that he had planned to link parsimoniousness to anal eroticism. Instead, he replaced the "exit from" with the "entrance to" the intestinal tract. Yet he did not act completely by oversight, for he explained: "When the child realizes that he loses (*sic!*) his feces, which represent to him a very precious substance, a part of his own body, he feels this is something that ought to be in my body, but it is outside now and I cannot put it back." Again he calls it "mine," which means I should like to put it inside my body, but that is impossible, so I declare it "symbolically-put-into-my-body." Obviously, a vigilant "Censor" suggested to Fenichel that he replace "my mouth" with "my body."

Fenichel did not intend to write a parody; he was deadly serious. But who is willing to believe that an art collector desires to put his Rembrandt into his mouth symbolically, or that a bride wants to devour symbolically all her wedding presents!

With his interpretation of possession as a symbolic account of incorporation, Fenichel has reached a position diametrically opposed to actuality. Unlike food, which passes through an individual's intestinal tract, possessions—as everyone knows and must acknowledge—are exchangeable; they may go from hand to hand, be bought and sold, bequeathed and inherited, jointly held by two partners or by thousands of shareholders. Possessions may be insured and stolen, kept in good repair or neglected, sent from factory to retail store, mailed and shipped. Only someone blinded by a biased dogma could ignore those characteristics of human economy. There is always a danger that absurdity poses as profundity.

I do not plan to follow Aeneas on his descent to the Acheron. I shall not try to illuminate the *tenebrae* of Hades with sparkles emitted from a homemade flashlight. Instead, I shall turn my hermeneutic endeavor to the surface phenomena, namely, the anthropological structure of possession and money.

II

As THE MODEL for our discussion of possession we select the property that is rightly called "real estate."

A forest, a pasture, or a field does not, as such, constitute a
possession; the claim made by someone to use that land as his to
the exclusion of anyone else turns the territory (that is, a segment of *terra*, earth) into a private seizin. It makes no difference
whether the claimant who puts up a "No Trespassing" sign is an
individual or a group or a family or a city, whether the owner
resides on his property or is an absentee landlord, whether his
claim is based on discovery and conquest or on cultivation,
trade, gift, or bequest. In each case the title rests on power—but
not on the physical power of the plow breaking ground or of the
axe clearing virgin forest; it is the power of arms and weapons
that establishes and sustains the possessor's right to prevent any
other person from entering or using the region claimed by him.

A possession always refers back to a possessor; there is a tie
between possession and possessor, between the *quid* and the *qui*,
to use Gabriel Marcel's terminology.[13] This tie has no physical
characteristics; it cannot be measured in terms of grams or
volts. There is nothing in the nature or structure of property that
would connect it necessarily and exclusively with a particular
person or possessor. The *quid* remains silent; the *qui* alone
speaks, making his demands. When Smith sells his house to
Jones, the house itself changes owners—their names are listed
one after the other in the County Courthouse files. There could
be no heirs if a possession did not outlast a possessor.

Unfortunately, the pronoun "mine" is used without proper
discrimination in reference to the possession and the possessor. I
cannot turn over to someone else what is truly mine as a living
creature.[14] I cannot give away my hand, nor receive another in

13. See Richard M. Zaner, *The Problems of Embodiment* (The Hague:
Martinus Nijhoff, 1964).

14. I believe it is not necessary to enter here into a discussion of the
problems presented by such technical accomplishments as transplantation
of organs, hormone therapy, or artificial insemination. Suffice it to say that
nobody would use a third kidney as he might use a third car or take a
spare foot along on a trip. A spermatozoon not joined to an ovum fades out
soon after ejaculation. True, a mother nourishing a baby gives "her" milk

exchange. My hand, my heart, my body, and my life are mine as possessor, a relation radically different from that which connects my possessions, my house, my car, and my books with me, and is also, by the way, at variance with the ties linking me to my parents, my wife, my friends, and my country. I may "lend" a hand, but not in the same manner that I could lend a book, which remains my property even on the borrower's shelf. Such books still "be-long" to me—a word that expresses very well the extension of the possessor's reach over a distance, which separates but also connects possessor and possessions. As long as my rights are valid, my property belongs to me even if I should never set foot in my house leased to tenants. However, while the younger generation may learn from the older one, while an apprentice acquires, i.e., incorporates into himself, skills taught by his master, he cannot sell them "over the counter." If someone steals a diploma, he cannot thereby carry away the knowledge certified by that document. Incorporation is not the ontogenetic model of possession.[15]

Because claim and fact are at variance, since the legal sign "No Trespassing" tries to block access actually open to a possession, a conflict necessarily erupts between the owner and the

---

to her child; a "wet" nurse may even sell her suck, but she could not sustain herself on her own product. She can give away her milk but not her breasts.

15. The terms "to take possession, to settle down, to reside" refer back to the moment when strife and occupation (from Latin *capere* = to take) have come to an end and a settlement has been reached so that the invader, the conqueror, the pioneer, can lay down arms, relax, take a seat (possession is related to Latin *posse sedere* = to sit down), settle, and thereby turn into a resident (*re-sedere*).

In olden days men probably felt that every act of usurping ground was an insult to the gods who dwell in forests and plains, in rivers and fountains. The founders of cities had to conciliate the gods through sacrifices brought into the "templum," that is, an area cut off from the common grounds and rededicated to the gods. According to the Bible, Cain (a tiller of the ground) "brought of the fruits of the ground an offering," while Abel (a keeper of sheep) brought the "firstlings of his flock and of the fat thereof." The Lord, the Bible continues, had "respect unto Abel and to his offering," but "unto Cain and to his offering he had not respect." Perhaps it is justified to relate this difference of respect to the different walks of life: the shepherd's vocation and the tiller's occupation. This view is confirmed—at least to some extent—through the Bible, which tells that Cain, the fugitive, protected by his "mark," built the first city and named it after his son Enoch. Checking the meaning of the name "Cain," I enjoyed reading that "Cain" means possession and "Cainan" means possessor.

"outsider." Although the conflict may remain latent in a law-abiding community, it never abates completely. Possessions are threatened from two sides: by the destructive elements of nature —fire, water, air (gales), and earth (quakes)—and by hostile neighbors. Obviously, modern owners are well aware of this precarious situation: witness the immense success of the many companies that offer insurance against various kinds of destructive and aggressive powers. Anticipating violent attacks, the owner takes his countermeasures; he erects a fence as a first line of "de-fence." [16] The stockades are followed by iron grilles and steel shutters, and finally by armed guards, hired to watch, so that the owner may go to sleep. Yet the incentive for illegal or semilegal assaults rises in direct proportion to the value of possessions. The sparkle of diamonds casts a shadow of theft. Finally, we are possessed by our possessions: "Where your treasures are, there also is your heart."

Overwhelmed by the fear of loss of property, the miser also seems to respond to the inherent structure of possession. Yet his attitude is but codetermined by the situation. His behavior cannot be interpreted as the typical reaction of a possessor, carried to its extreme. There is more to it; the miser enters the scene as a person who in his reaction distorts the very structure of possession.

In our country the good citizen need not rely on his personal strength alone. He is protected by the "law," embodied in the policeman. But in order to receive official protection the claims of possession must be made public, entered into the books in the owner's name as a member of the society. In just this respect the miser fails completely, for *his* tendency is to remain anonymous, unknown, almost invisible. His lack of a passport, so to speak, or his social camouflage forces him to forego public protection and to supplant it with personal devices, as the Collyers did.

To present oneself in public as a rich man demands self-reliance, at least to some degree. For good reasons, quite a few wealthy men prefer to travel incognito. However, the misers whose death and life the newspapers reported were not rich people measured by American standards. Even so, these Harpagons lived in a kind of voluntary seclusion, hermits without sanctuary. They preferred the densely populated districts of a

16. This is no play on words, since "fence" is an abbreviation of "defence."

large city, which provided anonymity, to the open countryside where they would have to brave the elements and face their neighbors. When they had to leave their hiding places to do some indispensable errands, they kept at a polite distance from people; they were lonely in the crowd. Langley Collyer and Pat Chary [17] left their homes only at night. When Langley had to go downtown once during office hours, he was overwhelmed by an agoraphobic attack at the entrance of the subway, although he was accompanied and supported by a lawyer.

One can understand that a man in Aichele's financial position wished to keep potential burglars away. However, in the course of twenty-five years, even the lawyer, in whom he must have put some trust, was never allowed to enter Aichele's apartment. One can also understand that someone living in an impoverished district of town would not be eager to reveal his superior living conditions to his neighbors. Yet the miser does not enjoy a good life behind closed doors; he does not use his means for himself. Without effort the miser resists the temptation to use anything for himself. To starve is for him a lesser evil than to eat and thereby to reduce his "pro-visions"; for to use something is identical with using it up, with consuming it. Supplies used are supplies spent. Paralyzed by fear of the future, the miser holds on to the past.

The miser's possessions are as a rule inherited, not obtained through personal efforts. But whether inherited or acquired, titles of ownership have been acquired in the past. Deeds must be dated accurately, indicating when the property changed hands and the possessions changed possessors. With inheritance, a transaction performed in the past is brought forward as a valid claim into the present. Possession has the temporal character of *perfectum present,* well expressed by the verb "to have." Rights and obligations are "brought forward" from the past in legal chronology.

The relation between possessing and having and the intrinsic conformity of their temporal structures have long been recognized in language. Words like "to have," "habit," "habitat," are striking examples. In other nouns, as for instance "debt," the relation is less obvious; the word "debt," however, stems from

17. Pseudonym for a patient mentioned by W. Betzendahl, "Ueber maskierte Verruecktheit und ihre Folgen," *Allg. Zeitschrift fuer Psychiatrie,* Vol. C, 1932.

the Latin *debit,* infinitive—*debere,* a shortcut for *de-habere*—not having. In German the auxiliary verb *haben* (to have) has been transformed into the noun, *die Habe;* a favorable bank account is called *Guthaben.* A poor fellow may be designated as a *Habenichts,* corresponding to the English "have-not."

When someone exclaims "I have an idea," or "I have an answer," he thereby indicates that at that very moment he has found a solution for a problem, and, having found it once, continues to have it at his disposition. The English "I have to do," "I have to leave," etc., likewise indicates that an order established in the past has to be complied with at present.

Titles to a possession obtained in the past and carried over as rights from generation to generation create an only too-well-known tension between the establishment and revolting youth, the conservatives and the progressives.

Property is meaningful only when it is used in some way. This is one of the essential differences between a "normal" possessor and the miser, who, hounded by the fear of using up, denies himself the usage of what he owns in abundance. We would all hesitate to use the last candle when the electric current fails. But under normal conditions we rely on our "re-sources." We are inclined to use something at the present moment, confident that a supply will be forthcoming in the future, whether by the grace of natural or supernatural powers or through our own effort and accomplishment. The miser, terror-stricken by the Medusa-like physiognomy of the world, spellbound by the irresistible passage of time, overwhelmed by the prospect of depletion, distrusting his own capacity to accomplish anything, haunted by a panic fear of the future, clings to the past: it is sacrosanct to him. The Collyer brothers never touched the bank account inherited from their mother. Pat Chary kept her mother's room like a mausoleum. The miser's predicament arises not from parsimony, not from possessiveness, not from frugality, but from an overwhelming fear of his future in an inhospitable world. Whatever has passed over his threshold must remain—and remain untouched.

A congeries of unused match folders, piles of old newspapers, a bundle of harmonicas, and a carton of unopened whiskey bottles would not have aroused the curiosity of reporters and readers; but an estate of $150,000—in denominations from one respectfully listed penny up to one-thousand-dollar bills—spread at random in a pauper's apartment was news well deserving of headlines.

Obviously, Aichele had never indulged in the pleasure of using the funds he could not take with him. A spendthrift enjoys abundance; admitting no limits and disregarding all future repercussions, he lives on the spur of the moment in full accord with his actions. Diogenes in his tub enjoyed his freedom from needs, praising his autarky. Saint Francis, the son of a wealthy family, espoused poverty, eager to enjoy treasures "where thieves do not break through nor steal." The miser, on the contrary, who does not enjoy spending the money so passionately accumulated, cannot be in harmony with his own attitude. Aichele, Shepard, the Collyers, are dead; but even if they were still alive and willing to cooperate, they couldn't tell us why they acted as they did—not because they were driven by unconscious motives, but because they responded to the hidden dynamics of money. Therefore, to understand the miser we must now turn our attention to money as a human creation. The finished product will teach us something about the inventor, as well as about the invention and its possible use.

Money is a human achievement. Animals have no genuine relation to money; a dog would prefer a piece of meat to a golden coin. Likewise, a child in the early years of life will stretch out his hand for a shiny penny rather than for a dollar bill. But at school age the capacity for accounting rapidly grows with that of counting. Looking around in public life today, we may well venture to define man as *animal monetare.*

Since money is a medium, a kind of instrument devised to facilitate the exchange of goods, we must take a step further back and first consider the situation of men in barter trading. The guiding principle in such trading is the mutual and voluntary exchange of goods—the *do ut des* (I give that you may give in return). The goods that change owners at a trading post must be on hand, obtained or finished in the past. "All things," Martin Buber said, "have the existential character of the past."

Since the traders must bring their goods to a place agreed upon at a date set in advance, barter is severely limited in regard to space and time. Lacking also is a scale that would permit the establishment of an equitable relation between the goods exchanged—a price. The invention of money was certainly an act of liberation.

Someone who had received cash for goods produced and delivered in the past is free to use that money at a later time, in a different locality, and in dealing with another partner. Money thereby immensely widens the temporal horizon of possible transactions. It opens the market place; it serves as means in a double sense—that of a medium term and that of an instrument of exchange. It permits the establishment of a quantitative relation between highly disparate goods. Money therefore made it feasible to eliminate serfdom and slavery; it provided the opportunity for the worker to offer his services (the word derived from the Latin *servus*, a slave) for a price.

To function as a medium of exchange, money must satisfy a number of conditions: (1) It must be desirable to everyone, everywhere, at any time. (2) Therefore it must be durable, that is to say, it must not be consumed by use. (3) It must be quantifiable. (4) It must be rare, available only in relatively small and controlled amounts.

These four conditions were fulfilled by the rare metals like gold and silver, which were desired because of their aesthetic charms, predestined for their role as mediators, and useful as means just because they are useless for all vital needs.

As reified promise, as potentiality materialized, money creates a paradoxical situation, for money accumulated but not spent is worthless, and money spent loses its potential power at the very moment of spending. The roles of seller and buyer in a regular business are by no means symmetrical in spite of their apparent symmetry! The seller, it seems, turns over goods and receives money; the buyer receives goods and turns over money. Yet, while for the buyer the transaction has reached an end, new prospects are opened for the seller; he is free to use the money received for many other items in the future. Let us assume that someone drives to town in the weeks before Christmas with a list of friends and relatives whom he plans to gladden with a gift. As it happens, he first stops at a fur store where he cannot resist buying a mink stole for his beloved. Suddenly all his buying power has vanished. He returns with just that one gift. Someone assured of his earning power will not hesitate to enter into that circular movement of spending and regaining. The miser, however, utterly convinced of his incapacity to make money, is painfully aware of the power lost. Whatever he has bought turns out to be a poor buy, since it will be subject to the "law of consumption."

Goethe, in his comedy, "Jest, Craft and Vengeance" (*Scherz, List und Rache*), which was planned as a libretto for a German *opéra bouffe*, anticipated my view. At the beginning of the second act the victim of the plot, a miser, counting money, talks to his treasures in a monologue:

> Most people seem to me
> Like never grown up children
> Who hurry to the market
> Eagerly with a few pennies.
> As long as the purse
> Still holds the little money
> Ah, everything is theirs:
> Candies and other sweets,
> Colorful pictures and the hobby horse,
> The drum and the violin.
> Heart, what more can you desire?
> And the heart is unsatiable!
> It opens wide the greedy eyes.
> But if for one of those seven things
> The little funds are spent
> Then adieu to all those golden wishes.
> All you hopes, all you desires, farewell!
> You all have crept into one little piece of gingerbread.
> Child, now go home!—
> No, no, it shall never happen to me.
> As long as I own you, all treasures of the earth are mine.

There is, however, one exception to the general law of consumption: money begets money in the form of interest. Aichele and Shepard, nevertheless, kept a considerable sum of money idle.

If Aichele had invested his cash in a savings account, the interest it drew would have provided a modest subsistence with a minimum of risk. To be sure, all securities are fraught with a certain degree of insecurity. Thus, in choosing a bank Aichele could not escape making a decision of his own, a decision requiring a detached evaluation of existing conditions. Yet a miser is poorly prepared for a sober appraisal; flabbergasted by a confrontation with the world, the resulting stupor renders him practically stupid.[18] The miser would have to give away cash for the mere acknowledgment of credit in the books of a company. Although it would be a legally well-protected right, he would lose the company of his individual treasury notes. It seems that in our days misers are no less fascinated by dull and dirty bills than their predecessors—"wallowing in gold"—were by shiny and glittering coins. They do not imitate George Washington, who supposedly said, "It is not a custom with me to keep money to look at."

The transition from gold to paper money, begun during the French Revolution, was more than a mere exchange of materials; it was a transition from goods on hand, which had been accumulated in the past, to credit—that is to say, to faith in a promise that was to be fulfilled at a later date. To Buber's statement, "All things have the existential character of the past," one may add "all things except paper money, which has the existential character of the future." Representing merely quanta of buying power guaranteed by the authority of a state, paper money is valuable only as long as it is recognized by an organized society and therefore accepted by its members. The miser, however, frightened by the future, coy in relation to his fellow man, mistrusting his own decisions and capacity to act—this pusillanimous man treats paper money as if it were in itself a valuable thing.

"Orderliness," as listed in Freud's triad, refers to personal conduct and appearance. Yet someone may be accurate in business matters and nonchalant in personal affairs. His drawing room may be arranged properly for the reception of guests, while the area entitled "living room" may present a quite different aspect. Since order is a generic term, and since orderliness may be manifested in many variations, some further distinctions are in order.

The alphabet and the numerals are schemata of order used to order other material. In a telephone directory the alphabet is applied to the initial letters and reapplied to all the following

18. Balzac in his novel *Eugénie Grandet* presents the father in the double role of a ruthless, enterprising businessman and a miser tormenting wife and daughter. Balzac probably combined, for the purpose of dramatization, mutually exclusive attitudes in one person. Also, great writers are not immune to error.

letters of a name. The order thereby established permits us to locate with certainty a person's name among many thousands and so also to locate his "number" in the numercial system that in turn orders the network of wires for technical purposes. In the yellow pages the alphabet is used once more for an additional purpose. Obviously, in all those cases order is in the service of a given purpose—one that is pragmatic. At a dinner table, plates, glasses, spoons, and forks are set for the convenience of the guests. After the meal, when the table is cleared and the dishes washed, they pass through a different arrangement, until they are finally stacked in a cabinet or placed in a drawer, once more at hand for the next setting of the table.

Although we do not expect to find a drawing room, reserved for social representation, in the dwelling of an Aichele or a Collyer, we were surprised at first by the degree of disorder encountered in their rooms. However, we finally understood that the miser's chronophobia paralyzes intending and planning and thereby eliminates any incentive to keep order or to accept the often tedious business of clearing and cleaning up for the sake of possible future usage.

In every respect the miser reveals himself as a fugitive from the demands of human existence.

By a happy coincidence, a clinical observation has recently been published, a case history presenting—though without the author's intention—the cardinal traits of misers, including disarray, so typically that it may well serve here as a kind of summary.[19]

Walburga H., a 64-year-old spinster, was sent to a psychiatric hospital with the tentative diagnosis of "involutional depression, with delusions of pauperization." Walburga, the youngest of three daughters born to a butcher, "yielding to her father's wishes," renounced plans for a teacher's career and worked instead, without any financial remuneration, in the butcher shop for twenty years until her father's death. She then continued to serve her mother until finally, after her mother's death, she tried to carry on the business alone but failed and quit at the age of fifty-five, probably because she needed help but was unable to accept for herself the role of owner and boss. Walburga's sexual life was completely barren. Although described as an attractive

19. H. Dietrich, "Über Sammelsucht" ("Collector's Mania"), *Der Nervenarzt* (June, 1968), pp. 271–74.

blonde in her teens, she never searched for, never found, and supposedly never missed, a male companion. Having inherited from her parents an apartment house, she could have carried on a comfortable life by using the rentals; actually, she lived below even moderate standards *in order to save money.* She even accepted a job, it seems, as a housemaid.

When she failed to report for work, an older sister became alarmed, like Aichele's lawyer and Collyer's grocer. However, the sister did not call the police; instead she went to Walburga's home, where she found Walburga still alive but reluctant to open the door. When she was finally allowed to go in, she "found the two-room apartment in complete disarray, filled to the ceiling with paper, rubbish, garments, old carpets, shoes, and umbrellas, collected, or gotten by begging, in nearby boarding houses. Just as crammed as these rooms were the former butcher shop and the basement. The toilet was blocked so that it could no longer be used, and Walburga had had to resort to buckets. The bed was covered with old clothing, forcing Walburga to sleep in an old armchair. She dated the beginning of her compulsion seven years earlier (soon after she had lost her mother). At that time she began her bad habits of accumulating things and taking them home; she collected the shoes and newspapers, and especially clothes and underwear, discarded by guests in nearby boarding houses; she picked the things up at pretty regular intervals and brought them home on her bicycle. She thought that those things might still be used by someone else; actually she never gave anything away. Her action appeared senseless to her; yet she continued collecting and never reached the point of placing all the stuff infesting her home into the trash. During all the years of compulsive collecting she never permitted anybody to enter her apartment." [20]

While the newspaper reports about Aichele and the Collyers, though suggestive, do not permit us to put a diagnostic label upon the miser, Walburga's history provides us with a deeper insight into the so-called involutional depression. In his report, the author first gave the description I have just quoted of Walburga's "collector's mania" and then added to it an all too fragmentary case history, presenting poorly connected data of a curriculum vitae. He failed to recognize the morbidity of the

20. My translation.—E.W.S.

premorbid personality. Yet seen in a proper perspective, Walburga's life developed *uno tenore* in a crescendo of missed opportunities, silent retreats, and concealed disappointments. From early youth Walburga, who in the course of 60 years never passed the limits of the city of Munich, was dominated by fear of an encounter with people and with the world, a "cosmophobia." She spent the prime of her life, between the end of World War I and the beginning of World War II, in her father's butcher shop. Obviously, the services rendered to her father and mother were no sacrifice on her part. Rather, Walburga took refuge in this situation, as a kind of sanctuary. Condemned to independence, she failed in business, in spite of West Germany's fantastic economic recovery under the Marshall Plan. After the death of both parents she tried to retreat completely, arranging clandestine feasts, celebrated in the company of the empty wrappers of unknown people she never dared to face in person. She had good reason to keep these quasi-fetishistic and necrophilic orgies strictly secret. After years of ever renewed attempts to combat the *horror vacui,* her efforts to fill the existential void, doomed to failure from the very beginning, ended in complete despair. Clinical treatment and—last but not least—asylum in her sister's house, where she was kept like a captive for her own protection, prevented suicide.

Walburga's case history reveals the ties that connect involutional depression with cosmophobia and "the unsunned heaps of misers' treasures."

10 / Monetary Value and Personal Value

George Schrader

ONE OF THE MOST INTERESTING and, to my mind, fruitful developments in recent philosophy has been the turn toward descriptive analysis—including descriptive metaphysics. Having tired of their perennial attempts to construct the world either on the model of an original blueprint or on conventional logic, philosophers have turned increasingly to the world as it is. Often, to their surprise, they have found it highly interesting. At precisely that point where philosophy was on the verge of having as its content only the forms of its own discourse, it is reappropriating, little by little, segments of the world which it had long since relinquished. To accept the world, for the sake of analysis, as already there poses the fundamental question to which phenomenologists have addressed themselves, namely, how it is constituted. It seems obvious enough that it is indeed there, and, further, that a basic understanding of the received world and our involvement with it is presuppositional to any subsequent theorizing. Descriptive analysis and phenomenological understanding cannot, however, constitute a total philosophical program. We are immediately confronted with the additional problem of how we are to respond to the world. It is never simply there as something frozen, nor is our participation in the world simply that of stationary observers. On the contrary, we are active participants in a dynamic world even as we seek to know and understand it.

The theme of this volume of essays is the "lived world." I take the "lived world" to be the unreduced world of human experience. It is neither the world causally beneath nor the world speculatively beyond the world as we live in it. In this essay, I want to consider a pervasive value aspect of our ordinary world and for this purpose have chosen to focus on monetary value. Through a descriptive analysis I hope both to elucidate the everyday meaning of this mode of value and to make explicit its relationship to personal value. I will also attempt to specify some of the problems that are posed by these contrasting modes of value and to suggest alternatives for responding to these problems. Rather than start with a philosophical conception of value, I shall begin with an everyday mode of value and attempt to understand it in its own terms.

At the moment there are two major world crises—or possibly two aspects of a single crisis—which focus on a pervasive feature of our contemporary value system, namely, the dollar crisis and inflation. The stock market ticker and the Consumer Price Index are two of the barometers which we consult to see how the economy is faring. The anxiety evidenced with respect to these indicators suggests that our manifest value system is economically constituted. If we are to proceed phenomenologically with our analysis of value, we must begin with the most pervasive and conspicuous determination of value, namely, the economic.

It would, of course, be nothing short of foolhardy for a layman to venture forth in the territory of the economic theorist and statistician; surely he dare not do so without the most expert and reliable of guides. Still, the philosopher need not concern himself directly with the science of economics in order to take cognizance of the bearing of our socioeconomic system on the status of value, any more than he is required to embark upon the pursuit of physics in order to consider the overt aspects of man's relation to nature. Karl Marx had a philosophical interest in the problem of value and a prophetic insight into the transformations which were occurring in the disposition of goods. It is regrettable that, by and large, subsequent philosophers have veered away from this entire area of concern, leaving it almost completely to the economists. I cannot expect to redress the balance in this essay, but must content myself with pointing up the importance of the problem and the need for a full-scale philosophical exploration.

Nothing is more obviously true about our society than the fact that money is the most conspicuous measure of value. It has long since reached the point where we not only require money as the currency for almost any operation or activity, but we could hardly expect to survive for very long without it. Conversely, with money we can expect to meet virtually any of our needs, including love and recognition. It need not be argued that almost everything we confront has a designated monetary value; it is hard to think of many things that do not. For our purposes it is sufficient to note that money is the most insistent value factor with which we must contend in our everyday activities. On leaving the house in the morning we must take care that we have not forgotten our wallet, our checkbook, or, if we are somewhat more felicitously accommodated to the system, our credit cards. On entering a foreign country, the first thing we must do is convert our currency. Money is prima facie the primary value and the measure of most other values. The questions are: Just what is the value of money itself? And how does it measure the value of those things which have a monetary price?

In the days when gold and other precious metals served as money, we could make a fairly easy connection between the value of our coin and that for which it was exchanged. Gold was, and to some degree still is, valued because of the rarity of its occurrence in nature and because of its intrinsic properties. Moreover, so long as paper money had a direct relation to gold or silver, we had some idea of its value in relation to natural processes. With the severance of currency from any such precious metals as gold and silver, money must obviously be estimated in quite a different way. This means, in the first instance, that money has whatever value it is declared to have. The value of a dollar is a dollar, a dime is the tenth part of a dollar, and so on. Each monetary unit has a value in relation to the monetary system. Yet in another sense money appears to have no value in itself at all. If Aristotle could argue that money is valuable only as a means, that point could be urged even more strongly today. Valueless in itself, it somehow serves as the measure of true value and the standard medium for the exchange and conversion of goods.

Ten dollars, one might say, has no value whatever in itself and is worth only what it can buy. It is not to be viewed as a "good" but only as a token to be exchanged for "goods." If so, we can presumably estimate the value of our monetary units by reference to the prices of things which they can be used to buy.

Ten cents means chewing gum, a candy bar, or an hour's parking. Yet when we make such an attempt to estimate the value of our standard of measure we find ourselves involved in a rather frustrating circle. If I am supposed to find the true value of a dime by seeing what it will buy, I must then look around me to see what things can be purchased for ten cents. I thus obtain what appears to be a rough measure in terms of goods and services for estimating the purchasing value of the dime. But, alas, the only value I find attached to these items is precisely the price which I am attempting to estimate independently. In other words, ten cents buys a package of Dentyne and, by the same token, a package of Dentyne is worth ten cents. Why? Because that is the amount of money it takes to buy the gum. In short, we have come upon a pretty bald tautology, namely, that a dime will buy whatever costs ten cents. The worth of the dime is, then, just what we already knew it to be, a dime, or ten cents. As a matter of fact, the gum is worth ten cents only to the buyer as buyer. If we were to turn around and try to exchange the gum for a dime, we would probably have great difficulty in doing so. The price means one thing to the seller and another to the buyer. There is, and apparently has to be, a discrepancy between the price and hence the monetary value to buyer and seller, or there would be no motivation to engage in the exchange. But that is not the point in which I am interested; it is rather the seeming arbitrariness of the price that concerns me.

If we cannot determine the true value of our currency by looking to the price of things, can we look to the value of the goods themselves and thus, possibly, give an account of pricing? To attempt this means, of course, that we have provisionally reversed our position and, instead of assuming that money is the primary value, now regard it as secondary and derivative. Instead of measuring goods in terms of money, we will seek to measure money in terms of goods. To succeed in this project we must be able to find some way of converting the real (nonmonetary) value of goods into a price which reflects that value. The relation between monetary value (price) and real value must be nonarbitrary, or we have no standard for making the conversion. In exploring this relationship we have to consider the very different perspectives of the consumer and the producer. As we shall see, they confront the question of the worth and price of goods in quite different ways. One facet of the problem, therefore, will be to find a rational way of converting worth on the part of the producer in terms of worth to the consumer.

So far as the producer of goods is concerned, the basis for calculating monetary value would appear to be fairly simple—or at least based on a clear and straightforward process of cost accounting. He must know what he paid for the materials he has used and what further expenditure of money is required to process the goods. In addition, he must determine what return or profit he requires in order both to continue his business and to reward his own efforts. Once those calculations are made, he knows what price to charge for his goods. But notice that we have done nothing more in making this computation than break down price into costs or, conversely, constitute price from costs. This sort of computation doesn't get us much further in estimating the true value of goods, since we start with prices that are already determined. We begin our calculations on the basis of the price of raw materials, labor, advertising and selling costs, and so on. Cost, after all, is but another term for price, namely, the price of that which we buy. Since we are seeking to find the basis for pricing, we have to go beyond cost accounting to uncover it. At the very least we must find a nonarbitrary way of determining the cost of raw materials and of labor.

Is there some way in which we can estimate the true monetary value of raw materials and labor? Take tobacco, for example, which provides essential material for one of our largest industries. What is the real value of raw tobacco? We might conjecture that the price of raw tobacco depends on such factors as the cost of producing it, the supply available, and competing demands for the available supply. Tobacco can be grown only in selected areas where soil and climate are favorable. It requires intensive cultivation, and only one crop a year can be grown. With respect to the price paid to the grower, there are at least two ways in which this could be determined: (a) If the grower uses sophisticated business techniques, he knows what he must charge for his crop. By calculating the cost of his land, machinery, labor, etc., he can estimate his costs in much the same way as the processor and eventually arrive at the price that is to be assigned. But if he operates in that fashion, we have only added another stage to our cost-accounting procedures and are no better off than before in assessing the value of goods as a basis for price. We need only assume a prevailing cost of land, labor, machinery, etc., in order to calculate the price of raw tobacco in precisely the same way as we calculate the price of cigarettes. (b) Alternatively, the grower might simply put his goods on the market and ask whatever price he thinks he can get. The price would then be simply market price, a function of what he hopes to get and what the processor is willing to pay. If we assume that the processor wants to keep the grower in business, it would be reasonable for him to pay enough to cover the grower's cost, plus an incentive margin for profit. But even if that is assumed, price is based on a rough estimate of costs and the situation is not significantly different from the first alternative. Clearly the price of labor and raw material may be calculated regressively from the projected price of the marketed product; or, the price of the marketed product can be calculated by adding up the accumulated costs of labor and materials. On the second alternative we introduce a potentially irrational and speculative factor since the market permits free play between selling price and buying price.

Supply and demand are said to exert a decisive influence on market price. But to say that still does not explain the resultant monetary price of goods. Insofar as supply and demand are contingent variables, determining price is rather like predicting weather. If a larger supply of tobacco can be produced more cheaply by virtue of improved farming techniques, this could rationally affect the price of raw tobacco. But if, on the other hand, the supply is larger in any given year simply because more has been planted and the weather is more favorable, this would not affect the cost of producing the tobacco and could have no rational effect on price. For either supply or demand to help us in establishing a rational price, some monetary value must already be attached to the supply of goods and to the demand itself. So far as the goods are concerned, this can be done in terms of the cost of production. The monetary value of demand, on the other hand, seems to depend upon the price one is willing to pay for goods desired. In the case of the processor, the dollar value of demand must be calculated backwards from anticipated yield. In short, he is anticipating what the consumer will pay for the marketed product. We still have made no significant progress in breaking out of our circle of cost and price.

Technical questions concerning the complex processes which determine the price of goods are admittedly more pertinent to the science of economics than to philosophy. The philosopher might well pay more attention to these processes than he usually does, but he should not confuse issues in economic theory with philosophical issues. This declaration of modesty having been made, however, there remain basic philosophical questions about value which involve both the philosopher and the economic theorist. Insofar as we have no fundamental understanding of the basis for converting real or goods value into monetary value, the economy in which we live must appear as an arbitrary and irrational system. The fact that it is thoroughly rational in itself does not entail a rational basis in human experience. If it should turn out that there is not *in principle* a rational basis for converting the value of goods and labor into monetary terms, our economic system is necessarily nonrational.

The problem is whether, without begging the question by appeal to costs and prices which have already been determined, we can find a basis for making the conversion into monetary terms. Put in its most general terms, this looks very much like the familiar problem of converting quality into quantity. It also poses the problem of quantitative measurement. The latter problem is, of course, far easier to deal with than the former, and hence it is a better starting point. We are able to measure length, for example, by use of a metric system. To use such a system we must establish a scale and calibrate that scale. Once that is done, we can make our calculations in terms of metric units. But even so we must be able to mark units on actual lengths of material, land, etc., so that the relationship is established between the measure and what is measured. From a mathematical point of view, the actual length in a material sense is of no importance. But for the operation of measurement it is of critical importance. What we are measuring is length of spatial extension in one dimension. The mathematical meter is ideal and may never be perfectly matched by any length we can mark off. Moreover, there is a certain arbitrariness in the measure itself since we could have measured in feet and inches or on any one of a number of different scales. A meter is not, therefore, a purely natural unit of length in that natural objects don't come in meters or perfect fractions of meters. This does not alter the fact, however, that in an important sense length is measured in terms of itself.

We are in no doubt that it is length or spatial extension we are measuring, nor are we in any doubt as to how we come by or use the measure. We know that we can measure any log in terms of any piece of a log. In letting our metric unit stand for such a length as a short log we only abstract from the crude unit of measurement so as to make it systematically elegant and precise.

To be sure of having two pieces of wood exactly the same length, we can measure one of them against the other. Indeed, our measurement by use of a tape measure would be immediately suspect if it did not afford precisely that result. Measurement does not, therefore, translate quality into quantity. By abstracting from material units which could be carved out of natural materials, it substitutes a scale for those units themselves. We do abstract in a sense from the qualities of the materials to be measured, and for good reason. In measuring we are concerned about only one quality, namely, length. Although we have chosen a crude example, the same point could be made by reference to physics, where natural events are taken as units of measurement.

There are, of course, both technical and philosophical issues with respect to measurement, but they are all of quite a different sort from those involved with the conversion of quality into quantity. Weighing a pound of butter, for example, is quite a different operation from pricing a pound of butter. They appear to be much the same, since in both cases we attach numbers to the butter—one pound at eighty-nine cents. The difference is that we weigh the butter in order to determine that it is a pound before attaching the pound sign to it; we perform no comparable operation in determining what price to assign it. In other words, the pound weight is the value of the butter in terms of a physical property of the butter itself. Although a pound is a specific quantity of butter, in designating it as a pound we have in no sense converted butter into another type of value. We have only measured the weight of the butter.

Now one could say that in attaching a price to the butter we are only measuring the worth of the butter and, hence, not doing anything basically different from weighing it. Or, if you prefer, we are simply weighing it on a different scale. To say this is, of course, to speak figuratively and metaphorically, for there is no literal scale on which to weigh it with respect to its price. Any grocer knows the difference between these two operations. We can measure any length by part of itself or, for that matter, in terms of another length. We cannot make the same translation of a material good into monetary terms. A dollar, for example, is in no sense a unit of that which is priced. We can't interpret monetary units as abstractions from real units of value, save, of course, with respect to gold or silver. If the value of a dollar bill were a specific quantity of actual gold, the monetary scale would be quite similar to the scale by which we measure length and weight. The quantity in question would be a quantity of gold; a unit of gold would thus be the measure of any other amount of gold. Thus the quality of gold would no more be altered or translated into quantitative terms than weighing butter translates it into qualitative form.

From a philosophical point of view it is fairly easy to see why there has been genuine concern about the so-called gold standard. It may well be that to maintain a gold standard such that all currency is actually redeemable in gold is no longer feasible or desirable in our economy. The question is whether in giving up the gold standard we have given up the last real tie between money and that which it is used to measure. In what sense can money be regarded as any kind of a measure of those things which are assigned monetary value? We began our consideration of money value by noting that money is the most conspicuous of all value scales in the contemporary world. If, however, our monetary units have no basis in any natural good, it is by no means clear that money constitutes a genuine measure of anything at all.

Before concluding categorically that there is no rational connection between money value and goods value, we need to explore the possibility that money, even though no longer based on gold, still has a real and rational connection with material goods. Surely our currency must depend on something other than itself for its value, since, save for coin collectors, the actual value of coins or paper money is hardly equivalent or even significantly related to the monetary value it bears on its face. Or is that, perhaps, a nonsensical statement? Can we even significantly ask about the relation between the real value and the monetary value of a coin or a dollar bill? In making the above, possibly nonsensical, statement, my intention was to emphasize that the material out of which the coin or bill is made has no significant relationship to the money value it bears. Though a dollar is worth a dollar, it is a dollar only because it bears on its face that declaration. Or, to make the same point differently, the cost of coining a dollar may not, and quite likely does not, amount to a dollar. Or, more precisely, the cost of coining the dollar has nothing whatever to do with the fact that it is worth a dollar. On the face of it, knowing the monetary worth of a dollar bill would appear to be the easiest value problem imaginable.

If, then, there is no significant relationship between the monetary value of a coin and the material from which it has been made, there must surely be some other relationship between our currency and natural goods. Tying our currency to gold or silver might have been artificial. Such odd things as feathers have been used, after all, as a medium of exchange. Perhaps the shift from the gold standard was simply a recognition that money is related not only to gold but to the whole array of natural goods available in our society. Thus wheat, oil, iron, and even butter might have as good a claim as gold and silver to serve as the basis for our currency. Our money, it doubtless would be argued by economic theorists, is simply backed up by the gross national product—including not only raw materials but manufactured goods. If a dollar bill is not redeemable in gold, it may still be redeemable in goods of comparable value. Since to use dollars on the gold standard we had to make comparative judgments of value, e.g., between gold and butter, we should be able to broaden our material base by backing up dollars with all sorts of marketable goods. A dollar is thus a token that is redeemable in the form of any goods whatever with the sole proviso that their worth be measured in dollars. Is the dollar scale, then, basically any different or more arbitrary than the metric scale as a system of measurement?

I am afraid that it is different, and for the following reasons. Let us assume, first, that various articles in specific amounts are priced at a dollar. In the move to generalize the basis for our currency, we are taking a multiplicity of goods rather than a single good as our basic unit. A dollar, let us say, is the price of a pound of butter, a pound of coffee, ten pounds of sugar, and so on. We could simply exchange a pound of butter for a pound of coffee or exchange either of them for a dollar and then exchange the dollar for butter or coffee. Money would then become a measure of sorts, namely, of units which can be exchanged for each other. It would be optional, therefore, whether we related money to butter, coffee, or gold. So far so good—but there are bothersome complications.

In the first place, we are using a general measure for the comparison of incommensurables—which is something like trying to find a common measure for height and weight. So long as we know that a dollar is equivalent to a portion of gold, we know what we are doing when we exchange butter for dollars— even though there is in fact no common measure between the two. Note that we have at least one constant in this case, since gold remains the stable unit of value. Butter or any other item to be exchanged for gold may vary in monetary value but we still know the value of the money itself, in the sense at least of being certain of the amount of gold backing it up. If we universalize our base in relation to goods, something of this situation might still obtain, *provided* that the units remained constant. In other words, the basis for exchange would be similar to the gold standard if and only if each unit involved remained constant in relation to the dollar. But if, on the other hand, no unit, even gold, remains constant, the value of the dollar is obviously independent of the value of goods. In short, the value of goods must be fixed in relation to dollars and, conversely, the value of the dollar in relation to goods.

It is perfectly obvious that money does not and cannot serve as a common measure in quantitative terms of the value of goods. If it were such a measure, then by appeal to monetary standards we ought to be able to determine the dollar value of butter, coffee, ice cream, and so on. The fact is that the dollar value of these items varies constantly, and, further, that each item varies independently of the others. It is more or less like measuring lengths of rope, leather, and linen, and finding that a foot of each is different at different times and of different length as between rope, leather, and linen. Our monetary scale simply does not provide a measure of monetary value. It is precisely this situation which the housewife and the householder find so utterly baffling. They have no way to convert the price of butter into eggs or, indeed, of anything into anything. Since money has value only in relation to goods and since the value of goods is in constant flux, there is no stable measure of goods in relation to money or of money in relation to goods.

There are two further complicating factors which make it even more difficult to relate money to goods. Inflation can occur either because new money is introduced into the economy or because the price of goods is increased. If there is more money relative to goods available, the dollar will obviously buy less. And if prices are increased and the money supply remains constant, it is also the case that the dollar will buy less. Inflation is a threat not only because it endangers the entire economy but also because it makes any rational estimate of monetary value exceedingly difficult.

Now if we were to consider the economics of the matter more fully, we would have to take into account the role of taxation in backing up currency. In lieu of taxes, property or goods can be taken by the state to redeem the currency. The base is not gold, then, but the national wealth as a whole. This still leaves us in our circle, however, for goods can be taken in lieu of money for tax purposes only at the prevailing market value. In other words, we have no fixed relation between money and goods to appeal to in backing up our currency or in assessing taxes.

But let us return to the question of quality and quantity to see what, if any, rational basis there is for converting one into the other. If money is not a measure in the sense of constituting a scale like the metric system, it must be differently related to the goods to which it attaches. As we have seen earlier, we can find a rational basis for assigning price once we are given fixed costs to work with. It is this fact about our economy which gives pricing its appearance of rationality. Viewed as a closed system of cost and price accounting, it is thoroughly rational and subject to exact methods of computation and analysis. It is only when we go outside the system to consider how the original costs are determined that fundamental questions arise. If, for example, a pound of butter is priced at a dollar and that price is not justified by reference to the cost of milk, of buying and keeping the cow, of transporting and processing the cream, and so on, then it is a purely arbitrary price. In principle it would be no different from putting a price tag of $1,000 on an oil painting.

It might, of course, be frankly admitted that there is in fact no rational basis for assessing monetary value so far as the original determination of price is concerned. We need not be particularly disturbed over this fact, however, since virtually everything has a price which can be used as a reference point. Moreover we have pragmatic ways of attaching initial price to goods. An artist, for example, may have very little to go by in pricing his work. He can estimate whether or not it falls in a general class with the work of other artists and can set his initial price on that rough basis. From there on it is largely a question of what he can get for his paintings, as well as how eager he is to sell them. On the face of it, works of art would seem to be the most difficult goods to price; in fact, we have succeeded so well in pricing them that they constitute one of the more stable investments—possibly even a hedge against inflation. If, therefore, we can price works of art without insuperable difficulty, there should be no serious problem with more mundane articles which come on the market. Although we cannot determine on a theoretical basis the initial or intrinsic monetary worth of any goods, we can do so pragmatically. We have simply to price them, submit them to the market, and adjust the price up or down as required to meet the conditions of exchange. We can then convert that price into other goods which might be purchased with the return in order to judge whether or not it is worthwhile to continue to produce and market the item in question. Suitable reward for one's effort is thus a crucial factor in judging the adequacy of price.

What is being said here is that money value is essentially exchange value. Although there are no fixed reference points save the numerical monetary units themselves, and possibly the quantity of money in circulation, the exchange system affords sufficient stability for us to assess price on a periodic basis. Prices are generally moving upward at the moment, and are constantly changing within the system. Still, on a day-by-day basis we know the price of things. Moreover, we are able to make sufficiently rational projections of prices to operate with respect to the immediate future. The basis for determining the value both of money and of goods is, then, the system itself. There are, however, such additional factors as labor, management, and demand which condition the operation of the system. These extrasystemic factors refer to human need and human effort and thus to the individual man who lives in and with the system.

We have made oblique reference to the role of human labor at various points in the discussion thus far. To simplify matters we have deliberately avoided the question of assigning monetary value to labor itself. Labor presents a problem in that it accounts for a major part of the cost of goods and yet is far less tangible than goods themselves. Marx was concerned to the point of preoccupation with the role of labor in affecting the value of goods. He formulated and defended the now generally discredited "labor theory of value." There were several major difficulties with Marx's theory. In the first place, the value of goods depends to a considerable extent upon the bounty of nature rather than upon the work of man. Diamonds and gold, for example, are rare in nature, and are the product of complex processes extending over a comparatively long time. The human labor used in mining and processing them is of far less importance in determining their value than is the manner of their occurrence in nature. Secondly, the natural supply of goods, as well as the ease or difficulty with which they can be appropriated, affects their value. Most important of all, however, is that the market has a decisive effect on the actual monetary value of all goods. In large part Marx was, I think, trying to make a *moral* point by recourse to economic theory, namely, that labor *should be* the decisive factor to be taken into account in the pricing of goods. The fact that it is not the decisive factor in no way nullifies the strength of Marx's moral thesis—though it is unfortunate that he confused the two considerations.

Labor, like goods, has its price. We face the same question of the basis for pricing labor as in the case of goods, save that there are even greater difficulties involved. There is, in the first place, a problem in determining what constitutes a unit of labor. Is it, as is often said, a "man-hour"? If we could assume that a man-hour is a constant and identifiable unit of work we might be able to estimate it by some standard. Unfortunately, this seemingly objective unit is misleading in that it takes no account of the work done. Suppose, for example, that a man is simply turning over shovelfuls of sand on a beach. Such activity might be construed as work and can be measured in hours, yet it accomplishes nothing. If, on the other hand, the man is digging a canal or excavating a cellar, the work can be measured in relation to the objective of the task. Work construed simply as diligent and conscientious activity has no worth at all—in fact it is utterly pointless. It is only when work is interpreted as the carrying out of an assigned or self-assigned task that it is meaningful and of value. In the latter instance the value can be appraised in relation to the task performed, for example, the canal dug or the cellar excavated. We can then say that a normal healthy man, suitably experienced and conscientious in his work, would have to devote so many hours to the completion of the task. Work thus has the double meaning of activity and task to be completed. The performance of a task is work in the economic sense if a price is to be attached to it or if it is done for a return in money or goods.

Marx calculated that in a capitalistic economy the worker will be paid only enough to keep him available as needed on the labor market. Marx believed, of course, that the worker should be paid on the basis of his contribution to the value of the goods he helps to produce. The organization of labor and the minimum wage have altered the situation, as has our more enlightened regard for the welfare of the laborer. Organized labor wants wages to be determined on several bases, including the cost of living for the worker, the value of the goods produced, and the profits made on these goods when sold. Thus so far as organized labor is concerned, the price of labor depends very heavily on the cost of living, and in many instances wage increases are formally tied to the cost of living index. The price of goods is increased to provide for the cost of labor, which in turn is estimated on the basis of the cost of living—which means the price of goods. Labor is no more exempt from the circle of price than are raw materials. Inflation increases the cost both of labor and of goods such that each is constantly being adjusted in relation to the other.

In most instances the individual laborer in a large concern can make no realistic appraisal of his contribution to the finished product. He must depend upon his union to make estimates for his work group as a whole on the basis of the same cost-accounting techniques used by the company. The labor share must then be divided up among the workers in terms of hours worked, relative skill, and whatever additional considerations they agree upon. Not infrequently the laborer must take it on faith that his work contributes to the material output of his company. The more important the system becomes, the more the enlightened laborer is inclined to expect his return from the system as a whole. If there is no rational basis for estimating the monetary value of his labor, no clear relation between his effort and the monetary value of the finished product, it is reasonable for him to view himself as participating in a system which should reward him in relation to his needs and its ability to satisfy them. More and more the state has assumed the role of distributing the fruits of production to the populace, often with only a pretense of rewarding tangible effort or work done. The average worker has no more satisfying basis for estimating the monetary value of his work than the monetary value of the goods he buys. To survive he must maintain the best equilibrium he can between the two.

It appears that for all practical purposes we have gone off the labor standard of value as well as off the gold standard. There is simply no basic unit of labor output that can be used in determining the value of labor. Both its real and its monetary value are within the economic organization in which it is performed. The laborer's wages depend on the fortunes of his company, and even more on his bargaining and political power. He knows that he must have marketable skills, but he no longer attempts to estimate their real worth. Political and pragmatic considerations thus determine the initial price of labor in a way that is similar to the initial pricing of goods. In neither case is there a real or natural unit of nonmonetary value to which appeal can be made in determining cost or price.

Demand, as we have seen, is the essential counterpart to supply in determining price. Perhaps this factor, which we have ignored thus far, can provide us with the foundation for which we have been searching. Here, of course, our attention shifts from the perspective of the producer and marketer of goods to the consumer. Is there, perhaps, some way in which human needs can be analyzed so that the value of goods can be estimated in relation to them? Can a housewife, for example, exercise control in a supermarket or a discount house by estimating her real needs and those of her family in relation to the goods available? Or can a cigarette smoker estimate the value of his need to smoke in relation to the cost of a package of cigarettes? The housewife can in an important sense estimate the real value of the goods she buys in relation to the needs of her family. If she wishes to provide them with balanced and appetizing meals she will shop carefully with that end in mind. Milk and bread, let us assume, are essentials which she can and must buy without deliberation. The question is whether considerations of that sort help her in any way in estimating price. So far as she is concerned there are two fundamental controls operating with respect to her shopping. First, the prices of items are already marked on the shelves, and, second, she has a limited sum set aside for the day's marketing. She has to select among the available goods in such a way as to stay within the amount she has allocated. It is clear that she must compute the prices of the items she selects, and in choosing some items must exclude others. Her problem as a consumer is to remain within the limits set by the money she has available to spend and the price of the goods she buys. Within that bracketed region she has freedom to choose and to determine priorities. In view of the fact, however, that very few of the items she is likely to buy could be called essential in that they are required for the sustenance of her family, there is no clear basis on which she can adjust need to the price of goods. For one thing, in deciding whether to pay more for frozen and ready-to-eat foods she has to put a value on her own leisure. In choosing or not choosing soft drinks for her children she must estimate quite artificial needs. If she buys a soft drink, say, at ten cents a bottle, how can she decide that it is actually worth ten cents? Isn't she forced simply to balance off one set of prices against another, thus operating within the sphere of predetermined value?

There does not appear to be any basic unit of need which can be converted into monetary terms to provide a rational basis for estimating the adequacy of price. Needs are, in the first place, tremendously diverse, and, second, many of them are artificially stimulated or induced. Advertising, which is so essential to our economy, trades on its ability to create needs where none exist or to potentiate needs which are already operative. Our desire to buy and our willingness to pay for a given product depend increasingly on the emotional associations we have with the item in question. Successful merchandising thus tends to create its own market, including the readiness to accept the stated price. In an affluent society, to the degree that available income exceeds the amount necessary for essential goods, the consumer tends to become acquisitive—actively looking for a bargain or merely for something to buy. Often it is the package more than the product which is important in soliciting the consumer. A great many items are worth only a fraction of their cost—if they can be sold at all—once they are removed from the shopping center. Our conclusion must be that, like labor and raw materials, there is no rational basis for assigning monetary value to consumer needs and, hence, no rational connection between need and price. The consumer is but an intermediary in the system whose role it is to transfer money from one unit to another.

What conclusions are we to draw from this crude sketch of our economic predicament? If our analysis is correct even in the broadest outline, there is no direct relationship between natural goods, human effort, human need, and monetary value. Money, in spite of appearances to the contrary, is no true measure of any of these factors. The system floats freely, as it were, with only a tenuous and highly pragmatic relation either to man or to nature. It would be nostalgic to try to reestablish a rational connection by returning to the gold standard. Nor is the overturning of the monetary system as a whole a feasible alternative; such a complete negation would require a reversal of the major economic developments of the past century. Short of that, we must find some way of coming to terms with the system so as to recover our ability to assess the real value of things—goods, labor, need, etc.—in human terms.

Although the upshot of our analysis appears to be negative and discouraging, that is but the first and most obvious result. It is disillusioning in the literal sense of the term, but that is precisely the positive result. Discussions of capitalism, communism, and socialism have for decades been couched in moral terms. The defenders of enlightened capitalism, no less than the defenders of socialism and communism, have appealed to the moral foundation and moral rectitude of their favored system. The time has come when we must regard such debate as mere posturing and as failing utterly to understand the sort of alienation which results from the systematic economic organization on a universal scale of production and consumption. Problems internal to the system are primarily theoretical and technical. The moral and political problems concern the relation of the individual to the system as a whole—a system which in one version or another constitutes the fate of contemporary man. It is simply naive to believe that under any modern system man will be more directly related to the products of his work or that the value of goods and the value of money will be any less artificially connected. The question is, then, what alternatives do we have for interpreting our work, our needs, and the material goods with which we are surrounded?

One possibility is, as we have noted, for the individual to set himself against the system, but such a project for contemporary man is a mere posturing, a tilting at windmills. Even the artist not born to wealth must sell his work or be supported by a foundation. To make use of Heidegger's term, this is the mode of man's inauthentic existence, a mode of life which is as necessary as it is everyday (*alltäglich*). The system about which we have been speaking is neither ruled by nor the creature of any one man or group of men. Its most conspicuous attribute is that it is self-organizing and self-generating, comparable for modern man to the terrible power of nature and no less frightening or intimidating. Taken in and for itself it is the sphere of the impersonal, where human choice and human freedom count for very little. The danger is that it be taken as the most fundamental reality for man in terms of which he must define himself as a person. To the extent that he accepts his participation in that manner, he has surrendered all possibility of an authentic personal existence.

If the system itself is not to be overturned, shall the individual simply turn a double somersault, as Kierkegaard sometimes appears to suggest, and turn inward? Is the sphere of his freedom the space of his privacy, the slight room for maneuvering as he plays his role within the system? Are the two alternatives revolution and subjective retreat, or, as some have thought, Marxism and existentialism?

These are, indeed, the two fundamental alternatives, namely, to modify the system in relation to society as a whole or in relation to the individual member of society. We should hasten to note, however, that these are not incompatible alternatives. Moreover, both the Marxist and the existentialist response presuppose and make use of human transcendence. Marx's moral passion and basic humanistic concern are evident throughout his writings. More than any other factor they motivated his research. One of the most important results of Marx's work was the discovery that the organization of the means of production constitutes a system with implications for every aspect of human endeavor. This humanistic concern has become even more prominent in neo-Marxist writings. We have learned from Marx how our participation in the systematic organization of production and consumption affects the mode of our everyday existence. As we find ourselves in the everyday world our values are thus initially *constituted* by the prevailing system. To know

this, however, is the first step toward the recovery of our freedom. Understanding is itself a mode of transcendence, and
moral concern is an even stronger expression of human freedom. We can hope to humanize the system only if we have an
exact understanding of the way it operates. Only when we recognize that the economy is not to be regarded as a morally developed teleological system are we in a realistic position to decide
how it should be controlled. The real and pressing moral and
political problems at issue here concern the relationship between
man and the system. That we are free to take enlightened and
concerted action on this front can hardly be in doubt. Revolutionary activity remains a defensible alternative provided that it
is not a mere abstract negation shading off into nihilism.

If Marxists have tended to address themselves to the system
as a whole as it relates to man, existentialists have concentrated
on the relation of the individual to the world in which he lives.
No matter what large-scale revolutionary change takes place,
revolution cannot be an end in itself or fail to issue in a reorder-
ing of the economic system. The individual is thus faced at every
moment with the question of how he is to relate to any systematic and objective order. Since to opt out is in effect to attempt to
exist independently of the objective world and, hence, altogether
unrealistic, his only alternative is to choose how he is to participate and, within limits, what his activity is to mean. It is here, I
believe, that Camus's notion of "revolt" is particularly apt. To
exist in perpetual personal revolt in that sense is essentially to
refuse to compromise. It is, in other words, to refuse categorically to allow one's personal values to be determined by the
system of monetary value. To recommend such a stance is but to
urge that the individual recover and assert his personal freedom
to know and appraise his own real needs, the value of his effort,
and the meaning of objects and persons. Although he need not
reject the objective order by attempting to dispense with monetary value, he can stubbornly refuse ever to construe it as a
measure of true worth. Only in that way can he free himself
from the dominance of what must otherwise be an overwhelming and dehumanizing power. The absurd for Camus is the
measure of human transcendence. Only by constantly reminding
himself of the intrinsic incompatibility of the values determined
by the monetary system and his own human personal values can
the individual preserve the necessary space for his freedom.

Man's authentic existence must be, therefore, a modification of the inauthentic—that is, of his objective existence as a participant in the prevailing order. His hope lies in his steadfast refusal to be seduced.

Throughout this essay I have contrasted monetary value with real or human value. I have not meant to suggest that we can expect to dispense with monetary value or a system of monetary exchange. The problem for contemporary man is, I believe, to free himself sufficiently from the tyrannical dominance of monetary value to be able to judge in his own terms what things are worth to him as an individual with his own needs and purposes. To do this, he must programmatically turn aside from the prima facie monetary value of his own needs, his labor, and the goods he confronts and look toward that dimension of himself and his world which stands in contrast to the entire domain of monetary value. He must ask such simple questions as: Do I really care that my clothes should be so white? Do I really wish to look so pretty? What do I really care about, and what will in fact and not simply in representation answer to that concern? Only by insisting on asking such questions can he avoid having all of his values decided for him. And only thus can he have his own world.

11 / Individualisms

W. L. McBride

PHENOMENOLOGISTS and various philosophers of human existence have often been criticized for their alleged "individualism," which the critics take to be an intellectual (and, ultimately, a social) crime. Marxists, who frequently preface the abstract noun with the adjective "bourgeois" in applying the individualist label to opponents, have been among the most consistent critics of existential philosophies on this point.[1] In France, the current fad of structuralism brings to the surface somewhat similar charges against a majority of that country's most eminent twentieth-century thinkers, though I am convinced that the structuralist challenge to "individualism" must remain quite different in its inspiration from the Marxist one, despite attempts to bring them together. The widespread reaction to philosophical emphasis on the human individual has become extremely thoroughgoing in some quarters. If an Adam Schaff, for example, can still uphold a Marxist "philosophy of man" against what he considers the excessive individualism of existentialist-inspired humanisms,[2] an Althusser puts radically into question the value of humanism as such.

1. "This central point around which accumulate, as around an axis, all the other differences of opinion between existentialism and Marxism is the manner of approaching the conception of the individual, central problem of every existentialist tendency" (Adam Schaff, "Sur le marxisme et l'existentialisme," *Les Temps modernes*, No. 173–74 [August–September, 1960], p. 400 [author's translation]).

2. Adam Schaff, *A Philosophy of Man* (New York: Monthly Review Press, 1963).

John Wild, whom we are celebrating in this volume, certainly appears to qualify as an outstanding proponent of the philosophical emphasis in question. On page after page of his writings, the themes of human freedom and individual integrity, of opposition to purely impersonal, objective treatments of the phenomenon of man, recur. But John Wild is also the philosopher who has written, among other things, *Plato's Modern Enemies and the Theory of Natural Law* and *Human Freedom and Social Order*. He is therefore not at all oblivious, as perhaps Søren Kierkegaard or even to some extent Albert Camus might legitimately be charged with having been, to the claims and the positive importance of the *group* with respect to the life of the individual. If the individual ought ultimately to be made the focus of the philosopher's attention, this is not equivalent to making the false contention, as Wild shows, that the individual is *prior* to the group either ontologically or historically.[3] Anthropological studies prove, as he points out, that primitive societies lacked the modern conception of individuality.[4] The emphasis on the individual, then, is of rather recent origin. But the massive, ineluctable reality of the group is at least as intrusive in our times as in any past era, and in some respects the power of one type of group, the state, has clearly become more awesome than ever. Moreover, the type of existence that characterizes most groups seems to be of a very different order—among other things, to be inherently more conservative, more self-perpetuating—from that of the contemporary man who is conscious of some of the possibilities of human freedom.[5] These are some of the basic themes with which John Wild has dealt in his writings, and the mere listing of them already belies the contention that anyone who adopts his philosophical standpoint has *ipso facto*

3. John Wild, *Existence and the World of Freedom* (Englewood Cliffs, N.J.: Prentice-Hall, 1963), pp. 190–91.

4. It is interesting to reflect on the fact that the greatest popularizer of structuralism, himself an outstanding anthropologist, very consciously denies to the study of history any place of privilege in comparison with other disciplines, such as his own, and regards "historicity" as a concept that often serves as "the final refuge of a transcendental humanism." See Claude Lévi-Strauss, *La Pensée sauvage* (Paris: Plon, 1962), pp. 347, 338 ff. (author's translation). The distance between his position and that of most existence-oriented thinkers, such as Wild, is quite considerable.

5. John Wild, *Human Freedom and Social Order* (Durham, N.C.: Duke University Press, 1959), pp. 185–217.

chosen to disregard the problems of social existence and the limitations of the individual and of individualism.

But is it not true that individualism is, and perhaps of right ought to be, a declining phenomenon and a losing cause today? Should we not subscribe to the essential, though rather vague, truth of those vast historical generalizations which regard the growth of individualism and subjectivity in the West as having been linked first with a special type of philosophizing that sprang up in Greece, then with the Christian emphasis on the individual soul, and later and most paradigmatically with the peculiar structures of the capitalist economic system? If we follow this line of thinking to its allegedly tragic denouement in our own day, must we not admit that the processes of self-destruction have reached advanced stages in all three domains—Western philosophy (in which the violent criticism of its past has attained a point of apparent apogee), Christianity (where an unprecedented crisis of both practice and doctrine has engulfed even the once stable institution of Roman Catholicism), and capitalism (which is clearly under severe attack even from within the memberships of its most successful national systems)? As for individualism itself, if all its theoretical and institutional props are decaying, and if the generous but self-effacing call for increased social commitment, heard on all sides, is to be taken as a rejection of it, must it not begin to be treated as the relic of a very long but now completed epoch? These are most serious questions, even though they elude treatment with the precision, rigor, and neatness that many philosophers would like to impose upon their world. Our cultural life-world is not, alas, of this sort.

In refutation of the thesis about the decline of individualism that I have just been suggesting, however, one can enumerate a number of salient contemporary phenomena that point in a rather different direction. Though motivations are always complex and each particular situation can only be fully evaluated within its own context, it seems unquestionable that one of the themes most frequently articulated by student and faculty protesters throughout the contemporary Western world is their opposition to the treatment of themselves and/or others as things or as ciphers. The impersonality and vastness of modern institutions—corporations, universities, war machines, etc.—

have at last called forth a greater response, one more frightening to the proponents of cipher civilization, than what prevailed only a decade ago, let us say. It is in the name of "the individual"—that is, of a conception of each human being as having a unique, worthwhile set of goals, "his own thing," which is to be respected, and which cannot be captured even by the once-important but too abstract and legalistic notion of "rights"—that this response has most forcefully been made.

The ambiguity that I have just sketched concerning the place to be attributed to "individualism," both descriptively and as a norm, in a survey of contemporary cultural patterns and especially of social movements that are considered "progressive" or future-oriented can perhaps be focused more sharply if we briefly consider some of the principal currents in contemporary social theory that claim to draw some inspiration from Marx. There are now many such currents, of course, but let me outline the typologies of two of them, the directions of which seem, on many issues, to be very nearly opposite. Neither type should be attributed, in its purity, to any single writer or group. The first type of Marxism is humanistic: it insists very strongly that Marx's ultimate vision is, after all, that of a society in which, as a result of the overcoming of scarcity through a combination of technological progress and the elimination of the wasteful utilization of resources characteristic of past and present social systems, all individuals will at last be liberated from institutional and even psychological restraints in order to work in a manner most in keeping with their own possibilities. In light of this vision, it is a scandal if movements that have seized political power in the name of Marxism do not make every possible effort to bring about such a state of affairs, even though, since this is still a transitional period, total success cannot as yet be expected. This Marxism finds congenial intellectual company in much of existentialist thought, as the examples of Sartre, Petrovic, and Kolakowski illustrate in diverse ways, and it regards students protesting against outmoded institutions in France and in favor of their reform government against Russian invaders in Czechoslovakia as being equally laudable. Recently, the writings of Herbert Marcuse have seemed to many to epitomize this kind of Marxism, though his essay on "Repressive Toleration" [6] makes

6. Robert Paul Wolff, Barrington Moore, Jr., and Herbert Marcuse, *A Critique of Pure Tolerance* (Boston: Beacon Press, 1965), pp. 81–117.

it very clear, if there had ever been a doubt, that his theory is not all velvet glove, and though I suspect that a period of sharp criticism of it even by former defenders is at present beginning. Surely, the type of Marxism that I have just outlined glorifies the individual as the ultimate focal point of values.

The second type can be called, for want of a better label, antihumanistic. It insists on the criminality of individualism in a century in which the vast majority of the world's masses, particularly in the former colonies, still live in subhuman conditions. It does not expect the alleviation of these conditions to be magical or to come about very soon, and so it stresses the theme of permanent revolution for the foreseeable future in order to destroy all the vestiges of privilege of a capitalist system that even now, though it has begun to be on the defensive, overwhelmingly dominates the world's economic resources for the benefit of a relatively insignificant percentage of its population. This struggle, it is pointed out, requires great discipline, both theoretical and practical. Even those theoretical enterprises that might be shown, in some abstract way, to be valid because unexceptionable from a scientific point of view may frequently have to be disallowed as frivolous, idiosyncratic distractions from the principal (revolutionary) work of our era, both the validity and the far greater importance of which are beyond any reasonable doubt. Most of the French student leaders of May 1968 are to be condemned rather than congratulated, according to this type of Marxism, since they constantly emphasized their own demands with very little regard, until it was too late, for the legitimate needs of the masses of French workers. The Czechoslovakian affair is somewhat more complicated. Though the theoretical inadequacies and bourgeois, individualistic tendencies of many of the Czech students and their government leaders were blatant, some holders of this version of Marxism may nevertheless approve of their actions because of the nature of the enemy against which they were directed, namely, the homeland of state monopoly capitalism, the U.S.S.R., whose new consumer-goods orientation gives further proof of its betrayal of revolutionary principles in favor of its own form of humanism and individualism. "Antihumanistic" Marxists may be rigid and dogmatic, but they are not necessarily stupid. Louis Althusser, for example, has provided brilliant defenses of *some* of the themes that I have suggested in this second typology; against him, the middle-of-the-road, mediative efforts of the former official French Communist Party theoretician, Roger Garaudy, display an obvious theoretical inferiority.

And so contemporary Marxist discussions and divisions bring into focus, in a particularly clear and comprehensible fashion, some of the dilemmas posed by the espousal of individualism, or at least the emphasis on the human individual, in our world.[7] The level of polemics has been high, that of clarity not always so. In particular, the concept of individualism itself has figured more frequently in slogans than in rational arguments.[8] In consequence, having indicated the importance of the role assigned to the individual in any investigation of the life-world, as well as some of the specific forms in which ambiguities concerning that role are receiving concrete expression today, I now propose to make some effort at clarification by proposing and distinguishing three possible meanings of individualism. These are: (1) individualism as a descriptive and normative philosophical *theory*, exemplified both in the writings of John Locke and in the watered-down Lockeanisms that pervaded "genteel" opinion in the society, for example, in which Karl Marx lived; (2) individualism as a particular *method*, namely, the device of starting one's phenomenological descriptions with the isolated individual; and (3) individualism as a *leitmotif* in formulating judgments concerning *importance*—most generally, the judgment that the individual is of primary importance for philosophy and social theory. The elaboration of these three meanings of individualism will occupy the middle portion of this essay, with the third receiving the greatest amount of attention. Needless to say, the three meanings are not intended to be exhaustive. In the concluding section, I shall outline certain errors that should be avoided once the decision to emphasize the individual has been taken.

7. Here in the United States, debates within the Students for a Democratic Society between proponents of the participatory democratic ideal favored by many of its founders and proponents of the militant, antihumanistic Progressive Labor Party line mirror many of the same divisions.

8. See, in this regard, John Wild's interesting discussion, "What Is an *Existential* Argument?" in *Existence and the World of Freedom*, pp. 203–6.

II

IT IS AGAINST INDIVIDUALISM as a philosophical theory about the nature and goals of man—a systematic world-view that pretends to be both descriptive and normative—that most of the strongest nineteenth- and twentieth-century reactions have in fact been directed. When *this* sense of individualism is in question, it soon becomes clear that the philosophy of John Wild, like that of most other major existentially- and phenomenologically-oriented thinkers, permits very little sympathy indeed for "individualism." I shall try very briefly to spell out some of the systematic assumptions of the ideology (for so it must be regarded) in question, and I shall, at the same time, give some indication as to why it has rightly fallen from favor in so many intellectual milieus today.

Probably the most important historical source for individualism as an ideology is, as is widely recognized, seventeenth-century English political theory. That was the century of Hobbes, of Locke, and of the rise of the market economy. In a work of scholarly interpretation that has already become almost a classic, C. B. Macpherson has shown some of the common assumptions about man and society that seem to underlie not only Hobbes's conservatism and Locke's liberalism, but even the more genuinely democratic, quasi-popularist thinking of the Levellers.[9] The theme upon which Macpherson focuses is the conception, never made fully explicit by any of the writers in question, of individuality, personality, as being essentially a type of *property*. If this way of defining man was indeed as fundamental to the "possessive individualists" as Macpherson claims, then it is no surprise that the famous states of nature imagined by Hobbes and Locke bear remarkable structural resemblances, upon close analysis, to the market or capitalist society that was beginning to emerge during their lifetimes: their ontologies of the individual predetermined their social models. And these biased social models then served the cause of seeming to justify certain social and political forms (in Locke's case, moderately

9. *The Political Theory of Possessive Individualism: Hobbes to Locke* (Oxford: Clarendon Press, 1962).

"progressive" forms for their time) that their authors favored; that is why they can be called "ideological."

There are many words and phrases that have been employed to capture the essential characteristics of the ontological type of individualism, the roots of which I have just been recalling. Perhaps none is more familiar or more satisfactory than the epithet "atomistic." The analytically disjointed world of Hobbes is something of a paradigm of this approach: he treats even his various "endeavours" inwards and outwards,[10] to say nothing of human individuals in the state of nature, as if they were nearly discrete quanta. And although it is true that this ontological model can be contrasted, on the level of the group, with the more traditional organic conception that is evident in the frontispiece of *Leviathan* and in several important passages of the book, it is just *because* Hobbes's world-view is fundamentally so atomistic that he feels constrained to grant the Leviathan so much power to keep the fragments together.[11] Locke's human atoms are presented as if they were more friendly than those of Hobbes, but there is little firm basis within the later writer's ontology itself to justify the mood of greater optimism. The self-sufficiency and discreteness which Locke's presocietal individuals are supposed to have,[12] and which constitute the core of liberal individualism as an ontological theory, are ascribed on the strength of what appears to be one of the most sustained attacks of wishful thinking to be found in the writings of any major philosopher. Who but Locke, for instance, would speak with apparent insouciance of "the turfs my [i.e., his] servant has cut" in a chapter in which he is supposedly describing the rugged presocial individual in the early stages of property creation? [13]

It is wishful thinking of a rather less innocent sort that leads to the second aspect of the philosophical theory of individualism

10. Thomas Hobbes, *Leviathan,* ed. Michael Oakeshott (Oxford: Blackwell, 1960), Pt. I, Chap. 6.

11. Cf. two interesting references to Hobbes by John Wild, one in *Existence and the World of Freedom,* Chap. 10, "The Individual and the Group," *passim,* the other in *Plato's Modern Enemies and the Theory of Natural Law* (Chicago: University of Chicago Press, 1953), pp. 123–27.

12. "If man in the state of nature be so free, . . . if he be absolute lord of his own person and possessions, equal to the greatest, and subject to nobody, why will he part with his freedom, his empire . . . ?" (John Locke, *Second Treatise of Civil Government* [New York: Appleton-Century-Crofts, 1937], Chap. 9, p. 82).

13. *Ibid.,* Chap. 5, p. 20.

that I have been discussing, namely, individualism as a social norm. Central to this conception is the sanctioning of unlimited self-aggrandizement on the part of "the" (in reality, the *favored*) individual, the acquisition *à l'infini* of power or wealth or some other more or less quantifiable attribute. On this point, Locke seems to have been somewhat more aware of what he was doing. In his theory of property, which is so crucial to his entire view, he treats the introduction of money as the historical turning point, after which no more moral restraints upon accumulation need be thought to exist. But neither Locke nor those numerous educated people who took his principles as their own during the century or two after his death were unaware of the fact that both natural and monetary resources remained relatively scarce, and that therefore the self-aggrandizement of a proportionate few could only occur at the cost of drastically depriving the many others who lived in the same world. No serious philosopher could, of course, formally and completely identify the deprived with the depraved, but *traces* of this underlying assumption are to be found in the thinking of more than one philosophical individualist of the sort that I have been describing, to say nothing of the prevalence of this attitude among those who had no need of explicitly declaring it in published form. It is not possible, it seems to me, to salvage this normative individualism by contending that its connection with defenses of gross inequalities and injustices in property distribution was a historical accident, and that, let us say, the traditional liberal theory of freedom is completely separable from accompanying theories about ownership; rather, the terminal norms—in other words, the conceptions of the best human possibilities—remain tainted by the original assumption that a man *is*, in essence, a kind of self-owning property, and more adequate views of freedom and ethics in general are rightly to be regarded as requiring a different ontological basis.

Most of what I have just stated is well known, but it has been important to reconsider quickly the descriptive and normative aspects of traditional philosophical individualism here in order to see how far removed it is from the "individualism" (if the label should not ultimately prove too misleading) for which many philosophies of existence are noted. The falsification of the *descriptive* strands of the outmoded theory is being carried out from many different points of view. The phenomenologist, for example, insists on the intersubjective element in all human experience that is suggested by the "world" part of the expression "life-world," while the psychologist may speak of the impossibility of understanding the individual without reference to his environment. Rejection of *normative* individualism of the kind that I have treated comes with a deeper awareness of the more extended possible meanings and concrete expressions even of many of the norms that the individualist theorists themselves espoused—values such as equality, freedom, and self-government. In the strongholds of Western capitalism, there are those who still accept some version of this theory, and perhaps there may yet occur temporary revivals of it in even more blatant forms in some of those parts of the globe where drastic economic deprivation has been the rule until now. But the future does not lie with this ghost from the past.

III

VERY DIFFERENT from individualism as an ontology, though not logically incompatible with it, is the use of the individual person as the methodological starting point of one's philosophy or other theory. Most frequently identified with Descartes [14] among earlier historical figures, this methodological choice is also, though in a much modified version, the one made by Husserl and many of his followers. The choice has seldom been an arbitrary one, of course. Descartes, for example, thought of the *cogito* as providing the sole Archimedean point of absolute certitude from which the removal of all essential doubts could eventually be effected. Similar motivations were operative in Husserl's case, though it goes without saying that his conception of the *cogito* is very different (since it is supposed to include the *cogitata*) and that he is far from intending to make any presup-

14. Though F. A. Hayek, in *Individualism: True and False* (Dublin: Hodges, Figgis; Oxford: Blackwell, 1946), contrasts the "true, anti-rationalistic" individualism of Locke, Mandeville, and others with a false, rationalistic individualism that he traces to Descartes. It should also be noted that "methodological individualism" has become a current expression in some contemporary discussions in the philosophy of the social sciences. Though it is used in this context to refer to a very different, more limited group of thinkers, its basic meaning has much in common with that of the concept that I am about to explore.

positions about the nature, or even the individuality, of the I that thinks. Nevertheless, Husserl's original choice can in some important sense be called "individualistic." [15] That there is a choice but not necessarily an ontological commitment involved in starting one's philosophy with the individual, and that there are *dangers* (which are not the same as errors) inherent in such a choice, are the two principal points that I wish to note concerning this second type of individualism.

Husserl's original choice, like the choices of the rest of us, took place in a historical and cultural context not of his creation. There were, for example, the proponents of a false theory about mathematical entities, psychologism, with whom it seemed important to him at the time, as soon as he came to realize the theory's falsity, to do battle. Thus, the early Husserlian focus on the contents of subjective consciousness, rather than, let us say, on the social, cultural, and historical questions that preoccupied him to a greater extent toward the end of his life, was a freely chosen response on his part; yet, at the same time, as a *response*, it was determined in a negative way by the movement to which he was opposed. Of course, Husserl made a considerable effort to ensure that the personalistic connotations often associated with the mention of consciousness in ordinary discourse would be set aside by his readers as they pursued the investigation of the *eidē* with him. But those connotations, with all their individualism, remained ineradicably associated with the very language that Husserl, despite his often painful circumlocutions, was still forced to use. This is simply one way of describing the ultimate failure of the strict conception of the *epochē*, the ideal of pure presuppositionlessness.

Whether and to what extent ontological commitments concerning the ego were made in some of Husserl's later writings (a controversy in which I do not wish to become involved here), it can safely be said that there were no such commitments—certainly none bearing directly on any possible theory of individualism as descriptive of the nature of man—implied in his original use of Brentano's conception of intentionality. There was, as I have said, simply a methodological choice of starting point, a starting point from which, it was hoped, exploration could even-

15. Husserl himself deals at length with the limitations of Locke's "egology" in Part II of his *Erste Philosophie, Husserliana* VII (The Hague: Martinus Nijhoff, 1956), pp. 78–140.

tually be made of the entire range of real and possible "intentions." Many of Husserl's disciples began, quite naturally, by using the same starting point, but divergences of approach became apparent very early in the history of the movement that he initiated. Such divergence has been, I think, a welcome development, and it is not opposed to that part of Husserl's original inspiration (itself so incompatible, in some respects, with his onetime view of philosophy as a unitary, rigorous science) to the effect that philosophers could function much more effectively if they liberated themselves from the strait jackets of a priori systems. If one were (with tongue in cheek) to do a content analysis comparison of one of Husserl's early writings with those of some recent writers who have been influenced by him, I suspect that the number of instances of the word "consciousness" would be found to have declined considerably in the latter group. This would coimply, I would argue, a decline in the "methodological individualism" to which I have been pointing. John Wild, for instance, lays considerably more stress on the *Lebenswelt,* the Husserlian term that very appropriately serves as the focal point of this volume; the extent to which the very use of this term points away from methodological individualism and toward a differently conceived starting point for philosophical reflection (even in Husserl's own, later *Krisis,* where it comes fully into its own) hardly needs to be mentioned. And one of John Wild's former students, Wilfrid Desan, has developed quite explicitly, though in a fashion that is still somewhat more suggestive than definitive, the possibility of a nonindividualistic starting point for a phenomenologically inspired philosophy. Desan's *The Planetary Man* (a book better known in its recent French translation than in its original American version) begins with the assertion that it is possible "to take the viewpoint of the totum," [16] rather than of the individual subject, in working toward a tentative and undogmatic understanding of our world. Though Desan's book runs the obvious risk, which he himself clearly recognizes and struggles to avoid, of postulating a collective consciousness, the very existence of his enterprise is one more strong contemporary testimonial to the fact that there is nothing apodictic about the methodological choice of the individual as the starting point for one's philosophy.

16. *The Planetary Man,* Vol. I: *A Noetic Prelude to a United World* (Washington, D.C.: Georgetown University Press, 1969), p. 5.

If there are serious dangers to be avoided in the procedure of beginning with a more intersubjective than solipsistic perspective on the life-world, it is also true that the dangers encountered in adhering to the latter point of departure, especially if one proposes to go on from there to construct an ontology, are at least equally grave. On this, my final point concerning individualism as a *method*, the example of Sartre's philosophical development is particularly instructive. Sartre began the productive part of his academic career as a disciple of Husserl's, wrestling with problems of philosophical psychology, and the culmination of all his early researches, *Being and Nothingness*, raises a highly individualistic *pour-soi* to a degree of autonomy seldom before achieved in the history of philosophy. Of course, Sartre's first ontology is not nearly so uncompromisingly individualistic as many of his commentators would have us believe, and at any rate it is far different in its foundations, its description, and its ethical implications from the individualism of Locke and other liberals. Sartre now writes frequently in Marxist terms, and his *Critique de la raison dialectique*, while it contains no explicit renunciation of the earlier philosophy, asks a radically different set of questions and makes no pretense of adhering to the Husserlian methodology. Even the *Critique*, however, begins its investigations with the isolated individual, who is said to embody dialectical reason at its most incomplete or abstract, and so critics of many persuasions [17] continue to ask whether Sartre has really ever escaped from the shadow of Descartes. That he desperately wished to do so is clear, for page after page of his political essays expresses solidarity with the wretched of the earth and a revulsion toward "bourgeois" individualism. Surely, if it is still possible to misconstrue Sartre as being an individualist in anything resembling the ontological sense that I outlined earlier, it must be because he has never fully managed to overcome the initial disadvantages, for a social philosopher with his present concerns, of *methodological* individualism.

When Adam Schaff rejects Sartre's claim to be a Marxist on the ground that the French philosopher fails to take the collective as his starting point and that this is the only possible Marxist starting point, his meaning is somewhat ambiguous, but he may well be primarily criticizing the methodological individual-

17. Among these, one may count, for example, both Schaff and Desan.

ism of which I have been speaking. If that is the case, then this does not seem to me to point to a crucial difference in *theoretical* propositions (descriptions, generalizations, etc.) between the two philosophies in question. The historical instances to which I have alluded may suggest that the use of the individual as a methodological starting point makes it somewhat difficult for the philosopher later to develop an adequate theory about collectives, but these examples do not and cannot point to any fundamental incompatibility between methodological individualism and a social philosophy that would eschew ontological individualism. Clearly, much more discussion than I can undertake here is needed concerning the possible effects of the simple original choice of where in the world to begin philosophizing, or where to begin one's phenomenological descriptions, on the eventual outcome of one's philosophy; clearly, too, alternatives to Husserl's early "solipsistic" point of departure are deservedly achieving greater attention and popularity today among philosophers interested in exploring the life-world.

IV

A THIRD POSSIBLE MEANING of individualism, a version that I would like to defend, has to do with a crucial kind of normative judgment that must constantly be made by theorists of all sorts, especially those who deal with social phenomena, namely, the judgment concerning relative *importance*. Here, "individualism" is a characterization of an author's philosophy (or other type of theory) with respect to the phenomena that he has chosen to emphasize in his writings; an individualist in this sense, of course, would simply be a theorist whose "ultimate concern," or one of whose ultimate concerns, was the human individual. This may at first sound like a rather trivial and obvious point, but I do not think it is. Rather, the importance of basic judgments about importance has been too much neglected in philosophy and in the social sciences.[18]

The question of "emphasis," it should immediately be

18. Alfred North Whitehead once wrote an interesting, brief essay on the subject. See *Modes of Thought* (New York: Macmillan, 1957), Chap. I.

pointed out, is not measurable in a purely quantitative way. When I wrote above, somewhat facetiously, about doing a content analysis on some works of Husserl and of later phenomenologists with respect to the word "consciousness," [19] it was with a full realization of the limitations of such a procedure. A writer could not, to use a simple example, be adjudged an individualist in my third sense of the term just because the word "individual" occurred frequently in his writings, nor could he be disregarded just because it occurred rarely. I wish, in this section of the present essay, first to consider the general logical force of any arguments for or against this type of individualism, then to consider specific arguments against it, and finally to consider reasons, which to me are more compelling, in its favor.

A philosopher who separates the way of truth from the way of appearance or opinion may still, as Parmenides is said to have done, write fascinatingly about the latter; the reason is, of course, that the appearances have a legitimate truth of their own. The contemporary philosopher who argues that the "way of truth" is to be sought in the direction of discovering some ultimate, impersonal, natural scientific entity, and who devotes the bulk of his professional attention to exploring the logic of this vaunted search, may be faulted in some details of his logic and may be challenged concerning the metaphysics of his fundamental assumption, but it would be completely inappropriate to attempt to "disprove the validity" of his enterprise as such. (There may be some question within the philosophy of science itself about the meaningfulness of speaking of absolutely ultimate entities, but this would not necessarily denigrate from the value of our philosopher's original quest, either, for a clearly negative finding might also be worthwhile.) The same individual may perhaps envisage a future time at which, under the impact of a drastic language reform, terms referring to natural scientific entities would constitute an increasingly large proportion of ev-

19. A recent employment of a somewhat different content analysis technique was presented in a paper read by Alastair McKinnon at the December, 1968, meetings of the American Philosophical Association, Eastern Division. Excerpts from several of Søren Kierkegaard's pseudonymous works were compared by computer with passages from works whose authorship Kierkegaard acknowledged, in order to establish a hierarchy of resemblance and difference among the pseudonymous works. As the chairman of the symposium pointed out, Kierkegaard would have found this procedure most interesting.

eryone's vocabulary, whereas the language of today's life-world, particularly those parts of it (questions about freedom, value, and so on) that are of most concern to philosophical individualists of my third type, would become increasingly rare; he may even advocate such an evolution. In this case, the philosopher's suggestion can be *disproved* only if it can be shown that any such development is *totally* impossible. This, I think, would be extremely difficult to show. After all, there have been certain limited areas of academic discourse, notably in the social sciences, that have recently undergone developments of just this type, in which references to allegedly scientific or quasi-scientific entities have been systematically substituted for references to the more individual-oriented, value-colored phenomena of the social life-world itself. The results, of course, have frequently been unsuccessful and sometimes even disastrous, for they have skewed the originally desired relationship between the social scientific investigation in question and the phenomena themselves, often at the price either of irrelevance or of ideological rigidity. (It should be recalled, for example, that some of the earliest protests at Nanterre in April 1968 centered around sociology students' objections to the so-called American sociology for reasons of this kind.) But this judgment of failure is precisely my point. It is not that the substitution of a quasi-scientific language for language more directly related to the life-world has been shown to be entirely impossible, for indeed such substitution has been effected within limited domains and has been followed by some persons working within those domains for at least some limited periods of time; but it is rather that the enterprise itself, at least when considered as a general program for the intelluctual community and the world at large, can be shown to have extremely serious disvalues. In other words, the negative judgment concerning the proposed abandonment of the world of "appearances" is primarily not a judgment of factual truth or (in this case) falsehood, but it is rather, at base, itself a value judgment.

Importance is, as I have said, a central and much-neglected value in the formation of such a judgment. There are some thinkers, such as John Wild, who, in contrast with the attitude adopted by the imaginary philosopher described above, consider the human individual, as he exists in ordinary life with his world of projects, relationships with others, past history, and so on, to be the phenomenon of truly central importance for philosophical inquiry. It goes without saying that this judgment does not entail the denial of the possibility of conceiving of *anthropos erectus* as a complex conglomerate of natural scientific entities; indeed, a valid description of this type is certainly conceivable. But which of these two possible kinds of descriptions (the two worlds in John Wild's "The War of the Worlds" [20]) is more important? Or, if this way of phrasing the question seems too vague to permit the perfectly certain answer that philosophers love to seek, which kind of phenomena is it more important for the philosopher today, or for me personally, to emphasize? Annoyingly enough, no matter how hard we try to narrow the question, there is no clear-cut, logical proof that one or the other answer is "correct." I may be able to resolve the question (through action) in my own case, of course, but proof involves generality and objectivity. And a question of this kind is simply not susceptible, it must be concluded, to any such proof.

To admit the impossibility of absolute proof, however, is not identical with saying that no good reasons can be given for one or the other choice. This point applies to the general choice between emphasizing the life-world and emphasizing the natural scientific world in one's philosophizing, and it applies equally well to the choice between individualism and collectivism as judgments concerning importance. In fact, as we shall see, there is a close link between these two sets of choices. Some good reasons can be given for placing priority of emphasis on the collective or the group, and I shall first consider two of these. After that, I shall point to two excellent, rather familiar reasons for insisting on the priority of the individual. The choice between these sets of arguments will not be one, I repeat, that can be made in terms of universal validity, but this fact should not be as disturbing as some philosophers have found it.

Two of the most compelling arguments in favor of laying greater stress on the group than on the individual in contemporary philosophical reflection are what we may call the argument from the need for radical reform and the argument from quantifiability. The first returns us to the typology of "antihumanistic" Marxism that I presented near the beginning of this essay, for it is in such milieus that this argument is presented with the greatest passion and cogency. Emphasis on the individual, so the

20. In *Existence and the World of Freedom*, pp. 80–97.

argument goes, is a luxury that we cannot afford today, if we are to bring about the needed world revolution. When one thinks in terms, quite literally, of hundreds of millions of individuals who are in a condition of overwhelming economic, cultural, and almost every other conceivable kind of inferiority in relation to a much smaller number of privileged persons who live primarily in the technologically developed countries of the world, then the contemplation of the problems of "the individual" would seem to constitute a diversion, one with clearly ideological motivations. Individualism, even if it is only an individualism of philosophical emphasis and not of ontology or methodology, is said to slow down the progress of social change and to perpetuate the belief of the bourgeois intellectuals that they, along with other members of their class, are the only really *important* individuals. Even Ernst Bloch, who is by no means considered antihumanistic among neo-Marxist thinkers, has written an extended argument along somewhat parallel lines against a particular manifestation of this sort of individualism, Freudian psychoanalysis.[21]

In reply to these charges, the thinker who has chosen to concentrate his attention on the individual can give a number of different answers, many of them at least as compelling as the criticisms. He may say, for example, that he is looking toward a different future at least as much as is the antihumanist radical, but that he is perhaps more concerned than the latter with the *kind* of future that those who are at present underprivileged will experience. If his type of philosophical emphasis—if, indeed, intellectual endeavor itself—is at the present time a luxury that is practically unavailable to the underprivileged, he wishes at least to use his position of privilege to build up models that will aid in their deeper understanding of their own individualities when a more equitable world society comes into existence. (There is no way of denying, apropos of this answer, that Marx's own vision of the future "reign of freedom," elaborated most explicitly but not, I think, exclusively in his early manuscripts, is a highly individualistic one.) The individualist may further express his concern lest his opponent fall victim to the force of habit: if he now neglects completely the phenomena of individuality in favor of mass-oriented activities, he or his successors may be unable or unwilling to reorient their thinking when

21. *Das Prinzip Hoffnung* (Frankfurt a.M.: Suhrkamp, 1959), Chap. 13, esp. pp. 71–74.

conditions more conducive to individualism come about, and so the opportunity for making the best use of these conditions may be lost. (A process somewhat resembling this seems to be taking place in those countries of Eastern Europe that are at present undergoing a partial re-Stalinization.[22]) The philosophical emphasis on the problems of the individual *can*, of course, serve as ideological self-gratification, but it need not do so, according to its defenders. Furthermore, adherence to such an emphasis need not entail total neglect of the peculiar structures of groups, such as classes; rather, the individualist of the third type contends, as we shall see, that groups can be best understood through a deeper analysis of certain characteristics of human individuals. For example, psychoanalytically-oriented therapist-researchers, through the painstaking application of their techniques to a number of individual poor people, can incidentally make a major contribution to the understanding of poverty as a class phenomenon by bringing to public attention the high incidence of mental illness among the very poor.

The second argument that I shall mention against individualism as a choice of philosophic emphasis is what I have called the argument from quantifiability, and it is directly related to the gap between the "two worlds" of which John Wild has spoken. It is, simply, that facts and statistics about aggregates are much easier to obtain, neater and clearer to compile, and in some ways more impressive than the tentative, ambiguous phenomena that must be dealt with when one discusses individuals. There is a sense of the word "importance" that is quantitative, referring to numerical magnitude. In this sense, the collective obviously is more "important" than the individual. For instance, a political opinion poll that shows, let us say, 85 per cent of the American public to be rather hawkish in its views about a particular war at a particular time is thought by many to be tremendously significant, even if a similar poll conducted six months later should show a reversal of the percentages. By comparison, a phenomenological analysis of various types of reactions to opinion polls, pointing up the ambivalences in individuals' attitudes toward both poll-takers and governments and the varied effects on them of learning, through published polls, what "everyone else" is thinking, might seem considerably less respectable, from a "sci-

22. The writings of Leszek Kolakowski frequently refer to this paradoxical dynamic.

entific" point of view, and at any rate far less conclusive. And far less conclusive it would, indeed, be. One of the fundamental demands of the scientific attitude is for ever vaster generalization, and so, in approaching the problems of society, the collectivity appears to be a far more promising domain than the individual for scientific activity. When one speaks of the "life-world," one must be aware of the fact that this world is at least a little bit different for each individual, and this is very discouraging to the lover of quick and easy quantification. Of course, the two types of approach are not totally incompatible; they can be combined, and some very interesting contributions to knowledge result from such combinations as that illustrated by the psychoanalytic research mentioned above. But the temptation to revel in the quantitative and general is so great among certain social scientists today that an emphasis on problems of the individual appears to many to be mere obscurantism. Any resolution of this conflict of attitudes is complex, and requires great tolerance on both sides.

What, now, are the positive reasons, other than defenses against opponents' arguments, that the philosopher who has chosen to regard the individual as more important than the group can offer on behalf of his choice? I would like to single out two, which are closely related to each other. The first has to do with the relationship between individuals and groups in the life-world, the second with one of the peculiar characteristics of individuals that groups do not exhibit.

Perhaps the whole philosophical terminology, inherited from the Greeks, of "priority" ought to be reconsidered periodically. At any rate, there is in John Wild's essay on "The Individual and the Group" a passage, to which I alluded at the beginning of this paper, which may be misleading because of its employment of this terminology. He says: "The individual is in no sense prior to the group. Both ontologically and historically, the group is prior to the individual." [23] The assertion of historical priority, traced to the conditions of primitive societies, is unexceptionable. But ontological priority is a different, more complicated matter. There is a very important truth to the latter assertion, to wit, that most large groups can be conceived as continuing without any gross, noticeable changes in their identities after the remov-

23. In *Existence and the World of Freedom*, p. 190.

al of any particular individual member, whereas no individual remains conceivable when one tries to abstract entirely from his relationships with the group or groups to which he has belonged throughout his life. But, from another perspective, it is the individual who is logically or ontologically prior (I am not sure which adverb to choose, since both are so ambiguous), as evidenced by the fact that institutions exist only on the basis of "acceptance" by their members, even though this acceptance is always of a passive, unreflective type in primitive societies and frequently so in modern societies.[24] Sartre has expressed this in a somewhat different way in his *Critique* by insisting, much to the dismay of some of his more rigid Marxist critics, that group praxis is always *constituée* and never, like the praxis of the individual, constitutive. I doubt that John Wild would seriously object to either of these formulations, but it seems to me that they do constitute a concession of a certain ontological priority to the individual, though one which bears little or no resemblance to the Lockean theory of ontological individualism that I sketched earlier. If so, we see the beginnings of a cogent argument in favor of considering the individual to be of greater importance than the group.

The recent historical events to which I have alluded on several occasions in this essay, namely, the series of strong student and other dissents from the policies of various large "establishments," provide some further evidence for this argument and bring it out of the area of somewhat abstract philosophical speculation to that of the life-world itself. Temporary setbacks and stabilizations do not detract from the probable long-range effects of these events. I doubt that the United States as a set of political institutions, for example, will ever be quite the same as it was before the build-up of determined, conscientious opposition to its Vietnam policies that began with the actions of some relatively isolated individuals, even though the temporary beneficiary of their partial success has been the political party that was generally more united in condemning them and defending the policies at the outset. These events have, it is to be hoped, contributed to the more widespread realization of the fact that the individual is, in a meaningful sense, "more real" and for that reason more important than the group, despite all

24. See W. L. McBride, "The Acceptance of a Legal System," *Monist*, IL, No. 3 (July, 1965), 377–96.

the contrary indications to be found in the world around us. In the ambiguous life-world of the ordinary contemporary individual, there exists a healthy resistance to the propaganda of the many giant institutions that are engaged, whether directly or indirectly, in continually asserting his insignificance. The more reflective individual recognizes this assertion to have no more truth than he, together with the other individuals in society, chooses to permit it to have. It is important for *some* philosophers, at least, to add more detailed and disciplined substantiation to this recognition, and thus to defend the third type of individualism that I have discerned.

On the other hand, it does not seem to me advisable, in pursuit of this aim, to draw too sharply the conceptual line between the group and the individual. Apart from the largely terminological point previously mentioned concerning "ontological priority," it is in my belief that John Wild has occasionally done just this that I find some ground for disagreeing with his generally very sound treatment of this entire issue. In his chapter on "The Gap between Individual and Social Action" in *Human Freedom and Social Order,* he is especially insistent on the necessary rigidity of institutions. Among his contentions are the following: The institution is "always governed by self-interest and impersonal reasons of its own, *raisons d'état*"; "political deliberation concerns means only and never the end"; and political action "is governed by a backward-looking hope." [25] Though he has already spoken of an "I-Thou group" which does not follow this pattern, and though he concludes by proposing ways of bridging the gap and of judging political institutions in accordance with the amount of freedom of action that they permit their members, it seems to me that the original assertions that I have cited suggest something approaching a sense of necessity about the patterns of group action that certain social and political groups, for at least brief periods of time, have managed to elude. If the political domain, which someone like Reinhold Niebuhr (whom Wild criticizes) [26] appears to regard as hopelessly corrupt, is not to be given up, then the possibility of a forward-looking group, capable of reevaluating its own ends and not oriented primarily toward self-perpetuation, must be left open. This is the ideal of what has sometimes been called "par-

25. *Human Freedom and Social Order,* pp. 189, 203, 208.
26. *Ibid.,* p. 210.

ticipatory democracy." It would permit the cultivation of individual members' freedom that John Wild calls for, and yet it would be a group because it would be engaged in joint endeavors. To stress this possibility and thus to diminish the gap between the individual and the group is not at all, I think, to yield on the fundamental issue concerning the greater importance of the individual.

A second argument for the individual, closely following from the first, can be put very succinctly. Individuals, not groups, are the ultimate sources of value judgments, including, in particular, judgments concerning importance. If it is true that a group is always *constituted* by its members, even though many of them may not be conscious of their creative roles, then the group can never be the originator of judgments as to what is important. A social scientist who decides, for instance, to treat gross political phenomena in as complete abstraction as possible from normative considerations may be mirroring the judgments of the majority of members of his professional association that such considerations are unimportant for their purposes; but it is clear that it is the *members,* and not some eternal Form of a social science association, who have chosen to adopt this particular scale of importance, and furthermore that the individual in question is free to challenge that scale and perhaps even, if he is successful, to effect its eventual revision. There do exist, then, group standards of importance and group values, but this is simply a shorthand way of talking about certain complex interactions of individual value judgments. If all judgments concerning what is important in general are eventually traceable to the choices of individuals, does this not provide additional support for the advocacy of the third type of individualism that I have been describing, the individualism rooted in the value judgment that it is the individual who is most important?

To conclude my discussion of this third type of individualism, I would like to point out that, although it may often be found in combination with one or both of the other types, it is logically independent of them. The "Lockean" ontological type, at least in certain versions and on certain issues, is susceptible of disproof. The methodological individualism which consists in taking the individual as the starting point of one's philosophy may be shown, from historical examples, to be dangerous. But the choice to emphasize the problems of the individual as being the most important for philosophy, while it is not the sort of matter that can be "proved," seems to be a very worthwhile and *important* one in our contemporary world. This is the very honorable type of individualism that can, it seems to me, be attributed to John Wild. Before one attempts to criticize Wild or other like-minded persons for their individualistic stances, one should take account of the sorts of distinctions among individualisms that I have been making.

V

MY FINAL SET OF COMMENTS consists of a cautionary note in the form of a postscript. Once a philosopher has made the choice to treat the individual as the subject of greatest importance for his philosophical inquiries, he ought to avoid the strong temptation to lapse back into the quantitative ways of reasoning that, as we saw, served as one of the principal arguments in favor of attributing greater importance to the group. For, once it has been acknowledged that the individual's importance is greater (but obviously not in a quantitative sense!), then questions immediately arise concerning the relative importance of individuals among themselves. If, in response, the philosopher chooses to generalize about the importance of *all* individuals in a quantitative fashion, without bringing in any reference to their particular qualities, then two possibilities are open: (1) all individuals are of infinite importance; or (2) all individuals are of absolutely equal importance. (A third possibility, that individuals are of zero importance, has been excluded by hypothesis.) Both of these ways of trying to quantify my third type of individualism have long histories, with the second being particularly popular today.

The view that each individual is of infinite importance is closely associated, historically speaking, with Christianity, though in its Christian forms this statement must always be understood within a wider ontological framework. Besides individuals, for the Christian, there is also, of course, God, and so any assertion of the infinite importance of individuals is usually qualified by the phrase, "in the sight of God." This notion achieved its high-water mark of formalization in the philosophy of Leibniz, each of whose monads was said to "represent" the entire universe, with only the comparative unclarity of human monads' representations standing in the way of their being equivalent to deities.[27] In the ethical sphere, Kant's view of every individual as being ideally a pure end, never a means, has similar origins. The principal difficulty with this way of quantifying the importance of the individual is that, in viewing the individual both too formally and in too ideal a fashion, it runs the risk of making any real, existing individual appear more or less irrelevant. If every individual is of infinite importance in God's sight, then, it might be concluded, since we are so far removed in perfection from God, this alleged fact can be disregarded, for all practical purposes, by us. Even if it is true that every monad does, for the most part unconsciously, represent the entire universe, yet the monads with whom we have contact in the life-world give so little evidence of this infinite power that its alleged existence makes no difference to us. If, ideally speaking, other individuals are never in any way to be treated as means, then, since such treatment does in fact occur, often in what we would otherwise call very innocent fashions, dozens of times each day in our ordinary relations with others, it may seem that the abstract exhortation has no relevance to our ordinary ethical lives. Such are some of the dangers of mathematicizing the assertion of the importance of the individual by holding that each individual's importance is infinite.

The topic of equality is being widely discussed these days; a postscript such as this can barely touch on the issues. Suffice it to say that a value judgment concerning the overriding importance of the individual does not entail the belief that no individual is either more or less important than any other. Neither is it a warrant for ideological justifications of existing social inequalities, of course, as the first argument that I cited in favor of the importance of the group would wrongly have it. Interestingly enough, one of philosophy's clearest, most reasonable brief indictments of the quantitative conception of total equality as a social goal occurs in Marx's early writings, in his discussion of the "crude, egalitarian" form of communism.

"One man, one vote" may be a useful lawyers' and legislators' slogan for the purpose of alleviating certain gross injustices in a

27. *Monadology*, #60.

particular political system at a particular time, but the global implications of absolute egalitarianism that are sometimes drawn, quite unreflectively, from this slogan are clearly invalid. The references that I have made in this essay to the evaluative concept of "importance" may be of help in discovering the exact locus of the invalid inference. Absolute egalitarianism, as I understand it here, is the judgment that the importance of every human individual is in every respect identical with that of every other human individual; but such a judgment could legitimately be made only as the outcome of an extremely complex, ongoing, never completed investigation of *all* individuals, and not by an a priori fiat. Relative importances are simply not quantifiable, though it may be very reasonable, in a given set of conditions, to assume or postulate the quantitative identity of individuals *in a certain respect,* as my very familiar example from contemporary politics demonstrates.

This final *caveat* against relapsing into quantification even after one has made the choice, as a philosopher, in favor of emphasizing the individual involves no assumptions whatever about the existence of elites. Quite the contrary, for, in order to belong to a true elite, one would have to be superior to "the masses," either in every single respect or at least in every "important" respect. All human experience testifies against the likelihood of the first-mentioned state of affairs, and any discernment of the latter state of affairs must itself depend on a challengeable, never fully demonstrable decision as to which particular qualities of individuals are "truly important." The attempted combination of the type of individualism that I have been defending with any systematic elitism can only be the product of the invalid subordination, against which I have been warning, of qualitative evaluations to the deep-seated impulsion to try somehow to quantify them.

And so philosophies which emphasize the human individual are left with a life-world that is, if one chooses so to regard it, "sloppy," that is, unreduced to any easy formulae or systems. There are many different theories and variants of theories that have been called "individualistic" and that have nevertheless fallen victims to some such reductions. In addition, philosophies that systematically eschew individualism, in the sense of the term in which I have been defending it, usually appear to exhibit a more "orderly" world than the one that an individualist such as

John Wild is able to describe. But that more orderly world is not *our* world, the one in which we live. I hope that my analysis of several species of individualisms has helped to indicate why the individualism that I have attributed to John Wild and other like-minded theorists, far from constituting either the erroneous ontology or the conservative ideology that it has sometimes been labeled, is at base a very crucial aspect of their efforts at maintaining the integrity of philosophy itself.

12 / Sartre the Individualist

Wilfrid Desan

THE INTENT OF THIS PAPER is to trace some of the aspects in Sartrean thought which more than any others bring to the fore, I believe, the great contribution of the French existentialist. I shall attempt to show that the overriding character of Sartre consists in his defense of the individual. It may appear that this defense is also his weakness. I shall not attempt to refute what I consider deficient, for the refutation is already taking place elsewhere through the formulation of contrary ways of thinking, such as the neo-Marxist trend in France, the structuralism of Claude Lévi-Strauss, and the interpersonalism of Lacan. Even Teilhard de Chardin, although older in years, in some way constitutes a corrective to the existential position. It is not this turning point which interests us at present, but rather that which in Sartre gave rise to it.

II

IN HIS BRILLIANT AUTOBIOGRAPHY, *The Words,* Sartre wrote:

Every man has his natural place; its altitude is determined by neither pride nor value: childhood decides. Mine is a sixth floor in Paris with a view overlooking the roofs. For a long time I suffocated in the valleys; the plains overwhelmed me: I crawled along the planet Mars, the heaviness crushed me. I had only to climb a molehill for joy to come rushing back: I would return to my symbolic sixth floor; there I would once again breathe the rarefied air of belles-lettres; the Universe would rise in tiers at my feet and all things would humbly beg for a name; to name the thing was both to create and take it.[1]

This already is the Sartre of later years: "To name the thing was both to create and to take it." *Being and Nothingness* is the forceful illustration of a thought where man is presented as organizer of a world, where he is made not to be ruled but to rule. Man is a meaning-giving center: without man nature would be deaf-mute.[2] Sartre would agree with Heidegger in claiming that "knowledge is the world"[3]—not in creating the world in the strict sense of the word but in causing it "to appear." No one has emptied consciousness as much as has Sartre—for him it *is* "*néant*," yet paradoxically this consciousness, which has nothing to be, has everything to *do*. It ensures that there is being; it ensures that there is *this* being; it makes time; and, juxtaposing this thing to that thing, it makes space. All the so-called categories—unity-multiplicity, whole-part, more and less, outside of—are ideal manipulations of things, which leave reality itself completely intact. They are different ways in which the For-itself, or individual consciousness, "attacks" and organizes the "apathetic indifference" of things.[4] Meyerson was wrong when he accused reality of a "scandalous diversity." It is man who is responsible, man who stands at the center of reality and constitutes a world.

III

Children played in the Luxembourg Gardens. I would draw near them. They would brush against me without seeing me. I would watch them with the eyes of a beggar. How strong and quick they were! How good-looking! In the presence of those

1. Jean-Paul Sartre, *The Words*, trans. Bernard Frechtman (New York: Braziller, 1964), p. 60.
2. Wilfrid Desan, *The Marxism of Jean-Paul Sartre* (Garden City, N.Y.: Doubleday, Anchor Books, 1965), p. 41.
3. Wilfrid Desan, *The Tragic Finale* (New York: Harper Torchbooks, 1960), p. 49.
4. *Ibid.*, p. 55.

flesh-and-blood heroes, I would lose my prodigious intelligence, my universal knowledge, my athletic physique, my blustering shrewdness. I would lean against a tree, waiting. . . . To save me from despair, [my mother] would feign impatience: "What are you waiting for, you big silly? Ask them whether they want to play with you." I would shake my head. I would have accepted the lowliest jobs, but it was a matter of pride not to ask for them. She would point to the ladies sitting in iron chairs and knitting: "Do you want me to speak to their mothers?" I would beg her to do nothing of the kind. She would take my hand, we would leave, we would go from tree to tree and from group to group, always entreating, always excluded. At twilight, I would be back on my perch, on the heights where the spirit blew, where my dreams dwelt.[5]

At that moment the famous play *No Exit* was born. "L'enfer, c'est l'autre!" Sartre's theory of the *look* grounds the theory of the Other—the Other who looks at me, annihilates me as a subject, and reduces me to the rank of object. No rational demonstration proves it, but feelings like shame, envy, resentment, etc., make it manifest. The presence of the Other is hostile: in some ways he limits my own consciousness. Where Spinoza says that thought is only limited by thought, Sartre would claim that awareness is kept within bounds through awareness. But—and this is important—this limitation is active: it encloses me, it surrounds me, and yet I never reach it. For Sartre, the Other no less than I myself is center, his whole life is a continual disposition of the world around himself. The Other is an "absence-presence," a mysterious being which ought to be handled with care. "I want him to stay *object* and I hate to see him *subject* again! He makes it nevertheless from time to time. The dead alone stay object for ever." [6]

IV

IT IS BANAL by now to stress the element of freedom in a global view of Sartre's philosophy. Let us merely mention that it is part of his concept of nought. What is not, is free; what is not, is not and cannot be caught within the laws of a mechanistic world like any being other than consciousness. In being

5. Sartre, *The Words*, p. 134.
6. Desan, *The Tragic Finale*, p. 72.

nothing, individual consciousness knows that which is and at the same time escapes determinism. Man is the future of man. This implies that since there is no weight of the past on him, man is condemned at every moment to invent man. Consequently, "There is no action of things on the subject, but merely a signification (in the active sense), a centrifugal *Sinngebung*." [7] This attitude of total freedom and of incessant departure is also Sartrean. It is a pleasant feeling, of course, but it may be illusory. "At the age of ten, I had the impression that my prow was cleaving the present and yanking me out of it; since then, I have been running, I'm still running. For me, speed is measured not so much by the distance covered in a given time as by the power of uprooting." [8]

Sartre went to the *lycée* and to the university, where, as is well known, René Descartes dominated the philosophical scene. Sartre, like anybody else who went to school in France in those days, was a Cartesian and at his best a Bergsonian. No less than any other Frenchman but with far more talent than most, Sartre has carried on a lifelong struggle to protect what the French have so aptly called *la lucidité*, which is of course Descartes's old *cogito*, the privilege that mind alone has of not being earth, or any kind of matter. In the depths of his doubt Descartes discovered one certainty, namely, that he thinks, and therefore is a spiritual being. *Lucidité* is that unique light that, containing a world of sense data, itself stands outside and above the world. This is Descartes's defense against a world that is myth—*mundus est fabula*—and Sartre, as a descendant of the Cartesian tradition, introduces it into his own life and doctrine as the negation of matter. Mind alone is supreme and free. In the Cartesian view, thought contains the complex activity of perceiving, knowing, willing, and desiring. Yet knowing is not exactly desiring, since the latter has no limits. Only because you know as a man can you desire as a god. Sartre has inherited this view, but he has eliminated God from his inheritance and replaced him by man, who now has absolute freedom. The conclusion of Sartre is obvious: man must take over the freedom of God. [9]

So there we have Sartre, the philosopher maturing out of the

7. M. Merleau-Ponty, *Phenomenology of Perception*, trans. Colin Smith (New York: Humanities Press, 1962), p. 436.
8. Sartre, *The Words*, p. 232.
9. Desan, *The Marxism of Jean-Paul Sartre*, p. 262.

child, taking as his cornerstones *subjectivism, conflict* with the Other, and *all-out freedom.* The method no less than the content stresses the superiority of the Self. The method is phenomenological, which means that one attempts a description of the world and oneself-in-the-world as they appear. Sartre has a method, but a method which only emphasizes his Cartesian seclusion.

Where is the Marxist in all this? There is none except in desire. No doubt as a young intellectual Sartre nurtured a strong opposition to the bourgeoisie. While a teacher at the *lycée,* he refused to wear a tie, as if he could shed his class with his tie and thus come closer to the worker. For this he deserves no blame. Like the *petit bourgeois intellectuel* that he is, he uses more words than the workers, words with which he can analyze their status and rebel in their name. His concern for the worker is the reverse side of his contempt for the strength of the bourgeois; his concern with man is the fight against anything that humiliates man, and his rebellion the reaction against all power. The freedom and power and esteem of the subject that are so deep in Sartre revolt against the suffering itself, whether that suffering results from the egoism of the Continental bourgeoisie or from oppression preached in the name of Marx and of Lenin. Sartre virtually grew up writing and attempting to publish his writing, for he was devoted to literature, not as art for art's sake but as a means whereby man justifies himself and at the same time fills a need for others.[10]

Sartre now stands at high noon: we are in the 1950's, and he has reached world fame as a philosopher, a playwright, and a novelist, but has not yet committed himself in the domain of social studies and ethics. He will do so in another magnum opus, *Critique de la raison dialectique,* 755 pages of small print which came off the press in 1960, unbelievably difficult and chaotic, with one central message: Marxism is the answer; existentialism is merely a correction. Sartre declares himself a Marxist.

V

IN THE *Critique* the concept of need is presented as concrete, and human reality is called a "being of need" (*un être*

10. *Ibid.,* p. 3.

de besoin), a being that is, which must have an object capable of assuaging its hunger in order to live. This of course is Marx: "Hunger is a natural need: it requires therefore a nature outside itself, an object outside itself in order to be satisfied and stilled." [11] Hunger is only one need. Man also seeks clothing, sex, habitation, etc. All these needs are inseparable from material production. We can assert, therefore, that material production lies at the beginning of history. On all this Sartre agrees. He does add, though, that it is in a world of scarcity (*dans un monde de la rareté*) that need originates; because there is not enough of certain things, need originates. This correction may seem merely redundant. It is not. It is, on the contrary, important, for it is because there is not enough of certain things that the Other is transformed into a menace. The Other for Sartre, more than for Marx, is the opponent who threatens me in my very survival.

Need thus lies at the beginning of the dialectic between man and matter, man and man. The dialectic continues and transforms individual man into the common man (member of the group), the organization man, and the institutionalized man. Proceeding along that road, his freedom has dwindled, yet his power is hundredfold. When the moment comes that all will share alike in the abundance of things, freedom itself will again triumph in all its sovereignty. That is the dream of tomorrow. As for today—and on this Sartre seems to agree with Marx—the need to unite has clipped the wings of freedom.

As far as the opposition of Sartre is concerned, it is directed not so much against Marx himself as it is against a modern interpretation of Marx by certain present-day Communists who in his opinion have distorted the pristine Marxist view.

Sartre is dead set against what he calls the *Marxist rigidity* which so often in the past has forced the ways of living of a country or of an individual into a prearranged scheme without regard for their peculiarity or uniqueness. He calls this the sclerosis of modern Marxism. Examples are, among others, the repression of the Budapest revolt in 1956 and the interpretation of cultural achievements like those of Paul Valéry or Gustave Flaubert. It is naive to call their achievement merely an expression of bourgeois idealism or a result of economic factors. Such

11. Karl Marx, *Economic and Philosophical Manuscripts of 1844*, bd. with Erich Fromm, *Marx's Concept of Man* (New York: Frederick Ungar, 1961), p. 182.

generalities explain everything and nothing. Although Sartre has no wish to deny the relation between culture and economics, he wants to deepen the meaning of that relationship in trying to show that both are "mediated" through the individual. In Sartre's opinion, the modern Marxist has forgotten that a case is something unique, that it is not just money which shapes man but the way in which he is directed in and by the individual, in and by his parents. Childhood and growth play a role, and they may in one way or another alter the impact of economic factors.

This commutation of the economic situation by the "mediating" individual must be understood in the light of some of the views developed in *L'Etre et le néant,* where man is seen above all as capable of "going beyond" a given situation through his "project," which is precisely his attitude toward the multiple possibles open to him. "To say what man is, is to say what he can," and, conversely, "To say what a man can is to say what he is." [12] Man surpasses his given, and in this sense surpasses the merely mechanical.[13] It is through his "project" that he surpasses the given and looks toward the future as to that which needs to be fulfilled.

Even the worker's rebellion implies in depth that attitude, for it presumes a "going beyond" toward the possibility of change in his situation. Because the worker is not a "mere" thing, his act of rebellion plans and fulfills a new set of possibles.[14] If one would object that the material conditions of his existence determine the number of possibilities which are open to man, Sartre would agree. Yet, although limited, there is a choice of possibles from which he can positively realize one. The subjective in man can surpass one objectivity and reach unto another and, in doing so, define him. It is in his *project* that man is defined.

It is paramount, therefore, to discover this (fundamental) project which will reveal the uniqueness of the self. In order to do so, Sartre suggests a return (regressively) to the beginnings of the self, and from there, with the knowledge obtained, a climb back to the deed itself, where the project is fulfilled in a work or a book or some other accomplishment. Man must be studied as

12. Jean-Paul Sartre, *Critique de la raison dialectique* (Paris: Gallimard, 1960), I, 64.
13. Desan, *The Marxism of Jean-Paul Sartre,* pp. 56 ff.
14. *Ibid.*, p. 57.

an entity which is in tension toward a future and an end to be fulfilled.

If we apply this method to *Madame Bovary*, the masterpiece of Flaubert, we shall discover that it is much more than the product of an epoch. Going back to the genesis of the work, we shall discover who the author was and how his "project" was fulfilled, and how, in order to escape from himself and from his inner contradictions, he had to tell a story. Flaubert then will use this instrument to tell a story, but what a story it will be: "l'ouvrage monstrueux et splendide . . . Madame Bovary." [15]

VI

IT IS IN EXAMINING the growth of the collective in its different phases that Sartre attempts to show most clearly that indestructible something in the hearts and minds of men called individual freedom.

We are in Paris in Sartre's apartment on the corner of the rue Bonaparte, and through his window we are looking down upon a small crowd of people waiting for the autobus at the stop on the place Saint Germain des Prés.[16] What strikes us first of all in this crowd is the solitude of the individual members. These people neither know one another nor care about one another; as Sartre quotes from Proust, "Chacun est bien seul." All this fits into the spirit of the modern metropolis, where the individuals are interchangeable, yet in their solitude somehow protected, as, for example, behind their newspapers on the bus. The local limitation (the sidewalk, the sign around which they gather) and the similarity of purpose unify them in a loose way. Of course, the autobus itself is the central link, what Sartre calls the *collective entity*: as object, it overflows its inert materiality and is full of meaning, with a future and a past in the life of the travelers. In the present, it is also that which will dictate the *seriality*: for this is indeed what this gathering is, a series; it is

15. Sartre, *Critique*, I, 94.
16. For more detail and for close references to Sartre's *Critique*, Vol. I, refer to my book, *The Marxism of Jean-Paul Sartre*, from which the following pages are partly borrowed.

not a group. It is a series, and by this is implied that through this object, which is the bus, the potential passengers become interchangeable, their internal qualities are negated, and they become simply *Other among Others.*

It becomes immediately apparent that the *seriality* is not structured; in contrast to the *group,* which, as we shall see later, is within itself structured and hierarchical, the Other is never the subordinate or the superior but simply the Other. In this series gathered together by the approaching bus, the factory owner is equivalent to the lowest clerk, the duchess to the charwoman; each one is leveled, each takes his anonymous place in the line. The multiplicity—the waiting crowd—finds in an inert (but man-made) object—the bus—its unity of exteriority, that which makes them Other among Others. Yet the gathering implies a certain unity, a serial unity, or what Sartre calls *une unité en fuite,* a gathering loosely held together and constituted only by way of not being a structured group. The seriality comes from the practico-inert multiplicity of individuals, all of whom are equivalent to one another, yet compelled to give in to a certain order of succession—I get on the bus first, you second, and so on. It is the bus which makes them *inert* beings-outside-themselves, and Other among Others. As Other among Others, they are linked in powerlessness; the seriality, lacking any organization or intercommunication, is inert, powerless to act or move.

Nevertheless, the serial structure should not be considered as just an ideal, fictive entity or a mere concept, for it is something very real. This becomes apparent in the case of Jewishness. In a society which persecutes Jews, to be a Jew is not a fiction. The plurality of Jews as an object of scorn is on this basis a unity and constitutes a seriality. The individuals exist in solitude next to one another and are interchangeable; they belong to the collective only by virtue of their Jewishness, not by virtue of their *individual* internal qualities. The series once more is a collection of people related to one another only through their common Otherness and common being-an-object-of-scorn to those not in the collection. Examples of seriality are many, such as, for example, the listeners to a radio program, the readers of *Figaro,* and so on.

But the seriality can become much more complex, as when it constitutes a certain milieu, whether this be the unorganized cohesion of individuals, as Others, working within a certain profession, living within a certain section of a city, or belonging to a particular business collectivity. Milieu is structured only through the *Other*, although there is a certain unity—we all live in the 16ème *arrondissement*, we are all small grocers of Montmartre—but it immediately appears that this unity is a fleeting one. *C'est une unité fuyante.* There is a form of container in which one finds oneself Other among Others but where no attempt toward any grouping is made.

We are now in a position to understand what a "class" is, for it, too, is a collective with a practico-inert character, while the individual himself as a member of the class is a powerless member of a seriality. Man discovers his being-outside-himself as his truth and his reality. It is the practico-inert or the ponderosity of matter in and around him which catches hold of man and places him in a social class; this inorganic presence, strangely enough, both describes and is man. This "weight" of the practico-inert which defines the individual man also classifies him socially. One can truly say that the worker who spends eight hours a day in a monotonous and fatiguing job, from which his needs are barely fulfilled, has no other essence outside this frustrated self; he truly is what he does. These conditions are part of his individuality and actually define it. *They make him what he is and hold him where he belongs*, Other among Others. The loose, unorganized unity of individuals is built around an object—in the case of the proletarians, the machine.

Yet—and this is a hopeful sign—there is something incomplete in this ontological identification of one's self with the practico-inert of one's career. No essence is ever completely rigid, and one may very well revolt and attempt to go beyond it. Sartre wishes always to make clear that the individual on this globe, although caught in many ways, as for example the impotent member of the seriality, is *not unfree*. This should never be forgotten: although the individual in the series is a prisoner, he can always go beyond his impotency through the consideration that the present condition is *provisional* and *relative*. The proletarian is powerless now, but he *will change a world*.

At a certain moment the exploited or serialized man feels the pain of his alienation and, under some stimulus, the ineptitude of the seriality breaks up and the group is formed. We have seen this happen. Take the case of the bus-riders in Alabama, when the Reverend Martin Luther King stepped out of the seriality and organized his fellow Negroes into a resistance against the inequality with which they were treated. But we are stepping ahead. All that should be made clear at this point is that the riders may be inert, Other among Others, prisoners of their particular seriality, but the potentiality of changing that situation, of going beyond, gives them a measure of freedom, even within their present prison.

Oddly enough, however, the walls of that prison will only fall with the formation of the group.

VII

IN OUR APPROACH to this matter, we come back to a recurrent theme of the *Critique*, one which is basic to Marxism itself, and observe that at the start of all change lies a *need*.[17] Need is the stimulus for all human activity—man's work begins in order to fulfill his basic needs, and his *project*, engendered by "what is lacking" (above and beyond the means for bare physical survival), carries him always beyond-himself-toward. The need is such that it results in the impossibility for the individual to remain what he is. One must change, that is, one must break the ground of what is *forbidden*. Yet this conquest of what is forbidden contains a paradox, since upon the basis of scarcity one thinks of oneself and not of the Other. How can it be explained that in a situation where all that matters is the survival of the *self*, the *group* has come into being? In answering that question, let us remember that it is an *object* which brings men together. It was the common object, e.g., the bus, which resulted in the vague unity of the seriality, and in the same way it is an object which will provoke a closer unification, and ultimately the formation of the group itself. To show this, we return once more to Paris; this time we bring our imagination to the eve of one of the most striking events of the French Revolution, the days before the capture of the Bastille.

It is July 12. There is a state of insurrection in Paris. We observe several things. The Parisians, still juxtaposed in the manner of seriality, are hungry and tired. They are not sup-

17. Desan, *The Marxism of Jean-Paul Sartre*, p. 127; Sartre, *Critique*, I, 385 ff.

ported by the government. On the contrary, the king and his ministers are set against them, provoking some form of unity in the Parisian seriality in an effort to strengthen its opposition. Paris is surrounded by the army, and this physical fact accelerates the unification. Everyone in Paris discovers that he is a "particle of a sealed-off materiality." All of these factors—mutual discomfort, the opposition of the government, and the siege of the army—strengthen the cohesion of the people: everyone sees himself as Other in the Other, and yet as himself.

At this moment the arms depot is looted. This is, no doubt, a positive deed against the king. The gathering has acted, and in this *free deed* it has suddenly discovered that it was fusing into a *group*. This is as far as the past is concerned. As for the future, they prepare a self-defense with their weapons, positing a new act of free self-assertion, *qua group*. The dissolution of the seriality is now manifest for everyone. It is not yet a group in the full sense of the word, but it can be called *un groupe en fusion*. Sartre, borrowing a term from Malraux, calls the mystique of the collectivity tumbling into the phase of group formation *un apocalypse*. Sartre chooses his epithets with great care at this moment. Using Jaures's beautiful expression to focus on these moments of pressure, he calls them moments of *haute température historique*.

The menace now becomes more precise in one section of the city, namely, in the neighborhood of the Bastille, the so-called quartier Saint Antoine. Since the inhabitants of the quartier Saint Antoine will have to defend themselves against the enemy in front of them coming from outside the quartier, and against the enemy in the rear posted in the Bastille, they are more pressed than others and must act as a group if they want to survive. They come out on the street.

Let us stop for a moment and philosophize upon what happens, for what matters above all for an existentialist way of looking at group formation is the avoidance of a positivistic interpretation.

What happens is this. Up to now I have always totalized my quartier from the outside, and by this I mean that, although inhabitant of the quartier, the mental act by which I considered its totality was an englobing act which automatically left me out. At present, however, under the menace of the planned attack from the outside, I am integrated in this (totalized) totality.

There is a strange contradiction in my mind; I, the totalizer of my quartier, now become, under menace of the advancing army of the government, the passively totalized one. The human subject is not an object which is pushed around like a robot. He is subject and must fulfill his dignity in freedom. The inhabitants of the quartier Saint Antoine come out on the street, each one constituting the mental synthesis englobing the totality; in this act of totalization they constitute the unity of the group and at the same time are part of it. A concrete example will clarify this point. Someone, while running toward the Bastille, gives the *mots d'ordre* "Stop," "Go ahead." These *mots d'ordre* are not strictly orders; they are simply manifestations coming from the "third man" (myself or the Other in the group). One cannot call these *mots d'ordre* products of the group; they come from an individual, but, in the act of understanding and of executing them, I, who did not give the orders, recognize myself, and my free choice confirms them. If the *mots d'ordre* are followed, it is because each member has himself given them. There are in the *groupe en fusion* hundreds of individual syntheses; yet they are, as multiplicity, dialectically negated in the very act of constituting the group. Each act can be said to be a free individual development—it is Sartre's constant worry to protect individual freedom—yet it is such through the *group*. The group alone makes the act efficient and is instrumental in its success. Although it can be said in truth that the individual freely joins the group, it is no less certain that if he wants to survive, he has to do so. Salvation is where the group is. And while, as we saw above, the seriality was always elsewhere, or, as Sartre puts it, *en fuite,* it can be said now that salvation is *here.* The *we* expresses the ubiquity of the *me* as interiorized by the Others, which was not and is not at all the case in the seriality.

Although there is at this stage of *groupe en fusion* no leader, there is a strong solidarity and a common action, which although internally diversified—I do this, you do that—keeps all of us subordinated to the common purpose. Once the victory is achieved, which in our example is the capture of the Bastille, some form of frustration is not excluded, but this only comes later. In this case it will be fear: at night the group settles down among the old stones, but it does so uneasily, for the old fort, although tamed, is still a menace.

There is in this phenomenology of the *groupe en fusion* no

super-organism tying the group together, nor is there any hyper-synthesis transcending the individual act; but there is the individual synthesis, which knows itself to be identical with any other individual synthesis. This synthesis or totalization happens from within, in freedom. It is from within, then, through the individual choice, that the plurality becomes unity. A group, or better still a group formation, is nothing but a multiple and ubiquitous presence of the individual synthesis, hundreds of syntheses holding together the group and embracing its totality in freedom.

From the outside there is of course the object, the common danger to be avoided, the Bastille to be taken, Paris to be defended, the common purpose to be fulfilled. The group, to be alive, needs a purpose, offensive or defensive. This purpose indeed challenges the individuals, but their response is not a deterministic one, nor is it a mechanistic necessity as positivism would have it. It is, on the contrary, an act of self-determination performed by the individual; it is his internal choice and approval, his cooperation in the whole move toward the Bastille down the boulevard Saint Antoine. In all this, existentialism discovers the individual subject, whose dignity asserts itself and freely responds to the impact of the future upon the group.

Since the group was merely action, and since in this action it was sufficiently unified, the group did not feel the need to reflect upon its status. Once, however, it has done what it had to do, it becomes more conscious of itself. Now that the Bastille is taken and the group is sitting on its laurels, the need for a new form of integration becomes urgent. It is very important for the survival of the group that I, for example, who am a guardian during the night after the taking of the Bastille, keep alive the awareness of the group as a common reality. The interiorization must survive, but it will have to struggle against solitude and fragmentation.

VIII

AT THIS MOMENT a new qualification appears; it is called the *oath* and will be the protection against the menace of atomization.[18] The oath brings with it a new form of inertia and

18. Desan, *The Marxism of Jean-Paul Sartre*, p. 139; Sartre, *Critique*, I, 139 ff.

abridges freedom. The group becomes its own inertia as a protection against seriality. I can also call the oath a form of reciprocity in the sense that through the oath I protect myself and the third man, the one through the other. But this reciprocity is mediated by the whole group: my oath is only a guarantee when taken for granted by the others as well. This definitely modifies the group, for the clear implication is that from now on *I can become* a traitor. The group, to avoid fragmentation and dissolution within its own ranks, through the oath exerts pressure upon its own members. The members themselves are in danger *within* the group. If the group has a political coloring, we call this group pressure *terreur,* and a traitor is not only dismissed but, as is well known, is eliminated as well. The oath implies punishment or death as a possible destiny, since it really means this: if the individual weakens, the group will take care of him, in one way or another. There is in each of the members a solicitude for the other, but it is a fatal solicitude. Yet underneath all this, freedom is not dead: it was and is my free choice which at present is being protected. It is a common freedom, a freedom which belongs to all, but it is a freedom which, as a result of the oath, must be protected by violence. It should be added that the oath at times has a sacred and noumenal character and that ceremonies are used as the means through which that sacred character reaches me. But the oath does not necessarily have this explicit exteriorization and may very well be implicitly present although never performed as such.

IX

WE NOW STEP into a new phase, which is called the *organization.*[19] The oath having cemented the unity of the group, the distribution of tasks within this unity requires a differentiation of the members. The function individualizes, no doubt, and in this sense limits the freedom of the individual. The player on the team who is chosen to be the goalkeeper automatically has his freedom restricted, since he has that particular function and no other. But if it is his duty, it is also his privilege and his right.

19. Desan, *The Marxism of Jean-Paul Sartre,* p. 142.

We notice also how, within a group, a function is a determining limitation in the way a *tool* acts. We discover that a tool is a contact with the world, implying both a sovereignty upon a portion of the world and a restriction of my own world. Take, for example, the airplane in Saint Exupéry's *Terre des hommes*. To be a pilot is to be a pilot only, but within this function the possibilities are great. In the same way the individual, caught in the praxis of the group and confined through the oath, can exercise his common function in an uncommon way. The road is free toward that achievement. But in whatever way it is done, it is negated and absorbed in the common end of the group. Each individual function creates a situation within the group and through the group with each one of its members. We members of the group are all brothers tied together by this complex dialectic of each toward each through the group. One can also specify the functions of X with an eye upon Y, or one can point at the functions of Y with an eye upon X. There is indeed a form of brotherhood at work, but it is, as was implied above, *une fraternité terreur*. When one speaks of the organized group, one does not mean that every member is indispensable, even though his function is. Sometimes the indispensable member is thrown out after a purge; sometimes he is kept on as a mere unit, thus proving that he was not indispensable.

Because of the fact that groups within the society are very complex—e.g., the intricate relation within one city of the productive and nonproductive elements, such as children and old people—it remains true that a mathematical logistics can be made up of the mutual actions and reactions, of growth and decline. Only when A freely decides to marry B does he begin the complicated logistics of relations between cousins, nieces, parents, aunts, and uncles. In other words, the possibility of using mathematics results from a free decision of Peter or perhaps of Mary.

When the child is born, it is born into a group. To be born *into* implies acceptance of the group. This is the rationale behind the practice of baptizing a child at his birth and making a decision for him. Sartre here surprisingly, but no less consistently for that reason, takes a stand in favor of the French Catholic who, although perhaps not practicing his religion, wants baptism and first communion for his children. This indeed implies some passivity in the individual, but allows for later interiorization or internal acceptance of these ceremonies once the child has become an adult. Freedom is not denied; actually it still is part of the group as such, since the group in Sartre's conviction is not an objective totality or organic reality by itself, but merely the result of subjective synthesis or totalization, or better still of the interiorization or acceptance of the total activity as such. The individual is still alive, as is the group. The individual is still alive but under menace, for the next stage of development is the institution.

X

THE GROUP, sadly enough, will become an institution. The deeper reason for this final change is the fact that the organized group does not and cannot live within a spatial container.[20] Its practical unity, which is a unity for action, requires a sort of ubiquity in space and time. The individual member in the very exercise of his duty is led geographically out of the group. Against this the oath is of no great help, for contact with the Other is a necessity. It is a strange paradox which affects even the religious group, namely, the fact that the group requires unity, yet its action is impossible without dispersion. The group was made for action, yet dissolves in the action, and here once more we put our finger on the fluidity and freedom of human participation. The individual subject, which actually is everyman, is never entirely in the group, nor is he entirely out of the group. Every act could be a refusal of the oath.

Against this menace the group reacts and becomes an institution; and the common individual becomes the institutional one. This may appear to be an unavoidable evolution, but it is quite often far from progress in the full sense of the word.

What characterizes the institution is, first, that from now on what counts is the *function*, which becomes essential, while the individual is unessential and is merely perpetuated in the function. The immediate result is a great rigidity and an increase of the *inert*. From now on any individual who proposes a change is suspect, since that very proposal is already a manifestation of

20. *Ibid.*, p. 171.

freedom and a revelation of individuality. The institution clearly wants impotency toward alteration. It is in a way a return to seriality, where the individual is merely Other; yet it is more powerful, since it keeps active toward a common objective. The trend toward the same and common objective remains, because the praxis (or action) remains, and the praxis remains because it is a praxis under command.

This is a second feature of the institution. The institution has *authority*.[21] The remote foundation of authority has to be sought in the *groupe en fusion*. The people of the quartier Saint Antoine, who, as you will remember, were "on the run" toward the Bastille, have a third man regulator. Leadership was present but very vague. Later on, it became more specific but not stable. Authority becomes permanent only when the institution is born. According to Sartre, authority does not come from God, nor does it come from the people as a direct expression of their wishes; it is merely a concession of the masses. According to his existentialist view, "every man is sovereign," but there is one who becomes *the* Sovereign, and he is the Sovereign because he is the mediator of communications and obtains this particular function through explicit or implicit concessions. He becomes the *indépassable* entity: One cannot go around him, since he stops the flow of circularity. An imperative ordering me to work in a specific way toward the common cause reaches me through him. We commonly call that an order. From now on my freedom is alienated, or rather my freedom is *in the sovereign*, because I want it to be so.

At this moment, the *unity* of the group still lies in its object and its purpose; it lies in the members *qua* inert; it lies in the Sovereign. It is *not* in the group. There is power in the group, but this power paradoxically lies in the impotency of its members. This impotency constitutes a power of inertia. During this phase, the aims of the group are still fulfilled, but they have become destiny. What matters now is consolidation of power in the hands of the one regulator or Sovereign. If he is omnipotent and incarnates both State and Party, he is worshiped as a god. The phenomenon is known as personality cult, and its most notorious example is of course Stalin.

The Sovereign wants unity and he gets it, but notwithstand-

21. *Ibid.*, pp. 176 ff.

ing this unity, or rather because of it, he remains distrustful. "His right hand trusts his left hand and no other hand." This beautiful quotation reveals one thing clearly: in an institution-alized group with authority, even with, as Sartre calls it, *une autorité terreur,* the Sovereign remains suspicious, because he cannot prevent humans from being what they are, namely, at heart free. In and through the institution my freedom is alien-ated, or rather my freedom is in the Sovereign, because I want it to be there. Yet can I say farewell to what I am? Although quasi-inorganic, inert and submissive, *perinde ac cadaver* ("like a corpse"), shall I forever remain that way?

Here we are, at the end of the long duel between man and the inert, which attempts to immobilize him but without which he cannot exist. Seriality, *group en fusion,* group under oath, organization, institution, authority—there are so many means which make the individual act with power, yet which also make him powerless, powerless but not unfree. Someday, when the time is ripe, perhaps the Bastille will be taken again.

In conclusion, Sartre basically accepts dialectic as the infra-structure of sociological growth, but he looks at this dialectical procedure with a critical eye. His book—and this must be kept in mind—is a *Critique de la raison dialectique.* The dialectic which moves through history *is not merely a deterministic one* to which man must blindly submit. At every stage the subject intervenes; even in the seriality man chooses to an extent his prison, and if the walls become too confining, he, in unison with others, is driven to escape and to form a group. In the case of the bus passengers, they chose to embark at a certain point and to disembark at a particular destination—they were of course com-pelled to stand and wait for the bus which would take them there. One might say that they were caught, but, on the other hand, there is always the possibility of going beyond. Thus, we have already seen that the Negro riders in Alabama might al-ways have accepted unequal service, which as members of a series they were forced to do—but they did not; they united. There is always the human element; man is caught, yet free. He is not the mere helpless pawn of a dogmatic dialectic, as the Marxists would have us believe. Furthermore, Sartre would have us always be *aware* of the events which are operating, as now when we observe the genesis of the group as a *rational* and *intelligible* procedure. It is the intention of the entire work of

Sartre to lay all this before us, to bring it out of the darkness into the light; but as we have said before, others may—and must—do it also. It has always been a preoccupation of Sartre's to investigate how much a person is conditioned by his class and how far he is self-determined.

The obsession of the *Critique*, not always overt yet always there at least subterraneously, is that the individual is *center* and that the Other in one way or another is a menace. In the analysis of the sociological development, Sartre makes it abundantly clear that the group is born through *me as individual* and for *my* protection. When the Other is no longer a help, he becomes in the world of scarcity a menace. In a world such as ours, where there is not enough for all, he appears as a menace, a scandal, a perpetual opponent.[22] Having erected an impressive defense of the subject, Sartre has exploded the concept of the intersubjective. The foremost French existentialist has no philosophy of the group *as an ontological totality*. As long as he installs the individual as sovereign and refuses to accept the group as ontological entity, the existence and the accomplishment of which surpasses the being and the activity of the individual self, one must conclude that Sartre has not really and in depth given us the speculative basis on which to build a philosophy of the collective.

Where then lies Sartre's merit? Sartre's merit is precisely the glorification of his sin, namely, of the self. Sartre, more than his predecessors, has drawn attention to the individual, to his freedom and his creation. Marxism had not sufficiently seen this (and in stating this, I merely repeat Adam Schaff). At present the power of the Subject comes to the fore. Besides the indubitable impact of economic factors, there is also in individual man that ineffable something which escapes quantification, which is irrepressible, starts anew, affects and mutates a surrounding world and in this very deed creates. In this Sartre corrects Marx. But to correct does not necessarily mean to become.

22. *Ibid.*, p. 265.

13 / The Nature of Social Man

Maurice Natanson

THE HISTORY AND PHILOSOPHY of social man are inseparable, for history encompasses philosophy and philosophy includes the critique of historical experience. No priorities in chronology are appropriate here. Nor is it possible to understand the
relationship between history and philosophy without recognizing
the special sense in which philosophy is included in the historian's province. The arguments of the philosophers are part of the
subject matter of history only to the extent that they are deemed
relevant to the age, to the events considered worthy of recollec-
tion, and to the transformations of societal structure. The arguments themselves, strangely enough, are left alone; or, more
strictly, they are left to the puzzlement, the haggling, or the
bemusement of the philosophers. Hegel's thought is certainly
important to the understanding of nineteenth- and twentieth-
century history, but it would be odd to suggest that it is the
historian's responsibility to vindicate or refute Hegel's philosophy. He must know *about* Hegel; he is not professionally committed to philosophize with Hegel. It is possible, then, to learn a
great deal about the history of philosophy—what the major
thinkers said—without fully encountering the conceptual problems which worried them or turning to the phenomena which
occasioned them and to which the arguments are directed. Philosophy stands in a qualitatively different position. Its concern is
with the assumptions and presuppositions of historical experience, not with the factual content of what happened or with the
orderly narrative reconstruction of the significant past. It is not

the leavings of history to which the philosopher turns but to the leaven of the unexamined and the unformulated. The embrace of history is then a selective enclosure of philosophy's formulations but not of its conceptual content. The latter remains untouched by observation and report, almost, one is tempted to say, as a poem transcends print or music a score. On the side of philosophy a corresponding distinction is called for. As a critique of historical experience, philosophy restricts itself to the meaning of our ordering of the past and is not interested in the description or analysis of the events involved. Occasionally we have individuals who are both historians and philosophers— R. G. Collingwood, for example—but the disciplinary difference remains. The inseparability of history and philosophy is far from constituting a unity. Indeed, the inseparables live very distinct though related lives. In the restless ménage of knowledge, the historian and the philosopher live together without sharing either board or bed.

The difference between history and philosophy is directly reflected in their formulations of the nature of social man. A history of social man would face the overwhelming task of ordering materials into a coherent account of much of world civilization, but there would be no problem in the identification of the subject matter—man as a social being. Understanding, interpreting, analyzing, comprehending, and explaining social man are demanding and troublesome ventures, but there is little suggestion in history that man himself is a problematic phenomenon or that the social is inherently elusive. In fine, the recognition of social man is historically taken for granted. The historian's professional enterprise begins—properly and necessarily— where the philosopher's craft ends. The issue, the bond and yet the contention between them, is the nature and status of the public, readily available, common-sense world of everyday life which we all share as mundane beings. For the historian, the real world all of us inhabit is the unchallenged ground and foundation for the events which comprise the story he tries to tell. For the philosopher, it is the very reality of our world which calls for scrutiny. The central terms of discourse, then, must be subjected to inspection: "man," "world," and "sociality" are necessary as well as proper themes for inquiry. It is not a question of definition, at least in the usual sense of offering a few carefully formulated sentences which explain how each term is being used. At best, philosophers end with definitions; they cannot begin with them without endangering their quest. The reason is simply that in trying to define such fundamental concepts as social man the terms of discourse are already inflected with philosophical attitudes and commitments. If we were to start defining man "as a being who . . ."—for example—we would be presupposing a difference between beings and Being, and would be treading on ontological ground. Being is no problem for the historian; it is perhaps the most basic question for the philosopher. If we cannot start by simply defining our terms, we can begin by sketching the large outline of certain thematic issues which may lead to a philosophic understanding of social man.

Amid the variables of human experience, there are certain features of man's existence which are essentially unchanging and, I believe, unchangeable. It is a constant of human being that each of us is born into a world already inhabited by Others, fellow-men like ourselves. It is a constant of mundane reality that each of us is born into a historical and cultural order, that we have language, that we experience the limits of existence in terms of the religious or the magical, that we grow older together, and that we are destined to die. But it is also true that each of us can say "we," that we are able to share selected aspects of reality—appreciate the same poem, respond to the same music—without reducing them to idiosyncratic expressions or private contents of consciousness. And it is a prime fact of daily life that we take communication with fellow-men for granted, that is, we perceive the world and act in it on the unstated, completely immanent assumption that Others see the world essentially as we do, that the one umbrella of reality serves us all. We are not, of course, at the level of individual or sociocultural differences. Rather, we are trying to grasp the conditions necessary for the very possibility of experience in the social world. In these terms, the individual's knowledge of an experience of his fellow-men emerges as the definitive theme of social reality, and the essential features of intersubjective experience are what provide the basis for understanding social man. The "social," let us say, is located by way of the philosophical problem of intersubjectivity. Once again, it is the privileged responsibility of the philosopher to look after this issue. "And he's welcome to it!" an unfriendly voice may catcall. Before proceeding any further, we should face the not uncommon charge that the philosopher who worries about intersubjectivity is like a man going down in a sinking ship who asks whether Archimedes' principle really holds water.

The charge amounts to this: given the actuality of war, riot, assassination, famine, overpopulation, plague, revolt, oppression, prejudice, and apartheid, how dare the philosopher ask whether there are really other people in the world or how it is possible to have knowledge of them? Isn't that a continuation of the same inconsequentiality philosophers indulged in centuries ago when they asked how many angels could dance on the head of a pin? If I may be permitted one aside, I would like to put in a good word for the angels and suggest that their discussion by St. Thomas Aquinas and Maimonides is well worth study by those who are willing to exchange the jingling for the genuine. But whatever other failings philosophers may have, they are not guilty of triviality in turning to the problem of intersubjectivity. On the contrary, there is hardly a theme in their discipline with more immediate and vital implications for the scene of human action. To set matters straight, it must be said that the philosopher is not an innocent, nor is he isolated from the harshness of the world. The best man in the history of our profession died in jail. Since the fourth century B.C., working conditions for us may have become better but certainly not less complicated. When we ask about fellow-men, then, we are not wondering whether there is anybody else around besides ourselves, nor are we suggesting that social life is somehow unreal. *Of course*, there are Others, and *of course*, we communicate with them. The difficulty is in understanding how the obvious is possible, how the givenness of sociality is to be explained. The choice is not between affirming or denying intersubjectivity but between taking its philosophical structure for granted or trying to account for it. The choice is between assumption and explanation. What we are really asking is what "of course" means when we bank on its certitude. Nor is there any simple option in choosing between common sense and philosophy, for, as I hope to show in quite some detail, common sense is built on philosophical commitments, and the purpose of philosophy is to illuminate its structure.

I have contrasted common sense with philosophy. Whatever account we give of philosophy, we are at least on mutual ground when it comes to common sense, for it is, at first approximation, our natural habitat, the arena of work and love, of everyday performances. It is the world we are all wise to, whatever our station in life. Most simply, common sense is the typical; common sense is the familiar. To avoid one possible misunderstanding, however, it should be understood that in the context I am relying on, common sense refers to the structure of man's action in daily life, not to the quality of his judgment. Interestingly enough, even when we do have judgment in mind when we speak of common sense, there is a quantitative rather than a qualitative ascription made. We say that someone has a "lot" of common sense or else "very little," and we may also say, "He showed good common sense" on that occasion. But the last would seem to translate into "He showed a great deal of common sense," for what would it mean to say—and could we possibly say—"He showed bad common sense"? It would seem that common sense is always good, though often in short supply. In invoking it we are not appealing to a special faculty of mind but to the character of social order, its traditions, its formulas for handling problems, and its recipes for action. Common sense is not so much a personal possession as a mark of sociality, an emblem of man's involvement in the public world. It is this social pull that common sense responds to which leads us to speak of its structural dimension. Rather than common sense, perhaps we should more properly speak of the common-sense world. In any case, what we have before us as a problem can be formulated fairly simply. Each of us lives in a world which is organized along typical and typically taken for granted lines. The content of that world varies from individual to individual, from culture to culture, and from one era to another, but its formal properties, its underlying guidelines, remain universally secure and pertinent. What we called the constants of man's existence hold for common sense: from birth to death we are plunged and immersed in the currents of a meaning-laden sociality, created by Others and sustained by intersubjective resolve and complicity. How are we to understand the forms and forces of social reality? How is a philosophy of the common-sense world possible?

To be clear about our procedure in presenting a philosophy of common-sense reality, it is instructive to note what we are *not* concerned with. No effort will be made here to account for the genesis or causal development of the social world. There are valid and urgent questions of causation related to man's mundane existence, but we are explicitly setting them aside for our purposes. Further, no attempt will be made here to evaluate or promote some judgment of what is right or wrong, good or bad, about social structure. Again, judgments of value are profoundly relevant to some of the topics we are examining, but not in our context. We choose, then, to set them aside, along with many other dispositions and interpretive attitudes men share in their appraisal of life, in order to turn directly to the structure of the common-sense world so that we may describe its terrain and determine its constitution. Positively stated, we are embarked on a descriptive enterprise which seeks to render the world of man's social being an explicit object of scrutiny and which is concerned with uncovering the thick and often hidden meaning of social reality by a radical conception of consciousness. In its distinctively modern form, this philosophical orientation is known as phenomenology. In what follows, as in what has already been said, I am indebted to the work of the founder of phenomenology, Edmund Husserl, and to the phenomenologist who has subsequently done most to develop a theory of the social world, Alfred Schutz. If I have not credited them with particular notions already presented it is because I have done so elsewhere, and because it is tiresome to have to say, "as Husserl showed" or "as Schutz maintained," and, finally, because I am not simply expositing their views but utilizing them in my own way, a more nearly existential way than either man would have cared to be associated with. To get started, though, I will appeal to Schutz for an initial depiction of social man. He writes:

> Let us try to characterize the way in which the wide-awake grown-up man looks at the intersubjective world of daily life within which and upon which he acts as a man amidst his fellow-men. This world existed before our birth, experienced and interpreted by others, our predecessors, as an organized world. Now it is given to our experience and interpretation. All interpretation of this world is based on a stock of previous experiences of it, our own or those handed down to us by parents or teachers; these experiences in the form of "knowledge at hand" function as a scheme of reference.

Furthermore:

> Man finds himself at any moment of his daily life in a biographically determined situation, that is, in a physical and socio-cultural

environment as defined by him, within which he has his position, not merely his position in terms of physical space and outer time or of his status and role within the social system but also his moral and ideological position. To say that this definition of the situation is biographically determined is to say that it has its history; it is the sedimentation of all man's previous experiences, organized in the habitual possessions of his stock of knowledge at hand, and as such his unique possession, given to him and to him alone.[1]

Expressed in first-person terms, I am thrust into a world which is always "already" in process, that is, for me, the actor on the social scene, the participant in daily life, there is no point at which it could be said that the slate is clean, experience is untouched by the past, or everything is just starting. At any moment of reflection, I can look back and locate the ground or source of the present; in fact, reflection by its very nature presupposes a something prior, a something already there to which attention is to be given. A pattern of intention and attitude, merged with memorial notes and sly expectancies, underlies even the most casual elements of experience. Nothing is presented to me which is pristinely stripped of association and implication, nor is anything received by me which enters my perceptual doors without ringing a bell that reverberates throughout my being. I am speaking of the social, not the physical. A light flashed in my eyes during a medical examination produces a characteristic response, a reflex reaction, without presenting a challenge to my being as a person. A light flashed in my eyes during a police investigation provokes a different kind of response. The pupil contracts in the same manner in both instances, but the meaning of the light derives from the situation of authority and privacy, and reaction gives way to response. The moment of reflection, then, is bound to the total reality of my continuity as an individual and cannot be understood apart from the unity of my being as a person. But each time something happens which occasions reflection, the event is appropriated by the categories and schemas of common-sense interpretation. As a social being I am always in the midst of experience and always undergirded by the structure of mundanity. The seemingly and even genuinely novel is irretrievably

1. Alfred Schutz, *Collected Papers* (The Hague: Martinus Nijhoff, 1962), I, 7–9.

caught in a matrix of the familiar. William James, speaking as a pragmatist, made essentially the same point in a different way:

Our minds . . . grow in spots; and like grease-spots, the spots spread. But we let them spread as little as possible: we keep unaltered as much of our old knowledge, as many of our old prejudices and beliefs, as we can. We patch and tinker more than we renew. The novelty soaks in; it stains the ancient mass; but it is also tinged by what absorbs it. Our past apperceives and co-operates; and in the new equilibrium in which each step forward in the process of learning terminates, it happens relatively seldom that the new fact is added *raw*. More usually it is embedded cooked, as one might say, or stewed down in the sauce of the old.[2]

If we grant the force of the traditional in the sphere of common sense, it is still necessary to determine the relationship between the general field of social life and the concrete reality of the individual. What is the point of access each of us has as an individual to the typified world of social man? The reply I will give may appear both eccentric and out of keeping with what has been said so far. Explanation will follow swiftly, but the immediate answer is: my body!

As a purely physical phenomenon, my body is measurable and classifiable chemically and biologically. Its physics is that of a remarkable but faulty machine. It may be understood qualitatively in the same way that other animal machines are studied and explained. Apart from incidental differences, my guess is that an autopsy on my cadaver would, were it performed soon, reveal unexciting, rather mediocre results. I'm afraid that my case records would be indistinguishable from hundreds of thousands of others. Since I have no hopes for posthumous medical glory, I am resigned to seeking other fields of conquest. A more positive domain is that of my body as an expressive rather than a sheerly physical reality. By that I mean my body as a primordially experienced means through which I am able to insert myself in the world, through which I am able to achieve both intimacy and distance, and whose immediacy is the agency for my locating objects and persons, events and feelings, as *here* and as *mine*. To be sure, the body is the functioning sensory screen which enables me to contact the world and respond to it. At the

2. *Pragmatism* (London and New York: Longmans, Green, 1940), pp. 168–69.

same time, however, it may be understood as the active instrument which brings to life, which activates and indeed creates, the resplendent and baffling variety of human involvements: work, love, disease, and death. There is a terrible familiarity about the body which tends to disguise its centrality to the individual's organization of the world. First, it has always been with us; second, it is always there when called on; third, it seems as though it invariably manages to be there when we arrive. In between awareness of it, times when we inspect it or self-consciously utilize it, it hovers, an obedient wraith. When it fails, in disease, in trauma, in extreme conditions, we tend to think of the body in beast-of-burden terms: we speak of having to drive, push, propel ourselves. Or, if we are seriously incapacitated, it is as though insurrection had occurred: the body revolts, is crushed, defeated. Apart from the more obvious circumstances of pathology or injury, there is the oblique dimension of the body's relationship to us. Familiar, ally, friend, despot, slacker, troublemaker, it sustains us and betrays us, bears us and abandons us. The discussion of the existential motility of the body in Sartre and Merleau-Ponty is extensive and, I think, impressive even to those who might not be persuaded by the larger philosophical positions advanced by those authors. Rather than rehearse those theories, I prefer a more direct route to the point they make, the active and integral relationship between person and body. Quoting Whitehead's phrase, "the withness of the body," as a motto for his poem, Delmore Schwartz says in "The Heavy Bear Who Goes With Me":[3]

> The heavy bear who goes with me,
> A manifold honey to smear his face,
> Clumsy and lumbering here and there,
> The central ton of every place,
> The hungry beating brutish one
> In love with candy, anger, and sleep,
> Crazy factotum, dishevelling all,
> Climbs the building, kicks the football,
> Boxes his brother in the hate-ridden city.
>
> Breathing at my side, that heavy animal,
> That heavy bear who sleeps with me,

3. Delmore Schwartz, *Selected Poems: Summer Knowledge.* Copyright 1938 by New Directions. Reprinted by permission of New Directions Publishing Corporation, New York.

Howls in his sleep for a world of sugar,
A sweetness intimate as the water's clasp,
Howls in his sleep because the tight-rope
Trembles and shows the darkness beneath.
—The strutting show-off is terrified,
Dressed in his dress-suit, bulging his pants,
Trembles to think that his quivering meat
Must finally wince to nothing at all.

That inescapable animal walks with me,
Has followed me since the black womb held,
Moves where I move, distorting my gesture,
A caricature, a swollen shadow,
A stupid clown of the spirit's motive,
Perplexes and affronts with his own darkness,
The secret life of belly and bone,
Opaque, too near, my private, yet unknown,
Stretches to embrace the very dear
With whom I would walk without him near,
Touches her grossly, although a word
Would bare my heart and make me clear,
Stumbles, flounders, and strives to be fed
Dragging me with him in his mouthing care,
Amid the hundred million of his kind,
The scrimmage of appetite everywhere.

The discovery of my body, myself incarnate in the world, mysteriously and paradoxically strapped to something I both am and am not, is achieved or avoided within common-sense existence, for the "here" of my body has no place on any official map. It is, however, the null point, the center zero, of the mundane coordinates which mark my position in everyday life.

At every moment of my life, I occupy some "here," marked by the locus of my body. Obviously, the "here" keeps changing as I move about, yet it is perpetually renewed. From that "here" the shape and organization of the world is discerned or hypothesized by the individual as a mundane being. Right now, the world opens up before me, around me, from *Here,* where I stand; and what I perceive as near or distant, as within or out of reach, as *There,* is defined by the place of my body. That I can move from Here to There, that I can have a new Here, means that a principle of exchangeability tacitly underlies the location of the individual in the world, for not only is it the case that I can move from Here to There but I take it for granted that from the new Here the world will unfold, be structured in essentially the same way it was before, in my old Here. Exchangeability is not a physical directive; it is an axiom of social life. What it posits is the thesis that all transformations of the placement of the body will yield an unchanging and stable world in which the individual will have everything laid out before him essentially as he did before. Certainly, the new vantage point may present a very different, sometimes a surprisingly new, view of some event or situation, but transformation rules are available which take the altered circumstances into account and enable the individual to confront the "same" segment of reality he perceived before. What remains constant in the transformation is the principle of centrality, that in the exchange of places from Here to There the null point remains the same. The most vital implication of that presupposed constancy is that the individual who is Here can change places with his fellow-man who is There and that both of them will find the transposition continuous with the flow of their prior experience. The constancy of the null point is thus not a geographical but a sociological insight. I regard it as decisive for the constitution of intersubjectivity.

A closer examination of the insertion of the body in the world reveals a major difference between the assumption the individual makes about his own transposibility from Here to There and the supposed analogous counterpart he thinks is true for his fellow-man. In first-person terms, I have direct evidence regarding my own transposition but none regarding my alter ego. I simply take it for granted that what is true for me is also true for him. In that act of "animal faith," I take the first, the crucial step in the epistemic journey which leads to intersubjectivity. That act is unsupported by any argumentation, it is not based on inductive procedures, and it cannot be accounted for by a chain of causal reasoning. Rather, it is more modest to say that belief in the sameness of my and the Other's standpoint in the world and faith in the reciprocity of our world-organizing principles are already evidenced in the experience of the social world within whose limits questions about the individual's relationship to his fellow-men arise. It is within the intersubjective world of daily life that our inquiry into its structural possibility emerges. And it is through the body that the outlines of that world are initially glimpsed and gauged. If that is so, then the act of faith which takes for granted the sameness of the Other's placement in the world must take its clue from the appearance of *his* body. How then is the body of the Other perceived? It might appear reasonable to answer, "Why, just as I perceive my own." But that won't do for a number of reasons. First, I don't perceive my body directly. In fact, there are parts I have no direct visual access to without artificial aids: my face and my back. Second, even those parts I can see directly are features of the body which is seeing, that is, they are integral to my presence as a perceiving being; they are *me!* By a special effort I can, of course, observe my hands or my toes or my teeth, but they are then removed from the taken-for-grantedness of my bodily stance and rendered objects for inspection, like soldiers on parade. My body, then, is the vital instrument through which perception takes place; it is not in its mundane being a phenomenon for perception. The Other's body presents itself to me in altogether different circumstances. It *is* an object for my perceptual experience, but it is an object of a special sort. Unlike my seeing and touching sticks and stones, my awareness of the body of the Other is suffused by a recognition that it is *the Other,* a fellow-man, I greet when I catch his eye, touch his hand, hear his voice. All apparent evidence to the contrary, the fishiest handclasp ever offered belongs to a man, not a fish. But just as the movement from the Here of the individual to the There of his fellow-man is based on the assumption of the reciprocity of null points, so we may say that the recognition of the body of the Other as animately *his* is grounded in the perception of the Other as a presence whose cognitive and affective life manifests itself in simultaneity with the presentation of his body. We do not see flesh and infer a human being inside it; we confront a psyche in seeing a man. The Other lives and is recognized at the focus of his glance, in the space he warms, and in the void his language fills. In this bodily presence the sociality of man achieves its primordial expression.

The discussion thus far of the body might tend to give the impression that even if it does offer a valid starting point for the understanding of intersubjectivity, the model it is based on—man confronting fellow-man—is too narrow to serve as a paradigm for all sociality. That is quite true, and I hasten to turn now to an equally important aspect of the problem, that of time. If it is true to say that the body is the clue to social man, that is certainly not the whole truth, for man's being articulates itself in temporal no less than spatial terms. To the Here of bodily presence must be added the Now of social encounter. The immediate liberation that results from introducing this category should be evident, for we can share a temporal reality with fellow-men we do not see and cannot touch, not only those at great distance from us but those who died before we were born and even those who will be born after we die. The social world is made up of predecessors and successors no less than of contemporaries. Not only are we influenced by them and oriented to them, but we share with them the history of sociality, for each of us is destined to be a predecessor and a successor as long as a social world goes on. Moreover, our relationship to contemporaries with whom we have a face-to-face relationship is marked by the temporal roots which anchor our social immediacy. Those seen now may move off and drop out of all perceptual contact. Those once encountered may return. In a sense, the social world is constructed out of interruptions and mortared with expectancies; it is a patchwork of presence and departure. If this were the end of the story, it might well appear that all we could say about intersubjectivity is a bland and unrewarding, "Here today, there tomorrow." I propose an altogether different refrain as a preliminary conclusion to these proceedings: Here means type, Now means form. The analysis of the body brings us to the concept of typification as the form of social existence. It returns us also to social man as a being immersed in as well as generated by the taken for granted and the familiar. Once again we turn to Alfred Schutz as a guide to the phenomenology of typification. He writes:

> The factual world of our experience . . . is experienced from the outset as a typical one. Objects are experienced as trees, animals, and the like, and more specifically as oaks, firs, maples, or rattlesnakes, sparrows, dogs. This table I am now perceiving is characterized as something recognized, as something foreknown and, nevertheless, novel. What is newly experienced is already known in the sense that it recalls similar or equal things formerly perceived. But what has been grasped once in its typicality carries with it a horizon of possible experience with corresponding references to familiarity, that is, a series of typical characteristics still not actually experienced but expected to be potentially experienced.[4]

4. Alfred Schutz, *Collected Papers*, I, 281.

Applied to the social world, we may say that our experience of each other is typified not only by common-sense attitudes and expectancies but more fundamentally by the very perceptual process through which apprehension and interpretation occur. In seeing the embodied Other, I am presented, strictly speaking, with only an aspect of his being, his face, his intonation, his gesture; but that glimpse is enough for me to perceive him as an individual having a multitude of attributes, all of which are features of a being *like* myself. That "likeness" is the initial typification which permits me to commence the movement from I to we. But the typification of the Other goes far beyond the immediacy of our bodies in face-to-face situations. As I have said, in addition to the Here of immediacy there is also the Now of transcendence. The Other who is *not* present is also typified. Indeed, our knowledge of predecessors is largely limited to knowledge by way of type, and what we surmise of our successors is completely restricted to typified expectancies and fantasies. The insertion of my body in the world is then only the beginning of a long and complex series of performances which account for the construction of a social world. Within the larger present of contemporaries with whom I do not share common space, there is an infinitely complex system of typifications which enable me to understand them and their activities and permit me to translate their demands and offers in appropriate ways. With Joseph K., most of us will never penetrate to the high courts, but we organize our lives in terms of that exclusion. What remains as the field of our social action is similarly typified: whether it is City Hall or the State Department, the local police force or the United States Army, the university, the movies, the stock exchange, or the Library of Congress, most of us know about the workings of these local or national organizations and institutions only in typified ways. Some of us may know one of them intimately, but then the rest are known vaguely, hypothetically, and indirectly. The remainder of contemporary experience, the entire sociocultural world now in process, is known in essentially the same manner. The result of such typification is that the strange and the foreign are accommodated in mundane terms. We may never meet any of the great heroes of our times, but we know about them in common-sense terms, and that *is* the way they enter our lives and become part of our reality. Neither may we ever meet the men who handle the mail, who repair telephone lines, who unload freight, or who grow wheat, but we have typified concepts of them and their jobs. They are no less contemporaries than the pedestrians we pass on streets or the crowds we mingle with on public occasions. If, as I have suggested, the typical is the clue to mundane existence, then it is possible to say that it is also the secret of the familiarity of common sense. Rather than the familiar being defined by the concrete actuality of what each of us has directly experienced, it is more nearly the opposite case: the familiar is what is typically possible, what is potentially experienceable. Common sense is a tissue of possibilities.

If we have stressed our relationship to fellow-men so far, it should not be thought that the existence of the individual has been sacrificed on the altar of sociality. Nor should it be concluded that typification applies only to the Other. Man is a self-typifying no less than an Other-typifying creature. If it is only an aspect of the Other which manifests itself to me, it is also only a fragment of my own being I am aware of or have come to terms with, and only a facet of myself which presents itself to my fellow-man on any occasion. Once again, this fragmentation is taken for granted in common-sense life. We don't ask clerks questions which are appropriate for priests, nor do we go to the corner newsstand in search of rare first editions. Most basically, we know, as common-sense men, that certain forms or types of behavior are called for in certain situations, and we all serve an apprenticeship in the academy of daily life which trains us for taking the roles we must inevitably play in social reality. Roles and role-playing are the forms that typification takes in moving from the beginnings of intersubjectivity in bodily presence to the schemas and constructs of the public world in the regions of distance and absence. Whatever interpretations and explanations social scientists may give to roles, the primal status they enjoy is expressed in mundane life, in the midst of common-sense experience. There man and fellow-man, understood as actors in as well as observers of the social scene, build the reality within whose limits all history is lived. To locate the uniqueness of the individual, the existential sphere of the person, we are obliged to honor common sense rather than to sidetrack it. The whole point of our discussion of typification is that it provides a wedge into the nature of social man. It would be a misreading of my words to conclude that common sense and personal identity are antagonists. Before we can say that there is enmity between them we must first make certain that the relationship is understood in its positive sense. Where, precisely, do we locate the concrete individual in the matrix of societal typifications? Having discussed the body and the dialectic of intersubjectivity, having stressed the familiar structure of mundane existence and the world at distance from us, where at last shall we find the pulse of a single, actual, splendidly or miserably existent human being? Where in the castle of social man can we find our own small bedroom?

Let me turn to an example for help. Years ago I had to pass reading examinations in French and German in order to fulfill requirements for the Ph.D. I remember the German exam especially well because of an incident which disrupted it. A group of doctoral candidates were given the test together in one room. Among them was a graduate student, quite a bit older than the rest of us, a married man with several children, who had come back to the university late in academic life, who was an able and a hard worker but whose nemesis was German. He had failed the examination twice and was given a special dispensation to try a third time. He had passed all other requirements for his degree but would be forced to abandon his career if he failed German a third time. We all knew him, liked him, admired his spirit and fortitude, and were hoping he would make it this time. He had worked with a private tutor, spent a great many hours in preparation, and had, he thought, a decent chance to pass. As soon as the text for translation was distributed, we all set to work. The room was a cube of perfect silence, but seconds after we got started, I heard a small but peculiar noise. One of the examinees had a rather full, laden nose and was snuffling. I wasn't particularly disturbed but I noticed that our last-chance friend, who was sitting next to the sniffler, was upset. He gave him two or three withering looks, tapped his pencil vigorously, rearranged his chair severely—all to no effect. The offender seemed immune to all signals, lost in the complexity of some endless German sentence. And the noises went on. Indeed, by some strange nasal chemistry, the sounds grew not only in volume but in variability. Little bubbles seemed to erupt from time to time with tiny explosiveness, inhalation was accompanied by liquid grunts, and the perilous moment when what was there seemed about to flee its tunneled prison was obviated by a quick save of almost passionate intake. Meanwhile our friend was frantic. Unable to concentrate, at a disadvantage under the best of circumstances, under the added pressure of the time limit of the examination, confronted with the knowledge that it was now or never in his career, undoubtedly aware of the years of work he had already put in and the hardships his family had suffered on his behalf, poised at the linguistic Rubicon, his face screwed into a torment of ire, he slammed his fist on the table and screamed at the villain: "JESUS CHRIST! BLOW YOUR NOSE!"

How does one go about understanding such an outburst? How does one account for an otherwise mild person exploding into paroxysm? And how is it possible to distinguish between *this* individual and the typified class of "men of that type"? It would seem that the most natural way of proceeding to answer these questions is to turn to the background of our friend, to study his past, work up a detailed analysis of the pressures on him, and, having come to terms with the causes and motivational grounds of his personality and behavior, offer an explanation of the examination events consistent with the causal conditions which produced them. My insistence on a phenomenological framework for analysis has ruled out that general line of explanation for the present context. Committed as we are to a structural and descriptive account of social man, we shall have to look to other sources for help in assessing his action. To understand the examination scene—limited as that example may be—it is necessary to locate our friend in the midst of what existential philosophers call a "situation," that is, an ensemble of forces and projects defined by the constants of man's being, the goals he has set himself, and the freedom he displays in choosing the meaning of what limits and liberates him. If we assume that a present action is explained by certain states of affairs in the past, then explosive behavior is the "result" of tension, pressure, and frustration. However, if we allow for present action being defined by present choice, stemming from the continuous decision the individual makes in interpreting his world, then irruption proves to be the point of departure for reconstructing some causal history of a human career rather than the other way around. Nor is it then possible to file away men according to their "type" and say, "Well, after all, what can you expect of him? He's a choleric." There are times when we are surprised by a moderate voice when we expect the Other to be enraged, and there is no assurance that a typified expectation will in fact yield the expected result. Part of the fund of common-sense knowledge is the distinctive recognition that the unexpected is always possible and that fellow-men, ourselves included, are always capable of breaking out of the circuit of the taken for granted and the condoned and of acting in novel and sometimes erratic ways. The prime lesson of common sense is that we must comprehend man in his situation if we are to understand him. The performances of social man are shadow plays apart from the meaning human action has to those who are actors situated in mundane reality.

It is the status of meaning which marks the center of the network of problems we have been examining and which provides the basis for a solution to the puzzle of sociality and the paradox of identity and typicality in common-sense life. Meaning, we suggest, is a function of the interpretation an actor on the social scene gives to his own act. The ground of meaning in the social world, then, is not the observer's explanation of the actor's behavior but the participant's understanding of his own acts. In seeking to grasp the meaning of his alter ego's action, the individual tries to determine what the Other's action means to him, the one who performs that action. Now there is no claim being made at this point that either the actor or his fellow-man has a full comprehension of his own or his alter ego's action. As we have insisted on before, all action is expressed in fragmentary modes, all understanding arises through the typifications the individual makes of his social reality. But within the limits of fragmentation and typicality, the actor constructs a world whose form and content are composed of the interpretation he gives both to his own acts and to the action of Others. To say that such interpretation is *situated* is to suggest that the "same" behavioral act is not at all necessarily the same social act. I understand the meaning of an act when I determine what it signifies to the actor. The Other understands my action when he determines what it means to me. That much determination is partial and faulty is precisely the truth of social existence, for the necessary reliance on typicality—the very construction of common-sense life—is a recognition that we know ourselves, let alone Others, in partial and hidden ways and yet are bound, if not condemned, to find our way in the world within the restrictions of an opaque sociality. At the same time, typicality rewards us with a certain freedom and a measure of consistency. The anonymity of types assures the steady flow of social traffic, the commerce of everyday needs and desires, the business of our surface involvements. I can deal successfully with much of the content of everyday life because its typified form permits *any* individual in a certain societal position to act in a routine way. Identity and typicality need each other.

The location of meaning in the actor's intention, in his interpretation of the meaning of his own act, not only makes his situation the definitively important focus of social life but places a major stress on participation rather than observation as the proper point of departure for understanding social man. By this I mean only that the field of social action is initially that of the actor. To be sure, the actor is also an observer, but, as I have tried to show, his observation is directed in action to the situated reality of his fellow-man. His observation is an effort to interpret the meaning of his alter ego's action. The observer in this context is a participant because he is geared into his fellow-man's reality and shares the social scene with him. His history and that of his fellow-man mesh with a communal order; they share certain sectors of the same situation because they are immersed in the common-sense world. However, if we mean by observation the role of the scientist who takes human beings as objects of inquiry, then the meaning of observation changes, for the scientist is a participant in the scene he observes only in a special and quite restricted way. To the extent that he fulfills the role of scientific observer, the individual scientist relinquishes the Here and Now of mundane reality, gives up the placement of his body in the arena of social action, suspends the history of his biographical situation, renounces the demands of his project at hand, and identifies himself totally with the methodological commitments of his discipline. Two cautions are immediately necessary. First, even if it is agreed that such abstention is the ideal goal of the scientist, it hardly follows that he in fact realizes that goal in his actual work. Second, and more significant, the scientist does not cease to be a human being while he operates professionally. I am not saying that when he "does" science he is transformed into a weightless wonder, a free-floating phantom. The point is that the scientist elects to stand outside of common sense when he commits himself to taking the role of the professional observer. That such a choice involves conflict and compromise, that it is horrifically difficult to succeed in disengaging oneself from the sources of sociality, that the entire realm of value orientation and value commitment presents intense ambivalence, is granted. The qualitative difference in mundane and scientific role-obligations remains. And, of course, it is the social scientist who is caught most cunningly in the crosscurrents of disciplinary commitment and mundane estrangement. He is compelled to face a problem which is not unknown in the natural science but which has its strongest expression in the study of social reality: man's inquiry into himself. With that theme we come to the relationship between the natural and the social sciences and are led in turn to the question of the similarities and differences between human beings and animals.

At this point I must confine the discussion to a table of conclusions and forego the discussion necessary to support them. I hope that the analysis of everyday experience which I have developed will be sufficient to give some ballast to what otherwise might appear to be a scantly burdened vessel. The root difference between natural and social science is in the world that both investigate. The natural order is fundamentally one discovered and explored by man; the social order is paramountly one preinterpreted by its inhabitants. The models and constructs the natural scientist makes are of the first degree, that is, they are schemas of objects and events themselves unschematized; the interpretations of the social scientist are constructs of the second degree, schemas of realities already schematized. The self-interpretation of social man takes place by way of the typifications of common-sense life, and, as I have argued, the locus of everyday existence includes a very powerful temporal dimension: ours is a world of predecessors and successors no less than of contemporaries. The preinterpreted world of common-sense experience is then historically oriented in its very texture, for it is impossible to turn to social reality without finding the sedimentation of meaning, the memorial residue, left by our ancestors and their action. Language is one of the cardinal instruments by which we come to appreciate the history of meaning which grounds our social being, but there are other structures of mundanity to be considered. It is possible for man to move from the world of common sense to the worlds of religion, art, fantasy, and dreams because the immediacy of Here and Now can be transcended by means of a reflective decision. Transcension does not mean permanent abandonment. Quite the opposite: we are able to pray and to imagine because our position in mundane life as common-sense men can always be regained. The movement from life to art presupposes the possibility of interrupting the mundane and then rejoining it. Alternation makes us human. Animals, to the contrary, live in a permanent present; for them it is always Now. To shove the point to a final resting place, it should be said that common sense is a distinctively human achievement because it depends on a subjunctive capacity of consciousness. Let me explain.

Typification as the ground of intersubjectivity, the condition of the social, is an "as-if" mode of cognition. If a voice could be given to consciousness in its perceptual activity it might be heard to say: There is a fellow-man, standing before me, waiting for me to join him. His presence co-presents his world, his action, his interpretation of me and of our shared and unshared situation. Were he to say this, I would reply with that; were he to do this, I would do that. Since it is only a part of his world that shows itself at this moment of our meeting, I assume that a host of typicalities would manifest themselves in his action were I to get to know him over a long period of time and were we in close touch with each other. Even further, the very perceptual acts through which I have experience of the Other are selective and formative, for consciousness is an active partner in the construction of the social world. In setting aside the detailed specificity of the Other and seeing him in typified terms, consciousness deploys a hypothetical mode of awareness and revels in the liberation of the subjunctive. Animal consciousness is dominated by the indicative tense. And it is destined to enter a world which is perpetually renewed as the same. That nonhistorical constancy is the animal substitute for common sense. The hypothetical is precluded by the mechanisms of instinct and habit. I do not mean to strip the animal world of its variety, subtlety, and richness. Nor do I mean to treat its denizens as automata. The refreshing and remarkable gifts the animal world offers its human associates and observers are perhaps possible precisely because the situation of Here and Now can always be generated in the same way. I'm not sure we have as much to offer the animals, but, for better or worse, humanity is enmeshed in a historical order which utterly transcends the comprehension of our closest and most intelligent animal companions.

For man, then, mundane reality is historical reality; that is at once the reassurance and the anguish of his situation. How does social man stand with respect to himself? It is here that the convergence of phenomenology and existentialism is most dramatically evident. Our answer will retrace the course we have followed and will offer a glance beyond. To understand ourselves and our fellow-men as social beings it is necessary to examine the philosophical presuppositions of mundane existence. In the taken for granted attitude of daily life, the historicity and inter-subjectivity of the public world are assumed to be both obvious and valid. Whatever special problems arise for consideration are already taken to be within the horizon of *our* common world. But to come to terms with the meaningful structure of social reality it is necessary to set aside our believing in the obvious and call to scrutiny and account the basis for our beliefs. When we turn our critical glance to the social world we inhabit, we find that its epistemological center is the domain of common sense, understood as the matrix of typification and familiarity. From that center arise the constructs which organize our experience of life and toward that center are directed the problems and crises which disturb or plague our being. We find our direction in mundane reality by the coordinates of space and time at whose zero point lies our body, and it is from that orientation that we discover the bodies of fellow-men and are able to move from personal to intersubjective interpretation. Both self-understanding and the appreciation of Others involve a recognition that social action is meaningful initially to the actor himself and that no human act can be comprehended apart from the situation in which it has significance for the human agent. Participation rather than observation is the prime moment of the dialectic of social life. Accordingly, the task of the social scientist is to honor the preinterpreted order of common-sense experience by discerning and describing its structure and by trying to illuminate its relevance for the total range of man's historical and cultural reality. Our being in the social world is above all a thematic problem for us, concrete men in action in daily life, not a topic for social science. It is in our reflective potential that common-sense experience emerges as strikingly human, for in reflection we are able to transcend the Here and Now of social immediacy and encounter the full complexity of the possibility, the subjunctive options, of the immediate and the actual. Within the orbit of the mundane, then, we find the freedom of social man. At the same time, we find a definition of his—our—nature. Man is the being who creates social order out of the typifications of common sense.

With that we reach the end of our phenomenology of social man and come in sight of those existential questions regarding human identity and choice which our discussion has pointed to without ever broaching directly. The creature at the null point of space and time, confronting the social world, is not a body without a personal core. It is yourself or myself who awaits the philosopher's rendezvous. Yet the approach to that self is possible only by the discipline of knowledge. Therein lies the paradox of thought. How is it possible to capture social man without destroying his spontaneity? Isn't the analysis of common sense damaging to its autonomy? At this point we can do no more than raise the question and transpose it to the sphere of valuation we explicitly bracketed out of our discussion at the outset. There is little profit in saying that man is always social man because he cannot be otherwise. There is certainly a sense of the social which is normative and which is a measure of the distance which separates man's accidental birth from the attainment of dignity and justice. The social, in these terms, is as much an ideal as it is an attribute. It is somehow always left to final paragraphs to pay tribute to the spirit of man, his final mystery, and his ultimate transcendence. It is rather like saying, "Don't misunderstand me, I'm for man." Existential philosophy begins with the ambiguity of self-assessment and confronts the strangeness of having to account for ourselves. If I have centered the discussion on the structure of the mundane, it is not because I prefer to avoid existential concerns but because I am convinced that the secret of individual identity is locked in the nature of the social world. If common sense is the region in which our sociality is grounded, it may also be the existential locus of our normative possibilities. And if history is the covenant between man and God, daily life is the record of its fulfillment. There in the unexalted chronicle of the familiar is disclosed the image of what we may still become.

PART IV
SUBJECTIVITY AND OBJECTIVITY

14 / The Problem of the Will and Philosophical Discourse

Paul Ricoeur

THE ORIGIN OF THIS ESSAY lies in the dissatisfaction I feel when after almost twenty years I consider the type of analysis of the will I presented in *The Voluntary and the Involuntary*.[1] I intended this work as a phenomenological description of such phenomena as purpose, motive, gesture, and so forth. When I now consider the great philosophies, from Aristotle to Nietzsche, which stand out as landmarks in the history of philosophy on the path that passes through the Scholastics and Descartes to Kant and Hegel, and if I admit what I think must be admitted, that these philosophies have said something significant about the will, then a question arises: Do these disparate philosophical statements about the will belong to the same type of philosophical discourse, or are there several types of philosophical discourse? This in turn raises a question about the unity of philosophical discourse. My working hypothesis in this paper is that the philosophy of the will requires at least three types of discourse, each with its own rules, kind of coherence, and mode of validation. I call the first type *phenomenological discourse* (this already implies an extension of what I have previously called phenomenology). The second type is *discourse about meaningful action*, a type which we must identify with some kind of dialectical discourse. The third type is an indirect ontology and requires a kind

Translated in collaboration with the author by Peter McCormick.

1. *Freedom and Nature: The Voluntary and the Involuntary*, trans. Erazim V. Kohák (Evanston, Ill.: Northwestern University Press, 1966).

of *hermeneutic discourse,* that is, a discourse in the form of an interpretation.

II

THE FIRST TYPE OF DISCOURSE goes back to the third book of the *Nicomachean Ethics,* which is devoted to the principal notions of voluntary and involuntary action, of rational preference, and of the wish. This first phenomenology has not yet found its unity since there is not yet a unified concept of the will and since the concept of the will as such is perhaps not yet even formed. Moreover, it has not found its justification as phenomenology unless dialectical method in Aristotle's sense, that is, as a confrontation of opinions which is arbitrated by the work of definition, can be considered as the ancestor of phenomenology. Despite this fault in the analysis and this lack of a complete methodological justification, the third book of the *Nicomachean Ethics* can be called with good reason the first phenomenology of the will. It has a relative autonomy among the treatises which constitute the *Ethics.* The development of the phenomenology of the will can be followed like a straight line from Aristotle to post-Husserlian phenomenology because of the kind of continuity and relative autonomy which allows this discourse to preserve its identity even when inserted in different philosophical problematics.

I want to recall here only the principal instances of this phenomenology of the will. It appeared first in Greek philosophy with the Stoic conception of assent as an active counterpart of a passive image. This articulation between an active pole or term and a receptive pole constitutes a working model which will reappear in the famous Fourth Meditation of Descartes. While Aristotle organized his phenomenology around the central act of preference as applied to means in contrast with the wish as an evasive impulse directed toward ends, the Stoics reorganized the entire field of the psyche as a function of the polarity between activity and passivity. All the subsequent phenomenologies of the will, including the subtle analyses of the Scholastics and the elegant, simple description of Descartes, will remain faithful to this double phenomenological determination of the concept of the will: articulation of means and ends in purpose and articulation of a more or less passive understanding and the power of decision in the act of choice. From Saint Thomas to Descartes (who does not break with the Scholastic tradition in what concerns the phenomenology, properly speaking, of the will) the phenomenology of the will appears as a continual refinement of the Aristotelian and Stoic descriptions. This phenomenology culminates in the concept of decision, a concept which implies (1) purpose as an intention of the will; (2) choice insofar as the act itself points to the purpose; and (3) the decisive alternative as content of the act, what the Scholastics called power over contraries.

This tradition was not lost during the great period of German Idealism from Kant to Hegel. The description of the will as arbitrary (*Willkür*) is never lost sight of even if *Willkür* as arbitrary is now subordinated to another dimension of the will, the *Wille* properly so called, which according to Kant cannot be elaborated within the same universe of thought or on the same plane as purpose, choice, and the arbitrary. (We will come back to this turning point of the Kantian analysis of the will when we consider the second type of discourse about the will.)

The phenomenology of the will found its justification in Husserl and its fulfillment in the post-Husserlian literature. Husserl himself hardly wrote about the will. This fact, as we will remark later on, may have an important bearing on what concerns the limits of the phenomenological method. Essentially the Husserlian analysis rests on the priority of objectifying acts, and, among these, on perception. For this reason phenomenology is principally a phenomenology of perception and of assertive statements. Nonetheless, phenomenology has given to the classical type of discourse about the will a justification and a foundation. Thanks to the phenomenological reduction, all the naturalist statements about things, facts, and laws are bracketed and the world appears as a field of meaning. This reduction makes the phenomenon of the will as such possible. The notion of purpose appears as a particular case—and the most striking one—of the intentional character of every psychic life. Purpose has its noetic side in choice itself and its noematic side in purpose as something which must be done by me and which can be fulfilled or not. The relation of purpose to instincts, impulses, and affects is subordinated to the general concept of motivation, which is neatly set off from natural causality by the phenomenological reduction.

All the phenomenological traits of the will find in the Husserlian method an appropriate descriptive instrument elaborated neither in Aristotle nor in the Scholastics nor in the Cartesian tradition. However, not only is the phenomenology of the will justified by the Husserlian method, but the Husserlian method in its turn is extended beyond its classical expression. We may say here that the primacy of the phenomenology of perception gives a powerful impulse to the phenomenology of the emotions and to the phenomenology of the voluntary and the involuntary.

At this point in my reflection I should like to say that it is on this level of the first type of discourse that a confrontation occurs between the phenomenology of the voluntary and the involuntary and the conceptual analysis devoted to the notions of intention, purpose, and motive by the generation of English-speaking philosophers influenced by Wittgenstein's *Philosophical Investigations*.[2] I have in mind Anscombe's *Intention*,[3] Hampshire's *Thought and Action*,[4] Austin's admirable "A Plea for Excuses,"[5] and Taylor's *The Explanation of Behaviour*.[6] In fact, conceptual analysis is a phenomenological study to the extent that it does not imprison itself in a study of statements but, as these authors say, attempts to approach the complexities of life through a more exact knowledge of precise distinctions and the complex relations discerned by ordinary language in the course of the centuries. On the other hand, phenomenology is a conceptual analysis to the extent that it claims to apprehend not so much lived experiences as lived but the essence of lived experience, its articulations and its connections. I would say that today the future of this first type of discourse lies in an interpenetration of phenomenological description and the conceptual analysis of ordinary language.

2. L. Wittgenstein, *Philosophical Investigations*, trans. G. E. M. Anscombe (New York: Macmillan, 1953).

3. G. E. M. Anscombe, *Intention* (Ithaca, N.Y.: Cornell University Press, 1957).

4. Stuart Hampshire, *Thought and Action* (New York: Viking, 1960).

5. John L. Austin, "A Plea for Excuses," *Philosophical Papers* (Oxford, 1961), pp. 123–52.

6. Charles Taylor, *The Explanation of Behaviour* (New York: Humanities Press, 1964).

III

NONETHELESS THIS FIRST TYPE OF DISCOURSE does not and cannot exhaust the philosophy of the will. In fact, phenomenological discourse about the will has always been just an aspect of a much broader type of discourse which I propose to call discourse about responsible or meaningful action. Free choice has never been the principal problem. Rather the question is: what kind of action makes sense?

Let us go back for a moment to Aristotle because it is he who founded the philosophy of the will. What we have called his phenomenology is only an abstract segment within a treatise on virtue, its nature, its acquisition, and its conditions for actualization. With the concept of virtue, or, better, with that of excellence, the problem of the meaningful achievement of human life is raised. This problem constitutes, so to speak, the concrete envelope of the phenomenology of the will. More precisely, we learn from Aristotle that the architechtonic science which this description is subordinated to is politics, inasmuch as the good of the city is more general and more concrete than the good of the individual. In this sense phenomenological discourse is only an aspect of ethico-political discourse. It is only this discourse that is autonomous. The description of preference is an ingredient in a whole constituted by the determination of ethical life, which is also political life. The accent thus must be transposed from what is arbitrary in choice to its norm within the framework of a theory of the will. In this respect the treatise on prudence (*Nicomachean Ethics,* VI) constitutes the pole of the second type of discourse, just as the treatise on preference (*Nicomachean Ethics,* III) was the kernel of the first type. I will not consider here the details of this theory of virtue. I will stress only one point, the famous definition of virtue as "something mediated," as a point of equilibrium between two extremes, as a mean between excess and deficiency. The proper tension of the act, says Aristotle, is the norm. The mean between excess and deficiency is this proper tension.

This analysis anticipates with its relative formalization (the extremes and the median) the more radical formalization which reigns in Kantian philosophy of the will. For Aristotle, only the will regulated according to the principle of the mean and animated by the virtue of prudence (which plays the role of the categorical imperative) makes complete sense and is for that reason truly will. This continuity between Aristotle and Kant cannot be perceived at the level of the first type of discourse, but it can be perceived at that of the second level, that is, at the level of discourse about meaningful action. The revolution of thought which characterizes Kantian philosophy of the will takes place within a single and identical universe of thought and of discourse, that of meaningful action. The question which opens the *Groundwork of the Metaphysic of Morals* [7] is put this way: what makes a good will good? This question must be put on the same plane as the Aristotelian question: what is virtue, what is prudence? This kind of question implies that the arbitrary moment which constitutes the will as such on the phenomenological level articulates itself at the normative moment which constitutes the will as such on the second level. This duality between *Willkür* and *Wille,* between the arbitrary and the normative will, constitutes the central difficulty of the Kantian philosophy of the will. But before this duality brings about the ruin of Kantian philosophy it shows its strength. *The Critique of Practical Reason* [8] is nothing else than a transcendental analysis of the good will, that is, of the conditions of possibility for a good will, in the same way as the first *Critique* bears on the conditions of possibility of a true judgment of perception. This transcendental analysis of the good will is not only a new approach to the problem of meaningful action, but it radicalizes a tendency already present in Aristotle's work—and perhaps in the definition of virtue already formalized by Plato in Book V of *The Republic*—and brings us to the definition of the will as practical reason.

But this radicalization is at the same time at the origin of a paradox which steers Kantian philosophy of the will to shipwreck. The paradox is this. According to its intention *The Critique of Practical Reason* aims at explaining how a representation produces a real effect. In other words, the problem is the actualization of thought on the plane of action, the problem of the difference between nature and freedom, the first consisting in an action according to law and the second in an action

7. Trans. H. J. Paton (London, 1948).
8. Trans. Lewis White Beck (Indianapolis, Ind.: Bobbs-Merrill, 1956).

according to the representation of law. Thus freedom is a kind of causality which produces events in the world. But the result of the *Critique* destroys its intention. When the principle of rationality is cut away from the concrete ground of impulse and desire, the will as the unity of desire and rationality is broken in two. The will is no longer a kind of desire, a rational desire, but a variety of reason. At the same time, the will is separated from its goals since ends cannot be given a priori but belong to the sphere of desire. Hence Kantianism appears as a philosophy of division. From this it becomes very difficult to understand how the movement of contingence, of subjectivity, and of choice, which is *Willkür* itself, can be reintroduced into the field of the will. The first theorems of the second *Critique* presuppose in an axiomatic fashion that the duality between the will in general (which is determined by law) and human will (which is undetermined in its intimate movement) is a given, the ethical fact par excellence. The duality constituted by an objective will determined by law and by a subjective arbitrary will is the philosophical result of the second type of discourse about the will. This duality cannot be deduced from a phenomenology of the subjective will (or of free choice or of power over contraries). The discord between the two kinds of will, we might say, culminates in the *Treatise on Radical Evil*. Evil appears here as the most extreme divergence between the maxim of free choice and the determination of the objective will by law. One might be tempted to say that the *Treatise on Radical Evil* represents the return of free choice to the forefront of a philosophy of practical reason which has been constructed on the principle of the subordination of free will to the will of the law. This priority of the will for the law was the basic principle of discourse about meaningful action. Evil means breakdown in this type of discourse.

This antinomy of the will raises the question of the authentic nature of discourse about meaningful action. It seems to me that we have to recognize the dialectical character of this type of discourse.

In the same way that Husserl represents the phenomenological method, which is employed for the description of the will as purpose, preference, and choice, Hegel represents the dialectical method, which is the only adequate method for the problematic of meaningful action.

If the history of the philosophy of the will is considered from this viewpoint, then it must be recognized that this history raises a series of questions which cannot be resolved without a dialectical method, that is, without some means of overcoming antinomies by mediation. The dialectical situations implied by a discourse about meaningful action might be summarized in the following way.

First of all, the will is a transition from desire to rationality. When Aristotle defines the will as "deliberating desire," this expression itself implies that the natural reality summed up in the word "desire" is negated and yet retained within a reality of a superior order connected to rationality. Indecision requires a dialectical conception of reality according to which the root of desire is sublimated in the energy of decision. Such is the first dialectical situation. It is represented in Hegelian philosophy by the transition from a philosophy of nature to a philosophy of mind. Here is the second dialectical situation. The Scholastics and Descartes conceived of judgment as an interaction between two faculties, the understanding and the will. The interaction is conceived on the model of the relation of mutual causality. The understanding moves the will and the will moves the understanding. What can be seen here is a predialectical expression transposed into the language of a psychology of the faculties which itself flows from a cosmological concept of causality. This dialectical situation has not disappeared either with faculty psychology or the cosmology which supports it. The Kantian distinction between theoretical and practical reason only gives a new expression to this old problem, and everyone knows the formidable difficulties this dichotomy raised at the threshold of the third *Critique*. This second dialectical situation constitutes what is essential in the philosophy of subjective mind in the *Encyclopedia*. And the third dialectical situation is as follows. It concerns the transition from subjective will, which was the object of phenomenology, to objective will, which is the object of ethical and political determination in Aristotle and Kant. This dimension is lost in a simple psychology of decision where only the individual will is taken into account while the political dimension emigrates beyond the field of the philosophy of the will and constitutes the kernel of a political philosophy under the title of a theory of power or of sovereignty. Hobbes, Machiavelli, and the Spinoza of *The Political Treatise* witness to this other philosophy of the will which constitutes itself beyond the field of the psychology of decision. The dialectical unity of the problem of the will as individual and collective, as psychological and political, is lost. Aristotle was not ignorant of this unity, but he did not have the logical apparatus to master the problem of the relation between a phenomenology of preference and a political philosophy. This third dialectic is the center of what Hegel calls the philosophy of objective mind. The elevation of the arbitrary will to rationality is its principal concern, while at the same time it attempts to resolve the problem of the actualization in a human world of a freedom which will be at the same time both rational, that is, full of meaning, and real, that is, effective. This third dialectic comprises the authentic philosophy of the will at the level of discourse about meaningful action.

As can be seen in *The Philosophy of Right,* which develops only the section of the *Encyclopedia* devoted to objective mind, this dialectic of a freedom both meaningful and effective is itself a succession of dialectical movements. It is useful to recall at least two or three elementary dialectical movements within this global dialectic of objective mind. The first threshold of objective will is the contractual relation which links one will to another in a reciprocal relation. This duplication of the will constitutes a specific relation which cannot be derived from a simple phenomenology of the will based on the concepts of purpose, motivation, and voluntary motion. With this relation of one will to another new determinations come into play, principally because this relation is itself mediated by things as the object of an activity aiming at possession. The solitary will in the act of taking possession of something is again the arbitrary will. In the case of a contract each will renounces its particularity and recognizes the other will as identical with its own in the act of exchange. While things are universalized in the abstract representation of their value, the will is universalized by the contractual exchange of things. Thus the thing effects a mediation between two wills, while the will of the other effects a mediation between the will and the thing possessed. Such is the first threshold in this meaningful history of the will as objective mind. The connection with things in which my freedom is actualized is as important as the connection between the wills themselves.

Only a will which has undergone objectification in this sense is capable of recognizing itself as the responsible author of its acts. Here is the second threshold in the dialectic of objective mind. Freedom is not actualized in things insofar as they are possessed but in the deeds and works which represent freedom in the world. Beyond simple intention the will must pass the test of success and failure and link its fate to some phase of history. There is no effective purpose without this test of the real, without this judgment exercised by other men, and finally without the judgment of "the world's tribunal."

The will appears then as an interior dialectic between an infinite exigence which reflects its limitless power of self-assertion and the task of self-realization in a finite reality. Individuality is nothing else than this confrontation between the endlessness of reflection and the finitude of actualization. This will alone has the right to be held responsible only for what it has done and not for everything which has happened through its action.

As it is easy to see, it is in this framework of thought that the philosophy of the will can do justice to Kant and his distinction between the lawful will and the arbitrary will. However, it is not just an abstract rule, the law, which makes the difference between objective and subjective will, but the concrete course of intentional action in which subjective and objective aspects are intertwined, desire and rationality reconciled, and the quest for satisfaction linked to the quest for rationality. A simple ethic of intention, cut off both from the depth of life and from trial by the real, is just an abstract segment in the total process of the actualization of freedom.

Finally, a philosophy of the will conceived as a discourse about meaningful action culminates in a theory of concrete communities in which the will is capable of recognizing itself. This objectification of the will in the family, in civil society (that is, in economic life), and finally in the state realizes the Aristotelian project of a philosophy of the will which is at the same time a political philosophy. Rousseau and Kant are once again justified. There is no state, no political philosophy, without this equation between the sovereignty of the state and the power of the will. Rousseau's problem was the state which is not an objective will but which remains a strange and hostile reality. Hegel resolves this problem with other resources than the contract which belongs only to the abstract layer of the will.

To say that discourse about meaningful action reaches its goal in a political theory is to say that man has concrete responsibilities, concrete virtues, only when he is capable of situating himself within historical communities in which he recognizes the meaning of his own existence. We may be as critical as we like of the Hegelian hypostasis of the state, but the problem Hegel raised remains. Is there any reasonable mediation between the individual power we call free choice and the political power we call sovereignty? If political life is this mediation, then the dialectic between the individual will and that of the state makes sense and with it the discourse about meaningful action as well.

IV

MUST IT BE SAID NOW that discourse about meaningful action exhausts the task of a philosophy of the will? It seems to me that we have not yet reached the roots of the problem. The free choice which phenomenology concentrates on goes back to the task of actualizing freedom through personal and collective action. In its turn this second type of discourse points to a new kind of research which requires a new type of philosophical discourse.

What research and what discourse?

The notion itself of act, action, activity, says something about a mode of being which neither ethical theory nor political theory does justice to. In human activity the character of being as act is revealed, made manifest. An approach to the basis of being as creativity is discovered. This is the ultimate implication of a philosophy of the will. But do we have an appropriate type of discourse for expressing this emergence of being in a univocal language which would compete with the phenomenological distinction of project and with the kind of dialectical discourse displayed by the theory of meaningful action? Whoever is aware of the misfortunes, to say the least, which have overtaken ontology in the past must recognize that this type of discourse is at best a kind of broken discourse, full of ambiguity and having more affinity with variations of interpretation than with the coherence of absolute knowledge. Nevertheless the problem is whether interpretation might not receive philosophical status as a specific type of philosophical discourse. This is the wager that motivates the third part of my paper. If someone should ask why this third type of discourse is a broken discourse, the first response that must be given is that the awareness of what might perhaps be called "modes of being" is linked to a history which in turn seems to be inevitably linked to the manifestations of these modes. This depth history, it seems to me, cannot be linked simply to a change in theory which is itself linked to a cultural change, and even less to an ideological change. The history is, in a certain way, the history itself of the modes of being, the history of the manifestation of being. It affects not only the solutions but the questions as well. It comes to the surface of the history of philosophy under the guise of new ways of questioning. It affects the problematic itself. To give some idea of this deep history let us go back one more time to Aristotle. Here the three layers of discourse are easy to disengage. We have the discourse about the voluntary and the involuntary, which constitutes the phenomenological kernel of the *Nicomachean Ethics,* III. This discourse is incorporated in a much larger type of discourse which Aristotle designates as the architechtonic science of politics. And this type of discourse in its turn goes back to discourse about being. But how? By the determination of ethical inquiry as inquiry about the *ergon,* about the works of men. This *ergon* is the veritable emergence of being as *energeia.* Aristotle says that there is a task or work for man as man, a task which is not exhausted by the different *technai,* the different skills and professions, a task which unifies human action and which gives life its human meaning. The *Ethics* points then toward a deep layer where human praxis finds its basis. There is something, Aristotle says, like a human *energeia,* "a life according to activity" (*kata energeia, Ethics* 1098), because being itself is activity. Or, better, it is in the virtuous life, life lived according to virtue, that something is revealed of the determination of being as act. All the allusions of the *Ethics* then about the notions of act and of activity must be referred to the ontology of the potentiality of the act in the *Metaphysics* (chiefly Book 9).

But at the same time we modern readers of Aristotle are necessarily struck by the discordances between the moral philosophy of praxis and the ontology of the act. In the end, the act par excellence, act as act, excludes change and movement and is no longer exemplified by human activity but by the divine activity of thought, and thus by contemplative activity which in man is the closest approximation to the "thought of thought." Thus human praxis floats between natural "movement" and the "act" par excellence without any specific foundation in being. This lack of a mediation between the ontology of *ousia-entelechia* and ethics explains to a certain extent the absence of any concept of freedom in Aristotle, and indeed of any unified concept of the will even on the phenomenological level. These inadequacies are evident to our eyes as modern readers of Aristotle because we are heirs to a metaphysical age in which the will was identified with another mode of being, with being as subjectivity.

This is the first time I have mentioned the word "subjectivity." This was not an oversight. I think that subjectivity is not merely a feature in the phenomenological field or even a component in a theory of meaningful action. Subjectivity may occur as a dimension in the two previous types of discourse because it is primarily a mode of being which belongs to a metaphysical age, that of being as subjectivity. Finally, the emergence of the will as a philosophical problem expresses the progressive emergence of subjectivity as the predominant mode of being. That is why there is a subterranean history of the philosophy of the will which expresses on the phenomenological and dialectical levels a deep history of the modes of being.

This depth history does not coincide with the conceptual articulations of the other levels. It has its own structure. Or, rather, it implies a series of thresholds which do not necessarily coincide with progress in phenomenological description as is the case with Descartes.

I would like to underline three of these thresholds between Aristotle and Hegel. First of all, if the will is to become objective in the strong sense of the term, it must be conceived as infinite. This infinity is unknown to Aristotle. The power of choice for Aristotle is effective only in the limited field of deliberation in the midst of finite situations. Deliberation, as Aristotle says, bears on means rather than on ends. Virtue itself as a mean between two extremes defines the rules of finite action. Thus a revolution is produced which reverses the relation between the infinite and the finite. This first reversal, as Hegel says in *The Philosophy of Right* (§124), is the turning point between the Greek world and the Christian world. This turning point can be recognized in Augustine. *Voluntas* shows itself in the experience of evil and of sin as a power of denying being. This terrible power is the infinite power of the will.

A second threshold in the emergence of the will as subjectivity is represented by the Cartesian *cogito*. With the *cogito* the subject is that for which the world is a representation. But the will which we have described in the first part, within the same framework of thought as the Aristotelian description of "preference," appears now as the emergence of the *cogito sum*, as the existential freedom of the *cogito* as such, as free thought in the most fundamental sense of the term.

The third threshold of this conquest of subjectivity as a fundamental mode of being might be constituted by the recognition of the antinomy between freedom and nature. This antinomy could not be conceived so long as nature itself was not unified under a unique legislation. Freedom is now exiled to the plane of nature. No longer is a systematic unity capable of embracing within a cosmological unity both the notion of an effect according to nature and the notion of a free act that can be ascribed to an ethical subject. It was necessary for speculative thought to be submitted to the test of the antinomy. This antinomy cannot be recognized within a phenomenology of decision or in a discourse of political and ethical life. The antinomy is the critical point in the third type of discourse about the will.

Having come to this point one might be tempted to ask: have we not surmounted all the antinomies of the Kantian type of discourse in a Hegelian discourse? In one sense, yes; in another, no.

In one sense Hegelian reason has overcome Kantian understanding, in that the dialectic of meaningful action constitutes in itself this overcoming. Moreover, it is perfectly possible to read Hegelian philosophy as an attempt not only to overcome the antinomy of Kantian philosophy but to overcome the antinomy of Western philosophy as a whole. Considered retrospectively, from the Hegelian point of view every history of philosophy is a struggle between philosophies of substance, illustrated by Aristotle and Spinoza, and philosophies of the subject, illustrated by Descartes and Kant. The philosophy of the will and all the dialectic it develops—between desire and rationality, representation and volition, subjectivity and objectivity—implies some sort of reconciliation between substance and subject. In Hegelian terms, substance is subject.

This reconciliation, we know, is the key to the Hegelian concept of mind. But can one say that a philosophy of mind has exhausted the history of the modes of being? Is not this concept of mind the cycle of another reduction of the basis of being, a reduction which the qualification of idealism points to? The basic difficulty with a Hegelian philosophy of the will concerns the relation between will and truth. Hegel's principal concern at every stage of the dialectic is to show the truth of each moment. Each moment has its truth in the following moment, that is, in another moment in which its contradiction is mediated and overcome. In the end every process of overcoming contradiction can be considered from the viewpoint of a backward look which begins from absolute knowledge and recapitulates the cumulative process. Thus every moment has its condition of possibility in the position of a philosopher, in his advance with respect to a total development; in a word, it is placed in an absolute position at the end of the process. This demand of the philosopher to situate himself somewhere, both beyond and in the milieu of process, inside it and outside it, must be questioned as a pretension.

This questioning is perhaps the basic event in the post-Hegelian period in the philosophy of the will. It primarily concerns the relation between will and truth. If truth itself is an aspect of the will as a "will to truth," is there not a kind of inquiry that looks for truth in a certain quality of the will? As we have already seen, this kind of inquiry was inaugurated by Nietzsche. He opened a new phase in the philosophy of the will. In one sense this phase manifests what the philosophy of the will has always attempted to do, to reveal the ground of being as act, as energy, as power and not just as form, as essence, as logos. Something of Aristotelian philosophy is not only preserved but magnified, something which the philosophy of mind has in some way devitalized, emptied of its force. I mean the priority of act over form, of energy over essence, of power over logos.

But in a more radical sense this rediscovery of an archaic intuition precipitates a crisis in philosophy, a double crisis. First of all, there is a crisis in the concept of subjectivity which had ruled classical philosophy of the will. As Heidegger has shown in his great work on Nietzsche, Nietzsche has the ambiguous importance of having completed the philosophy of subjectivity and of having opened another field, another quarry, for another mode of being. The will to power has the ambiguous importance of bringing to a kind of paroxysm the claim of subjectivity and of breaking this exigency by means of powerful symbols which are no longer symbols of subjectivity but cosmic symbols of the Eternal Return of the Same, Dionysus, Zarathustra. The notion of the *Übermensch* witnesses to this ambiguity of a philosophy in which subjectivity reaches its culmination and collapses at the end of a self-destructive process that Nietzsche calls nihilism.

This is the first crisis that Nietzsche precipitates in the modern philosophy of being. He situates modern inquiry about the will between two times—the time of subjectivity which has been the time of classical philosophy from Plato to Hegel, and the time which he speaks about only in a kind of kerygmatic way.

The second crisis expresses the first at the level of philosophical discourse.

This crisis might be formulated in these terms. If the relation between will and truth must be inverted, if, as the inverse of what Hegel maintained, truth itself or the search for truth manifests a quality of the will (perhaps the worst, the quality of a weak will looking for comfort and security), what kind of discourse can we articulate concerning the will itself, its strength, its weakness, its power of affirming itself, its strategies in vengeance and resentment? Only a discourse which qualifies itself as interpretation, that is, a type of discourse linked to symptomatology and to philology: a discourse in the form of semiology.

This crisis in philosophical language is not necessarily unhealthy. It can even become extremely wholesome if we rethink it in connection with the ambiguity of being itself. Aristotle already knew that being must be used in many ways. This ontological polysemy is recognized in a philosophy which characterizes itself as a philosophy of interpretation. Now this recognition raises more questions than it resolves. If Hegelian philosophy raises the question of the place of the philosopher when he speaks the truth, the absolute truth, a philosophy of interpretation such as Nietzsche's raises the question of the criteria of an interpretation which claims to be the correct interpretation. I leave this last question open. I leave it open as a wound at the heart of philosophical discourse. I will confine myself to suggesting that the key to a response, as I see it, lies in looking for a better understanding of the relation among the three kinds of discourse in which philosophy is capable of speaking of the will: phenomenological discourse, which simply describes the will as project and choice; dialectical discourse, which articulates in a logical fashion the degrees of meaningful action; and discourse in the form of interpretation, which recognizes behind the changes happening in the two previous fields the depth history of the modes of being in which being itself is both concealed and disclosed.

15 / Structuralism and Humanism

Mikel Dufrenne

AT THE VERY HEIGHT of its development, technological civilization is for the first time being seriously questioned in nearly all modern industrial societies. Will this probing lead to a new humanism in its search for expression? This is possible, but any new humanism will be opposed, especially in France, to philosophies which are avowedly antihumanist. These latter prove to be indifferent toward, if not in fact accomplices of, the reign of technocracy, failing to prepare for the advent of a new civilization.

These philosophies are commonly grouped together under the heading of "structuralism." This word is equivocal, since structuralism may mean simply the scientific recourse to a conceptual apparatus with a high degree of rigor and effectiveness. In this way the mathematical notion of structure has been introduced into linguistics, anthropology, psychology, and aesthetics. We do not challenge this move, which is made by experts; the philosophy of science has no choice but to acknowledge it. But structuralism as a philosophy belongs to the epigoni—to those who exalt scientific thought without practicing it and who operate with a vague and confused sense of the term "structure," which they treat more as a banner than as a program. The elasticity of this term also facilitates doctrinal alliances. In fact, the bond that unites structuralist philosophies is first of all a form of scientism similar to that which was dominant around

Translated by Edward S. Casey.

1880, even though contemporary scientism is based on a radically transformed group of sciences.

In the view of scientism, scientific knowledge alone is authentic, rigorous, and effective; everything else, including philosophy, is fantasy, delirium, or poetry. What is disquieting in this view is that it leads to an allied antihumanism, the other common denominator in much recent philosophy.[1] The primary reason for this is that the "human" sciences today promulgate an idea of the human which denies man the prerogatives of subjectivity. Of course, these sciences have the right to determine their own field of research, constructing the concepts which appear to them the most rigorous and operative. For example, in using the concept of the unconscious they say that the "id" speaks in man rather than man himself. Generally speaking, man is seen in the same way as is a particle in physics: as a network of relations without relata. Man himself is no longer productive; he is merely the arena (*lieu*) where relations of production function—an arena itself determined by institutional and cultural systems. Yet man is not supposed to realize this determinism; whatever he says about his situation or about himself is never true, and what he thinks he does is never what he really does. In this light, humanism, understood as the idea of man possessed spontaneously by all men, becomes the epistemological obstacle par excellence. It is only natural that Michel Foucault should proclaim the "death of man"—not as a matter of genocide, but in order to announce the disappearance of a certain concept of man from the field of modern *epistēmē*. In the place of this concept are substituted, on the basis of certain methodological options, other concepts usually made explicit in a structuralist language. Antihumanism, as seen most conspicuously in Louis Althusser or Jacques Lacan, thus results from scientism—i.e., from the decision to consider as true only what science says today, even if science does not itself make this demand.

Several decades ago, scientism was allied with Anglo-American positivism. But in France philosophy is less vulnerable than in English-speaking countries; and antihumanism might not have flourished as much as it has if it had not found philosophical backing. Thus, in the case of philosophers like Foucault, epistemological themes are revealingly mixed with philosophical

1. For an elaboration of this theme, see the author's *Pour l'homme* (Paris: Seuil, 1967).—Trans.

or lyrico-philosophical themes borrowed from Nietzsche or Heidegger. In this fashion, philosophers themselves, at least as they are often interpreted, also proclaim the death of man. Many themes converge in this gospel, for the meaning of the acts by which man reveals himself and of the mediations he uses can be wrested from him and turned against him. An inordinate use of capital letters shows this clearly. Thus, "man thinks" is interpreted as "Thought thinks in man"; "man discovers being" as "Being reveals itself to man"; "man speaks" as "Language realizes itself in man"; "man creates works" as "Art passes through the artist"; "man is free" as "The Freedom of Being transfixes man"; "man is mortal" as "Death inhabits man." Of course, this is somewhat exaggerated; the analyses of the philosophers in question are, on the contrary, admirably subtle and obscure. Moreover, the very image of being which they propose is haunted by distance, absence, and emptiness. Just as the concept is substituted for the object instead of designating it, the fascination with nothingness replaces the feeling of presence: idealism becomes pathetic. Non-being in this vision is not a moment of a dialectic, but the asphyxiating element in which the destiny of man is consummated. Accordingly, such an ontology conspires to dethrone man and to deny him all initiative, reducing him to a receptacle or an instrument of extrahuman powers; man becomes the "shepherd of Being," in Heidegger's words. Here we find an echo in philosophical discourse of what the sciences are doing legitimately and effectively in their own domain. We do not find what the sciences exclude: irreplaceable lived experience. This is why antihumanistic philosophies seem to me needlessly mystifying or alienating. They thrust the nonhuman directly into the human, placing man at the service of an outside force; by rendering man a stranger to himself, they are at the same time condemning him to death.

In my view, they are expressing in their own language what is unfortunately a historical reality in our time—the dilemma of "mass man": abstract, atomized, depoliticized, homeless, and lacking self-identity. His only refuge lies in individual consumption; but this consumption is itself directed by technocrats, who define man's needs arbitrarily, and by advertising, which manipulates mass men so as to subordinate them to the interests of production and capitalist profit. Man does not fully appropriate the objects he uses, for these objects become fetishes or symbols of social status. Even his work, which is forced labor, does not belong to him; his leisure is prescribed, and his culture telecommunicated. His spontaneity and creativity are stifled. The city has ceased to be the place where he is truly recognized by others and can express himself to them. The very individualism which he sometimes asserts in attempts to revolt against this depersonalization is marked by the same seal: it becomes a position of mere withdrawal or exile. Thus the relations of man to the world and of man to man become falsified in the consumer society.

Contemporary antihumanism both reflects and supports this situation: it speaks of the death of man and brings it about under our very eyes, within ourselves. Must philosophy endorse this action?

I believe that philosophy's role is assuredly not to save man —for man is quite capable of saving himself—but rather, on the reflective level, to restore his just due (*droit*). This is what humanism strives to do, and what was already undertaken by the existentialism which Sartre considered a humanism, at a time of tragic engagement in history when man did not allow technocrats to determine his destiny.

Nevertheless, humanism has subsequently acquired a bad reputation. Why is this? Largely because it has been reduced to paternalistic humanism, as in the case of those who persist in defending the teaching of Latin in the name of the humanities. Such a humanism is often linked with a theology: man is assigned a fixed nature, which bestows on him a definite place in the system of creation, along with rights and duties (and usually more duties than rights). A corresponding rhetoric has triumphantly invoked an eternal man bound to eternal values.

Science itself reacts triumphantly to this concept of man, which it sees as abetting certain official values or the ideology of the dominant class; and it contrasts this concept with its own system of concepts, which it elaborates in constituting its object. The humanism that I wish to defend has nothing in common with a theologically-oriented humanism. Nor has it anything in common with science, whose harsh strictures it eludes. For its task—the task of philosophy itself, at least in the form of phenomenology—is not to repeat, contest, or orient science. Rather it seeks to make explicit what the epistemological rupture deliberately ignores: lived experience (*le vécu*), especially perception. This humanism is not so much concerned with the concept of man (a concept said to be moribund) as with the experience of man. Such irrecusable experience is as unavoidably relevant today as at the dawn of humanity, and it proceeds more from the encounter with the other person than from reflection on oneself. Yet why turn toward the past? Are not the first truths also the first errors? This question touches the heart of the issue, as Gaston Bachelard saw in his double role as philosopher of science and literary critic. For the crux of the matter lies in the crystallization of our first contact with the world "there" where we are rooted in the very soil of the perceived which the scientist *qua* knower continually excavates. The crucial point is that we come to the world as capable of the world, already armed for knowing it and recognizing ourselves in it.

Therefore, encountering the other person is the occasion of recognizing, rather than knowing, him. Out of this encounter arises a knowledge of man which is not conceptual and which philosophy can make explicit without conceptualization. The idea of human nature is thus restored. There is no reason to be ashamed of this, so long as this nature does not lead us to deny man's freedom (on which existentialism put so much emphasis) or his individuality. If it is a fact that I always recognize man— as when the child who plays with her doll distinguishes it from her younger sister, or when a precivilized man who accosts a stranger *knows* that the stranger is "strange" only because he is also a man—this always occurs in the case of a particular man whom I recognize. Man *is* the irreducible individual whose uniqueness and individuality come from an interiority (whether this be considered conscious or unconscious). In accordance with the scientific dissolution of the object into a network of relations it is unquestionably popular today to say that man is only a region (or, as Heidegger said, the "there"), an absence or emptiness: the place where something happens, where desire encounters Law, where the word is spoken and Thought takes place, as well as the place where social and economic determinations occur. Yet if something happens through man it also happens *in* him: man as place is already situated, circumscribed, and singular, and the place possesses the consistency and density of the individual. This individual is nature; he has a nature which identifies and particularizes him.

This nature, however, is not the nature of a thing. It is first of all transcendental: I know the other as soon as I see *him* seeing, e.g., seeing me. The transcendental appears impersonal or disincarnate only when reduced to a system of logical conditions such as Kantian categories. But before this occurs, the transcendental is the capacity to open oneself to the world: it is the very being of the flesh in which the flesh of the world is duplicated, the being of the eye and ear which puts me in touch with a world I know from the distance of a glance. I am also no further away than speech: language introduces an interval not only between the signs of a code but also between words and things; yet this difference is originally initiated by the incantatory powers of the poetic word. It is the same nature in the same movement which is transcendental and articulate; Nature comes to language through man in accordance with *his* nature. Language is not only a law, or the countenance of law, for man; it is the law *of* man. Even if Nature proposes, only man disposes and speaks of his own destiny.

Moreover, human nature as voluntary is unpredictable. To understand this phenomenon, philosophy must return to primordial experience. Such experience is not found in the reflective consciousness of my willing, but in the immediate consciousness which I possess of the other person: the being in whom the effort of all being to persevere in its being becomes conscious, who wills without always knowing what he wants, and who is capable of decisions and affirmations to the point of obstinacy. Of course, I cannot clearly distinguish between the voluntary and the involuntary in the other, or differentiate desire from will (if this is even necessary). In any case, man wills; he wills himself, affirming himself both as value and as the source of values he discovers in the world. He also wills himself as source of himself. For just as a transcendental nature is a nature open to the world, a voluntary nature is a nature open to oneself: *natura naturans* as well as *natura naturata,* a being who has to become what he is. Man is the future of man, as both Ponge and Sartre have said; he finds his image only in exercising his will to power.

But this future is always uncertain; the will can be impotent, and desire may remain unsatisfied. Not only does the real resist us, but the individual exists only in society. Man asserts himself in separating himself from the world, but he is always linked to others—to a community and to a culture which regulate his conduct and his relations with others. Community and culture mold the appearance of things to the point that the social and natural worlds become interchangeable for him. Just as man maintains an ambiguous rapport with the world because he never totally abstracts himself from it or fully submits to it, so the individual is related ambiguously to society. The human milieu which surrounds man can become inhuman; the culture informing his nature can denature him. The very meaning of his *praxis* can be taken away from him, and the system he animates can turn against him in what Sartre calls an "antidialectical" movement. We are experiencing all of this acutely at the present moment. But this does not mean that man is annulled or that all resiliency has been removed from his nature. When the system becomes for him only a means of livelihood—when it is experienced as unlivable—man can still refuse it. He can still at least become conscious of his alienation, and work to change the institution by inventing a new language, new human relations, and a new notion of law. Humanism cannot accept a philosophy of history which effaces man by denying him all initiative.

When man strives to liberate himself—to liberate man within him—he is achieving his own nature. Yet this is not accomplished through a definitive break with Nature. The oppressive and alienating features of culture arise precisely when culture ceases to be a second nature in accord with man's own nature—when, independently of the latter, culture violates Nature instead of celebrating it. The relation of man to Nature is essentially ambiguous. Man would like to be the mirror in which only man is reflected, but he also wants (and is perhaps summoned) to be the mirror in which Nature is reflected. In willing himself through knowledge and power, man does not want to make the world in his image; he does not really want to become God. It is incomparably better merely to possess hands for grasping, eyes for seeing, sexual differentiations for loving. Nietzsche spoke of the body as a "marvel": a sensing, desiring, imagining flesh within the flesh of being itself, inviscerated within the Nature from which I am born.

The insertion of man in Nature unquestionably provides him with an equivocal destiny in terms of the countenance offered to him by Nature—i.e., in terms of his relation with it. To be part of *natura naturata* is to be nature as destined to accidents and coercions, even to the point of becoming merely the locus of scientific determinations. But to be born of *natura naturans* is to possess a nature—i.e., one's own powers and a unique becoming—with which to unlock a history intimately bound to life's dynamism. From this point on, man is called upon to emancipate himself, yet without ever severing the umbilical cord of Nature. No matter how high he flies, he must return to earth; however abstract his thought, he never ceases to perceive; however pure his will, he is carried away by desire; however Herculean his labors, he remains an Antaeus: he turns back continually to the life-giving source where subject and object, the real and the imaginary, meet and flow together. Man never loses his nostalgia for primordial identity. His desire to create man is always tempered by a desire to return to the origin, to the emergence of a primary meaning, a dawning sense in which Nature expresses itself through man rather than the converse. Art constantly effects this pilgrimage to the source; it liberates the word in restoring its primordial power, the image as one of genuine origination, the gesture as spontaneous. As the origin of man's inspiration, art is celebration.

These reflections, in the form given above, are perhaps themselves inspired by events experienced in Paris in May, 1968. In these events, I discerned the gestation of a revolt, the beginning of an enduring effort to change life, to create a new civilization. I saw men attempting to liberate man. A philosophy of man cannot be indifferent to this movement. It too must move with its age: it must not remain enclosed within the present, but open itself toward the future.

16 / The Illusion of Monolinear Time

Nathaniel Lawrence

TEMPORALITY is one of those subjects in philosophy which defy direct description. As phenomenal it is both *sui generis* and pervasive. Language, therefore, which seeks to describe it is defeated from the outset. First of all, being *sui generis,* temporality yields only to clusters of metaphors, taken conjointly: flowing, moving, passing, and so on. There is no higher genus to refer it to, no classification of which it is a proper subdivision. The metaphors which we employ to rereveal it are themselves manifestations which presuppose it. For this reason we are likely to speak of objects or events as *in* time. It might be wiser to speak of temporality as *in* events, as Whitehead repeatedly suggests. Second, being pervasive of phenomena it does, however, lend itself to evocation and monstration. Even the "it" suggests, unfortunately, that "it" is something final, complete, closed, a proper entity. Any definition of temporality cannot meet, therefore, the canons of description insofar as these demand an entity bounded and classifiable.

As a starting point, let us place "temporality" in juxtaposition with two other pseudo-entities, "the world" and "consciousness," which share with it the negative property of being *sui generis,* binding the three terms together with a single metaphor which is often used for each. *Temporality is the basic passage in and through which consciousness, itself open-ended, and the world, itself forever only partly revealed, are in partial apposition.*

The groundwork of temporality, thus presented, is in conscious perception, and many of our conceptions of time are only derivatively related to such temporality. For example, if we ask about the size of units of temporality, they are relatively large— on the order of about 10^{-1} to 2×10^{-3} seconds, depending on what empirical procedures and criteria are used.[1] Physical time —i.e., the time of so-called fundamental physical particles— comes in much smaller bits, on the order of 10^{-24} seconds.[2] And mathematical time has no least units at all, being divisible without limit. We are not concerned here with these refined and exotic notions of time, but rather with the workaday passage of known and shared events. We will concentrate on this unique, commonplace temporality, putting aside physical and mathematical time. Such special modalities of time are distillates or extracts from ordinary temporality, and all existential claim which they make must be tested in the domain of ordinary temporality. Such ordinary temporality, at the point of primary appearance, is not divided serially into quantized units, however, nor is it a split screen with passing world on one side and passing consciousness on the other. Atomization and qualitative separation are both the products of reflective awareness.

1. The exact minimum threshold is an empirical matter, of course, but it also depends on definition. For example, what counts as a least unit of conscious perception? The length of a received sensation? The interval between two sensations? Data from a single sense? Data from several senses? How "natural" is the laboratory situation where attention and acuity have become artificially sharpened? And so on. The extremely small figure of 2×10^{-3} seconds is from H. Pieron, *La Sensation guide de vie*, 3d ed. (Paris: Gallimard, 1955), p. 396. It is for apparent motion between two sound sources placed some distance apart and emitting a "rapid succession of excitations applied to both ears." This and other data are reviewed in Paul Fraisse's excellent work, *The Psychology of Time*, trans. Jennifer Leith (New York: Harper & Row, 1963). See esp. Chap. 4, from which the preceding quotation is given (p. 113). If the least unit of temporality be defined as the least unit dividing two distinguishable sensations in isolation from other sensations, then 10^{-2} seconds seems to be the threshold, acording to Pieron and, independently, O. Klemm, "Über die Wirksamkeit kleinster Zeitunterschiede," *Arch. ges. Psychol.*, L (1925), 204–20. Other senses and mixtures of senses give minimal durations as large as 10^{-1} seconds.

2. This unit, the so-called chronon, can lay claim, with some justice, to being a natural constant, in the physicist's sense of "natural," since it is derivable from two relatively distinct computations. See G. J. Whitrow, *The Natural Philosophy of Time* (London: Nelson, 1961), pp. 156. 236–37.

II

EQUALLY A PRODUCT of reflective awareness, but less exotic and less laborious, is the differentiation of temporality into its aspect as revealed in the living self and its aspect in the changing world, those two standpoints which are delineated in the above definition of temporality. If we ask ourselves how these separable but not isolated aspects of temporality are in actual juxtaposition, the answer is: through perception and action. The revived awareness of the intimacy of perception and action is a recognition-characteristic of twentieth-century philosophy of many kinds, not merely of phenomenology.

For example, in the context of closely related themes, both Santayana and C. I. Lewis comment on the interdependence of perception and action, the one in exposing the sterility of parlor solipsism, the other in the exposition of the self as active. Santayana says:

Ideas become beliefs only when, by precipitating tendencies to action, they persuade me that they are signs of things; and these things are not those ideas simply hypostasized, but are believed to be compacted of many parts, and full of ambushed powers, entirely absent from the ideas.[3]

C. I. Lewis puts the same point tersely, without Santayana's Latin elegance:

Only an active being could draw any line of demarcation between what is self and what is not self. . . . Without activity, everything given would be equally willy nilly and just there, and all on one plane of fact. . . . only for an active being could anything be possible except what is actual and actually given.[4]

Where Santayana speaks of ideas, Lewis speaks of the given; where Santayana speaks of action, Lewis speaks of active beings and activity; where Santayana speaks of ambushed powers, Lewis speaks of the possible. But the theme is the same: there is

3. G. Santayana, *Scepticism and Animal Faith* (New York: Scribner, 1923), p. 16.
4. *An Analysis of Knowledge and Valuation* (La Salle, Ill.: Open Court, 1946), p. 17.

no world of sheer definitive presentation; rather, since it is also a world of action in which I act, it is fraught with possibility as well. And the possibility is perpetual and immanent. In a remarkable passage, which might almost have come from Sartre, or even from Bergson, Santayana says:

> The fact of experience then is single and, from its own point of view, absolutely unconditioned and groundless, impossible to explain and impossible to exorcise. Yet just as it comes unbidden, so it may fade and lapse of its own accord. It constantly seems to do so; and my hold on existence is not so firm that non-existence does not seem always at hand and, as it were, always something deeper, vaster, and more natural than existence. Yet this apprehension of an imminent non-existence—an apprehension which is itself an exciting fact—cannot be trusted to penetrate to a real nothingness yawning about me unless I assert something not at all involved in the present being, and something more remarkable, namely, that I know and can survey the *movement* of my existence, and that it can actually have lapsed from one state into another, as I conceive it to have lapsed.[5]

The passage is striking for its contrast between being and nothingness. There are two other important points, however. There is a tendency here to save the term "existence" for human existence, perhaps even personal existence, and to speak of that existence as a *movement,* which can be surveyed as having "lapsed." But this is to speak of it as in some sense having gone its temporal way. On the other hand, to speak of *surveying* the movement is to present the same movement as not sweeping everything away with it. There is some arrest, some stoppage, some present grasp of what, in some sense, is no longer present. This fundamental contrariety is not to be resolved by speaking blandly of memory or recall, for we are then called upon to anatomize how present memory holds what is not present, and the problem appears all over again. Moreover, a complete physiological account of the residual memory would in itself be quite useless—even if it were technically possible, which at present it is not. Analytically, it would be no more illuminating than an analysis, say, of a Picasso blue into wave frequencies; namely, we might guess how to induce it or predict it. But secondly, we could not really compare a present state of consciousness with

5. Santayana, *Scepticism and Animal Faith,* p. 24.

the effect of brain activity in a recording device, for both the state of consciousness and the brain activity as electronically signified would have to be in the immediate past, and moreover would be drawn together by a further act of present consciousness which synthesized them for our comparison.[6] There is always a regression to the synthesizing, correlating consciousness, which objectifies and recalls its prior states but not itself.

Strictly speaking, the present act of consciousness cannot grasp the self which is in the act of grasping. The physiological account at best gives a correspondence between the recent memory of such an act and the physical correlate rendered explicit by some one of various kinds of machines.

But the alternative to the physiological-correlation type of account results in the paradoxical situation of which Santayana speaks. If the (relative and subjective) non-existence of myself is to be brought to a "real nothingness," then it must be through a survey which includes my then-states into one present now-recognition. Such then-states cannot, by definition, include the now-recognition among themselves, yet this now-recognition depends upon them for its existence and still is different from them. Somehow the "I" of consciousness bridges this disparity. Sartre's characterization of the *pour-soi* as not being what it is and being what it is not seems to follow Santayana's formulation almost as if it were merely a summary. Sartre's extreme phrasing seizes logic by the forelock and reminds it—as Humpty Dumpty says he does with words—who the real master is. As a gesture, it has a certain charm. Moreover, it undoubtedly carries a rude truth with it. But since we are acclimated to depending on logical discrimination, announcements of the Sartrean sort makes us feel that somebody has taken away our lantern, even if his motives are good. I shall return to Sartre in a moment, but I want first to examine the problem of consciousness and temporality at the point where it receives its modern formulation,

6. See Erwin Straus, "On Memory Traces," for a critique of this point. This important article, which came to my attention after the central idea of this essay was developed, first appeared in January, 1962, in *Der Nervenarzt*. It was translated by Richard Krambach for *Tijdschrift voor Filosofie*, XXIV (1962), 91–122. It is reprinted in *Readings in Existential Phenomenology*, ed. Nathaniel Lawrence and Daniel O'Connor (Englewood Cliffs, N.J.: Prentice-Hall, 1967), pp. 54–74. It should further be noticed that Straus speaks briefly of "bi-temporality" without much elaboration, thus touching intimately, in a different way, on the subject of the present essay.

namely, in Kant's categories of relation. The examination will be, necessarily, at points somewhat close-grained. Kant's thoroughness as a craftsman and his unmatched capacity to outrun even his own firmest convictions expose the problem in a systematic detail that has not been duplicated since his time. Whitehead said of the history of philosophy that it was to be understood as a series of footnotes to Plato. It is not unfair to suggest that the modern history of the problem of time and consciousness is a series of footnotes to Kant.

It is in Kant that we find some recognition of a presence of an empirical temporality, which is there, seriatim, for perceptual experience, and a nonempirical temporality, which must be the condition of the unifying process of synthesis. This synthesis, unlike the perceptible processes which it conditions, is not itself an item within experience. Kant explicitly considers breaching the Newtonian monolinear time but discards the idea as nonsensical.

III

FROM THE METAPHYSICIAN'S POINT OF VIEW the dialectical struggle in Kant's treatment of the categories of relation is a classic struggle between Kant's early commitment to the rightness of a substance philosophy and his emergent realization of the necessity for a process philosophy. From the point of view of a transcendental critique of knowledge, however, this same dialectic is the struggle between the static of the categories as structures and the dynamic of the categories as actively employed. In short, it is a form of the ancient quarrel between structure and function. Structurally, the categories derive from logical form alone. Functionally, they require a temporal schematism.

In Kant we find that both in his account of the Analogies of Experience generally, and in the individual examination of them, there is an unsuccessful effort to cling to a substance metaphysics. But, a bit at a time, the concept of action takes over and leaves him with an unsolved problem about time.

First, about the Analogies generally, Kant says, "The general principle of the three analogies acts on the necessary *unity* of apperception, in respect of all empirical consciousness, that is, of all perception, *at every time*." [7] The "unity of apperception," we recall, designates the spontaneous "I think" which accompanies all my empirical representations and can also be called "self-consciousness" (B132). But this consciousness of self is not the same as the knowledge of the empirical ego, which varies in time and is given through inner perception. In Kant the "unity of apperception" differs from the "empirical ego" in much the way that Sartre differentiates between *conscience de soi* and *connaissance de soi*. Kant's transcendental unity of apperception knows itself only, as he says, by its "identity of function" (A108). Kant also calls this identity the "identity of its act" (A128). No substantial agent for this action can be found or even searched for, because this act is transcendental, that is, does not lie within the experience which it unifies. Such action escapes the need to be categorized under the category of substance. Also beyond appearance and giving it objectivity is the unknown transcendental object.

To summarize, the transcendental unity of apperception provides the synthesis of appearance, but this is an action without an agent; complementarily the transcendental object supplies externality but otherwise remains unknown, and likewise is no substance. Thus is the Cartesian breach healed. The terms "function" and "act" refer to a unity which has no empirical and hence no substantial correlate whatsoever. In empirical awareness there is given only the changing self. The crucial question is *not:* What is this unchanging consciousness which acts to synthesize experience? According to Kant we are not to look, in the transcendental realm, for substantial entities. Substance is a category of a possible experience and nothing more. By Kant's own standards, therefore, as we move from the realm of empirical realism to that of a transcendental idealism, we have shifted from a substantialist metaphysics to a process metaphysics. We have here action without an actor. The question which is commonly ignored is: What is the nature of the temporality in which the transcendental action occurs? We seem to be presented with two temporalities: (1) First there is the one which—somewhat ambiguously—is the precondition of both inner and outer sense,

7. *Critique of Pure Reason,* trans. Norman Kemp Smith (London: Macmillan, 1953), A177; B220; Smith gratuitously inserts "instant of" before "time" (italics are Kant's).

as well as being the ground of the homogeneity between sensation and the categories, the condition of their being conjoined. (2) The second temporality is that passage in the transcendental realm from which the synthesis of experience springs. This is the home of the transcendental unity of apperception, a self-supporting process neither authorized by nor dependent upon any time-resistant substance. Kant's undertaking is, in short, only partly successful. He has refused to make of original consciousness a substantial thing, saving the term "substance" for its employment in the realm of perceptual experience. But in replacing the substantial self by a unique set of events, he leaves us wondering what is the temporal status of this unique set of events. They are not themselves perceptible, for by them unified perceptual experience comes into view, yet as occurrences they are by nature temporal in their essential structure.

Kant undertakes to dispel the Cartesian dichotomy, but instead he cuts off the hydra's head, for now he has a duality of ego, empirical and transcendental; a duality of relations, those within appearance and those between the appearance of the empirical object and the unity of apperception; and evidently a duality of times for the two kinds of events, phenomenal and transcendental.

In the first Analogy there is a momentary speculation about dual temporality, but it is rejected as absurd. In this analogy, substance is treated as that which is permanent. This permanence, says Kant, is "the abiding correlate of all existence [which] expresses time in general. For change does not affect time itself, but only appearances in time" (A183; B226). A few pages later he makes this point again, and says, "If some of these substances could come into being and others cease to be, the one condition of the empirical unity of time would be removed. . . . The appearance would then relate to two different times, and existence would flow in two parallel streams, which is absurd" (A188; B231). Kant is quite right; two times for one synthesis of *appearance* of sheer perceptual experience would be absurd. But in postulating two kinds of events, empirical and transcendental, he has postulated two different times, for activity devoid of temporal passage is meaningless. Moreover, he invests each kind of time with an appropriate ego.

Whether these two times can be called "parallel," to use his term, raises the question of how well the spatial metaphor can translate temporality.[8] It might be wiser to say that they must be set into correspondence with one another.

In the second Analogy the dominance of the category of action comes to the surface in use, even though it is not one of the magical twelve. The second Analogy holds that all alteration conforms to cause and effect. Inevitably Kant's treatment of objectivity shifts. In the first Analogy, objectivity rests on permanence. In the second Analogy, Kant distinguishes two types of synthesis. A subjective synthesis is at my disposal, as when I synthesize the presentations of a house. Objective synthesis, however, occurs where the time order of the assembly is not at my disposal. I must first see the boat upstream and then see it downstream. In this matter I do not have an option. Objectivity is thus found in the time-order of events, not in the time-resistance of objects, and it uses the language of events, *Wirklichkeit* and *Begebenheit*.

Furthermore, Kant now argues for the primacy of causality as the immediate aspect of phenomena, rather than for the primacy of substantiality. "Causality," he says, "leads to the concept of action; this in turn to the concept of force, and thereby to the concept of substance." And shortly he follows this by, "I must not leave unconsidered the empirical criteria of substance, insofar as substance appears to manifest itself not through permanence of appearance, but more adequately and easily through action" (A204; B249). The second Analogy gives us force and action as the primary encounterables in experience. Kant's arguments for substances in nature now reduce to the rationalistic insistence that there must be a substrate which does not change, but whose states change. But turning from what must be thought to what is actually encountered, the manifest phenomena are dynamic. Kant says "Action is a sufficient empirical criterion by which to establish the substantiality, without my requiring first to go in quest of its permanence through the comparison of perceptions" (A205; B251). The encounter with action in nature is thus both primary in perception and sufficient to establish the objective, without searching out permanences. In using the language of events, Kant here briefly anticipates Whitehead. In insisting on the primacy of action, he briefly anticipates the phenomenologists. But thirdly and most impor-

8. See Nathaniel Lawrence, "Time Represented as Space," *Monist* (July, 1969).

tantly, by translating substance into activity, he provides a basis for compatibility between the activity of unification, which is the transcendental unity of apperception, and the activities in the phenomenal world.

The third Analogy completes the picture. This analogy is the rule of the reciprocity among substances, insofar as they can be conceived in space. But the willingness to allow action as evidence of objectivity is still consistently applied. "The coexistence of substances in space," says Kant, "cannot be known in experience save on the assumption of their reciprocal interaction" (A211; B258).

Kant was concerned with defending crucial aspects of the empiricism of Locke and Hume while finding a place for the certainties of Newton. The third Analogy has for its target the justification of stable systems, such as those of our solar system, which apparently require postulation of action at a distance. Kant was writing at a time when the idea of physical space was a distinct idea, and he did not see that the conception of distance is derivative from action, both for its meaning and for its use. Nevertheless, he partially extricates himself from the ancient metaphysics in his analysis of actions and events, and by bringing both the spontaneity of consciousness and the immediacies of perception under the same category of act he lays the groundwork for a healing of the Cartesian breach between the self and the other, a healing more profound and inclusive than his own doctrine of appearance.

IV

YET A BREACH REMAINS, and we shall see that it is perpetuated in Sartre. First, we saw in Santayana and in Lewis the notion of existence as bridging idea and act, which are not allowed subsistent status independent of each other. Second, we turned to a basic problem in Kant. We might call it the case of the missing category, that of action. Kant derives from a supposedly exhaustive logical list twelve categories which supply the basic forms of intelligibility for all experience. Their structure comes from the side of logic. Their function, however, is discernible in experience. Basically the function is synthesis: to draw together the deliveries of sensation so that through the categories not only experience but science is possible. Such a synthesis is an activity, yet not an activity within experience, for experience arises from it. Activity is meaningless without temporality, but supra-sensory temporality transcends the temporality which provides the theater for sensory experience. Kant goes halfway in his analysis. He sees that he has defined substance in such a way that it cannot categorize the transcendental ego. Further, he sees that as far as experience goes, only a functional identity is needed for that ego. No substantial identity need apply. But the duality of temporality required by the presence both of natural processes within experience and of transcendent processes beyond the empirical world seems to him absurd and he says so. The missing category among the twelve is that of activity, action, process, or some cognate notion. This category does not appear in the logically derived list, but it is employed in the description of how the categories work—namely, synthetically. Yet when we turn, as we have seen, to the vital categories of relation—those of substance, cause, and reciprocity—this category emerges into a position of such dominance *within experience* that Kant says that action is a quite sufficient criterion for substance, without raising questions of permanence of the real in time, and moreover that substance manifests itself "more adequately and easily through action."

But a derivative problem remains. What is the link between the synthetic action which gives rise to experience, and action as a natural fact within that experience? If only one time is thinkable, then how can it embrace them both? I shall urge that the postulate of a linear time is inadequate and unnecessary. The absolute and irreversible sequence of indefinitely or finely divisible units provides a copious matrix for the passage of natural fact, but it hardly does justice to the richness of temporality. The smooth slippage of closed events in continuous progression along a time line is not adequate to the facts. Consciousness accumulates large patches of temporality into a variety of "nows" of many sizes. It synthesizes them in a great many ways beyond what Kant suggests and thereby generates the raw temporal materials from which many abstract meanings for time can be derived: mathematical, physical, perceptual, etc. In short, the conveyor belt metaphor of temporal sequence does not accommodate to the multiple modes of arrest and synthesis by which consciousness establishes both its open-ended quasi-identity and the continuous summation of the world-in-relation-to-consciousness. There is, of course, no exception in the sciences. Science must have observation and generalization. Let observation be as passive as you like, what is observed is held fast in one synthesis or else the generalizations which scientific law requires are not possible. The least moment of memory draws something out of the recession of the past, saves something from the flames that consume the trailing edge of the moving present.

Using a spatial metaphor, we may say that the shallowness of monolinear time cannot do justice to the depth of experience. Temporality has depth because experience has depth. Consciousness continuously transcends sheer, uninterrupted, steady passage. Human activity would be impossible if it were not so. Indeed, man would be impossible—not only because he hates and hopes, but also because he engages in such cold-blooded activities as remembering, predicting, and validating.

No matter how the matter of categorial derivation is settled, a persistent problem remains: How does the functional identity of a transcendental ego pass over into the given unity of an empirical ego? I have been maintaining that as long as we deal with time under the metaphor of spatial monolinearity the mono-dimensional temporality which results will never accommodate to both kinds of process.

V

THE PROBLEM ARISES in contemporary philosophy in strikingly similar ways. Husserl, in the work called *The Phenomenology of Internal Time Consciousness*, covers the same ground, more subtly in many respects. But when he comes to the subject of time, he says, "We have only one time—not only in the sense that things are ordered beside one another in a unique linear extension, but also that different things or processes appear as simultaneous. They do not have parallel similar times but one time, numerically one." [9] Like Kant, he considers and

9. E. Husserl, *The Phenomenology of Internal Time Consciousness*, ed. Martin Heidegger, trans. James S. Churchill (Bloomington: Indiana University Press, 1964), p. 164.

rejects the notion of two "parallel" times. Like Kant, in rejecting the idea of parallelness, he ends in insisting on only one time. Exactly like Kant, however, he cannot confine himself to this one time. In his analysis of objectification he says, "The consciousness of unity, spreading out in the pre-empirical flow of time, posits unity in the temporal flow of the exhibitive images." [10] What he is saying is that objectification of an object includes a temporal dating of each experiential item which reveals the object at such and such a time. But the act through which temporal unity is posited, and through which dating is made possible, is a process, requiring temporality very much like Kant's synthesizing unity.

Husserl's terms "pre-empirical" and "positing" lead us to Sartre, where the problem appears in its most recent form.

In Sartre the recognition of the problem is clearer than in any previous philosopher. He insists on one time only for the in-itself [11] but lays down three dimensions for the for-itself, that is, for consciousness as prereflective, prethetic. Sartre's architectonic offers little that is not found in Husserl's "protensions" and "retensions," or in Heidegger's "ek-stases." The three dimensions in Sartre turn out to be the past, present, and future, described in terms of the chronic contradictions which accompany all temporalization. The for-itself can present itself to itself in all three of these modes, but when it does so with the past, it seems to lose its ontological primacy, for it finds itself in what Sartre calls its "shocking solidarity with the foetus." [12] That is, insofar as it belongs to its body, consciousness seems scandalously dependent upon the priority of the foetus, but as being the ground of all temporality the for-itself has priority, since it provides the temporal framework within which the foetus is but a past, subordinate item. Thus there arises a fundamental duality in which I apprehend myself as a "unity of succession . . . I am conscious of enduring." Now, says Sartre, what is the relation between the "psychic temporality" that involves the sense of endurance and the "original temporality" which is the spontaneous basis of all three dimensions of temporality? [13] Sartre admits

10. *Ibid.*, p. 167.
11. *Being and Nothingness*, trans. Hazel E. Barnes (New York: Philosophical Library, 1956), p. 136.
12. *Ibid.*, p. 139.
13. *Ibid.*, p. 150.

that we are confronted with two temporalities which are incompatible. His effort to elucidate this incompatibility is subtle and difficult. It rests on the fundamental illogicality of the for-itself, which is a theme he wishes to strengthen rather than undermine, however, so that the elucidation becomes evidence for the illogicality, rather than an effort to penetrate the problem further and reduce the illogicality. He explains the duality as what he calls a "reflection-reflecting," but leaves the duality there, perhaps explaining or at least illuminating it by the suggestive mirror metaphor. Thus Sartre, making no structural advance over his predecessors, does go beyond them dialectically. But the difficulty remains, for "reflection-reflecting," be it taken as literal or figurative, also describes a process, and the temporality of this basic process is left unaccounted for.

At its roots this problem rests in a confusion about the idea of "one" in the phrase "one time." Both Kant and Husserl claim there is but one time, and each speaks of this time as unique and linear. *But of course it doesn't follow that because there is but one time it can only be metaphored by one dimension.* And each denies parallel times. Sartre is more subtle. He confronts two temporalities, and insists that they are coordinate. He imports something like the idea of parallelness in the use of the term "reflection-reflecting," and puts it to use as, for example, in the following passage:

> This psychic temporality as a projection into the in-itself of original temporality is a virtual being whose flow does not cease to accompany the ekstatic temporalization of the for-itself insofar as this is apprehended by reflection.[14]

In other words, the two temporalities—the original one, which founds all sense of temporal spread, and the psychic one, which is projected by the original and carries the sense of endurance—flow together, i.e., are in some sense parallel.

Sartre recognizes that there is a fundamental contrariety between the psychic time of the enduring self immersed in the in-itself and the original time of prereflective consciousness which he calls for-itself. But this contrariety is needed only on the supposition that a temporality must be uniquely linear. If we must deal with temporality under the spatial metaphor, we

14. *Ibid.*, p. 170.

should think of a plane or perhaps even of a solid, one of whose dimensions has a preferential direction. We will still be distorting our nascent temporality, of course, but in a less damaging way. This way we can get a more valid spatial cartoon of the temporality of consciousness. The fundamental problem is that consciousness regarded as caught up in the serial flow of monodimensional time cannot account for the presence of its own past in its now. If we take it out of the flow, making it transcendent, as in Kant and Husserl, it is in the implausible position of being engaged in nontemporal activity. If we have two temporalities, as in Sartre, either we need a common temporality to embrace them or we must suffer a bifurcation which is not much of an improvement on the Cartesian split. What must be rejected is the crippling metaphor of monodimensionality or, in Sartre's case, a bilinearity. Two unavoidable patterns confront us—the flow of the world's affairs, which is required for either sorrow or success, and the power of consciousness to control some of this passage, to hope and plan and undertake to rectify the past. But such control is hardly extratemporal. Arrest and alter it as we will, control is also from within the total passage.

Any metaphor which excludes these intercommitted patterns is prima facie false. The passage of temporality is real. Equally real is the conscious alteration of an otherwise relentless and meaningless chain of events. Both the unremitting passage and the conscious transformation of the world are temporal processes. The transcendence of consciousness means the gaining of perspective on the temporal flow, but it can hardly refer to withdrawal from that flow, for, as we have seen, consciousness is as much engaged in action as in idea. Or to repeat terms which perhaps now have more solid meaning: Human existence is a movement; it rests between the extremes of idea and act, requiring both, and thereby leads directly to the complementary otherness of the world as well as to consciousness which is not my own.

Sartre likes to talk of the "pre-positional" in recovering Kant's distinction between the transcendental ego and the empirical ego. What I have been discussing is a temporal depth which will accommodate both temporal passage and the arrests and actions of consciousness, themselves temporal processes. Accordingly, I shall speak of the self as transpositional. By "transpositional" I mean that aspect of self from which one can differentiate both a prereflective consciousness redolent with its native spontaneity and the postreflective *en-soi* self which has a certain finality and fixity about it and which instantly limits the self-creating self. Thus a minimum of two dimensions is needed in our spatial cartoon in order to account both for the fatality of selfhood and for its freedom. But this does not mean two absolute and objective axes or coordinates. For example, the same set of abstract facts may be "open" for a man of hope, "closed" to one of resignation or despair.

Sartre, the high priest of freedom as self-determination, nearly leaves the phenomenal scene entirely, because of a conviction that should we discern any structure at all in the freedom of the *pour-soi*, we smuggle in a disguised denial of that freedom. His wholly negative conception of freedom is also found in our current political attitudes. One of the great fallacies of the twentieth century is the conviction that political freedom is primarily negative, i.e., *freedom from*. Sartre ontologizes this concept of a negative freedom and gives us human freedom as being wholly nonstructural, the terrifying basis of its own values, damned to the task of forging values out of its own spontaneity, in a world otherwise devoid of meaning. There is a clumsy and admirable courage about this view, incarnated in the French Resistance and fierce in its resolve, but as philosophy it is a shade defective. It proceeds without reference to such obvious formative factors as the biology of perception, which is an activity—not a passivity—and varies mightily from species to species; the cultural standards and aims of the society in which my consciousness processively arises; and the finite and particular development of my historical temporal consciousness, insofar as there is a privacy in it. These factors are not restrictions on freedom, but embodiments of it. Pure negative freedom is a philosopher's toy. It bears an unhappy resemblance to prime matter.

Sartre appears to suppose that because I have only negative data for freedom, freedom can only be understood as negative. If I have free time, no obligation interposes. If I am free to choose my governors, nothing constrains me that I do not choose. A body in free fall does so because nothing impedes its course. But freedom does not therefore signify some absolute negativity, a pure nothingness. I do not refer to the Parmenidean problem of how pure non-being can be. This is a question in the logic of ontology, usually debated by philosophers who tend to regard time as shadowy or unreal. Nor am I referring to the epistemology of observation where—as in Kant's First Critique—there can be no difference to mere observation between a free act and an other-determined one. I am focusing on that level of phenomena more akin to Kant's restricted domain of moral decision, although this level overextends and includes moral decision. It includes aesthetic creativity, for example, and the closely related domain of religious self-transcendence. Such freedom is positive in character, embodied in self-realization, self-transcendence, self-making. Its negativity is relational, not absolute, in that its instances are different from the observationally presented data of perception. This freedom is grounded in what Santayana calls "surveying," an arrestive act that is not swept away by the past which it recaptures. But these free acts are also temporal. They have no other home than temporality. If they appear to be breaches in time conceived as a simple linear flow, without antecedent determination, illogical and mysterious, the fault lies in our original construction of the monolinear metaphor.

The difficulty is a technical one—one of technique, that is. It arises because I withdraw selfhood from the temporal flow of observable events in order to observe that flow, and then discover that there are no points or boundable segments into which I can reinsert the self as conscious. The conscious self is temporal, however; it is processive. It is not really removable from time. It follows that if I must choose a spatial metaphor it must be broad enough to accommodate both the distinctive and the related features of two factors: a consciousness whose occurrences assemble the world for order and action, for understanding and intervention, and an independence in the world which constantly declares the unendingly serial course of events.

17 / Can Grammar Be Thought?

James M. Edie

THE FOUNDATION OF PHENOMENOLOGY in the work of Edmund Husserl originally involved a renewal of the hoary rationalistic attempt to establish the bases of a universal logical grammar. This *Wiederholung* of a program of research, which goes back to Roger Bacon and the Franciscan theologians of the thirteenth and fourteenth centuries, to Descartes, Leibniz, and the Port-Royal logicians, was explicitly endorsed by Husserl in the Fourth Investigation and clearly motivated the work of his student, Heidegger, on the *Grammatica Speculativa* of Thomas of Erfurt.[1] Though Husserl's concern with this problem was somewhat marginal and not sustained in his later logical work, his statements on "pure-logical grammar" and a description of the place it would occupy in a fully worked out phenomenology of thought and reason remained as an embarrassment for some later existential phenomenologists. Merleau-Ponty defines Husserl's conception of an *eidetic of language* as a "universal grammar" which would fix the essential forms of the linguistic expression of meaning necessary and sufficient for any language to be a language. It would consist of "forms of signification" implied in the various natural languages men speak and of which these natural languages are only so many incomplete and confused realizations. Merleau-Ponty further claims that the ambition to discover such a grammar was abandoned in Husserl's later philo-

1. Martin Heidegger, *Die Kategorien- und Bedeutungslehre des Duns Scotus* (Tübingen, 1916), uses the concepts of phenomenology to explain this work, which was at that time still erroneously attributed to Scotus. Husserl cites it in *Formale und transzendentale Logik.*

sophical work, but he gives very little evidence for saying that this abandonment was necessitated by a change in Husserl's philosophical positions.[2] In view of the work recently beginning to be accomplished in the field of transformational generative grammar (which Noam Chomsky sometimes confusingly calls "Cartesian linguistics"), work of which neither Husserl nor Merleau-Ponty had the slightest premonition, this question must be reopened. In this paper I would like to make a preliminary, and more or less descriptive, contribution to the debate on "philosophical grammar" by examining what Husserl, Merleau-Ponty, and Chomsky have to say on the subject in an attempt to clarify what precise sense can be given to such an enterprise from a phenomenological point of view.

Merleau-Ponty once said that it would be a "very romantic way of showing one's love for reason to base its reign on the disavowal of acquired knowledge." [3] Therefore, to the extent that contemporary transformational generative grammar is elaborating a productive, empirical method, achieving empirical results, and forging new, nonbehavioristic, antiempiricist hypotheses (it is, perhaps, too early to speak of a "theory") concerning the acquisition and use of language, it must be accorded the same philosophical interest that is readily accorded to experimental psychology on the part of phenomenologists. The fact that Chomsky's critique of behaviorism and associationism in psychology (which does not concern us in this article) closely parallels that of Merleau-Ponty in some essential respects provides us with a persuasive, though supplementary, motive for examining his positive linguistic hypotheses from a phenomenological perspective. If phenomenology is the logos of phenomena, insofar as logos itself (speech and reason) is a "phenomenon," phenomenology must also become a logos of logos, a phenomenology of language, and this is a consequence fully in accord with the spirit of both Husserl and Merleau-Ponty.

Unfortunately, Husserl's remarks on "pure-logical grammar"

2. Merleau-Ponty argues for this shift (*Kehre?*) in Husserl's views in his essay, "On the Phenomenology of Language," in *Signs*, trans. Richard C. McCleary (Evanston, Ill.: Northwestern University Press, 1964), pp. 84–97. An argument against "universal grammar" is also contained in "La Conscience et l'acquisition du langage," *Bulletin de psychologie* (November, 1964), p. 254.

3. Maurice Merleau-Ponty, *The Primacy of Perception*, ed. James M. Edie (Evanston, Ill.: Northwestern University Press, 1964), p. 24.

are not sufficiently developed to be discussed independently of his general phenomenological architectonic. As befits a philosopher of experience, Husserl begins his logical studies with the *experience of language* and asserts that studies in logic must "be guided" by language. He does not mean by this that the empirical, psychological, physiological, historical, and cultural bases of language be incorporated into philosophy, or that logic is dependent on any given natural language, but rather that the study of "the grammatical" (not a given, empirical "grammar") is the *first level* of logical reflection. The two primordial types of intentional experience, according to Husserl, are (1) the experience of the world, and (2) the experience of language. The theoretical elaboration of the first (transcendental logic) is logically posterior to the theoretical investigation of the second, namely, *language.*[4]

To consider language in itself is to perform an implicit phenomenological reduction, i.e., to turn from the *Lebenswelt* of factual experience, in which meanings are instantiated in factual situations, to the separated meanings themselves, as they are experienced in their ideality, independently of any possible factual reference.[5] The experience of language is the experience

---

4. These two levels of analysis correspond in Husserl's logic to the *evidence of distinctness* (which is a purely formal consideration, established in the analysis of the grammatical and the logic of noncontradiction) and the *evidence of clarity,* or clarification (which requires the logic of truth, i.e., transcendental logic). See André de Muralt, *L'Idée de la phénoménologie* (Paris: Gallimard, 1958), pp. 115 ff.; and Suzanne Bachelard, *A Study of Husserl's Formal and Transcendental Logic,* trans. Lester E. Embree (Evanston, Ill.: Northwestern University Press, 1968), p. 18.

5. "We should never forget that meanings, essences, are directly expressed in language. *Language is the true locus of essences, of the ideal existence of meanings,* because language, taken in itself, abstracts from the factual existence of objects, and grasps only significations. This is the meaning of the excellent formulation by Merleau-Ponty: 'separated essences are those of language' [*Phenomenology of Perception,* trans. Colin Smith (New York: Humanities Press, 1962), p. xv]. In other words, a thought which moves solely on the level of language moves necessarily within the phenomenological reduction; it is on a level with the eidetic realm of pure, experienced meanings. This is why the *Logische Untersuchungen* which begins with an extremely careful analysis of language and its functions develops a logic which makes no reference at all to the phenomenological reduction but which nevertheless possesses an authentically phenomenological spirit. . . . this is necessary because, *from the moment that one considers language in itself, one has implicitly operated the phenomenological reduction*" (De Muralt, *L'Idée,* pp. 124–25).

of meaning par excellence; it is our route of access to the realm of "the meant," of "sense" and "signification." Now if one distinguishes the realm of significations (what Husserl calls "categories of signification" as opposed to the "categories of the object") from the realm of objects signified *through* language, one isolates within formal logic the territory of "apophantic analytics" or the purely formal study of the structures of judgment.[6]

Now, the *first level* of the implicit phenomenological reduction (if we can call it that) which is operated by the "linguistic turn" away from the world toward language itself is that of the discovery and analysis of *the grammatical*. Husserl calls this the study of the "pure morphology of significations" (*reine Formenlehre der Bedeutungen*) or "pure a priori (logical) grammar." Such a study is strictly a priori and purely logical, a study of "the grammatical" as opposed to the empirical and historical investigation of comparative grammars; it constitutes the first level of "apophantic analytics," to be followed by the second (the logic of noncontradiction) and the third (the logic of truth) levels of the formal analysis of signification. Now we cannot repeat here or justify the steps through which Husserl's thought moves to establish the conclusion that the proper and specific object of formal apophantic analysis is the *apophansis* (judgment, affirmation, proposition) taken in its strict formality as the fully explicit categorical judgment (*S is p*), which he considers to be the simple and necessary categorial structure of any possible judgment. That would require the recapitulation of large sections of the *Logical Investigations* and *Formal and Transcendental Logic*. What we are interested in is the sense in which the first level of the formal analysis of the judgment must be grammatical.

No philosopher can escape the a priori rules which prescribe the conditions under which a linguistic utterance can have a unified, intelligible sense. The study of grammar, in this sense, is necessarily philosophical. Pure logical grammar (or apophantic morphology) is, according to Husserl, that first branch of formal logic which establishes the formal grammatical rules necessary

6. *Logische Untersuchungen* (Halle, 1913), *Prolegomena*, Chap. 11, and the Fourth Investigation. Cf. Bachelard, *Husserl's Formal and Transcendental Logic*, p. 3. These remarks, to be fully justified, would, of course, have to be explained within a complete account of Husserl's philosophy of language. We are not, in this study, even scratching the surface of Husserl's philosophy of language as a whole.

for any statement to be meaningful at all; it is prior to and independent of all questions of the formal validity and the truth value of statements. Every judgment must, for instance, respect the a priori grammatical rule that in a well-formed sentence a substantive must take the place of S (in the primitive form S *is* p) and a predicate must be substituted for p. If this rule is violated, nonsense (*Unsinn*) results. We get strings of words like "King but where seems and," "this frivolous is green," "red is world," "a man is and," etc., which are devoid of any unified meaning; the words individually have meaning, but when they are arranged ungrammatically they have none. It is the purpose of pure logical grammar to derive from the originary form of judgment (S *is* p) the laws which govern the formation of potentially meaningful affirmative, negative, universal, particular, hypothetical, causal, conjunctive, disjunctive, etc., forms. It is in this sense that *das Grammatische selbst* founds the second and third levels of formal logic and establishes rules which are always already taken for granted in the logic of noncontradiction and truth. These purely formal grammatical laws are wholly independent of the truth or falsity of the statements which they rule and guarantee only that the statements formed in accord with them will be free of *Unsinn* (nonsense). They have no relevance to the material contradiction (*Wiedersinn*) involved in such well-formed sentences as "Squares are round" or "This algebraic number is green," and so on. The laws of logical grammar save us from *formal nonsense* only; it is the other levels of logic which save us from contradiction and countersense.

However, thus to vindicate the value of pure grammatical a prioris is not to assert that logic is based on ordinary language or empirical linguistics. Husserl insists on this: logic is founded not on grammar but on "the grammatical":

> It is . . . not without reason that people often say that formal logic has let itself be guided by grammar. In the case of the theory of forms, however, this is not a reproach but a necessity—provided that, for guided by grammar (a word intended to bring to mind *de facto* historical languages and their grammatical description) guidance by the grammatical itself be substituted.[7]

7. *Formal and Transcendental Logic*, trans. Dorion Cairns (The Hague: Martinus Nijhoff, 1969), p. 337. Cf. Bachelard, *Husserl's Formal and Transcendental Logic*, p. 11.

This is grammar raised to the level of the analysis of the formal conditions of thought. It is here that Husserl joins the seventeenth-century proponents of a *grammaire générale et raisonnée* in conscious opposition to the accepted views of his historicist and psychologistic contemporaries.[8] "Language," he wrote, "has not only physiological, psychological and cultural-historical, but also a priori foundations." [9] The validity and import of logical grammar is shown by the very fact that one can meaningfully ask such questions as: How does German, Latin, Chinese, etc., express "the" categorical proposition, "the" plural, "the" hypothetical, "the" modes of possibility, probability, "the" not, etc.? Its place is to study and furnish the a priori rules which govern the structural coherence of parts of speech with one another in sentences. Such grammatical rules are not just historical accidents or conventions but *necessary* conditions of meaningfulness and the avoidance of nonsense; they are not, without the higher levels of formal logic built upon them, *sufficient* conditions for the avoidance of contradiction and error:

> Nothing else has so greatly confused discussion of the question of the correct relationship between logic and grammar as the continual confounding of the two logical spheres that we have distinguished sharply as the lower and the upper and have characterized by means of their negative counterparts: the sphere of nonsense and the sphere of countersense.[10]

Husserl thus vindicates the place of grammar (*rein-logische Grammatik*) as a theory in its own right, within his phenomenological hierarchy of "sciences." But it is, so to speak, the emptiest and most formal of all. Its rules provide the barest minimal conditions necessary to avoid nonsense in forming linguistic statements. They exclude only the purest nonsense which, as Suzanne Bachelard says, it would never occur to anyone to

---

8. For an interesting comparison of how Husserl would reduce a complex sentence to the simple form (*S is p*) which is, in effect, equivalent to the procedures of the Port-Royal logicians, at least as interpreted by Chomsky, compare De Muralt, *L'Idée*, p. 136, with Noam Chomsky, *Cartesian Linguistics* (New York: Harper & Row, 1966), pp. 32–35, with regard to the transformation of nominalized adjectives into relative clauses and then into simple propositions. Cf. also Chomsky, *Language and Mind* (New York: Harcourt, Brace & World, 1968), pp. 25 ff.

9. *Logische Untersuchungen*, II, Pt. I, 338.

10. *Ibid.*, p. 341.

utter.[11] Pure grammar establishes rules which are always subunderstood and already taken for granted in all the formal systems which study and establish the sufficient conditions for meaningful expressions. But the fact that the uncovering of these conditions has no "practical" value, and even seems to make a science of what is trivially obvious, is no reason to despise it. Its theoretical value for philosophy, Husserl tells us, is "all the greater." Husserl takes pride in this discovery; he even glories in the fact that only philosophers are concerned with the "a priori," with the discovery of truths so fundamental that all the other sciences always take them for granted. It is, he believes, precisely such "obvious" trivialities as those expressed by the rules of pure grammar that mask the deepest philosophical problems, and he sees that in a profound, if paradoxical, sense philosophy is the science of trivialities.[12] The clear distinction which he was able to establish between pure grammar and the "higher" level(s) of formal analytics seemed to him to be a theoretical discovery of the first magnitude and a necessary point of departure for the elaboration of a phenomenological theory of consciousness.

It is all the more surprising, therefore, that this aspect of Husserl's phenomenological program has had so little influence on his successors. The language in which Suzanne Bachelard, for instance, decides *not* "to revive the debate over the possibility of a general and reasoned grammar" betrays a residual belief that the value of such an enterprise is highly dubious.[13] For his part, Merleau-Ponty not only rejects this aspect of Husserl's thought altogether, but confuses the historical record by claiming that Husserl himself came to reject his earlier idea of a purely logical grammar in his later work. This is far from certain,[14] but it will be of some interest to examine Merleau-Ponty's own position in this regard and the reasons behind it.

11. Bachelard, *Husserl's Formal and Transcendental Logic*, p. 6.
12. See Marvin Farber, *The Foundation of Phenomenology*, 2d ed. (New York: Paine-Whitman, 1962), pp. 331–32.
13. Bachelard, *Husserl's Formal and Transcendental Logic*, p. 9.
14. *Ibid.*

II

MERLEAU-PONTY'S REASONS for rejecting the notion of a universal logical grammar can be summarized under three headings: (1) Such a notion implies a false, "intellectualistic" conception of the relations between words and meanings; (2) it attempts to substitute an "ideal language" for natural speech; and (3) it cannot account for the preconceptual uses and meanings of language.

(1) Even if we disregard (as we should) the naive and loose talk about "innate ideas" and "Cartesian linguistics" which is uncritically suffused through Chomsky's writings, there are still several prima facie philosophical reasons to cause philosophers and historians of philosophy, who know the seventeenth century as well as Chomsky does, to have qualms about his claim to reinstate "philosophical grammar" as an explanatory hypothesis to account for the surface phenomena of our use and experience of language. Merleau-Ponty, perhaps the only consistent anti-Cartesian in the whole long tradition of French philosophy, would not be one to suffer gladly the surreptitious reintroduction of Cartesian metaphysics into twentieth-century philosophy. Chomsky's rhetoric is, indeed, in need of interpretation, but I would claim, nevertheless, that the substance of his argument is of serious philosophical significance. When we sort out what Chomsky really means to say from his eulogistic celebrations of "the century of genius," we will find that his basic contention is quite independent of the history of Cartesianism and that it deserves to be heard in its own right.

According to Merleau-Ponty, the Cartesian notion of consciousness is "intellectualistic" because it locates the experience of meaning (of "giving sense" to things and words) in an activity of pure reflexive thought; the *res cogitans* is the locus and the faculty of clear and distinct thought. All knowledge of the objective world, of other persons and of one's own body, is a projection based on the mind's experience of itself. Through a reflexive act of self-knowledge the mind raises itself to the level of the universal, of the clear and distinct ideas, without any detour through intersubjective encounters with other persons or any contamination from the body itself. The body plays no essential part in ideogenesis and has no other place before thought than that of another idea, fully objectified and exterior to the act of thinking itself. Language, being an objective datum for thought in like manner, lies necessarily outside consciousness; precisely because consciousness is self-consciousness there can be no necessary or internal link between consciousness and language. Words are to thought what the body is to the soul. Since words are the exterior (spoken, written) signs of concepts, they can have no intrinsic relation to the concepts they signify. No less than nominalistic empiricism, writes Merleau-Ponty, Cartesian intellectualism has to declare the relationship between concepts and the words which express them to be external, fortuitous, conventional. The mind in its splendid, isolated self-possession freely links its concepts to their verbal signs.[15] But such a view of the independence of thought from language is as untenable as the body-mind dualism which infects Descartes's metaphysics as a whole. Since the body can be shown to be not really just another object (*res extensa*) for thought, it cannot be "thought" like a concept. The body itself experiences or "thinks" and expresses meaning. Verbal language itself is an extension of the gestural system through which the human subject gives definition, form, and meaning to experience.

We cannot pause to justify this rapid summary of well-known theses from Merleau-Ponty. But we should stop for a moment at least to indicate, if not to examine in detail, the phenomenological evidence for the two positions here in conflict. Our first job, in any phenomenological investigation, must be to sensitize ourselves to the phenomenon at issue, in this case the *phenomenon of language*. In the case of language our attempt to "view the phenomena" is fraught with special difficulties. For one thing, like such primordial phenomena as the experience of time, of embodiment, of thinking itself, language is all-pervasive. Its structures pervade and include all the others; like our bodies and our acts of consciousness themselves, language is too close to us for us to be able to gain an easy distance from it to objectify it and lay it out before us. Moreover, language partici-

15. We are aware of the summary character of this argument, which presupposes the whole work of Merleau-Ponty, particularly his refutation of intellectualism and nominalistic empiricism in *Phenomenology of Perception*. For a more detailed summary see Merleau-Ponty, "La Conscience . . . ," pp. 226 ff.

pates in the reflexivity of thought itself in such wise that we can speak about speaking (as we can think about thinking) within language itself—with the result that a phenomenology of language can only be accomplished by means of language. Language is one of those primordial forms of experience which not only contain all the others but itself as well. The complexities of linguistic evidence are such that the elaboration of a fully completed phenomenology of language is something which must be relegated to the distant future. Who would say, even after Merleau-Ponty, that we have achieved a completed phenomenology of perception? Or, after Sartre, of the imagination? But we know where we must begin, namely, with those aspects and realizations of language which are *experienced*, in whatever way, and which, when taken together, constitute the essential structures of the indefinitely repeatable, open, ongoing, historical linguistic experience itself.

Moreover, this philosophical effort, this turn toward language, is not something that men have just recently thought of undertaking; philosophers for two thousand years have been attempting to come to grips with fundamental structures of linguistic experience and, although we cannot accept any one historically given theory of language as adequate, we must hope to incorporate into our final view and to explain any of the essential phenomenological distinctions which have already been made. Usually we find that past philosophers were too much impressed with one or another facet of the experience of language and therefore built their theories on too narrow a basis. We can even say that all theories of language which have been elaborated up to now are false because they are incomplete. They explain certain phenomena well but neglect others equally important. In the following considerations we will turn primarily to ordinary experience, therefore, rather than to philosophical theories, in an attempt to suggest some of the kinds of experiences which originally made this or that philosophical theory plausible.

Following Husserl, many phenomenologists argue that the central structure of language involves the intention of saying something to somebody about something. The distinctions between (1) *meaning* (what is objectively meant or intended), (2) *an object of reference* or a state of affairs (which would instantiate the meaning and to which it refers), and (3) *the linguistic vehicle* (the spoken or written utterance) are already given in such a general structure. We need not, hopefully, dwell on these hard-earned phenomenological distinctions here. (And for the purposes of this study we can neglect the hidden, and almost certainly false, premise in this definition of language: that language is essentially for communication.) At any given moment our language—as an objective linguistic system, as *langue*—is, for us, much more virtual than actual; in expressing ourselves we seldom advert to our language as such. As we speak, our language is almost never at the primary focal point of consciousness; rather, it is those things (events, thoughts, arguments) which we use language to think or speak about which are at the center of our attention. We attend primarily to what we mean to say, to what we are trying to say, to what we are talking about, sometimes to the person to whom we are speaking, or to the purpose for which we are speaking—these are what guide our speech. When the child begins to respond linguistically to its mother, it does not concentrate its attention on her lips from which the sounds to be imitated emerge but fixes her gaze with its eyes. Neither the orator nor the ordinary speaker has much reflexive awareness of the words and syntax he is using; like acts of consciousness, acts of speaking require a second, deliberate act of reflection to objectify them as such. This is why it happens that when we have engaged in a train of thought or attempted to present an argument, we seldom remember, a few minutes later, just which words we used to do so, though we could express the same argument again, in other words, any number of times. "Thus it often happens that we find ourselves knowing something which we have learnt by means of words without being able to remember a single one of the words which conveyed it to us." [16] This shows the evanescent, fleeting character of our sentences, which are nevertheless always composed of words with more or less solidly fixed dictionary definitions. We can always repeat an argument, but if we had to use again just the same concatenation of words, just the same sentence structures, just the same verbal images, just the same turns of phrase, we would normally be at a loss. Moreover, we frequently have the experience of knowing more or less clearly

16. Jean-Paul Sartre, *What Is Literature?* (New York: Harper & Row, 1965), p. 14. Cf. Anthony Manser, *Sartre: A Philosophic Study* (New York: Oxford University Press, 1967), p. 107.

326 / SUBJECTIVITY AND OBJECTIVITY

what we *want* to say without being able to find just the words necessary to express what we mean. We experience an impatience with ourselves and with our interlocutors; we experience ourselves being misunderstood. The exclamation: "That is not what I mean!" is followed by further words to make our meaning more clear. We try various linguistic alternatives; if we are brought to a stop, our interlocutor may suggest words or phrases (which we reject or accept as more or less satisfactory, more or less equivalent, or the best available, vehicles of what we mean to convey). Thus the relation of our psychological intentions, of what we *mean* to say, to the words we are able to use at any given time becomes problematic. There is no one-to-one isomorphic correspondence between words and thoughts; there is clearly a certain independence of the one with respect to the other which must be accounted for.

On the one hand, we cannot think without words; words are the embodiment and concrete actual realization of thought. Yet on the other hand, what we mean to say by means of words somehow transcends any particular verbal formulation of it. The irreducibility of thought and intention to words is at least part of the phenomenon of language which led earlier "intellectualistic" philosophers to locate meanings (as concepts) outside of language altogether as transcendent ideas, existing prior to and logically independent of any actual speaking. Merleau-Ponty attempts to account for the illusion that "thought" appears to enjoy priority and independence with respect to language by distinguishing the already objectified ("sedimented") meanings and forms of expression available to us in our maternal tongue prior to any actual use of these possibilities for expression from the actual utilization of these means of expression in speech (*parole*). The fact that our language is a historical and cultural instrument that was forged prior to our own use of it, that the world of thought was already instituted and structured when we came on the scene, and that this language is the *medium* through which we communicate with the thoughts of others, gives us the illusion of there being somewhere a realm of "fixed" meanings that preexist present and actual thought about them. This is the theory of language as the "instrument" of thought, and since language is clearly "instrumental," there is a truth of intellectualism. But it is not the whole truth; language is more than an instrument.

Available meanings, in other words former acts of expression, establish between speaking subjects a common world, to which new words actually being uttered refer, as gestures refer to the sensible world.[17]

Sartre and Merleau-Ponty join forces in bringing forth arguments against the possibility of thoughts existing independently of any actual use of language, though none of these arguments fully demonstrates that thought is not *logically prior* to its verbal expression. To say that thoughts are experientially *inseparable* from words, that the use of words is an absolutely *necessary condition* for thought, that we must express what we mean in words, even to ourselves, in order to know what we mean, even to deny that there is anything such as a thought or experience which is verbally ineffable,[18] is not *sufficient* to demonstrate, by strict implication, that the intention to speak and the conceptual purposes concretized and actualized in language do not enjoy a *logical* (and *ontological*) priority over their expression.[19]

But we can concede to Merleau-Ponty that these conclusions, if true, *are* sufficient to refute intellectualism, and that is all we are concerned with here. Communication is not the direct transmission from one mind to another of clear and distinct ideas by means of a system of unequivocal and fully learned, conventional word-signs. If this were the case, it would be impossible to understand the fact that the words we use are charged with infinites of subtle emotional, cultural, national, regional, idiosyncratic nuances (owing to styles of intonation, to rhythm, to historical circumstances and linguistic accidents, to accompanying facial and bodily gestures, to practical contexts, to moods and the intuition of purposes behind verbal utterances) which cannot be grasped without referring to *just the words* which now actually concretize them.[20]

17. Merleau-Ponty, *Phenomenology of Perception*, p. 186 (corrected).
18. Merleau-Ponty, *Primacy of Perception*, p. 30; idem, *Phenomenology of Perception*, p. 194; *idem, Signs*, p. 95.
19. See Merleau-Ponty's commentary on Husserl (*Formal and Transcendental Logic* and *Der Ursprung der Geometrie*) in *Signs*, pp. 84 ff. William James has a very interesting discussion of the "intention to speak" in *Principles of Psychology* (New York: Dover Publications, 1950), I, 241 ff. and esp. 253.
20. See Alphonse de Waelhens, *La Philosophie de l'ambiguïté* (Louvain: Nauwelaerts, 1951), p. 153 (on Sartre and Merleau-Ponty).

The meaning of words must be finally induced by the words themselves, or more exactly, their conceptual meaning must be formed by a kind of subtraction from a *gestural meaning* which is immanent to the word. . . . There is . . . a *thought in speech* the existence of which is unsuspected by intellectualism.[21]

Again, it is unnecessary (and, in any case, impossible) to repeat here all the arguments which Merleau-Ponty adduces to make this point. If a return to "philosophical grammar" requires the reinstatement of Cartesian intellectualism, either as a theory of knowledge or as a theory of language, it is clearly unacceptable, because this theory is incomplete and therefore false.

(2) I do not wish to dwell on the second reason which can be discerned behind Merleau-Ponty's rejection of the project of a "philosophical grammar." It involves his rejection of the attempts of logical positivists and other logicians to establish an "ideal language" (a sterile "algorithm," he says) *to take the place of* ordinary language. The reasons why he rejects such an attempt, which is today almost totally abandoned in any case, are not completely different from those of ordinary-language philosophers, i.e., because the logical form (or "system") which is realized in ordinary language "never exists wholly in act but always involves latent or incubating changes." It cannot, therefore, ever be fully translated into a language whose logical form would be fully explicit and fully rationalized on the level of fully reflexive, judging consciousness.

It [ordinary language] is never composed of absolutely univocal meanings which can be made completely explicit beneath the gaze of a transparent constituting consciousness. It will be a question not of a system of forms of signification clearly articulated in terms of one another—not of a structure of linguistic ideas built according to a strict plan—but of a cohesive whole of convergent linguistic gestures, each of which will *be defined less by a signification than by a use value [valeur d'emploi].*[22]

21. Merleau-Ponty, *Phenomenology of Perception,* p. 179 (corrected).
22. Merleau-Ponty, *Signs,* p. 87 (italics added). For Merleau-Ponty's critique of logical positivism see "La Conscience," pp. 242 ff. With respect to usage, he concludes: "The word is a *tool,* defined by *a certain use* to which it is impossible to give an exact intellectual formulation" (p. 253); and, "Each word *has* a meaning only in so far as it is sustained in this meaning-function by all the others. . . . For a word to keep its sense it has to be held in place by all the others" (p. 256).

This thesis, that the meaning of language lies not in some common, universal categorial structure but in its *usage,* is one which it would be interesting to examine from a phenomenological standpoint, but it is not to the point to do so here. The question here is only whether the project of "philosophical grammar" *must* be limited to a repetition of the "ideal language" experiments of logical positivism, or must, in some way, imply the same or a similar view of language. If the two projects can be clearly distinguished methodologically, as I believe they can, then this objection comes down to no more than a prejudice.

(3) The third range of considerations is the most important of all. It involves the nature of the acquisition and use of the linguistic instrument which is a natural language, and the best way to begin is to recall schematically a number of facts about language which have now been established beyond doubt by recent linguistic investigations and by the very important and synthetic work of Merleau-Ponty on the learning of language. Again, as phenomenologists, we must begin by looking at the phenomena.

Linguistic expression is specific to the human species; all normal human subjects learn to speak a maternal tongue as a process of ordinary social maturation. A child learns to speak as he learns to use his body, i.e., without ever reflexively learning the rules which govern such complex behaviors in the form of explicit judgments. When a child learns to smile he does not bring his bodily muscular control under a general concept through an act of judgment. Moreover, the ability of normal children to learn language (in the form of gesture and speech) bears no correlation to the degree of their native intelligence or to the efforts of their parents or those around them to "teach" them words and sentences.[23] Language is not, strictly speaking, *learned,* and it is certainly not *taught* (like swimming, reading, or arithmetic). Even the intellectually backward human subject develops (what the most intelligent apes do not) [24] the ability to

23. See for example the summary of recent empirical research in Ronald W. Langacker, *Language and Its Structure* (New York: Harcourt, Brace & World, 1968), p. 14 and *passim.*

24. Chomsky, *Language and Mind,* p. 9: "Language is a species-specific human possession, and even at low levels of intelligence, at pathological levels, we find a command of language that is totally unattainable by an ape that may, in other respects, surpass a human imbecile in problem-solving ability and other adaptive behavior."

utter and recognize grammatical (i.e., well-formed) sentences in his maternal language just from the fact of his being exposed over a period of time to the linguistic environment into which he was born. This ability extends systematically far beyond the empirical samples of correct speech to which he has been in fact actually exposed in the course of his chronological maturation. Here, we come upon an obvious empirical fact about the acquisition of language: it is an ability to utter a restricted system of sounds according to a certain well-defined style (i.e., grammatically) without explicit knowledge of the rules of grammar. The illiterate, medieval Russian peasant spoke a highly inflected, highly complex, and difficult language without the least knowledge of the rules of Russian grammar—rules which were scientifically codified only centuries after the language to which they apply was in existence. To learn a language is in some sense to be "imprinted" by the whole, given, historical language at once on the basis of very imperfect and incomplete factual examples of it. Each child, as we know, "reinvents" for himself the whole structure of his maternal tongue on the basis of his own perspectival, restricted experience of it, and, miraculously, this is just the language which his whole world understands and speaks.

A second, equally important, linguistic fact is that, though all human subjects learn to speak (and, in this sense, language is "species specific"), not all humans speak the *same* language. We find here, empirically, one of the motives for distinguishing between surface-grammar and deep-grammar. The particular phonological, morphological, syntactical style of any given natural language is not preestablished in the organism as such. We can go further. *Speaking* is not a "biological" but a "cultural" use of the human body. If the ability to speak is somehow "innate" in the human organism, its empirical forms are strictly indeterminate so far as the bodily organism itself is concerned. The physiological structures of the human organism do not prescribe any particular way of speaking, any *one* natural language, nor do they, apparently, prescribe the development of language at all. The organism, taken just as a natural entity and as a part of nature, has no need to speak. There is no organ which is used in speech, i.e., the lips, tongue, palate, throat, lungs, diaphragm, etc., which does not have a specific physiological function utterly independent of its superordinate and special employment for the purposes of speaking. Moreover, many scientists believe that, from the point of view of purely physiological development, there are certain other higher primates who lack nothing of the physiological apparatus which the human species employs for linguistic purposes.[25] Language is, therefore, a phenomenon of a higher order than biological life; it involves the use of biologically determinate organs for "another purpose," with another intention—in the words of Merleau-Ponty, "to sing the world." This much is true of the development of language in general, but we also know that it is not enough for two members of the human species to have the same organs or the same nervous system for them to make the same "natural" signs, to utter the same speech sounds, to use the same phonemes according to the same rules, i.e., to develop the same language. Our psychophysiological equipment leaves open many possibilities and is, in itself, indifferent to the use we make of it—whether to "sing the world" in English or in Japanese or in any other "natural language." Speaking is the using of a given physiological system, which has its own proper biological teleology independent of speech, for "cultural" purposes transcendent to the biological itself, namely, for the purposes of expressing, making sense of, and articulating experience in language. Thus there is an equivocation in the term "natural language." Though it is *natural* for men to speak, no *given language* is inscribed in human nature as such.

In one of his psychological studies Merleau-Ponty examined the way in which children learn to speak their mother tongue.[26] During its first months the child begins to make expressive movements, to utter sounds, to babble. This babbling is of an extreme richness and diversity and comprises phonemes of every conceivable variety, many of which do not exist in the language

---

25. See Langacker, *Language and Its Structure*, p. 142: "The fact that we vocalize in a highly systematic and coordinated manner, while they [the higher primates] do not, must therefore be attributed to neurological factors rather than to gross anatomical differences." This conclusion may be in need of refinement. I am indebted to Noam Chomsky for pointing out to me in a private communication on this paper that recent research (by Kelemen and Lieberman) indicates that the evolution of the peripheral physiological structures used in human speech may have taken place quite late and thus could be specific to man and his unique language capacity.

26. "La Conscience," pp. 226–59. This is the single most important study, but one finds parallel passages in the chapter on "The Body as Expression, and Speech" in *Phenomenology of Perception*, pp. 174–99; in the chapter "On the Phenomenology of Language" in *Signs*, pp. 84–97; and in the section on "Linguistics" in *The Primacy of Perception*, pp. 78–85.

being spoken in the child's environment. The child's babbling is a polymorphous and spontaneous language in which all the natural possibilities of the human organism are used to make sounds. When (around the age of two) the child moves from the stage of babbling to that of gradually learning to say his first *words*, in imitation of those speaking around him, he first of all begins to imitate the peculiar intonations, the conversational tone, "the melody of the phrases" of those in whose company he is speaking. Thus the German child begins to place the tonic accent on his babbled sounds which corresponds to the German accent, the French child babbles in French, the English child in English, and so on. Then, with the acquisition of closer and closer approximations to the kinds of speech sounds which follow the rules of the "natural" language of his environment, the child *greatly restricts* the number and quality of the phonemes he is capable of uttering and the rhythm and frequency with which they are used. If he is German, he begins to restrict the phonemes he recognizes and can reproduce to just those which are recognized and employed in the German language; and if, some years later, he is required to learn a language like English or French, which employs different phonemes according to different phonological rules, he will be able to lose his native accent only with great difficulty and effort, if at all. Learning to speak a given language, then, requires that the child grasp its distinctive phonetic style, and this requires a selection and *impoverishment* of the natural sounds his bodily organism could naturally produce. We see that this *selective activity*, even in a child of four months, involves the (of course unexpressed) *intention to speak*, and, in repeating sounds made to him in a conversational tone, and in producing quasi-linguistic effects, the child, without doubt, has the experience of doing just what those around him are doing and of fully participating in the world of discourse. Little by little, during the first years of his life, the child moves from his first words, which are really word-sentences of very global meaning-character, to sentences grammatically construed according to the morphological and syntactical regularities of his native language, until around the age of five or six he begins to grasp the symbolic and analogical character of language as such. We cannot here trace or analyze this linguistic development in complete detail. One of the things Merleau-Ponty is most concerned to show is that the child learns a language as an adult learns the style of a hitherto unknown work of art or of music. One first grasps it globally, as a whole, but very vaguely, and then, through further experience, is enabled to discover the articulated parts which constitute the whole and distinguish it from any other. Speaking originates in a personal affective and emotive gesticulation which only little by little, through a play of diacritical oppositions sufficient to distinguish one phoneme, one sound, one word, from another, begins to take on an increasingly explicit and determinate sense. In short, men begin to think through the most global and generic categories and, through these, descend gradually to the clear and distinct ideas of fully reflexive language.

What primarily impressed Merleau-Ponty, then, in his studies of language-learning was the fact that a language is grasped —through a period of "incubation" which begins to peak around the second year—"as a whole" (whose "parts" or elements are then capable of indefinite articulation in their interrelations with one another), as a *style* of expression which imposes itself and which contains an "inner logic" that is grasped dumbly and inarticulately (by an *"esprit aveugle"*) [27] prior to any ability to conceptualize the meanings for which it stands or which it enables us to express. Beneath the level of *words,* and beneath the level of *sentences,* spoken language is a coherent system of phonemic variations which render the existence of words and phrases themselves possible. Words and phrases are composed of phonemic "signs" which in themselves do not mean anything at all (in the sense that they do not designate or denote anything independent of this semeiological system itself) but are, rather, only the diacritical marks necessary to distinguish one word-sound from another according to certain patterns. The language, as a phonemic (semeiological) system, carries its meaning within it, as a global reference to the whole world of experience, capable of expressing an unlimited number of things, which only gradually take on a specific sense. Long after the child

27. "La Conscience," p. 255. Cf. *Phenomenology of Perception,* p. 185: "I do not understand the gestures of others by some act of intellectual interpretation; communication between consciousnesses is not based on the common meaning of their respective experiences, for it is equally the basis of that meaning. The act by which I lend myself to the spectacle must be recognized as irreducible to anything else. I join it in a kind of *blind recognition* which precedes the intellectual working out and clarification of the meaning" (italics added).

begins to learn specific words, he continues to babble ("to sing
the world") in a generalized way. What the child *means* to say by
such phonemic gesticulation is never *fully* expressed. There always remains an immense mass of subunderstood meaning even
in the most articulate, adult language, and adult speech, according to Merleau-Ponty, is only a continuation and gradual explicitation of the original phonemic babbling.[28]

The study of the acquisition of language leads us back,
according to Merleau-Ponty, to an activity that is *prior to cognition* properly so called. The acquisition of language is the acquisition of an "open system" of expression, which becomes a semeiological system capable of being used as the instrument to
designate, denote, refer, and speak about meanings transcendent to itself but which has an immanent sense to the speaker
prior to and independent of its categorial semeiological functions. Language is acquired not by means of any genuine intellectual operation (which would require an awareness of language as a "sign" of something else), but by means of a kind of
"habituation" to others through one's body and its phonetic possibilities.

> The speaking power the child assimilates in learning his language
> is not the sum of morphological, syntactical, and lexical mean-
> ings. These attainments are neither necessary nor sufficient to
> acquire a language, and once the act of speaking is acquired it
> presupposes no comparison between what I want to express and
> the conceptual arrangement of the means of expression I make
> use of. The words and turns of phrase needed to bring my signifi-

28. "La Conscience," pp. 230 ff. Merleau-Ponty suggests that certain
aspects of interior monologues in adults, the nonformulated thoughts that
precede and surround speech, are a continuation of this original babbling.
William James has an interesting section on a similar phenomenon in his
Principles of Psychology: "We think it odd that young children should
listen with such rapt attention to the reading of stories expressed in words
half of which they do not understand, and of none of which they ask the
meaning. But their thinking is in form just what ours is when it is rapid.
Both of us make flying leaps over large portions of sentences uttered and
we give attention only to substantive starting points, turning points, and
conclusions here and there. All the rest, 'substantive' and separately
intelligible as it may *potentially* be, actually serves only as so much
transitive material. It is *internodal* consciousness, giving us a sense of
continuity, but having no significance apart from its mere gap-filling
function. The children probably feel no gap when through a lot of
unintelligible words they are swiftly carried to a familiar and intelligible
terminus" (I, 264–65).

cative intention to expression recommend themselves to me, when
I am speaking, only by what Humboldt called *innere Sprachform*
(and our contemporaries call *Wortbegriff*), that is, only by a
certain style of speaking from which they arise and according to
which they are organized without my having to represent them to
myself. There is a "languagely" (*langagière*) meaning of language which effects the mediation between my as yet unspeaking
intention and words, and in such a way that my spoken words
surprise me myself and teach me my thought. Organized signs
have their immanent meaning, which does not arise from the "I
think" but from the "I am able to." [29]

It is the fact that words carry, beneath their conceptual
meanings and forms, an "immanent," "existential meaning," [30] a
"value of use," an "affective value," which is not merely *rendered
by* them but which *"inhabits them,"* that leads Merleau-Ponty to
question the possibility or validity of a universal grammar which
could ultimately dispense with the vicissitudes of empirical
speech.

If some sort of universality is ever attained,

> it will not be through a universal language which would go back
> prior to the diversity of languages to provide us with the founda-
> tions of all possible languages. It will be through an oblique
> passage from a given language that I speak and that initiates me
> into the phenomenon of expression, to another given language that
> I learn to speak and that effects the act of expression according to
> a completely different style—the two languages (and ultimately all
> given languages) being contingently comparable only at the out-
> come of this passage and only as signifying wholes, without our
> being able to recognize in them the common elements of one single
> categorial structure.[31]

29. Merleau-Ponty, *Signs*, p. 88. See also the essay on "The Child's
Relations with Others," in *The Primacy of Perception*, esp. p. 99.

30. Merleau-Ponty, *Phenomenology of Perception*: "Spoken or written
words carry a . . . coating of meaning which sticks to them and which
presents the thought as a style, an affective value, a piece of existential
mimicry, rather than as a conceptual statement. We find here, beneath the
conceptual meaning of the words, an existential meaning which is not
only rendered by them, but which inhabits them, and is inseparable from
them" (p. 182). "The link between the word and its living meaning is not
an external link of association, the meaning inhabits the word. . . . We
are therefore led to recognize a gestural or existential significance in
speech. . . . The human body is defined in terms of its property of
appropriating, in an indefinite series of discontinuous acts, significant
cores which transcend and transfigure its natural powers" (p. 193).

31. Merleau-Ponty, *Signs*, p. 87.

III

OUR QUESTION now must be whether these three reasons, and particularly the last one, for rejecting the project of a universal grammar finally undercut what Chomsky and his school of transformational grammarians are trying to do. Merleau-Ponty's conclusion that language is learned "as a whole" would seem to be in full accord with Chomsky's thesis that the learning of language is, in effect, the acquisition of a "highly restrictive schema" of linguistic possibilities, not only on the phonological but also on the syntactical and semantic levels, which is grasped in its *abstract generality* "on the basis of degenerate and restricted data [which are] independent of intelligence and of wide variations in individual experience." [32] Certainly Chomsky would agree that, on the surface level, there is no one innate "natural" language (otherwise there would be no need for a transformational grammar) and that the laws of phonemes are not as universal or coercive as the laws of physics.[33] However, he does argue that there are universal principles which govern not only "deep structures" but also "surface structures," transformations of these, and even phonology itself. Thus the *innere Sprachform* (which he also invokes) governs not merely the deep structures, which are, perhaps, the most abstract and "open" structures of language, but even the surface structures to which Merleau-Ponty limits his attention.

To argue this point, Chomsky bases himself on a primordial phenomenon of language which Merleau-Ponty likewise recognizes to be essential, namely, that people are able to speak grammatically without any *explicit* knowledge of the rules of grammar. This brings us to *the central semantic phenomenon* of using a language. Speaking is a rule-governed behavior in which the rules of correct usage are structural forms hidden deep in the collective subconscious of a given linguistic community. All the native speakers of a given language know the rules of their

32. Chomsky, *Language and Mind,* p. 53.
33. Merleau-Ponty, "La Conscience," p. 252. See also p. 250 for an extended discussion of the *innere Sprachform* in which Merleau-Ponty also sees the foundation of "universality." Compare Chomsky, *Cartesian Linguistics,* pp. 19 ff.

language in the sense that they can form sentences *according to them* without, however, being able to formulate, on the level of fully reflexive awareness, explicitly what these rules are. In no natural language has the grammar been fully fixed and codified up to the present time; this is a work of gradual clarification and explicitation which grammarians and linguists have been undertaking since the time of the Greeks (but not much before that) —a work which takes the form of making explicit what all the native speakers of a given language *already know* but *cannot say.*

Moreover, it is essential to the grammatical forms of any language to permit the new and spontaneous expression of meanings which have never been uttered before. Linguistic experience and grammar can be coextensive, perhaps, but *not identical,* precisely because there can be no rules for applying the rules of grammar. Merleau-Ponty calls this the "paradox" or "contradiction" of language: [34] it must proceed according to fixed rules, or understanding would be impossible; yet the rules themselves must permit the expression of what is as yet unexpressed, what has never before been said. In other words, we necessarily speak according to certain rules or we would not be understood, and in some sense we *know how* to apply correctly and effortlessly ("without thought") all the complex phonetic, morphological, syntactic rules which govern our native language. If we know how to speak, we know how to apply these rules at will, because that is what knowing how to speak means. But to apply a rule correctly is not itself a behavior which can be explained in terms of further, higher-order rules *ad infinitum.* This infinite regress must stop somewhere and it stops in the act of speaking. He who knows how to speak is one who is skilled in applying grammatical rules; he is not one who knows more rules for applying these, because there can be no rules for something which has not been done before, and to speak is to say what has not been said before. It is of the essence of grammatical rules that they be "generative" (in Chomsky's language), i.e., that they permit us to express what has never before been uttered. It is here that we come, then, to the threshold of the *crucial phenomenon* of language. And here, at least at the point of departure, we find Merleau-Ponty and Chomsky in agreement:

34. Merleau-Ponty, *Phenomenology of Perception,* p. 194.

The central fact [writes Chomsky] to which any significant linguistic theory must address itself is this: a mature speaker can produce a new sentence of his language on the appropriate occasion, and other speakers can understand it immediately, though it is equally new to them. Most of our linguistic experience, both as speakers and as hearers, is with new sentences; once we have mastered a language, the class of sentences with which we can operate fluently and without difficulty or hesitation is so vast that for all practical purposes (and, obviously, for all theoretical purposes), we may regard it as infinite. Normal mastery of a language involves not only the ability to understand immediately an indefinite number of entirely new sentences, but also the ability to identify deviant sentences and, on occasion, to impose an interpretation on them. . . . It is clear that any theory of language that neglects this "creative" aspect is of only marginal interest.[35]

And Merleau-Ponty writes:

I understand or think I understand the words and forms of French; I have a certain experience of the literary and philosophical modes of expression offered me by the given culture. I express when, utilizing all these already speaking instruments, I make them say something they have never said. We begin reading a philosopher by giving the words he makes use of their "common" meaning; and little by little, through what is at first an imperceptible reversal, his speech comes to dominate his language, and it is his use of words which ends up assigning them a new and characteristic signification. . . .

The consequences of speech, like those of perception (and particularly the perception of others), always exceed its premises. Even we who speak do not necessarily know better than those who listen to us what we are expressing. I say that I *know an idea* when the power to organize discourses which make coherent sense around it has been established in me; and this power itself does not depend upon my alleged possession and face-to-face contemplation of it, but upon my having acquired a certain style of thinking. I say that a signification is acquired and henceforth available when I have succeeded in making it dwell in a speech apparatus which was not originally destined for it. Of course the elements of this expressive apparatus did not really contain it— the French language did not, from the moment it was established, contain French literature; I had to throw them off center and recenter them in order to make them signify what I intended. It is

35. Noam Chomsky, *Current Issues in Linguistic Theory* (The Hague: Mouton, 1967), pp. 7–8.

just this "coherent deformation" (Malraux) of available significations which arranges them in a new sense and takes not only the hearers *but the speaking subject as well* through a decisive *step*.[36]

What any serious theory of language must account for, then, is the specific human capability "of generating new thoughts and of finding appropriate and novel ways of expressing them, in ways that entirely transcend any training or experience."[37] Chomsky agreeably mentions that Descartes made no contribution to this work,[38] and he pinpoints this methodological failure in its "unquestioned assumption that the properties and content of the mind are accessible to introspection."[39] What Descartes lacked was any conception of the prereflexive in experience (or, what is a more complex way of saying the same thing, any conception of the body-subject). Thus, despite Chomsky's eulogistic way of speaking of the Cartesians, his own investigations lead us to what Merleau-Ponty termed the "prereflexive" structures of experience.[40] In fact, the elaboration of a concept of

36. Merleau-Ponty, *Signs,* p. 91. See also *Phenomenology of Perception,* p. 194: "We must therefore recognize as an ultimate fact this open and indefinite power of giving significance . . . by which man transcends himself towards a new form of behaviour, or towards other people, or towards his own thought, through his body and his speech." See also Chomsky, *Language and Mind,* p. 18, with reference to the romanticist definition of language as that which makes infinite use of finite means (Humboldt), and the following citation from the Port-Royal *Grammar,* which calls language "that marvellous invention by which we construct from twenty-five or thirty sounds an infinity of expressions, which, having no resemblance in themselves to what takes place in our minds, still enable us to let others know the secret of what we conceive and of all the various mental activities that we carry out."

37. Chomsky, *Language and Mind,* p. 8.

38. *Ibid.,* p. 11.

39. *Ibid.,* p. 22.

40. This paper must, of necessity, assume both an elementary knowledge of phenomenology and an elementary knowledge of the claims of transformational grammar on the part of the reader. I have not, therefore, felt it necessary to begin at the very beginning and define such phenomenological terms as "eidetic a priori," "reduction," etc., and I have likewise taken for granted that the reader knows what "surface structure," "deep structure," "transformational grammar," etc., mean. But with the term "prereflexive" one has greater inhibitions. This term, as used by Merleau-Ponty, occurs in a multiplicity of senses. It can designate the non-actual or potential elements in my field of attention, all those things of which I have a "concomitant" but non-explicit awareness in my field of vision, for instance. It can also designate the consciousness I have of my own body in any conscious experience, that marginal awareness of being in a place, of my sensory-motor apparatus which is never absent, though frequently

linguistic competence, which is the chief theoretical goal of Chomsky's studies, should serve as a paradigm of what it means to thematize the prereflexive. Would it not be possible to understand what Chomsky calls "innate" ideas or capacities in terms of the more publicly observable and controllable eidetic a prioris discoverable in the factual experience of speaking languages? [41] If the whole sense of the term "innate" can be exhaustively accounted for in the elaboration of the necessary and universal a priori structures of linguistic experience, it is released from its hidden and "causal" status behind the phenomena to appear as the necessary structure *of* the phenomena. It is not something to be found by "turning within" but by an observation of behavior, by a bringing to the level of reflection the structures involved in moving from one level of meaning to another, from one language to another, etc.[42] Such structures are "prior" to experience only in the sense that they are prereflexively present within experience prior to their thematization. It is unnecessary to give them any ontological status independent of their structural function.

In this turn to the prereflexive, there is no essential dichotomy between the projects of Merleau-Ponty and Chomsky. Merleau-Ponty, following Saussure,[43] limited himself to the level of the semeiological system and the emergence of sense within the

---

ignored. In the usage of it here it has still a different sense (which is more strictly Husserlian): it is the sense in which the meaning-structure of an experience which is thematized in judgment (*Urteil*) precedes such full awareness in experience (*Erfahrung*). Husserl frequently used the term "prepredicative" in this sense. The prepredicative realm, of course, contains not only the ideal a priori structures which are thematized through posterior reflection, but the whole tissue of facts, states of affairs, etc., which constitute life-world experience in all its complexity. Thus, one of the urgent needs for phenomenological theory is to make the geography of this realm of the prereflexive better known.

41. Chomsky, *Language and Mind,* p. 24: "The study of universal grammar . . . is a study of the nature of human intellectual capacities. It tries to formulate the necessary and sufficient conditions that a system must meet to qualify as a potential human language, conditions that are not accidentally true of the existing human languages, but that are rather rooted in the human 'language capacity,' and thus constitute an innate organization that determines what counts as linguistic experience."

42. *Ibid.,* p. 72: "Any formulation of a principle of universal grammar makes a strong empirical claim, which can be falsified by finding counterinstances in some human language."

43. Merleau-Ponty, "La Conscience," pp. 232, 234, 242; and *Signs,* pp. 86 ff.

phonological system of signs which is realized in *words*. Chomsky—and this is his principal originality and specific contribution—goes beyond the level of words to the levels of syntax and semantics.[44] He is less concerned with the formation of words than with the formation of sentences. Without being cognizant of the implications of the fact, Merleau-Ponty limited his studies to the structures that bear on the emergence of meaning on the semeiological level of word-sounds.[45] Chomsky has shown that this is not sufficient and that, beneath this surface structure, there are *more abstract* semantic systems whose structures are not isomorphically reproduced on the surface level of natural languages. It is on the level of such deep structures alone that one can speak of "universals" of language, and pose the (Husserlian) question of how the Chinese, the German, or the Hebrew expresses conjunction, disjunction, negation, etc. Both of these levels of grammatical structure are prereflexive and thus "prior" to experience in the sense that their rules are already possessed by the speaking subject (without reflexive awareness) when he speaks; together they constitute his linguistic *competence*. The difference between them is one of degree of abstractness and generative power. It is not necessary to suppose that there is some innate, nonhistorical concept of language which can be formulated independently of any and all existing natural languages to account for what transformational grammar calls "deep structures." The deep structures are as open and contingent to historical experience as are the surface structures.

44. Chomsky, *Language and Mind*, p. 65. On the distinction between the emergence of meaning in words (on the semeiological level) and the meaning of sentences (on the syntactic level) see Paul Ricoeur, "La Structure, le mot, l'événement," *Man and World* (February, 1968), pp. 10–29. This extremely important distinction, which would lead to the distinction between objective language (*langue*) and speaking (*la parole*), and, ultimately, to the issues which divide structuralists from phenomenologists, will be the subject of a subsequent article, entitled "The Levels and Objectivity of Meaning."

45. I am not claiming that Merleau-Ponty did not understand the differences between words and sentences, or between semeiology and syntax, but that his theory of language is limited in its applicability to the level of the meaning expressed in the phonological system as such. It is for this reason that he necessarily remained on the level of what Chomsky calls "surface structure" and did not pose the question of the transformation of various "surface structures" on the basis of more abstract and general principles than those discovered by structural linguistics. But this assertion is not fully argued here and must be taken up later.

To discover the necessary structures of language, on whatever level, it is unnecessary to attempt to transcend experience toward some supposed and hypothetical source. Since these structures can be thematized only *after the fact*, it is essential to their thematization that there *be* languages and that there *be* speaking. In the last analysis the necessary conditions of speaking are as contingent as the fact of speaking itself, since they are the structures *of* historical speech. Let us grant, by hypothesis, that there are the universal structures of language on the various levels claimed by Chomsky. But there are still the natural languages themselves which employ and exemplify these structures in different ways, and it is possible that no *one* language exemplifies them all in their total complexity and completeness. The "concept" of language cannot, then, be thematized except through the investigation of the historical, factical expressions in which it is exemplified. Chomsky's approach to language has this in common with phenomenology—that it proceeds on the basis of an empirical, factual situation (the reality of language) to a description of the *ideal* and *necessary* conditions for the understanding of this situation. Given the experience of language, one sees that this experienced reality, if it is to be understood and insofar as it is understandable, implies realms of eidetic possibility which may never have been actualized completely or of which there are in fact no examples yet at all. But such ideal possibilities are *of the essence* of the various actually existing (past or present) languages and are eidetically necessary to our *present understanding* of what is presently given, and they are founded in *that*. If there be some innate capacity over and above what is given in its realizations, both factical and ideal, we can approach it only through its works, through an investigation and description of linguistic phenomena in their essential necessity.

Let us try to be more precise. When Merleau-Ponty states that "universality" is to be reached only "through an oblique passage from a given language that I speak . . . to another given language that I learn," [46] and that all empirical languages are "comparable only at the outcome of this passage and only as signifying wholes," he is not saying anything necessarily incompatible with the ideal of Husserl or the claims of transforma-

46. Merleau-Ponty, *Signs*, p. 87.

tional grammar. There is, after all, the fact of the translatability of languages, a fact which he recognizes, that I can move from one linguistic field to another. It is not necessary that there be *no* loss of meaning in such a movement, only that there be the universal, a priori rules which make such a movement *possible* at all. There is the further fact, which he also recognizes,[47] that *every* language is *capable* of expressing *everything* and that no language necessarily restricts or deforms thought. Thought has never been fully contained in or predetermined by what has been said up to now or by the (formal or material) linguistic structure of any given natural language. This kind of language relativism, interesting on the level of cultural anthropology, can never be the last word, and Merleau-Ponty recognizes this when he shows that the linguistic expression of experience manifests the ultimate "privilege of reason." [48] However, we must be clear as to what the "privilege of reason" is. It is not the isolated self-possession of a universal thinker who would precontain and predetermine, prior to speaking, the clear and distinct ideas which language attempts to express. It is rather the historical-linguistic experience of gradually making sense of a world of experience which will never be exhaustively expressed or clarified in any given language. But, no less than the experience of perception, the experience of speaking presupposes the teleological unity and ultimate concordance of all its possible forms. That all experiences of the world will ultimately coalesce and be found to be concordant with one another is a postulate of reason contained in the least historical experience, as a *telos* or goal evidenced in the experience itself insofar as this experience is intelligible. If we can interpret the "deep structures" or "universals of language" in this eidetic and teleological sense, as prereflexive structures of rationality which can only asymtotically and historically be brought to the level of full clarity, there is nothing in Merleau-Ponty's view which excludes the discovery of eidetic structures of language, any more than it excludes the discovery of eidetic structures of perception (which he made his principal life's work).

However, when Merleau-Ponty states that the study of language will always and necessarily stop short of the discovery of

47. *Ibid.*, p. 90.
48. Merleau-Ponty, *Phenomenology of Perception*, p. 190; and *Signs*, p. 96.

"the common elements of one single categorial structure," his viewpoint simply has to be corrected by the current discoveries in transformational generative grammar. He equated the notion of a "universal grammar" with the "ideal languages" of logical positivism and with the intellectualistic conceptions of language which would exempt us, by an appeal to eternal reason, from the investigation of the prereflexive and "embodied" structures of behavior which possess a "logic" independent of and prior to the rational consciousness of fully reflexive cognition. But insofar as Chomsky's transformational grammar is not truly "Cartesian," and is itself engaged in an attempt to bring to light the pretheoretical structures of thought as they are embedded in the *esprit aveugle* of linguistic behavior,[49] his notion of "universal grammar" is not the one rejected by Merleau-Ponty.[50] It seems clear that Merleau-Ponty was led into an overly restrictive conception of what grammar is by his devotion to the structural linguistics of Saussure [51] and his blameless inability to foresee the future

49. Chomsky, *Language and Mind*, p. 32: "The work of the past few years . . . suggests that all current approaches to problems of perception and organization of behavior suffer from a failure to attribute sufficient depth and complexity to the mental processes that must be represented in any model that attempts to come to grips with the empirical phenomena." "It is clear, in short, that the surface structure is often misleading and uninformative and that our knowledge of language involves properties of a much more abstract nature, not indicated directly in the surface structure." And on p. 62: "It seems clear that we must regard linguistic competence—knowledge of a language—as an abstract system underlying behavior, a system constituted by rules that interact to determine the form and intrinsic meaning of a potentially infinite number of sentences. Such a system—a generative grammar—provides an explication of the Humboldtian idea of a 'form of language.'"

50. *Ibid.*, pp. 75–76: "A generative grammar is a system of many hundreds of rules of several different types, organized in accordance with certain fixed principles of ordering and applicability and containing a certain fixed substructure, which, along with the general principles of organization, is common to all languages. There is no a priori 'naturalness' to such a system, any more than there is to the detailed structure of the visual cortex. No one who has given any serious thought to the problem of formalizing inductive procedures or 'heuristic methods' is likely to set much store by the hope that such a system as a generative grammar can be constructed by methods of any generality."

51. Chomsky gives a brief critique of Saussure (*ibid.*, pp. 17 ff.) which I find fully persuasive and one which, without mentioning him of course, explains why Merleau-Ponty, who was convinced by Saussure, could have no conception of universal grammar. That this critique of Saussure, if well justified, is also the refutation of the "structuralism" which he founded is a theme of great interest to phenomenology but one which we cannot take up here.

development of linguistic theory. This even led him to force the texts of Husserl into a denial of the project of a universal grammar—a project which Merleau-Ponty could not understand or account for but which recent developments in transformational grammar enable us to understand much better.

In conclusion, it seems perfectly possible and phenomenologically legitimate that the study of transformational grammar will give a new sense to the grammatical a prioris which Husserl saw exclusively as certain necessary formal conditions for the avoidance of pure nonsense. It can lead, beyond this, to the thematization of the "material" a priori structures of empirical languages. In this sense it is an eidetic inquiry into the experience of speaking which phenomenology, of all currents in philosophy, should find the most congenial and capable of theoretical justification. If what transformational grammarians refer to as descriptions of "innate" categories of reason can be interpreted as attempts at an eidetic analysis of a methodologically isolable realm of the prereflexive, i.e., the acquisition, possession, and use of language, then such research is *not* opposed to Merleau-Ponty's conception of phenomenology, as the thematization of the prereflexive, but in fact represents a good illustration of precisely what such a phenomenological program can mean. From such a viewpoint transformational grammar could, with respect to the phenomenology of language, play a role similar to that given by Merleau-Ponty to experimental psychology with respect to the phenomenology of perception.

18 / The Existentialist Critique of Objectivity

Samuel J. Todes and Hubert L. Dreyfus

EXISTENTIAL PHILOSOPHERS are popularly known to be concerned with dread, death, choice, and the self. It is less generally known, however, that this concern is due to the epistemological and ontological significance which existentialists see in these dramatic subjects. Primarily, existentialism is and claims to be a new understanding of the nature of truth. Since this understanding is new and has been worked out in opposition to the various philosophical positions held in the past, the existentialist understanding of truth is formulated as a critique of the traditional view that to discover the truth one must be objective. Thus to get at the heart of existentialism and evaluate it, we must consider and criticize the existentialist critique of objectivity.

It is difficult to speak of *the* critique, for there are as many critiques as there are existentialists. Although all are united in condemning objective knowledge, they differ in their account of it and of how it is misleading. There is, however, some order in this profusion. One can discern three stages in a deepening understanding and criticism of the tradition. Each of these stages is represented in its most original and developed form by a single thinker, and these three thinkers are related to each other in several interesting ways. Each includes in his work not only a critique of the traditional view of objectivity but also an implicit or explicit critique of his predecessor as still too traditional. Moreover, the work of the three men when taken together provides a critique of their common enterprise, for each thinker has an insight which, when combined with that of the others, suggests that objective knowledge is not as inadequate as each claims. These critiques, taken separately, undermine in various ways our belief in the *enterprise* of objective inquiry. But their collective import is, we shall argue, to undermine the traditional *interpretation* of the enterprise while leaving the way open to a defense of the soundness of the activity itself.

The traditional characterization of objectivity is fivefold. "Objective" knowledge is held to be: (1) impersonal, i.e., invariant from knower to knower; (2) disinterested, i.e., without regard to any interest the knower may have that something be so; (3) universal, i.e., applicable to all times and places; (4) eternal, i.e., not perishable like temporal things; (5) necessary, i.e., not conceivably otherwise, so that alternative conceptions would be logically unintelligible or would leave experience unintelligible.

The three critiques we shall consider are those of Kierkegaard, Nietzsche, and Heidegger. Each critique bears on all five characteristics; but Kierkegaard focuses mainly on the impersonality of objective knowledge, Nietzsche concerns himself mainly with its supposed disinterestedness, and Heidegger, insofar as he goes beyond his predecessors, deals chiefly with the supposed universality of objective truth.

KIERKEGAARD

PLATO WAS CONVINCED at the start of objective philosophy, and Kierkegaard was still convinced near what existentialists consider its end, that a pure objective thinker could arrive at truth. But Kierkegaard was also convinced by the skeptics that objective truth could not be attained by man. He held that science only *approaches* certainty by what he called "an approximation process." [1] And, remaining faithful to the original Platonic claim that for a proposition to be known to be true it has to be known with certainty, he never calls objective propositions attained by man "objective truths" but only "objective uncertain-

1. S. Kierkegaard, *Concluding Unscientific Postscript*, trans. D. Swenson and W. Lowrie (Princeton, N.J.: Princeton University Press, 1941), p. 37.

ties." Still, although Kierkegaard argued that truth could not be known by man, he held that it could be known by God (the infinite knower). In the *Postscript* he writes:

> An existential system cannot be formulated. Does this mean that no such system exists? By no means; nor is this implied in our assertion. Reality itself is a system—for God; but it cannot be a system for any existing spirit.[2]

It follows that in trying to know objective truths the existing knower is trying to identify himself with the completely objective thinker, God. What Kierkegaard opposes is not the meaningfulness or even the existence of completely objective knowledge but the pretension that man can attain it.

> The notion of the truth as identity of thought and being is a chimera of abstraction, in its truth only an expectation of the creature; not because the truth is not such an identity but because the knower is an existing individual for whom the truth cannot be such an identity as long as he lives in time.[3]

Or, again,

> The realm of pure thought is a sphere in which the existing individual finds himself only by virtue of a mistaken beginning; and this error revenges itself by making the existence of the individual insignificant, and giving his language a flavor of lunacy.[4]

Benefiting from hindsight into a long objectivist tradition, Kierkegaard was able to diagnose the lunacy in question. It had been supposed since Plato that true propositions were true for all people, hence that their discovery could in no way depend on the particular interests or biases of the thinker. It was only by divorcing himself from his moods, desires, wishes, needs, and tradition that a man could hope to recognize truths which would be accepted by any other thinker able to make himself equally disinterested. One could not be sure he had discovered an objective truth—a truth for everyone—until he had made sure that his personal needs and point of view played no essential role in the discovery.

2. *Ibid.*, p. 107.
3. *Ibid.*, p. 176.
4. *Ibid.*, p. 277.

There is a truth whose greatness, whose sublimity we are accustomed to extol by saying admiringly that it is *indifferent;* equally valid whether anybody accepts it nor not; indifferent as to the particular conditions of the individual, whether he be young or old, happy or distressed; indifferent as to its relationship to him, whether this truth benefits him or injures him; equally valid whether a man subscribes to it with his whole heart, or acknowledges it coldly and unemotionally, whether he lays down his life for it or uses it for poor profit; equally valid whether he has discovered it himself or only repeats what he has been taught. And only that man's understanding is true and that man's admiration is justified who grasps that what chiefly matters is this indifference, and who allows himself to be moulded in conformity with this indifference; being indifferent as to what happens to himself, or to some other person *qua* person, or *qua* special person.[5]

But Kierkegaard does not just rest with the skeptical view that there is no objective truth, nor does he simply add the "existential" point that even if there were such a truth it would be lunacy for an individual to pursue it. Instead, he turns his rejection of objective truth into a defense of a new sort of truth which, just *because* it is interested, first offers man the real possibility of satisfying, albeit in a new way, the old requirements that truth be impersonal, universal, eternal, and necessary.

This view is summed up in Kierkegaard's pronouncement that "truth is subjectivity." But to understand what Kierkegaard means by the subjectivity of truth we must first understand that he does *not* mean, as many seem to think, that truth is whatever we happen to believe. Kierkegaard is no Protagoras. To understand what Kierkegaard does mean by a subjective truth, we must turn to a passage in *Fear and Trembling.* There he describes "A young [prince who] falls in love with a princess, and the whole content of his life consists in this love."[6] This love defines who this prince is, as can be seen when the prince refuses to "forget the whole thing." "For the prince does not contradict himself, and it is a contradiction to forget the whole content of one's life and remain the same man."[7] The prince has

5. S. Kierkegaard, *Edifying Discourses,* trans. D. F. and L. M. Swenson, 3 vols. (Minneapolis: Augsburg Press, 1943–44), III, 71.
6. S. Kierkegaard, *Fear and Trembling* (Garden City, N.Y.: Doubleday, Anchor Books, 1954), p. 52.
7. *Ibid.,* p. 54.

become an individual through his relation to the princess. Moreover, his whole world is defined in terms of his princess. Kierkegaard notes that the experience in question need not be one of love: "[It could] of course [be] any other instance whatsoever in which the individual finds that for him the whole reality of actual existence is concentrated." [8] For the individual involved, i.e., for the person who has become an individual *through* the involvement, there is a new truth. In the case of the prince the new truth is, let us say, that the princess is adorable—although this formulation does not adequately express the prince's unique relation to the girl.[9] This new truth is synthetic a priori for the individual. It is necessarily true for him as long as he remains the person he has become. What he may do about his love, how he will express it, or whether he will betray it, are all open; so is the possibility that the girl may be lost (this poses the problem of *Fear and Trembling*). But it is assured for the rest of the prince's life, so long as he does not destroy his personality, that his world and thus everything in it will be defined in terms of this relationship.

In the *Concluding Unscientific Postscript*, Kierkegaard calls this sort of truth, which gives "absolute assurance," subjective truth, and the attitude by which it is achieved, infinite passion. It is contrasted with objective truth in the following way:

> The objective accent falls on WHAT is said, the subjective accent on HOW it is said. . . . At its maximum this inward "how" is the passion of the infinite, and the passion of the infinite is truth. But the passion of the infinite is precisely subjectivity, and thus subjectivity becomes the truth.[10]

This characterization of truth as infinite passion, suggesting as it does merely an intense feeling, has misled many into thinking of Kierkegaard as a romantic or, by implication, a sophist saying that whatever one believes is true. But such a reading mistakes the meaning of "infinite" here. "Infinite" does

8. *Ibid.*, p. 52.
9. Subjective truths cannot be adequately expressed in words, according to Kierkegaard, because they are truths definitive of an existing individual. To verbalize, he holds, is to abstract. In particular, it is to abstract from the individual. Thus the subjective truth must be witnessed in the life of the knowing subject, not proclaimed as a conviction. "The true knight of faith is a witness, never a teacher" (*ibid.*, p. 90).
10. *Postscript*, p. 181.

not simply mean very great. The "infinity" of the passion is meant to express what is new in Kierkegaard's view and differentiates him from the tradition. The "infinite" calls attention to the fact that the defining interest centers and outlines a whole world within which an infinite variety of experience can occur as significant for an individual. This infinite passion thus defines an individual in relation to a world which it opens up and lays out as real for him.

To differentiate this defining interest from any accidental interest, no matter how great, Kierkegaard distinguishes between a lower and a higher immediacy. "Lower immediacy" for Kierkegaard, like "immediacy" for Hegel, from whom he inherits the terminology, refers to wishes, desires, whims, etc. Kierkegaard is in complete agreement with Hegel and the tradition that such accidental biases can play no essential role in defining truth and must be overcome. But he has a new idea about how this purification is brought about. There is a passage worth quoting at length in order to silence once and for all the confusion of Kierkegaardian subjectivity with subjectivism:

> When one overlooks this little distinction, humoristic from the Socratic standpoint and infinitely anxious from the Christian, between being something like a subject so called, and being a subject, or becoming one, or being what one is through having become what one is: then it becomes wisdom, the admired wisdom of our own age, that it is the task of the subject increasingly to divest himself of his subjectivity in order to become more and more objective. It is easy to see what this guidance understands by being a subject of a sort. It understands by it quite rightly the accidental, the angular, the selfish, the eccentric, and so forth, all of which every human being can have enough of. Nor does Christianity deny that such things should be gotten rid of; it has never been a friend of loutishness. But the difference is, that philosophy teaches that the way is to become objective, while Christianity teaches that the way is to become subjective, i.e., to become a subject in truth.[11]

We can now return to the epistemological question. A Kierkegaardian subjective relation is a truth, not merely a belief, because it is definitive of the individual. As Kierkegaard puts it in a journal entry:

11. *Ibid.*, p. 117.

Ultimately everything must rest upon a postulate; but the moment it is no longer outside him, and he lives in it, then and only then does it cease to be a postulate for him.[12]

The same thought is expressed in the *Postscript:*

In this manner God certainly becomes a postulate, but not in the otiose manner in which this word is commonly understood. . . . The postulate is so far from being arbitrary that it is precisely a life-necessity.[13]

Here the Kantian transcendental turn of Kierkegaard's thought becomes evident. For Kant a synthetic proposition is a priori true of the phenomenal world if it expresses a necessary condition of the objective experience of a finite knower in general. For Kierkegaard a synthetic truth is a priori in an individual's world, his "sphere of existence," if it expresses a necessary condition of his existence as a particular individual. Like Kant, Kierkegaard is prepared to call such necessary conditions of the humanly knowable world "objective truths," even if they are not God's truth about the thing in itself.

There is a "how" which has this quality, that if *it* is truly given, then the "what" is also given; and that is the "how" of "faith." Here, quite certainly, we have inwardness at its maximum proving to be objectivity once again. And this is an aspect of the principle of subjectivity which, so far as I know, has never been presented or worked out.[14]

Our short excursion into Kierkegaard's thought has now equipped us to see more clearly how much he salvaged in his attack on the objectivist tradition. One pillar in the old temple of knowledge he pulls down: humanly attainable knowledge is simply *not* impersonal; the traditional pretension to the contrary is a ridiculous delusion. But the partially fallen structure has become a fit place for man. While somewhat altered, it remains recognizable, for, as we shall now see, the other four pillars of objectivity —disinterestedness, universality, eternity, and necessity—remain standing, albeit somewhat aslant.

(1) The tradition held that knowledge must be *disinterested,*

12. S. Kierkegaard, *The Journals,* ed. A. Dru (New York: Oxford University Press, 1938), p. 16.
13. *Postscript,* p. 179.
14. *Journals,* p. 355.

without regard to any interest the knower may have that something be so. The strength of this position rested on its repudiation of the instability of whim and the arbitrariness of idiosyncratic interests as incompatible with the eternity of truth and the discipline of knowledge. But this very strength was translated into a weakness with the supposition that all individual traits were of this order so that *all* interest must be discounted as irrelevant to knowledge. The result was to make knowledge pure but profitless. Kierkegaard counterattacks by basing himself on our common supposition, however obscure, of the human value of truth. He insists, therefore, on our essential interest in the truth. Agreeing that we are well rid of arbitrary and whimsical interests, he formulates his crucial distinction between two forms of interest and individuality of which only one is definitive of truth. "Lower immediacy" is distinguished from "higher immediacy"; the "aesthetic individual" from the "knight of faith"; the life of arbitrary interest and supposition from the life of interested belief "so far from being arbitrary that it is a life-necessity." In sum, the life and desires of the natural childish self with which we are each endowed by birth and upbringing are contrasted to those of the true self which each man needs to become through his own efforts. Kierkegaard thus, in effect, redefines the "disinterested" character of knowledge. Knowledge becomes "disinterested" in the sense of being independent of the superficial interests of the merely *natural* self. This form of disinterestedness implies the value rather than the valuelessness of knowledge, since it implies that the truth *is* crucially dependent upon the individual's true interests, the interests of his "true self."

(2) Knowledge was traditionally regarded as *universal* in being applicable to all times and places. The world-wide range of which human understanding is evidently capable was thus raised to a defining condition of all knowledge. This universality was attributed to universal laws or ideas held to be ingredients in all knowledge. Knowledge was considered to be essentially of universals, pure or applied. Abstract entities served as particularly fit objects for disinterested reflection since they are not in the real world of the existing individual, who therefore cannot hope to change his relationship to them and thus cannot take a live interest in them for their own sake. Thus the remoteness of truth from living men, so strikingly expressed in disinter-

estedness, appears also in universality. And Kierkegaard's critiques of disinterestedness and universality are correspondingly similar. He insists on man's need for truth and truth's existence for man, and on the consequent unacceptability of an epistemological tradition which alienates man from truth; at the same time, he shares the tradition's motivating conviction—in the case of universality, the conviction that man's ability to understand the world as a whole is somehow essential to his form of intelligence—and accordingly proposes some more acceptable solution. Specifically, he reinterprets "universality" as stemming not from universal laws but, as it were, from *universal particulars* incorporated in all knowledge. Knowledge is of the world as a whole because all knowledge includes knowledge of some epistemologically central facts such as the existence of some actual persons, relationships, or events which are locally in the world yet so decisive for the knowing subject as to be definitive of his sense of reality and of his world as the field in which things can be real for him. For Kierkegaard, in short, all knowledge is relevant to all times and places because it includes knowledge of some particular real thing such that relevance to this thing is at all times and places necessary and sufficient for anything's being real then and there.

(3) Kierkegaard's reinterpretation of the *eternal* character of truth, as not perishable like temporal things, proceeds in a similar manner. It is evident that beliefs may change; our convictions are continually bolstered, undermined, or altered in the course of further experience. But a change in belief is evaluated in respect to "the truth" being sought, which must be presumed fixed at least for the period of this change. So the truth is invariant with respect to changeable beliefs. Insisting on this point, and regarding *all* belief as changeable, the objectivist tradition concludes that the truth is entirely independent of human belief, that man might perish as he has lived without in the least affecting the truth. Kierkegaard sees that some beliefs are indeed changeable while the truth they aim at is not. But he distinguishes a special kind of belief for which this is not the case, namely, the subjective belief of infinite passion or faith. Kierkegaard distinguishes in effect between belief *in* something and belief *about* something or *that* something is the case. The truth is indeed invariant with respect to changes in belief *about* it. But with loss of a given belief *in* something, the correspond-

ing subjective truth *itself ceases to exist. Belief that* or *about* is changeable, while the objective truth to which it corresponds is not. But *belief in* is not changeable. To be sure, *belief in* may be had or not had, gained or not gained, preserved or lost. But it cannot be changed. It has but one state in which it exists if it exists at all. So the subjective truth, like the faith which founds it, is *perishable but not changeable.* Thus Kierkegaard preserves the "eternal" character of truth as unchangeable, while giving it human significance by showing that the eternal truth, like man himself and with man himself, is mortal.

(4) *Necessity.* Philosophers have perennially recognized that at least some truths seem peculiarly undeniable—undeniable because their denial is unintelligible or at least unbelievable. This was held to be more than a curiosity because truths of this sort seemed basic to all human knowledge. So questions about the nature of such truths—how they were possible, how they were related to other sorts of truths, and how we might know them—were tied to questions about the nature of truth and knowledge in general. In the objectivist tradition, as we have seen, truth is regarded as independent of belief because of its eternity. But if the truth is independent of belief then it is independent of man,[15] for it is through belief that man is related to the truth. Similarly, the objective truth simply *is* undeniable in the same way it *is* the truth, intrinsically, by itself and independently of whether or not anyone recognizes it. So, objectively speaking, the necessity of truth, like the truth itself, stands aloof, there for anyone who may come to know it. Kierkegaard's opposing interpretation of eternity leads to an opposing view of necessity. Because the objective truth is independent of belief, it and its necessity are the same for everyone. Conversely, because Kierkegaard's subjective truth is dependent upon the faith which founds it, it and its necessity exist only for *someone* who believes in it.

So Kierkegaard shifts the meaning of "necessarily true" from "undeniably true for everyone" to "undeniably true for someone." But with this he also shifts the meaning of "undeniable." If

15. Kant may seem an exception. For him, undeniable truth depends on the inner nature of man although not on man's belief. This view does reconcile independence of truth from belief with dependence of truth on *transcendental* and *noumenal* man. But truth remains independent of "man" in the common and Kierkegaardian sense of the term, namely, as an *existing individual.*

necessary truth is regarded as characterizing abstract propositions, their "undeniability" means the inability to conceive their
denial abstractly. But if necessary truths are, as for Kierkegaard,
the substance of individual persons in passionate possession of
themselves and their world, their "undeniability" means the inability to envisage their denial *concretely*—the inability to imagine, to feel what it would be like, to make it intuitively sensible,
that they be false. In short, the objectivist's "inconceivable"
means unintelligible as a possibility. But Kierkegaard's "inconceivable" means *unintelligible as a reality*.

We have now seen how Kierkegaard systematically alters the
traditional objectivist conception of truth in order to salvage
what remains as a form of truth which might for the first time
be actually attainable by man and really valuable to him. Kierkegaard begins by absolutely contesting the supposed impersonality of knowledge as implying its indifference to man and man's
indifference to it. This cardinal rejection moves Kierkegaard
throughout his search for a new form of truth, an interested or
subjective truth. Interest, for Kierkegaard, founds both the
truths that matter most to man and those which man can actually come to know. The whole shift which Kierkegaard effects in
the objective idea of truth may be seen to follow from his view
that truth is the passionate inwardness of a true self, i.e., "The
truth is subjectivity," or "An objective uncertainty held fast in an
appropriation-process of the most passionate inwardness is the
truth, the highest truth attainable for an existing individual." [16]

Kierkegaard accepts the traditional account of objective
truth, drawing the implications that it is so other-worldly as to be
unobtainable by man, and that even if it were obtainable it
would be pointless, of little or no interest or value to an existing
individual. "Away from the subject the objective way of reflection leads to the objective truth, and while the subject and his
subjectivity become indifferent, the truth also becomes indifferent, and this indifference is precisely its objective validity." [17]

16. *Postscript,* p. 182.
17. *Ibid.,* p. 173. A commonsensical or Aristotelian reader may deny
that objective truth is so purely disinterested in the first place. He may
claim that we have a natural curiosity, a desire to know for its own sake,
and that we find objectivity useful in the purposeful living of our lives. But
the Aristotelian ideal of objectivity did in fact give way in the history of
philosophy to a more ascetic, disembodied, and purely "disinterested"
ideal. What Aristotle said was outlived and replaced by what he had a

But the very clarity with which Kierkegaard spells out these implications leaves him with problems of his own. If the possession of objective knowledge is really so pointless, how can he understand the continual widespread interest in its pursuit? And if all one can know about objective truth is that it is lunacy for a finite knower to pursue it, why should finite knowers, including Kierkegaard himself, believe there are such truths at all?

NIETZSCHE

NIETZSCHE carries the existentialist critique of objectivity to what seems to be its ultimate conclusion. Instead of objective inquiry being uninteresting and incompletable for finite beings, as Kierkegaard claims, for Nietzsche there can be no objective inquiry at all:

> Let us, from now on, be on our guard against the hallowed philosophers' myth of a "pure, will-less, painless, timeless knower"; let us beware of the tentacles of such contradictory

---

right to say and should have said, granted his central views. Aristotle recognized that we do somehow understand particular things and events, not merely abstract forms. But he gave too Platonic an account of how, namely, by abstracting forms from particulars—with the aid of perceptions, to be sure, but the manner of this aid was left obscure. Understanding remained clear and itself understandable, on this account, only so far as it consisted of conceiving forms. Thus it is logical that Western philosophers working in this tradition eventually concluded that we can understand our understanding of particular things only by construing the "particular" as itself consisting entirely of formal relations (e.g., Descartes's purely geometric physical object; Leibniz' identity of indiscernibles; Kant's "object of experience" as a mathematical representation in outer intuition). Furthermore, Aristotelians held that all knowledge is had by a single impersonal cosmic knower ("active intellect") who uses all men's minds as his passive instruments. Such a cosmic knower was regarded as necessary in the absence of any other factor to assure the uniformity of truth for all men. This cosmic intellect is the recognizable ancestor of the "abstract thinker" whom Kierkegaard attacks as ridiculously unmindful of his individual existence. So the traditional attempt to make sense of concrete knowledge by real individuals collapses after all, when rigorously pursued, into an account of abstract knowledge by abstract thinkers who have forsaken all interests in order to know uninteresting things. Thus the *pure* "disinterestedness" which Kierkegaard ascribed to the objective attitude may strike common sense as being exaggerated, but it is implied even in the commonsensical tradition. And these implications had been clearly drawn by Kierkegaard's time.

notions as "pure reason," "absolute knowledge," "absolute intelligence." All these concepts presuppose an eye such as no living being can imagine, an eye required to have no direction, to abrogate its active and interpretative powers—precisely those powers that alone make of seeing, seeing *something*. All seeing is essentially perspective, and so is all knowing.[18]

Kierkegaard ridiculed human pretensions to complete objectivity; he left complete objectivity to God. For him, God's truth was unobtainable; for Nietzsche, it is self-contradictory. Nietzsche's pronouncement that God is dead is not primarily an observation about the role God plays in individual lives or the role of religion in the modern world; it is a claim that the notion of the objective truth—of the way things are in themselves—does not make sense.

The faith on which our belief in science rests is still a metaphysical faith. Even we students of today, who are atheists and antimetaphysicians, light our torches at the flame of a millennial faith: the Christian faith, which was also the faith of Plato, that God is truth, and truth divine. . . . But what if this equation becomes less and less credible, if the only things that may still be viewed as divine are error, blindness, and lies; if God himself turns out to be our *longest* lie? [19]

The same view is expressed in more epistemological terms in *Beyond Good and Evil:* " 'Absolute knowledge' and the 'thing in itself' involve a *contradictio in adjecto* [contradiction in terms]." [20]

According to Nietzsche, the claims that there are objective truths and that disinterested inquiry is possible are not just falsehoods; they are necessary lies. *"Truth is that kind of error without which a certain species of life could not live."* [21] These claims lead men to invent a disinterested knower who could entertain such truths:

The Eleatics, who . . . believed that it was possible also to *live* these counterparts . . . devised the sage as the man of immutabil-

18. F. Nietzsche, *The Genealogy of Morals,* trans. F. Golffing (Garden City, N.Y.: Doubleday, Anchor Books, 1956), p. 255.
19. *Ibid.,* p. 288.
20. F. Nietzsche, *Beyond Good and Evil,* trans. W. Kaufmann (New York: Random House, Vintage Books, 1966), p. 23.
21. F. Nietzsche, *The Will to Power,* trans. W. Kaufmann (New York: Random House, Vintage Books, 1968), p. 272.

ity, impersonality and universality of intuition. . . . They had to attribute to themselves impersonality and unchanging permanence, they had to mistake the nature of the philosophic individual, deny the force of the impulses in cognition, and conceive of reason generally as an entirely free and self-organizing activity.[22]

Nietzsche finds this ascetic knower as absurd as Kierkegaard found him ridiculous—and for the same reason:

The mischief has already reached its climax in Plato—And then one had need to invent the abstractly perfect man as well: —good, just, wise, a dialectician—in short, the scarecrow of the ancient philosopher: a plant removed from all soil; a humanity without any particular regulating instincts; a virtue that "proves" itself with reasons. The perfectly absurd "individuum" in itself! unnaturalness of the first water.[23]

In *The Genealogy of Morals* Nietzsche scrutinizes this ascetic ideal of disinterested inquiry in an attempt to discover what needs it satisfies. He discovers first that the ideal serves as a *means,* a way of concentrating our energies by channeling our wishes and whims. It thereby serves our most basic desire—the will to power, the need for self-expression. But existence *is* will to power. Therefore the ascetic ideal taken as an *end in itself*—the control of desire for its own sake rather than for the sake of eventual expression—must be pathological. It must serve a disguised need which Nietzsche as "psychologist" is concerned to root out.

This suppressed need is very hard to discover. If all knowledge is perspectival, why not admit it? If all our needs and drives are forms of the will to power (of self-assertion), how can there be a need to deny this basic drive?

An ascetic life is indeed a contradiction in terms. Here we find rancor without parallel, the rancor of an insatiable power-drive which would dominate, not a single aspect of life, but life itself. . . . Here we witness an attempt to use energy to block the very sources of energy. . . . All this is paradoxical to the highest degree.[24]

22. F. Nietzsche, *The Joyful Wisdom,* trans. T. Common (New York: Frederick Ungar, 1960), pp. 154, 155.

23. *Will to Power,* p. 235.

24. *Genealogy,* p. 253.

Nietzsche's resolution of this paradox is not very satisfactory. He claims that the ascetic ideal, the ideal of disinterested objective inquiry, is a form of resentment. Idealizing disinterestedness serves the needs of those who lack power to satisfy their interests and express themselves in a direct way. They are thus forced to make a virtue of not being able to satisfy themselves, and to claim that the highest truth emerges when one selflessly devotes himself to knowledge and tries as far as possible to eliminate his personal interests. Another way Nietzsche has of putting this point is that for some men in some ages the life force has become so weak that it must restrict its demands in order to preserve what force there is left. "Life employs asceticism in its desperate struggle against death; the ascetic ideal is a dodge for the preservation of life." [25]

So the ideal of objectivity as a moral demand is analyzed as part of the Judaeo-Christian slave revolt against the Greco-Roman splendor. But here Nietzsche's claim that our only need is individual expression, and thus that the pursuit of total objectivity must arise from the weakness of a certain kind of man, runs into trouble. Nietzsche seems to forget that it was the splendid Greeks, not the weak Hebrews, who expressed the ascetic ideal in its purest form. Of course, one could claim that the Athenians were weak too—at the time of Plato a conquered *polis*—but this ignores the fact that to make the theory work the Greeks should be the weakest of all. More generally, Nietzsche's trouble is that, like Kierkegaard, he cannot account for the evident universality of the pursuit of objectivity as an end in itself. To account for everyone's interest in being objective for its own sake Nietzsche would have to say that everyone is weak.[26]

Such a generalization, however, would amount to admission that the claims of objectivity and total disinterestedness satisfy a *universal* human craving. If so, one would like to know what it is. With discovery we would, according to Nietzsche, get over it,

25. *Ibid.*, p. 256.
26. It might be thought that Nietzsche could reconcile interest in objectivity with strong personality by claiming that some persons may be motivated to personal expression *in addition* to wanting objectivity for its sake. But this ignores the difficulty that if objectivity is *an* end in itself it must be *the* exclusive end. For it consists in the inhibition of all interest whose satisfaction might represent other ends. Nietzsche cannot accept the common impression that the valuing of objectivity for its own sake is *compatible* with the pursuit of personal ends.

for he tells us, "A matter that becomes clear ceases to concern us." [27]

That Nietzsche as psychologist has not satisfactorily done his job and made us aware of the repressed root of our deluded pursuit of total objectivity is suggested by the fact that this ideal still has such a grip on us—and on Nietzsche. We cannot help continuing to believe that we can set aside our whims, biases, and needs, and grasp truths whose validity does not depend on what we need to be true. And Nietzsche himself, instead of respecting interested truths, cannot help feeling that a truth which grows out of a personal need is somehow suspect.

> We have no intention of denying that man is saved by faith, but for this very reason we deny that faith proves anything. A strong, saving faith casts suspicion on the object of that faith; so far from establishing its "truth," it establishes a certain probability—of deception. [28]

Nietzsche's suspicion that the passion of faith betrays its untruth in betraying its basis in human need shows that in his understanding of subjective truth he is still a prisoner of the tradition. Perhaps Nietzsche would be the first to admit this, for he understood that it was not a simple matter to grasp and face the implications of the death of God (even Zarathustra does not claim to have done so). At any rate, Nietzsche, like Kierkegaard, implicitly accepts the traditional view that knowledge is ideally disinterested even though human knowledge is essentially interested.

In order to see more precisely how Nietzsche remains in the grip of objective truth we must reconsider his views in more detail, paying particular attention this time to how they change as he struggles vainly to free them of all traces of objectivity.

In all his thought, Nietzsche holds fast to the view that truth is a necessity of life. In an early stage of his critique of objective truth, however, he regards this necessity as rooted in "instinctive activities" and "physiological demands"; [29] "the bottom of us"; "something unteachable, a granite of spiritual *fatum* [fate], of predetermined decision and answer to predetermined selected

27. *Beyond Good and Evil*, p. 81.
28. *Genealogy*, p. 286.
29. *Beyond Good and Evil*, p. 11.

questions." [30] Thus, "whenever a cardinal problem is at stake, there speaks an unchangeable 'this is I'; about [such problems] a thinker cannot relearn but only finish learning—only discover ultimately how this is 'settled in him.' " [31] So "most of the conscious thinking of a philosopher is secretly guided and forced into certain channels by his instincts"; [32] and "every great philosophy so far has been . . . the personal confession of its author." [33]

For Nietzsche in this early stage the objectivist is right in holding that truth is fixed (at least for the lifetime of the knower), but wrong in believing that it is fixed in Nature at large rather than in human nature. In a transitional form of his doctrine, however, Nietzsche claims that "the most strongly believed a priori 'truths' are . . . *provisional assumptions* . . . a very well *acquired habit* of belief, so much a part of us that not to believe in it would destroy the race." [34] Being merely acquired rather than fixed in our nature, these necessary truths *could* then conceivably be discarded by a radically strong and free spirit. Such a spirit is finally envisaged in Nietzsche's portrayal of the man who is *instinctively skeptical* rather than instinctively biased:

> The great man is necessarily a skeptic. . . . Freedom from any kind of conviction is part of the strength of his will. Thus it accords with that "enlightened despotism" exercised by every great passion. Such a passion . . . permits itself convictions, it even *needs* them, but it does not submit to them. The need for faith, for anything unconditional in Yes and No, is a proof of weakness . . . of will. The man of faith, the believer, is necessarily a small type of man. Hence "freedom of spirit," i.e., unbelief as an instinct, is a precondition of greatness. [35]

"*Instinctive* skepticism" here means that freedom from *all* discoverable truth, subjective as well as objective, is itself the fundamental necessity or instinct of life—for those most alive and hence for life itself.

So there are really two stages in Nietzsche's critique of sup-

30. *Ibid.*, p. 162.
31. *Ibid.*
32. *Ibid.*, p. 11.
33. *Ibid.*, p. 13.
34. *Will to Power*, p. 273 (italics added).
35. *Ibid.*, p. 505.

posedly disinterested objective truth. First he holds that the truth is not objectively but subjectively fixed—that it is rooted not in some eternal world order independent of man but in the instincts of man himself. The truth is what it is because man can't help regarding things that way. More radically, however, particularly in *The Will to Power,* Nietzsche contests the fixity of truth in any form: the entirely free spirit, he proclaims, will reject enslavement not only to the values of others but also to his *own* past valuations. Just as he will not submit to the forces of public conformity, so he will not submit to "instinct," which he now sees as nothing more than the force of habit in himself. No particular truth is necessary in any sense. The truth is *whatever* it is because man freely *decides* to regard things that way.[36]

Thus Nietzsche discusses the ideas of truth as determined (1) by the world-order independently of man; (2) by the instinctive nature of man shaping his world; and (3) by man's will freely choosing the "instincts" or "values" that shape his world.

Corresponding to each of these ideas of truth is a certain degree of awareness that knowledge is "perspectival," i.e., that what we know reflects our ways and means of knowing it, what Nietzsche calls our "point of view." This perspectivity is difficult to discover because it has a tendency to self-concealment which insight must overcome. The "will to power," in ourselves and our interests, is responsible for this dissimulation of perspectivity: each impulse strives for exclusive domination and the elimination of all its rivals; and we delegate such absolute powers to our chief impulses in the interest of simplifying and controlling our experience.

36. Nietzsche is thus attracted to two incompatible forms of interested truth: truth as a function of fixed and discoverable interest; and truth as a function of provisional and created interest. Kierkegaard's distinction between a lower and a higher form of *concrete* self allows him to formulate a single kind of interested truth which—as, in effect, a creative discovery—reconciles and satisfies both of Nietzsche's desiderata. Nietzsche always sees that merely adopted beliefs belong to a lower order of self, a "phantom" self or "pseudo-ego" (*The Dawn of Day,* in *Complete Works,* ed. O. Levy, 18 vols. [New York: Russell & Russell, 1901–11], IX, 100–102). But, unlike Kierkegaard, he does not always see that "instinctive" biases instilled by nature are basically like received opinions of mankind in being *merely received.* And lacking Kierkegaard's idea of personal needs, which first become concrete and discoverable only through a "leap" creating a higher form of self, Nietzsche's only alternative to a self defined by merely received content is a self defined by *no* content but only by its willful domination over dispensable contents of its choice.

> Every drive is a sort of lust to rule; each one has its perspective
> that it would like to compel all the other drives to accept as a
> norm.[37]

All judgment is a product of this dissimulation.

> (T)he spirit *wants* equality. . . . *The will to equality is the will to*
> *power*—the belief that something is thus and thus (the essence of
> judgement) is the consequence of a will that as much as possible
> *shall be* equal.[38]

So we make our basic decisions in such a way as to blind
ourselves thereafter to all alternatives. And what we cannot see
seems to us not there. As a result, our decision, once made,
comes to seem called for by the world rather than imposed upon
it. This accounts for the total concealment of perspectivity in the
objective ideal.

The view that truth is determined by *instinctive* human
interests involves a *partial* concealment of perspectivity—what
we know is seen to reflect our "means" (via dominant interest)
but not our (willful) "way" of knowing it. Though our basic
decisions restrict *us* to seeing the *world* in a narrow spectrum,
they do not blind others nor do they blind us to the ("evidently"
false) claims of others. So the possibility of disagreement among
individuals prevents the tyranny of a narrow outlook from being
absolutely complete. Contrary judgments, if not contrary appearances, are liable to throw into question our narrowness. The
disagreement arises between individuals about the world. There
are then two plausible alternatives: (1) one judgment is right,
the other wrong: "evidence" is considered stronger than judgment, and the intrinsic character of the world is supposed to
decide—the objective ideal is supported against the challenge to
it; (2) both judgments are right: "evidence" is held to follow
from judgment so that each individual is right for "his world"—
the challenge to objectivity is upheld in the name of a subjective
truth.

How then is the remaining level of perspectivity (namely,
the willful basis of dominant interest) to be discovered? Blindness to contrary appearances, we have seen, is responsible for
blindness to perspectivity. Penetration of the objective disguise

37. *Will to Power*, p. 267.
38. *Ibid.*, p. 277.

is difficult since it requires seeing the *possibility* of contrary appearances for others in the face of actually *uniform* evidence from one's own experience. Now the question is how one may discover the willful variability of his *own* form of experience. One could do so, on Nietzsche's account, only by *actually* changing the axioms of his life. So it takes a radically free spirit to know the freedom which is the core of perspectivity in all human knowledge. The will to power conceals itself from itself in its weakness, and reveals itself to itself in its strength. It conditions everything but is itself unconditioned. It can be overcome, to be sure, but only by itself—by its own strength overcoming its own weakness. We can now see that the tendency to self-deception (to dissimulation of our perspectivity) stems from our absolutely unconditioned kind of self-mastery and existence, for our being self-conditioned means that we are always engaged in mastering deceptions we have manufactured for ourselves.[39]

We are now ready to reexamine Nietzsche's dictum that human truth, as interested truth, is (even in the last analysis) a "kind of error"; to see more precisely how this is meant; and to understand how even this conception remains to some extent bound by the idea of objective truth. Nietzsche considers human truth a "kind of error" because of its willful blindness to existing differences. Deception about the willful blindness of perspectivity is corrigible, as we have seen. But there remains a blindness due to perspectivity which is incorrigible because definitive of our very existence as perspectival beings.[40]

The absolutely unconditioned independence of the perspec-

39. It is true that Nietzsche ridicules the idea of unconditioned things-in-themselves, but in such a way as to *allow* rather than to rule out the idea of an unconditioned self: "There are no things-in-themselves! But even supposing there were an in-itself, an unconditioned thing, it would for that very reason be unknowable. . . . Coming to know means: 'to place one's self in a conditional relation to something'; to feel oneself conditioned by something and oneself conditioning it" (*ibid.*, p. 301). So *only* the self can be unconditioned (by anything else) and yet knowable, namely, as knowable *by itself* through being in relation to itself.

40. Even the corrigible deception is not corrigible once and for all. Perspectivity is the *delegating* of absolute power to one idea or set of ideas. This absolute power "corrupts" ideas into appearing valid "by themselves" —as if they *possessed* the power they merely *exercise*. So the appearance of objectivity is unavoidable. We can at best see through it again and again by constantly reaffirming the true source of power in our will. The distortion in appearances due to perspectivity, however, is not only permanent but *impenetrable*.

tivizing will is at the same time its absolute *exile* into a world of its own. Exile *from . . .* what? Not from the "true world" in the sense of a nonperspectival world. A perspectival world is not, by contrast, a merely apparent world. "In abolishing the true world we have also abolished the world of appearance." [41] A perspective, properly understood, is opposed not to a nonperspectival reality but to *other* (excluded) *perspectives.*

> Every center of force adopts a perspective towards the entire remainder, i.e. its own particular valuation, mode of action, and mode of resistance. . . . The "world" is only a word for the totality of these actions. Reality consists precisely in this particular action and reaction of every individual part toward the whole. [42]

Believing that life is a kind of blindness to existing differences, Nietzsche persistently recognizes "untruth as a condition of life." [43] But it is difficult for him to hold that there are unseen differences without presuming—against all else he writes—to know something objectively. His problem, in short, is to reconcile statements such as the following pair: "Logic is the attempt to comprehend the actual world by means of a scheme of being posited by ourselves"; and, "As if a world would still remain over after one deducted the perspective!" [44] He sometimes holds that "the actual world," which life distorts for its own purposes, exhibits [*sic*—to whom?] more *differences* from case to case than we can see; or more *change* than we can see. [45] But such formulations run counter to the main Nietzschean argument that something *is* the case by virtue of being so *exhibited,* and that exhibition occurs only *in perspective.* Life's "untruth" thus cannot be its blindness to certain "factors" or "conditions" intrinsic to the world, i.e., actual even though entirely unseen. It must be a blindness to *other interpretations,* to conditions apparent only in *other* lives. Nietzsche sometimes writes in this more consistent vein. For example, ". . . reason and Euclidean space,

41. "How the 'True World' Ultimately Became a Fable," *The Twilight of the Idols,* in *Complete Works,* XVI, 25.
42. *Will to Power,* p. 305. Nietzsche is not always master of his own thought on this point, as for example when he claims that our perspective "applies only to fictitious [*sic*] entities that we have created" (*ibid.,* p. 280); or when he refers to "the fictitious [*sic*] world" produced by our "power to order, simplify, falsify [*sic*], artificially [*sic*] distinguish" (*ibid.*).
43. *Beyond Good and Evil,* p. 12.
44. *Will to Power,* pp. 280, 305.
45. *Ibid.,* pp. 277, 280.

is a mere idiosyncracy of a certain species of animals, and one among many." [46] Or, "Facts is precisely what there is not, only interpretations. . . . The world is knowable; but it is *interpretable* otherwise, it has no meaning behind it, but countless meanings.—'Perspectivism.' " [47]

Life's incorrigible "untruth" can now be seen as of a piece with its corrigible tendency to self-deception. The same will to domination which operates *within* a given life to conceal its freedom from itself (as the condition of its own unconditionedness) also operates between various centers of interpretation to isolate and conceal rival freedoms from one another (as the condition of their mutual unconditionedness). So human truth is a "kind of error" because it is essentially the truth of *one* interpretive power blind to the truths of *all other* perspectivizing powers. Nietzsche turns out to be, in effect, a Leibnizian for whom there is no Leibnizian God but only a system of entelechies or monads which no one can know as a system.

How then does Nietzsche know that there *is* such a system ("totality of these actions")? And how can such an interplay of perspectives even be *conceived* except objectively (i.e., nonperspectivally)? Denying the objectivist view that our "togetherness" is nonperspectivally knowable, and unable to suggest how it *is* knowable, Nietzsche nevertheless cannot rid himself of the objectivist view that such a togetherness somehow exists—just as Kierkegaard, while denying that objective truths could be known by man, remains caught in the view that such truths do exist (for God).

HEIDEGGER

HEIDEGGER'S ACCOUNT of the history of Western thought makes just this point: although Nietzsche criticizes the traditional view of truth, he remains himself an exponent of it—indeed, for late Heidegger, its extremest exponent.

The tradition of occidental thinking is collected and completed in a crucial respect in Nietzsche's thought. . . . Coming to terms

46. *Ibid.*, p. 278.
47. *Ibid.*, p. 267.

with Nietzsche is coming to terms with the tradition as it has developed up to now.[48]

Heidegger himself is impressed with the profound error of this whole tradition. He sees a need to "destroy" or "overcome" it. He seeks a fulcrum on which he may challenge and overturn not just contemporary ideas but the whole Western tradition summed up in them. And this always implies "going beyond" Nietzsche. But Heidegger did not at first see how far beyond Nietzsche he had to go; he did not at first see how profoundly Nietzsche remained a prisoner of the very tradition he criticized. Thus in his early work, *Being and Time*, Heidegger sought only to extend Nietzsche's line of thought to a more complete repudiation of objectivity.

On Nietzsche's view the illusion of objectivity is universally needed in two ways: (1) to maintain the "ascetic" suppression required for powerful self-expression; and (2) to maintain the despotic rule of central "values" needed for organizing and dominating the world.[49] Truth remains a function of objective disinterestedness even if in the last analysis the truth is deceptive for appearing to be disinterested in one way, and false (a "kind of error"), as we have seen, for not being disinterested in another way (for excluding all other perspectives in blind partiality to its own). For the Heidegger of *Being and Time*, however, there is a pure subjective truth, free of all illusion of objectivity and free also of any objective limitation. It is the truth of our "being unto death," the truth that all our doings, all our purposes, continually point toward our annihilation as their ultimate end and thus as their deepest significance. What our life comes to in the end is, for Heidegger, always with us; it is with us not only at the end but also from the very beginning as the dominant theme of our life taken as a whole. Each individual is mortal. His deepest possibility is the possibility of having no more possibilities. And his own death is infinitely important to him in a way that it is to no one else. This finitude of ours is difficult and dreadful to discern, but it is nonetheless discernible. One who grasps this truth is, to be sure, always tempted to resort to an objective

48. M. Heidegger, *Nietzsche*, 2 vols. (Pfullingen: Neske, 1961), I, 13 (authors' translation).

49. *Some* (namely, weak) persons also need the illusion of objectivity in a third way: to maintain the ascetic ideal as a social force to prevent others from dominating them.

alternative. For he must "live" this truth (i.e., live in such a way as to be true to his insight) surrounded by the comforting norms of objectivity which are definitive of public life with its air of an everlasting *status quo* in which "one" (*das Man*) behaves conventionally as a shadowy non-entity who is nobody in particular. But the wise man resolutely spurns these temptations, nowise employing or depending upon them. Insight for Heidegger, unlike for Nietzsche, takes place, in short, despite the objective alternative—away from it rather than by way of it.

For Heidegger, truth is grasped by the individual insofar as he has the courage to stand apart from the mass. Just as for Kierkegaard, truth for Heidegger is individual and subjective. And just as for Nietzsche, its subjectivity is inevitably disguised. In *Being and Time*, the fundamental truth is held to be about actual things, as distinct from ideal or abstract entities. Such truth, we are told, consists in dis-covery (*alētheia*) of the "thing itself." No representation will do. The real object must be made to present itself bodily, to show itself as it actually is, in man's presence. Truth in this sense, the analysis continues, is based in the ability of man (*Dasein*) to discover things by way of and in terms of his practical concerns. These concerns are organized within a single context or framework, one might say a form of life. And we ourselves constitute—comprise as well as produce —this context, which Heidegger calls being-in-the-world.

> Being-true as uncovering, is . . . ontologically possible only on the basis of Being-in-the-world. This latter phenomenon, which we have known as a basic state of man, is the foundation for the primordial phenomenon of truth.[50]

Truths once revealed in our context of concerns are given verbal expression. So expressed, the truths which a particular person has discovered by his own efforts and in terms of his own interests can be mouthed by anyone, even persons unaware of these originating interests. Such truths, which can be bandied about by anyone, seem to be disinterested truths. They appear to be propositions or bits of information whose correctness consists in their correspondence to an independently existing reality. The assertion of such propositions retains no semblance of man's primordial power to *found* the truth by expressing it, to literally

50. M. Heidegger, *Being and Time*, trans. J. Macquarrie and E. Robinson (New York: Harper & Row, 1962), p. 261.

real-ize the truth by evoking certain things in an appropriate context so as to bring them into being there by making them emerge and present themselves there. The final step of objectification is taken by suppressing the ontogenesis of this superficial conception of truth. Truth is then regarded as essentially a property of propositions. And with the supposed primacy of this derivative conception of truth comes the objectivist ontology according to which what there is, is independent of any human knowledge of it.

Heidegger's account of why we are prone to make this last move—why, in Nietzsche's terms, we tend to conceal truth's perspectivity—is, as we have seen, that we tend to deny our involvement and to embrace an impersonal way of looking at the world because this helps us to forget instead of to heroically face the dreadful arbitrariness of our existence. The traditional conception of truth, then, simply makes explicit the ontology of an inauthentic way of life.

Thus in *Being and Time* Heidegger radically undermines objective truth. He agrees with Nietzsche in distinguishing objective truth from an underlying subjective truth. He agrees that this subjective truth appears to be objective and that this appearance is false and misleading. But whereas Nietzsche regarded the illusion of objective truth as a superficial expression of the underlying truth, Heidegger regards it as nothing but the concealment and repudiation of truth. For Nietzsche the illusion of objectivity is universally needed for the achievement of true insight. But for Heidegger this illusion is only a universal *obstacle* to authentic knowledge.

So in *Being and Time* Heidegger does not merely criticize objective truth but totally degrades it while putting forward a purely interested form of truth as our only access to reality. The traditional opposition between the world of illusory change and the realm of eternal truth is simply reversed. And Heidegger assigns an even lower status to eternal impersonal (scientific and public) "truths" than Plato assigned to the provisional "truths" of opinion and perception. For whereas Plato holds that mundane beliefs, however rudimentary, point at least *toward* the real truth, Heidegger holds that objective understanding, however refined, points *away*.

In his later work, after the period of *Being and Time*, Heidegger executes an abrupt "turn" (*Kehre*) in his thought. He makes an about-face involving a complete reversal of his early Nietzsche criticism. He comes to agree with Nietzsche that objective truth is an essential expression of subjective truth. But now he "goes beyond" Nietzsche in the opposite direction by insisting that objective and subjective truth are far *more* intertwined than Nietzsche ever suspected. For Nietzsche these forms of truth are loosely connected. The truth is basically subjective; but there are objective illusions which our subjectivity must have, though we need not be taken in by them; and there is, he implies, an objective truth which our subjectivity makes inaccessible. In the last analysis a remnant of objectivity infects subjective truth with untruth. In *Being and Time*, to be sure, man begins in a state of "falling" into the untruth of identifying himself with his public role even though he retains some sense of his individuality. But the authentic way of life lies in establishing a complete separation between truth and untruth.

> Dasein is already both in the truth and in untruth. The way of uncovering is achieved only in . . . distinguishing between these understandingly, and making one's decision for the one rather than the other.[51]

Late Heidegger, by contrast, claims that objectivity is completely *in*separable from subjectivity. From this point of view Nietzsche's error lay not in failing to separate them but in distinguishing them. Yet this was no simple mistake. It is no accident that subjectivity was sought, and sought vainly, as the way out of the Western metaphysical tradition. Both the reason and the wrongheadedness of this search—brought in *Being and Time* to what Heidegger later regards as its dis-illusioning completion—are finally made plain by the insight that subjectivity is itself the most profound tendency and guiding spirit of our tradition.

Rigorous examination of objectivity leads to subjectivity because subjectivity turns out to be the implicit form of objective truth. According to Heidegger, Nietzsche was the first to discern this subjective basis of objective truth. Though he thus drew out the deepest implication of objective truth, he nevertheless failed to recognize that he had done so. He failed to recognize that his own view was only an implication and not a transformation of

51. *Ibid.*, p. 265.

objective thought. What then is missing? What, more precisely, is the difference between Nietzsche's recognition of the subjective basis of objectivity and late Heidegger's claim that subjectivity is the very essence or *Grundzug* of objectivity?

The difference lies in Nietzsche's belief that the frankly willed truth of the "free spirit" is free of the main failings of supposedly objective truth, and in Heidegger's position that frankly willed truth merely carries these failings to the extreme. For Nietzsche, objectivity has some truth in it because it is to some extent an expression of the profound truth of the will to power. But for late Heidegger the sense of the connection is reversed: instead of objectivity benefiting from the validity of willed truth, willed truth suffers from the failings of objectivity. This can be seen most clearly in Nietzsche's and Heidegger's discussion of "nihilism," the general loss of value which both regard as definitive of modern times. For Nietzsche, our nihilism or valuelessness comes from our refusal to recognize what we are doing in valuing. But for Heidegger, it stems from the willful nature of what we are in fact doing. Hence for him, unlike Nietzsche, the more open and complete our covert and inhibited practices become, the *more* we will feel whatever terrible consequences arise from them.

For Heidegger, a culture is only gripped by its concerns when it has not conceptualized them as values. The health of a culture is judged by the number of things it takes for granted. But the commitment of Western philosophy since Socrates has been to clarify and conceptualize—to get before us—the principles by which we live, to make the horizon of our thought itself an object of thought. Therefore, we continually work to transform our concerns into detached values. But such values can no longer grip us; we come rather to possess *them*. Instead of being sustained by values to which we submit, we "uphold" them as values for us. But values merely insisted upon betray their willfulness and lose their value. A culture in which this happens, in which "the highest values lose their value," [52] is for Nietzsche in the stage of nihilism. Values seem merely imposed and cannot be believed in, even though they are imposed by the very heritage and culture of those on whom they are imposed. Nietzsche sees the "leveling" values of the ascetic ideal in this light, and cele-

52. *Nietzsche*, I, 35.

brates their forthcoming destruction as giving birth to a higher order of value, personal and spontaneous. But Heidegger sees that the fundamental form of nihilism stems not, as Nietzsche thought, from supposedly objective social or even biological values being imposed upon individuals but from values being imposed *at all*. Nietzsche's envisioned "transvaluation of values" is thus no escape from the nihilism of present values, for even the super-free spirit of *self*-imposed values lives with merely imposed and therefore impotent values. Nietzsche's *sup-posed* cure is in Heidegger's eyes the quintessence of the trouble. Willed value is without value. So, for Heidegger, "Nietzsche recognizes and experiences nihilism because he himself thinks nihilistically." [53]

In a similar vein, Nietzsche offers a profoundly disturbing analysis of the ascetic ideal of disinterested inquiry, an analysis with which Heidegger would agree:

> Finally the ascetic ideal arose to give [suffering] meaning. . . . No doubt that interpretation brought new suffering in its wake, deeper, more inward, more poisonous suffering. . . . All the same, man had saved himself, he had achieved a meaning, he was no longer a leaf in the wind, a plaything of circumstance, of "crass causality": he was now able to will something—no matter the object or the instrument of his willing; the will itself had been saved. We can no longer conceal from ourselves what exactly it is that this whole process of willing, inspired by the ascetic ideal, signifies—this hatred of humanity, . . . this longing to escape from illusion, change, becoming, death, and from longing itself. It signifies, let us have the courage to face it, a will to nothingness, a revulsion from life, a rebellion against the principal conditions of living. And yet, despite everything, it is and remains a *will*. . . . Man would sooner have the void for his purpose than be void of purpose. [54]

From Heidegger's point of view, Nietzsche is correct about the ascetic ideal. This ideal is an attempt to insist upon vanishing values; by demanding conditions which are in fact uncongenial and opposed to life, it does bring increased suffering to the life it is ostensibly meant to save; so in this sense it is in effect, all pretenses aside, a will for Nothingness, saving no reality but the will itself. But what Nietzsche fails to see, from Heidegger's

53. *Ibid.*, II, 54.
54. Nietzsche, *Genealogy*, pp. 298, 299.

point of view, is that in his analysis of the ascetic ideal he has laid bare the final meaning not only of *these* willed truths but of *all* willed truths. He has, in short, exposed the implications of the willfulness of willed truth. The Will to Power is nothing but the Will to Will. And the more frankly and ruthlessly it is pursued the more it brings "new suffering . . . deeper, more inward, more poisonous suffering," for it becomes ever more impossible for anything to retain the value ever more openly and arbitrarily imposed upon it. The more willful man's grasp, the less he grasps. And at the limit of willfulness lies the grasp of nothing at all.

In this critique of Nietzsche's nihilism, late Heidegger preserves after all something of his early view. In *Being and Time* he saw objectivity as a total failure—from which authentic subjectivity was supposed to be a complete escape. Nietzsche had seen objectivity as inextricably rooted in subjectivity—although he thought the latter comparatively free of the former's failings. Late Heidegger takes something from each view. Objectivity is a complete failure, as he early saw; but it is inextricable from a subjective basis, as Nietzsche perceived. So—this is late Heidegger's distinctive synthesis—subjectivity is also a complete failure. Subjective truth is utterly misleading (giving rise to the appearance of objective truth) only because it is itself an equally distorted form of truth.

Heidegger's deduction of the subjective basis of objectivity is built on two analyses absolutely fundamental to all of his thought: the analysis of "truth" and "being" as being un-covered (*alētheia* or *Unverborgenheit*); and the analysis of metaphysics as the view that beings derive their being from conformity to some eternal being (e.g., Plato's Idea of the Good, the Christian's God, or Nietzsche's Will to Power). Heidegger tries in several ways to show that the idea of metaphysics is mistaken because it is incompatible with the idea of truth as *alētheia,* and that objectivity and subjectivity belong together as the superficial and profound expressions of this mistaken metaphysical idea.

We have already broached Heidegger's idea of "un-covering" in discussing *Being and Time*. Fundamentally, Heidegger's point is that the "being" and "truth" of matters consists in their *presence*. Presence is understood as the presence of a thing. And the central feature of this presence is its *incompleteness*. A thing is present by standing out in a setting which does *not* stand out.

The background character of the setting is essential to the prominence of the thing. So, together with the appearance of something revealed (as thing), "presence" includes the concealment of something concealed (as setting). This concealment, however, is itself apparent. So the partiality of appearance is itself apparent. Hence the being of things involves both their revelation and their concealment. But things do not have their being by themselves. Man plays an essential role. In particular, it is through man that beings are revealed. But man is not alone responsible for the being of things. Things are not materialized out of nothing. They are *brought* forth (as prominent or salient) rather than *put* forth (as invented). Man's responsibility for the revelation of things involves his responsiveness to the concealment of things, which is not his own doing. Heidegger understands this essential concealment of things as the work of "Being as such." So man and Being together (as "belonging to one another" [55]) produce the being or presence of things as disclosed features on an undisclosed ground.

The pre-Socratics, according to Heidegger, understood "being" and "truth" in the way just explained. But Plato made a fundamental departure which inaugurated metaphysics and has proved decisive for all Western thought since, and indeed for the whole of Western civilization. Plato identified "truth" and "being" with the "Idea" as essentially a *completely apparent* being. To "be" and to be "true" was to be completely evident; to be concealed was not to be at all. From Heidegger's point of view this attempt to understand things in a context-free manner is a violation of the true being of things, requiring us to rip things out of the context in which they really belong. It requires us to isolate things from their setting in the concealment of Being. So the idea of Being-as-such is lost. It is replaced by the idea of metaphysics, the idea that things derive their being from relation to some chief thing rather than from their rootedness in some ground or condition which does not have the character of a thing at all. But the being of things as distinct from their setting consists entirely of their appearance or revelation, and hence is entirely the work of man. So the metaphysical "chief thing" from

55. Cf. "Alētheia (Heraclitus Fragment 16)" in *Vorträge und Aufsätze* (Pfullingen: Neske, 1954), p. 258. See also *Zur Seinsfrage* (Frankfurt a.M: Klostermann, 1956), pp. 27–30; and *Identität und Differenz* (Pfullingen: Neske, 1957), pp. 20–34.

which all things derive their being turns out to be the human subject producing the things he knows. Plato of course did not recognize this subjective implication of his metaphysics. He held that Ideas were *intrinsically* evident, luminously intelligible, whether men understood them (whether men were "looking") or not. But Heidegger insists that evidence as manifestation is the work of man, whatever Plato thought. The idea of "objective (i.e., intrinsic) evidence" is a contradiction in terms. So Plato's metaphysical legacy of "being" and "truth" as pure appearance was more decisive than his own objectivist interpretation of that legacy. And it is accordingly no accident that the metaphysical tradition begun by Plato eventually took a subjectivist turn in philosophers like Descartes and Kant, and finally reached the absolute subjectivism of Nietzsche. The basic truth will out; history is but the working out of essential truth. So the nihilism essential to Nietzsche's fully subjective metaphysics is to be understood as implicit in the general idea of metaphysics, and hence even in Plato's ostensibly objective metaphysics.

> *Metaphysics as metaphysics is the genuine nihilism.* The essence of nihilism *exists* historically as metaphysics, the metaphysics of Plato is no less nihilistic than the metaphysics of Nietzsche. In the former the essence of nihilism simply remains concealed, in the latter it becomes fully manifest.[56]

56. *Nietzsche*, II, 343 (authors' translation). But Heidegger's deduction of the subjective basis of objectivity does not rest merely on the implications for metaphysics of his own idea of truth and being as "uncovering" or *alētheia*. Seeing these implications, Heidegger knows what to look for and claims to find traces of nascent subjectivism in Plato himself. In *Plato's Doctrine of Truth,* Heidegger claims that Plato wavers between an objectivist criterion of truth as the "correct appearance" of Ideas by themselves, and a subjectivist criterion of truth as the appearance corresponding to a "correct looking" at these Ideas. Heidegger admits it is Plato's primary position that Ideas are real or true "by themselves" without regard to man's knowledge of them. But he holds that *alētheia* is so pervasive and fundamental that Plato could not help recognizing it to *some* extent. Since Plato did not recognize *alētheia* as first bringing Ideas into being, only one other way remained. Plato recognized "un-covering" as essential to knowledge of Ideas already in being. He did this by identifying Ideas with their correct appearance and construing the knowledge which uncovers them as correct looking. In doing so, according to Heidegger, he made the uncovering of Ideas somewhat responsible for their being, after all. For a "correct appearance" *is* an appearance to and for a correctly regarding subject.

Thus Heidegger's analysis implies that in our day of triumphant metaphysics we ought to see the furtive "correct looking" of Plato's

So metaphysics implied a subjective reality all along. At first in Platonism, and for much of its history since, an objective facade obscured this essential truth. But then came the rise of modern philosophy, culminating in Nietzsche. It paralleled the rise of science and industry, culminating in the overwhelming technology of the present age. And now in this age of "finished

---

thought everywhere boldly at work as the arbiter of reality *in flagrante delicto*.

In *Age of the World View* Heidegger recounts, in effect, how we do indeed find this to be so. What is currently accepted as real in our technological age is the product of a certain procedure of correct viewing. We first propose to ourselves some general scheme of things. We then understand the way something "really" is as the way it appears when fitted into this scheme. The reality of a thing consists in our "getting the picture" of it within some overall perspective or outlook we have adopted as axiomatic for all our experience. A thing *is* its appearance in perspective. The "truth" about things—the "correctness" of their appearance—is their fitting into perspective, their corresponding in this way to the ground rules we have laid down for ourselves in establishing and defining our point of view. In Heidegger's words, " 'Getting the picture' of something means not only that the existent is simply presented to us, but that, in everything that belongs to it and constitutes it as a system, it stands before us. . . . The existent as a whole is now so understood that it is existent when and only when and in the degree to which it is entertained by the person who represents and establishes it" (M. Heidegger, "Die Zeit des Weltbildes," *Holzwege* [Frankfurt a.M: Klostermann, 1957], p. 82. Adapted from Marjorie Grene's translation in *Measure,* Summer, 1951).

"Correct looking" is the only Platonic augury of the modern sense of reality which Heidegger discusses. But he might well have buttressed his argument by noting two others. Plato sometimes suggests that Ideas are *criteria.* He does this particularly in the early dialogues in which Ideas such as Justice are discussed primarily for the purpose of arriving at a satisfactory definition by which true and false examples might be recognized and distinguished. But criteria are essentially for application in judgment. So the "truth" and "existence" defined in terms of criteria are essentially products of the human subject adjusting given material to an accepted scheme of classification and discerning with precision its fitness or unfitness within that framework. Heidegger regards such discriminating "exactitude" as one trait of "getting the picture." A closely related point is that Ideas sometimes function for Plato as "values" in a Nietzschean rather than a traditional sense. They are not merely standards separating the "good" from the "bad" among that which is. They function as *ruling out of existence* whatever does not fit them. Whatever the previously discussed test of "exactitude" does not absolutely discriminate in favor of (as having perfectly satisfied the criteria employed) is radically discriminated against as banished from existence. All appearances to the contrary notwithstanding, there are no misfits and nothing is atypical. To be is to fit universal standards perfectly, and not to fit perfectly is not to be at all. Plato always holds that "to be" is to conform to Ideas. Normally, however, he suggests that all appearances are "saved" as reflecting Ideas to some extent. But occasionally he doubts, as when in the *Sophist* he (*vollendete*) metaphysics" the nihilistic subjectivity of truth and being is completely out: worked out, brought out, and played out. The idea of metaphysics holds no further surprises in store. But, according to Heidegger,

> Metaphysics lays the foundation of an age by giving it the basis of its essential form through a particular analysis of the existent and a particular conception of truth. This basis dominates all the phenomena which distinguish the age.[57]

So in these completely metaphysical times, if Heidegger is right, we may expect to see the full implications of the metaphysical idea widely and openly displayed and its nihilistic price fully paid, in all our distinctive forms of life such as our art, sex, religion, and society.

The subjectification of "truth" and "being" means that "everything must become experience for modern man."[58] Interest in works of art becomes interest in esthetic experience, interest in God becomes interest in religious experience, etc. These cultural trends follow in the wake of the leading technological trend of our epoch. More and more, objects are understood to exist only for and in our experience of them. If this trend were carried to the limit (which these cultural phenomena do not yet seem to have reached) we would experience nothing but other experiences of our own. Or, to make the point another way, the very idea of "experience" would be changed. Instead of being a way in which we are affected by things other than ourselves, "experience" would be understood as nothing but a way in which we affect ourselves, so as to "enjoy ourselves," for example, or "make ourselves miserable." As it is, in the "developing" phenomena of our age we tend merely to disregard the occasions of our experience while tacitly acknowledging their independent exist-

---

makes Socrates unable to decide whether there are Ideas for "inferior things" such as mud and hair. On such occasions Ideas tend to be employed in the manner we are discussing, as censors practicing a sort of eugenics of existence. This, together with discriminating "exactitude," comprises the *Gerechtigkeit* which Heidegger declares to be the essence of modern truth (*Nietzsche*, II, 332). He accepts Nietzsche's characterization of it as "constructive, discriminating, and annihilating" (*ibid.*, II, 322). *Gerechtigkeit* can well be translated as "justification." It is the idea of truth employed by a mode of thought—our mode of thought—for which there is existence by justification alone.

57. *Holzwege*, p. 69 (adapted from Marjorie Grene's translation).
58. *Ibid.*, p. 86.

ence. Still, we attend dramatic spectacles such as *Marat-Sade* solely for the effect they produce by playing upon our responses. What we relish on such occasions is not the spectacle to which we respond, but the responses evoked in us by the spectacle. As Susan Sontag puts it,

> Weiss' play is only secondarily an argument. There is another use of ideas to be reckoned with in art: ideas as sensory stimulants.[59]

We attend the public spectacle in order to enjoy the private spectacle we make (of and for ourselves) with the fireworks of our response. The private spectacle is what counts. This is what artists aim for in "exploring the possibilities of their medium" to produce interesting effects. McLuhan, in this vein, calls artists "experts in sensory awareness." Art that "has something to say" about the outside world *in* which the performance takes place is "square," old-fashioned, and dead. This is particularly evident in op art, where the patterns cannot be taken as depicting anything, even as forms interesting in themselves. They are enjoyed solely for the striking distortion they produce in our perceptions. Susan Sontag sums it up in expressing her own contemporary sensibility:

> A great work of art is never simply (or even mainly) a vehicle of ideas or of moral sentiments. It is, first of all, an object modifying our consciousness and sensibility.[60]

The world outside, which used to be identified with reality, is no longer noticed, has become a matter of indifference; only the inside psychic world is worth paying attention to, and hence "really counts," in the fundamental sense of counting as real. Such art gives us a whole world of our own for the moment—but no insight which endures beyond a given show. We go from show to show like Nietzsche's "free spirits" going from world to world. Each show means everything for the time being and nothing in the long run. So from an esthetic point of view we not only lose sight of the world in which we live, but also the thread of our life; the identity of the "I" who sees becomes an utter mystery to us, an emptiness in the empty time "between the acts." In having everything of many possible worlds, the "I" has

59. Susan Sontag, *Against Interpretation and Other Essays* (New York: Farrar, Straus & Giroux, 1966), p. 171.
60. *Ibid.*, p. 300.

made nothing of himself and his actual world. This is the price metaphysics exacts from art: one who takes art as "experience" loses himself and his world.

Sex too has entered the metaphysical age. Everyone feels he must have a fulfilling sexual experience. Women live under what Mary McCarthy has called "the tyranny of the orgasm." Devices for producing "profound" sexual experiences are advertised in our leading periodicals. Sex, like art, has become for us an "experience," and in the same sense of the word, as primarily an enjoyment of our own responses with comparatively little regard for what produces these responses in us. The cause of our responses is our sexual partner as an independent person. The old idea of sex was as a way of getting to "know" our partner in this sense, namely, as a person leading a life separate from our own. Now what we come to know is not our partner as cause of our response but our partner *in* response. We are interested in our partner only insofar as he shares our erotic experience. Thus the experience or "affair" of the moment tends to be the be-all and end-all of the sexual relationship. It constitutes a momentary world of its own. It has no import for the partners when they go their separate ways because to begin with they were not interested in each other as "real" partners who *could* go separate ways. One who takes sex as "experience" gains a more intimate (or at least seemingly more intimate) partner for the moment but pays the metaphysical price of losing a "partner for life."

For two thousand years Western man has waited for God to come again. Devotees of all denominations have hoped and prayed and prepared themselves to be moved by the Divine Spirit, and have felt helpless, degraded, and abandoned without Him. God the Creator was the source and object of all religion, and man was but His creature. But today the object of religion, what religion is all about, is a religious experience—a certain ecstasy. We find accordingly that religion has been taken over by man, who now sets *himself* the task of producing, e.g., by drugs, the blessings he once awaited from God. But though the mystical experience is thus made more readily available, the familiar metaphysical price is exacted: the "God" who can be summoned for the special experience when we are "turned on" does not remain to dwell with us in the mundane reality of our enduring life.

Contemporary art, sex, and religion thus display in a particularly striking and concrete way the *subjectification* of reality which Heidegger regards as rooted in the idea of metaphysics, the particular conception of "truth" and "being" that rules and molds our age. A second trait equally definitive of "metaphysics" is the *totalization* of reality, which is most strikingly displayed in that form of organization distinctive of contemporary society, namely, *totalitarianism.* We are most aware of totalitarianism as a political form in which all social functions are controlled and coordinated by a central political leadership such as that of Nazi Germany, Fascist Italy, or Soviet Russia. But the deeper meaning of "totalitarianism" is broader. Its essence lies in the overall coordination and control, in short, the centralized direction, of all social institutions as a single military-industrial-educational-political-financial, etc., complex. In this broader sense all "developed" countries, including the United States, are totalitarian. "Total mobilization," for example, which is feasible only in a modern society, was practiced by all the great powers during the Second World War.

According to Heidegger, "total mobilization [of social resources] as something disposable" is a symptom of our metaphysical times.[61] Elsewhere, in the same vein, Heidegger writes of Germany under Hitler:

> One supposes that the Führer in a blind rage of self-seeking established everything to conform to his own personal idiosyncrasies. In truth, however, this is the necessary consequence of the [metaphysical] distortion of beings. . . . Leadership (*Fuhrung*) is required for the calculated securing of the totality of beings.[62]

So Heidegger objects to totalitarianism as involving a "distortion" (*Irrnis*) of beings. His objections are not the conventional ones. The popular objection to the rationally efficient (totalitarian-technological) attempt at complete mastery of our social and natural environment is that it is doomed to such failure as producing *un*controllable pollution, *un*safe weapons, and *un*manageable cities. Heidegger, however, heralds the doom of an entirely well-managed planet, the tragedy of an overwhelming technological *success* that would organize the whole earth in an internationally totalitarian way.

61. "Die Zeit des Weltbildes," Zusätze, *Holzwege,* p. 89 (authors' translation).
62. "Überwindung der Metaphysik," § XXVI, in *Vorträge und Aufsätze,* pp. 93–94 (authors' translation).

Precisely if the hydrogen bombs do *not* explode and human life on earth is preserved, along with the atomic age a bizarre change will come over the earth.[63]

Heidegger's objection to totalitarianism is that it is metaphysical. From this point of view, it is no accident that Plato, the first metaphysician, is also the founder of a totalitarian social philosophy. And until we change our ideas of "truth" and "being" we cannot help taking an ever more totalitarian direction.

Thus, according to Heidegger, the idea of metaphysics—the idea that beings derive their being from conformity to some primary being, some single chief being—has two main implications. Objectively speaking, it implies that the truth is a totalizing truth, a truth about the whole system of coherently related beings, not a truth about things considered separately. Subjectively speaking, it implies an absolutely unconditioned subject by and for whom all truth and being are exclusively fashioned. This latter implication depends upon Heidegger's previously explained doctrine of *alētheia*, his view that "presentation," i.e., the singling out of beings from their context, is the function of man. If this view is assumed and if the law of totality holds—that *everything* is simultaneously re-presentable (as implied by the definition of metaphysics)—then being is entirely the work of man. And, conversely, again assuming Heidegger's doctrine of *alētheia*, if everything is the work of man as an absolutely unconditioned re-presenting (*Vor-stellendes*) subject, then what there is, is a totally object-ive reality.

Thus the hyperobjectivity and hypersubjectivity of our age are, for Heidegger, but two sides of the same metaphysical coin. The relation between these two facets—an absolutely unconditioned subjectivity and a thoroughly objectified reality—is effected by "reckoning" (*rechnende Denken*), the mathematically calculating mode of thought which prevails today. In order to see everything, we have to see things as a whole; and for this we have to make every single thing fit precisely in its particular place. We must calculate everything carefully. Our calculation is more basically practical than theoretical, for it consists not only of finding where each thing belongs, but of *making* a place for it in the world-order and *placing* it where it belongs.

63. M. Heidegger, *Gelassenheit* (Pfullingen: Neske, 1959), p. 22 (authors' translation).

The art of seeing everything is the ability to calculate which from the very beginning has entirely given itself over to the demand for steadily increasing order in the service of still further possibilities of order.[64]

The idea of truth that belongs to this "reckoning" mode of thought Heidegger calls *Gerechtigkeit,* which, as we have seen, connotes both exactitude and justification. The "truth" in this sense is the idea that can be justified as making its object fit exactly into the global scheme of things.

Thus in the final analysis Heidegger's idea of metaphysics implies three basic correlative ideas: unconditional subjectivity; totalizing objectivity; and a calculating mode of thought by which an unconditioned subject totalizes his objectified experience. This view is summed up, for the knowing reader, in the following quotation:

Metaphysics is the truth of beings as such taken as a whole. The metaphysics of completely unconditioned subjectivity thinks its own essence [as metaphysics] . . . the essence of truth as exactitude (*Gerechtigkeit*).[65]

So late Heidegger comes to see that the subjectivity he first favored as an alternative to the objectivist distortion of reality is but another facet of that very same "distortion." As such, it would be equally "false." But an idea is "false" only in contrast to a "truth" of which we have at least a general understanding. And in Heidegger's case our *only* idea of truth is itself held to be somehow lacking. So this lack cannot be understood as an error. For we lack any clear or positive idea of what it is that we lack. And with no glimmer of a conceivable alternative we cannot guide ourselves out of our predicament. Our idea of truth, then, is simply our fate (*Geschick*) to be lived through.

64. *Vorträge und Aufsätze,* p. 94.
65. *Nietzsche,* II, 332. The contemporary belief that we can computerize decision-making can easily be seen as an implication of this Heideggerian view. Computerization is possible only if seemingly incommensurate interests can all be related in terms of one parameter serving as one continuum of preference. Since Plato first objectified value, all values have become essentially objective. Being entirely objectified, all values are completely rooted in a subjective valuing of them. This provides the needed parameter, the subject's world-organizing will (or interest, preference, desire, choice) to have these values. Thus objectified, all our values become utility functions and all our decisions become optimizations.

The nihilism of our times is our experience of this lack. While it does not show us any way out—its worst horror consists precisely in its utter hopelessness—it is nevertheless instructive. The Nothingness that it reveals at the heart of our way of life shows us in a covert way that what we lack is "Being." This "Being" is not shown as the object of our need, something of a fixed nature unaffected by our lack of it. This would be to conceive of "Being" as *a* being, which is exactly the metaphysical kind of thought we need to escape. The Nothingness we experience *is* the-lack-of-Being; and Being today *exists only in this way,* as lacked. Being "belongs" to man. Being *is* its relation to man as expressed in man's idea of truth. Our modern nihilistic idea of truth expresses, accordingly, both that we lack Being and that Being in our day is *essentially* concealed. So the problem is not to "correct" our idea of truth, even if we could. For nothing exists to which any other idea of truth would correspond. The problem is to come into a new and more needed relation to Being which would at once transform Being and give us an entirely new form of truth that would not even involve "correctness" as we now understand it.

So the nature of truth, according to Heidegger, is historically relative. Man's need for truth is transhistorical—as may also be (this is unclear in Heidegger's work) the particular form of truth that man most needs. But the kind of truth there *is,* the truth that *exists,* varies from epoch to epoch. What the truth is, is itself a historical event; it is *the* decisive event (*Ereignis*) which is definitive of some historical epoch and outmoded in the next. For example, in our epoch stamped by the "event" of Platonic-technological metaphysics, truth, as objective, is universal in scope. But this universality is itself a historically provincial rather than a universal feature of truth. According to Heidegger it is a supposition of our particular epoch, but was not a supposition for the pre-Socratics and presumably will not be one for the forthcoming epoch. Kierkegaard and Nietzsche, as we have seen, disagreed with the common objectivist account of our epoch, that truths are universal because they embody universal laws which hold true independently of man. They nevertheless partake of our epoch, from a Heideggerian point of view, because they agreed, albeit for different reasons, that truths are universal (totalizing). Heidegger's break with the objectivist tradition is more radical than theirs on two counts: he denies specifically that the truth is always universal; and he denies generally that the truth has *any* fixed form for all of history.

Heidegger seems to believe that an epoch is inaugurated by some new idea of truth, guided by the progressive explicitation of this idea, and terminated by its fully concrete realization. Thus he holds that in our day, "With the end of philosophy [whose metaphysical program is now realized], thought is not also at an end, but in transition to another beginning." [66] So, sensing that we need a new form of truth and that we are ripe for it, Heidegger sets out to elaborate one by developing a new form of thought to replace the calculating (*rechnende*) thought of our closing epoch. As Heidegger sees it, this forthcoming struggle, which will constitute "another story," will not be, like ours, a struggle for the domination of beings; instead, it will be a struggle "between the might of beings and the truth of Being." [67] Preparing to take the side of Being, Heidegger attempts meditation (*besinnliche Denken*) instead of calculation:

> Meditation requires of us that we do not hold to a one-sided interpretation, that we do not go on and on with a one-track mind. Meditation requires that we go along with what does not at first appear to hang together.[68]

With this mode of thought, according to Heidegger, we become receptive to mystery and to things in their particularity. We thus gain the promise of "placing ourselves on a completely different footing in the world." [69]

But, basically, man must wait for Being itself to do the essential work of ushering in a new age. "No mere action can change things," [70] for Being is the ultimate agent in all action. Action cannot bring about a new advent of Being, but can only express whatever form Being already has.

> Change can come only through an event which lights and leads, makes man see it as it calls and needs man, thus bringing man in his mortality to the way of meditative thought.[71]

66. *Vorträge und Aufsätze*, p. 83.
67. *Nietzsche*, II, 262.
68. *Gelassenheit*, p. 24.
69. *Ibid.*, p. 26.
70. "Überwindung der Metaphysik," § XXVIII, in *Vorträge und Aufsätze*, p. 98.
71. *Ibid.*, p. 99 (authors' free translation).

Heidegger remains an ontological John the Baptist awaiting and prophesying, but not pretending to effect, the advent of a new truth and a new being in a new revelation (*Ereignis*). Any new idea of truth will be the work of Being, just as our present idea of truth, which seems entirely man-made, is also a deliverance of Being. Today's truth is willed. That this is so, however, is not itself willed by us but thrust upon us by Being's concealment from us.

The truth of Being remains transhistorically the truth man needs. This truth is, moreover, man's basic need, so that its concealment or uncovering is the chief determinant of human life. Today, according to Heidegger, the concealment of Being is about as complete as possible. So the mark of modern man is need. Less than ever do we know what we truly need. But more than ever do we know true neediness. Thus Heidegger leaves us with the implication that what we most miss and need is a true philosophy of need, that is to say, an understanding of truth as needing to be known, of being as needing to be, and of man as needing to meet these needs—not just for his own sake but for their sake as well. Man is not a mere object dominated by an objective world-order, nor yet the sovereign subject of an objectified world. Neither ruler nor ruled, man "belongs" in the world as responsible both for it and to it. He has to learn to live this way. In short, man needs to be at home in the world.

At the start of this paper we suggested that in spite of the existentialists' progressively radical criticisms, something positive concerning the character of objective truth emerges from their critique. It is now time to try to put the pieces together. If we accept Heidegger's "destruction" or "out-growing" of metaphysics as the logical outcome of this critique, it is hard to see what is left. In Heidegger's developed thought there is no account of a proper place for the ideal of pure objective thought or disinterested inquiry in human existence. The whole tradition of objectivity is regarded as a profound and undiluted nightmare whose very horror has finally awakened us. But before we throw out a possible baby with the murky bath water, we should at least try to save the seemingly valuable objective attitude by distinguishing it from its prevalent interpretation, which has had such a destructive influence in our cultural epoch.

Kierkegaard's central and lasting insight, as we have seen, is that whatever we believe because we must believe it in order to be ourselves is necessarily true.

Nietzsche's contribution is that belief in objectivity answers a general need definitive of human life.

And Heidegger sees that any conception of truth which is definitive of a human way of life cannot possibly be false.

The objective outlook would be compatible with these three insights if it could be understood to imply that reality is essentially an expression of human necessity. The stumbling block is that objectivity plainly disregards man's *personal* needs as an individual. It remains quite possible, however, that objectivity does express man's *universal* needs as a human being.

Three main questions arise in exploring this possibility:

1. What is this basic general human need for objectivity?

2. Why is the need for objectivity ignored by the tradition and by the objective outlook itself?

3. Is this account of objectivity put forth as objectively true? Or, if not, in what other way is it true?

To begin with, we must distinguish between the objective outlook and particular objective truths discoverable by employing this outlook. Although we need to look at things objectively, particular objective truths are disinterestedly known. There is a general human need for objectivity, but not for certain objective truths.

1. All three thinkers see the objective view as a way of hiding our mortality and general vulnerability. The need for this view is, indeed, to represent our really flawed reality as perfected, i.e., as more like what we need it to be. The objective knower is not mortal or vulnerable.

2. Since the objective knower is not mortal or vulnerable he cannot understand the need for having become what he is.

3. We cannot appreciate this need from the objective point of view, but only by reassuming the position calling for objectivity, as existentialism does by calling objectivity into question.

This general existentialist account of objectivity remains to be made fully clear and persuasive through a concrete philosophy of the human body. For we are limited, vulnerable, and perishable precisely because of our body.

BIBLIOGRAPHY

Bibliography

1. Books by John Wild

George Berkeley: A Study of His Life and Philosophy. Cambridge: Harvard University Press, 1936 (with three unpublished sermons).

Introduction to Realistic Philosophy. New York: Harper & Row, 1948.

Plato's Theory of Man: An Introduction to the Realistic Philosophy of Culture. Cambridge: Harvard University Press, 1948. Reprint. New York: Farrar, Straus & Giroux, Octagon Books, 1964.

Plato's Modern Enemies and the Theory of Natural Law. Chicago: University of Chicago Press, 1953.

The Challenge of Existentialism. Bloomington: Indiana University Press, 1955. 4th ed., 1959.

Human Freedom and Social Order: An Essay in Christian Philosophy. Durham, N.C.: Duke University Press, 1959.

Existence and the World of Freedom. Englewood Cliffs, N.J.: Prentice-Hall, 1963.

The Radical Empiricism of William James. Garden City, N.Y.: Doubleday & Co., 1969.

2. Articles by Wild

"The Unity of Berkelian Philosophy: A Reply to Mr. Luce." *Mind,* XLVI, no. 184 (1937), 454–64.

"Resurrection of Hedonism." *International Journal of Ethics*, XLIX (October 27, 1938), 11–26.

"Kierkegaard and Classical Philosophy." *Philosophical Review*, XLIX (September, 1940), 536–51.

"The Concept of the Given in Contemporary Philosophy." *Philosophy and Phenomenological Research*, I (September, 1940), 70 ff.

"Plato's Theory of *techné*: A Phenomenological Interpretation." *Philosophy and Phenomenological Research*, I (December, 1940), 255–93.

"Cartesian Deformation of the Structure of Change and Its Influence on Modern Thought." *Philosophical Review*, L (January, 1941), 36–59.

Report of the *Proceedings of the ACPA*. *Philosophy and Phenomenological Research*, II (December, 1941), 226–32.

"On the Nature and Aims of Phenomenology." *Philosophy and Phenomenological Research*, III (September, 1942), 15–95.

"The Church and the University Today." *Sewanee Review*, LI (January, 1943), 113 ff.

"Inversion of Culture and the World Revolution." *Sewanee Review*, LI (October, 1943), 449–66.

"Truth in the Contemporary Crisis." Report of the *Proceedings of the ACPA*. *Philosophy and Phenomenological Research*, IV (March, 1944), 411–20.

"What Is Realism?" *Journal of Philosophy*, XLIV (March, 1947), 148–58.

"An Introduction to the Phenomenology of Signs." *Philosophy and Phenomenological Research*, VIII (June, 1948), 217–33.

"Existentialism Old and New." Report of *Proceedings of the ACPA, 1946*. *Review of Metaphysics*, I (March, 1948), 80–92.

"The Divine Relativity." *Review of Metaphysics*, II (December, 1948), 65–77.

"Plato and Christianity: A Philosophical Comparison." *The Journal of Bible and Religion*, Vol. XVII (January, 1949).

"A Realistic Defence of Causal Efficacy." *Review of Metaphysics*, II (June, 1949), 1–14.

"Tendency: The Ontological Ground of Ethics." *Journal of Philosophy*, IL (July 3, 1952), 461–75.

"Natural Law and Modern Ethical Theory." *Ethics*, LXIII (October, 1952), 1–13.

"Berkeley's Theories of Perception: A Phenomenological Critique." *Revue internationale de philosophie*, VII, nos. 23–24 (1953), 134–52.

"An Examination of Critical Realism with Special Reference to C. D. Broad's Theory of Sensa." *Philosophy and Phenomenological Research*, XIV (December, 1953), 143–62.

"The New Empiricism and Human Time." *Review of Metaphysics*, VII (June, 1954), 537–57.

"Ethics as a Rational Discipline and the Priority of Good." *Journal of Philosophy*, IV (November 25, 1954), 776–88.

"Comments on Weiss's Theses Concerning Real Possibility." *Review of Metaphysics*, VIII (June, 1955), 673–75.

"Philosophy of Education in the West." *Harvard Educational Review*, no. 2 (1956), pp. 180 ff.

"Kierkegaard and Contemporary Existentialist Philosophy." *Anglican Theological Review*, XXXVIII, no. 1 (1956), 15–32.

"Existentialism: A New View of Man." *University of Toronto Quarterly*, XXVII (October, 1957), 79–95. (Chap. 2 of *Existence and the World of Freedom*.)

"Is There a World of Ordinary Language?" *Philosophical Review*, LXVII (October, 1958), 460–76. (Chap. 3 of *Existence and the World of Freedom*.)

"Realism and the Problem of Human Freedom." Paper read at fall meeting of the Association for Realistic Philosophy, October, 1959, at the University of Connecticut.

"Contemporary Phenomenology and the Problem of Existence." *Philosophy and Phenomenological Research*, XX (December, 1959), 166–80.

"Existentialism as a Philosophy." *Journal of Philosophy*, LVII (January 21, 1960), 45–62.

"The Exploration of the Life-World." (Presidential address, 57th meeting, Yale University.) *Proceedings of the American Philosophical Association* (Yellow Springs, Ohio: Antioch Press, October, 1961), XXXIV, 5–25. (Chap. 4 of *Existence and the World of Freedom*.)

"The Christian and Contemporary Philosophy." *The Christian Scholar*, XLV (Spring, 1962), 12–17.

"An Existential Argument for Transcendence." *The Journal of Bible and Religion*, XXX (October, 1962), 269–77. (Chap. 11 of *Existence and the World of Freedom*.)

"The Philosophy of Martin Heidegger." *Journal of Philosophy*, LX (October 24, 1963), 664–77.

"Questions Philosophers Ask Theologians." *Religion in Life,* XXXIII (Summer, 1964), 367–77.

"In Behalf of the Author (Merleau-Ponty)." *Pacific Philosophy Forum,* III (1964), 101–4.

"William James and Existential Authenticity." *Journal of Existentialism,* V, no. 19 (1965), 243–56.

"Being, Meaning and the World." *Review of Metaphysics,* XVIII (March, 1965), 411–29.

"Authentic Existence." *Ethics* (July, 1965), pp. 227–39.

"The Concept of Existence." *The Monist,* L (January, 1966), 1–17.

"Marxism and Existentialism." Symposium of the Society for the Philosophical Study of Dialectical Materialism, 1966. Unpublished.

3. ARTICLES BY WILD
IN BOOKS AND COLLECTIONS

"Husserl's Critique of Psychologism: Its Historic Roots and Contemporary Relevance." In *Philosophical Essays in Memory of Edmund Husserl,* edited by M. Farber, pp. 19–43. Cambridge: Harvard University Press, 1940.

Goals for American Education. The Conference on Science, Philosophy and Religion in Their Relation to the Democratic Way of Life, Vol. IX. New York: Harper and Bros., 1950. Wild's comments on pp. 14, 40, 148–49, 227–28, 254–57, 278–81, 325, 357–62, 381–84, 441, 468–70.

"The Present Relevance of Catholic Theology." In *Christianity and Reason,* edited by M. Myers, pp. 18–36. New York: Oxford University Press, 1951.

"Phenomenology and Metaphysics." In *The Return to Reason,* edited by J. Wild, pp. 36–67. Chicago: Henry Regnery Co., 1953.

"Education and Human Society in Modern Philosophies and Education." In *54th Yearbook of The National Society for the Study of Education,* edited by Nelson B. Henry, pp. 17–56. Chicago: University of Chicago Press, 1955.

"Can Christian Philosophy Be Taught in a Christian College?" In

Philosophical Study in the Educational Process. Evanston, Ill.: Christ the King Foundation of the Protestant Episcopal Church, 1958.

"L'Anthropologie philosophique et la crise des sciences européennes." In *Husserl,* pp. 270–306. Paris: Editions de Minuit, Cahiers de Royaumont, 1959.

"Man and His Life-World." In *For Roman Ingarden: Nine Essays in Phenomenology,* edited by Anna-Teresa Tymieniecka, pp. 90–109. The Hague: Martinus Nijhoff, 1959.

"The Concept of Man in Greek Thought." In *The Concept of Man,* edited by Radhakrishnan and Raju, pp. 47–131. London: George Allen & Unwin, 1960. Spanish edition, 1964.

"The Traditional View of Freedom: A Criticism." In *Experience, Existence and the Good: Essays in Honor of Paul Weiss,* edited by I. C. Lieb. Carbondale, Ill.: Southern Illinois University Press, 1961. (Chap. 6 in *Existence and the World of Freedom.*)

"Plato as an Enemy of Democracy: A Rejoinder." To *Plato: Totalitarian or Democrat?,* edited by T. L. Thorson, pp. 105–29. Englewood Cliffs, N.J.: Prentice-Hall, 1963.

"Christian Rationalism (Aquinas, Gilson, and Maritain)." In *Christianity and Existentialism,* by W. Earle, J. Edie, and J. Wild, pp. 40–65. Evanston, Ill.: Northwestern University Press, 1963.

"The Rebirth of the Divine." In *Christianity and Existentialism,* by W. Earle, J. Edie, and J. Wild, pp. 149–86. Evanston, Ill.: Northwestern University Press, 1963.

"Husserl, Life-World, and the Lived Body." *Symposium Sobre la nocion Husserliana de la Lebenswelt,* Proceedings of the XIII International Congress of Philosophy, Universidad Nacional Antonoma de Mexico, 1963, pp. 77–93.

"Devotion and Fanaticism." In *Process and Divinity: The Hartshorne Festschrift,* edited by William L. Reese and Eugene Freeman, pp. 445–69. La Salle, Ill.: Open Court Publishing Co., 1964.

"Husserl, Life-World, and the Lived Body." In *Phenomenology: Pure and Applied,* edited by E. Straus, pp. 10–23. Pittsburgh: Duquesne University Press, 1964. (The first Lexington Conference; includes a comment by J. de Boer, pp. 28–35, and a reply by J. Wild, 35–42.)

"Authentic Existence: A New Approach to 'Value Theory.'" In *An*

Invitation to Phenomenology, edited by J. Edie, pp. 59–77. Chicago: Quadrangle Books, 1965.

4. DISCUSSIONS BY WILD

Reply to Mr. Blake. *International Journal of Ethics,* L (October 28, 1939), 101–5.

In Reply to Mr. Read. *Philosophy and Phenomenological Research,* II (March, 1942), 410–14 (apropos the concept of the given).

On Professor Ducasse's Explanation of His Theory of Semiosis. *Philosophy and Phenomenological Research,* VIII (December, 1947), 239–41.

On the Distinction between the Analytic and the Synthetic, with J. L. Cobitz. *Philosophy and Phenomenological Research,* VIII (June, 1948), 631–37.

Reply to Professor Beck, with J. L. Cobitz. *Philosophy and Phenomenological Research,* IX (June, 1949), 728–31.

Comments on Mr. Hartmann's *The Epistemology of the A Priori,* with J. L. Cobitz. *Philosophy and Phenomenological Research,* IX (June, 1949), 737–41.

The Divine Existence. An Answer to Mr. Hartshorne. *Review of Metaphysics,* IV (September, 1950), 61–85.

Barber's Realistic Analysis of Possibility. *Review of Metaphysics,* VI (March, 1953), 487–501.

A Reply to Mr. Gale. *Philosophy and Phenomenological Research,* XXI (March, 1961), 377–83.

Reply to Father Adelmann on Professor Schrag. *Philosophy and Phenomenological Research,* XXII (June, 1962), 412–16.

Being and Time: A Reply to Harries. *Review of Metaphysics,* XVII (June, 1964), 610–16.

Reply to Professor Frankena. *Philosophy and Phenomenological Research,* XXVII (September, 1966), 97–103.

5. PREFACES AND INTRODUCTIONS BY WILD

Introduction to *Spinoza Selections,* edited by J. Wild. New York: Charles Scribner's Sons, The Modern Students Library, 1930.

Berkeley, C. "Unpublished Sermon of Bishop Berkeley: On thy

will be done." First published by J. Wild, *Philosophical Review*, XL (November, 1931), 526–36.
Foreword to *Existence and Freedom,* by C. O. Schrag. Evanston, Ill.: Northwestern University Press, 1961.
Preface to *What Is Phenomenology?* by P. Thévenaz, translated by J. Edie. Chicago: Quadrangle Books, 1962.
Preface to, with J. Edie, *In Praise of Philosophy,* by M. Merleau-Ponty, translated by J. Wild and J. Edie. Evanston, Ill.: Northwestern University Press, 1963.
Foreword to *The Structure of Behavior,* by M. Merleau-Ponty, translated by A. L. Fisher. Boston: Beacon Press, 1963.

6. Book Reviews by Wild

Neue Dialoge swischen Hylas and Philonous, by H. A. Wirmer. *Philosophical Review,* XLIX (October, 1940), 471–73.
Plato and Parmenides, by F. M. Cornford. *Philosophy and Phenomenological Research,* I (September, 1940), 233–40.
Plato's Earlier Dialectic, by H. Robinson. *Philosophy and Phenomenological Research,* II (June, 1942), 545–51.
Physics and Philosophy, by Sir J. Jeans. *Philosophy and Phenomenological Research,* IV (June, 1943), 559–65.
Platon. Sa Conception du Cosmos, by H. Perbe. *Philosophy and Phenomenological Research,* VI (June, 1946), 639–42.
Discovering Plato, by A. Koyré. *Philosophy and Phenomenological Research,* VII (March, 1947), 474–77.
The Doctrine of Imitation of God in Plato, by Rutengerg. *Journal of Religions,* XXIX (January, 1949), 75.
Being and Some Philosophers, by E. Gilson. *Speculum,* XXIV (1949), 573–78.
Problems of Philosophy, by S. Chatterjee. *Philosophy East and West,* I (October, 1951), 82–84.
The Philosophy of Rabindranath Tagore, by Ray B. Gopal. *Philosophy East and West,* II (January, 1953), 349–50.
The Concept of Mind, by G. Ryle. *The Philosophical Forum,* XI (1953), 19–27.
India's Culture . . . , by R. T. Raju. *Philosophy East and West,* III (October, 1953), 271–75.
The Origins and History of Religions, by J. Murphy. *Philosophy East and West,* IV (October, 1954), 276–77.

The Material Logic of John of St-Thomas, translated by Clanville Hollenhorst Simon. *Philosophy and Phenomenological Research,* XVI (June, 1956), 556–59.

A Companion to the Study of St. Augustine, edited by R. W. Battenhouse. *Speculum,* XXXI (January, 1956), 131–34.

Being and Nothingness, by J.-P. Sartre. *Saturday Review,* October 6, 1956, p. 26.

Modes of Being, by P. Weiss. *Review of Metaphysics,* XI (June, 1958), 610–36.

Irrational Man: A Study in Existential Philosophy, by W. Barrett. *Saturday Review,* September 6, 1958, pp. 12–19.

Being and Time, by J. Macquarrie and C. Robinson. *Review of Metaphysics,* XVI (December, 1962), 296–315.

7. REVIEWS OF JOHN WILD'S BOOKS

George Berkeley: A Study of His Life and Philosophy
   Jessop, R. R. *Mind,* XLVI, no. 82 (1937), 232–39.
   Lamprecht, S. P. *Journal of Philosophy,* XXXIV (September 30, 1937), 19–21.
   Mabbot, J. D. *Philosophical Review,* XLVI (September, 1937), 540–42.

Introduction to Realistic Philosophy
   Smith, C. *The Modern Schoolman,* XXVI (March, 1949), 254–57.
   Chisholm, R. *Philosophical Review,* LIX (October, 1950), 391–95.
   Kubitz, C. A. *Philosophy and Phenomenological Research,* XI (September, 1950), 265–68.
   Moody, L. A. *Journal of Philosophy,* XLVII (November 23, 1950), 717–19.

Plato's Theory of Man
   Mackay, D. S. *Journal of Philosophy,* XLIII (December 25, 1946), 688–97.
   Houl, A. J. *The Modern Schoolman,* XXIV (May, 1947), 246.
   Viastos, C. *Philosophical Review,* LVI (March, 1947), 134–93.
   Cherniss, H. *American Journal of Philosophy,* LXVIII (n.d.), 259–65.

Plato's Modern Enemies and the Theory of Natural Law

Stallknecht, N. F. *Philosophy and Phenomenological Research*, XIV (March, 1954), 426–27.

Robinson, R. *Philosophical Review*, LXIII (October, 1954), 596–99.

Chil, M. *The Modern Schoolman*, XXXII (May, 1955), 363–68.

Bobbio, N. "Ancora suil Diritto Naturale." *Rivista Filosofia Italiana*, Vol. XLVII, no. 1 (1956).

Friedrich, C. C. *Diogene*, no. 49 (April, 1965), pp. 118–35.

Corospe, V. R. *The Modern Schoolman*, XLIII (January, 1966), 143–78.

The Challenge of Existentialism

Collins, J. *America*, XCV (April, 1966), 205–6.

Human Freedom and Social Order

Thomas, H. *Philosophical Review*, LXX (July, 1961), 270–73.

McGill, V. J. *Philosophy and Phenomenological Research*, XXI (March, 1961), 407–9.

Existence and the World of Freedom

Langan, T. *Philosophy and Phenomenological Research*, XXV (March, 1965), 438–41.

The Return to Reason

Rematz. *Philosophical Review*, LXIII (July, 1954), 435–38.

Sellars, R. W. *Philosophy and Phenomenological Research*, XV (September, 1954), 104–11.

Collins, J. *The Modern Schoolman*, XXXII (January, 1955), 177–81.

The Radical Empiricism of William James

Thayer, H. S. *Journal of Philosophy*, LXVII (January, 1970), 52–55.

Edie, J. *Review of Metaphysics*, XXIII (March, 1970), 481–526.

8. Critical Discussions of Wild's Thought

Adelmann, F. J. "The Root of Existence." *Philosophy and Phenomenological Research*, XXII (March, 1962), 405–8.

Dreyfus, H. L. "Wild on Heidegger." *Journal of Philosophy*, LX, (October 24, 1963), 677–80 (Abstract).

Edie, J. "Recent Work in Phenomenology." *American Philosophical Quarterly,* I (1964), 115–28.

Ferm, V., ed. *A History of Philosophical Systems.* New York: The Philosophical Library, 1950. "Contemporary Thomism," pp. 454–70.

Frankena, W. "J. Wild on Responsibility." *Philosophy and Phenomenological Research,* XXVII (September, 1966), 90–97.

Haladus, J. J. "Realistic Philosophy and Its Future as Envisioned by Professor John Wild." Master's thesis, Faculté de Philosophie, Université de Montreal, 1966.

Harries, K. "A Note on John Wild's Review of *Being and Time.*" *Review of Metaphysics,* XVII (December, 1963), 296–300.

Hinshaw, V. "The Given." *Philosophy and Phenomenological Research,* XVIII (March, 1958), 318–25.

Kuntz, P. G. "John Wild's Plurality of Orders." *Proceedings of the ACPA,* XXXVII (April, 1963), 148–58.

———. "Mythical, Cosmic and Personal Orders." *Review of Metaphysics,* XVI (June, 1963), 718–48.

———. "Order in Language, Phenomena and Reality: Notes on Linguistic Analysis, Phenomenology and Metaphysics." *The Monist,* IL (January, 1965), 107–36.

Natanson, M. *Literature, Philosophy and the Social Sciences: Essays in Existentialism and Phenomenology.* The Hague: Martinus Nijhoff, 1962. "Phenomenology and the Natural Attitude," pp. 34–43.

Reck, Andrew J. "John Wild, from Realism to Existentialism." In *The New American Philosophers,* pp. 255–90. Baton Rouge, La.: Louisiana State University Press, 1968.

Rome, S. and B., eds. *Philosophical Interrogations.* New York: Holt, Rinehart & Winston, 1964. Interview with J. Wild, pp. 119–79.

Schrag, C. O. "John Wild on Contemporary Philosophy." *Philosophy and Phenomenological Research,* XXII (December, 1962), 409–12.

Sciacca, M., ed. *Les Grands Courantes de la pensée mondiale contemporaine.* Paris: Fischbacher et Marsonati, 1964. I, 478–79.

Spiegelberg, H. *The Phenomenological Movement.* 2 vols. The Hague: Martinus Nijhoff, 1960, pp. 635–36 (comments on *Return to Reason*).

Index

Abraham, Karl, 162
Abschattungen, 22 n. 8
Absolute, 73, 75
Abstraction, 101, 103, 106
Absurd, 199, 305, 308, 359
Absurdity, 88–90, 93, 98, 167, 305
Accident, 22, 35
Act, 125, 129, 137, 146, 147, 166, 236, 239–41, 243, 244, 250, 253, 258, 265, 266, 269, 275, 281, 283, 285, 287, 302, 304, 310, 312, 314, 328; of existing, 49; free, 286; intellectual, 7
Action, 3, 17, 18, 33, 92, 119, 120, 128, 136, 142, 149, 151–53, 163, 173, 178, 199, 205, 216, 231, 240, 241, 244, 245, 250, 252, 264–67, 273, 277, 282–84, 300, 301, 306–8, 312, 385; intentional, 282; involuntary, 274; meaningful, 277, 278, 289; social, 261; voluntary, 274
Activity, 112, 134, 142, 144, 145, 147, 148, 151, 152, 182, 193, 194, 199, 218, 238, 244, 247, 268, 274, 283, 284, 300, 302, 307–9, 312, 313, 335, 339; scientific, 220
Actor, 254, 265, 266, 304
Actuality, 29, 30, 67
Actualization, 17, 48, 126, 127, 282
Agnosticism, 61; Kantian, 13

Aisthēsis, 7
Alētheia, 369, 374, 376 n. 56, 382
Alienation, 110, 126, 131, 197, 237, 245, 246, 296
Althusser, Louis, 201, 205, 291
Ambiguity, 105, 122, 137, 204, 206, 219, 270, 283, 288
Anal character, 163
Analogy, 55; of being, 42, 54, 60
Analysis, 115, 116, 120, 125, 130, 132, 141, 143, 145, 147, 148, 180, 190, 197, 207, 212, 215, 227, 247, 249, 260, 264, 276, 308, 317, 320, 378; descriptive, 180, 181; eidetic, 345; ontological, 117, 118; phenomenological, 134, 219; transcendental, 278
Analytics: apophantic, 318; formal, 321
Anscombe, G. E. M., 276
Anselm, Saint, 41–43, 45–47, 49–61. *See also Monologion; Proslogion*
Anxiety, 116, 117, 122, 181; cultural, 108
Apophansis, 318
Appearance, 12, 13, 22, 35, 77, 89, 91, 104, 176, 215, 216, 259, 304, 305, 364, 365, 370, 375, 376
Apperception, 304; transcendental unity of, 304, 305, 307